AS IS

DG

Representations

Representations

Images of the World
in Ciceronian Oratory

Ann Vasaly

UNIVERSITY OF CALIFORNIA PRESS
Berkeley • Los Angeles • Oxford

University of California Press
Berkeley and Los Angeles, California

University of California Press, Ltd.
Oxford, England

© 1993 by
The Regents of the University of California

Library of Congress Cataloging-in-Publication Data

Vasaly, Ann.
    Representations: images of the world in Ciceronian oratory / Ann
Vasaly.

        p.   cm.
    Includes bibliographical references and index.
    ISBN 0–520–07755–5 (alk. paper)
    1. Cicero, Marcus Tullius. Orationes.   2. Speeches, addresses,
etc., Latin—History and criticism.   3. Mimesis in literature.
4. Rome in literature.   5. Oratory, Ancient.   I. Title.
PA6285.V37   1993
875'.01—dc20   92-18738
                                                        CIP

Printed in the United States of America
9 8 7 6 5 4 3 2 1

The paper used in this publication meets the minimum requirements of
American National Standard for Information Sciences—Permanence of Paper
for Printed Library Materials, ANSI Z39.48-1984.∞

Contents

List of Illustrations

Preface

Two passages that appear in the introductory pages of recent works on Cicero illustrate very well how differently the career of the orator appears to an ancient and to a modern historian. Thomas N. Mitchell, a distinguished commentator on the political landscape of the late Republic, opens his account of the early part of the orator's career with the statement that "the importance of the study of Cicero's political life and thought needs little illustration" (*Cicero: The Ascending Years,* vii). Neal Wood, on the other hand, whose interest in Cicero springs from his study of the history of political theory, begins his own interpretation of Cicero's political thought by posing the following questions: "Why should anyone today be concerned with the social and political ideas of the late Roman republican thinker and statesman Marcus Tullius Cicero? . . . Cicero's merit as philosopher has been so deflated and his popularity as sage and stylist has so declined that the endeavor would appear to be without intellectual or practical merit. Who today troubles to read Cicero, save a handful of Latinists and ancient historians, and an ever-diminishing number of students?" (*Cicero's Social and Political Thought,* 1). As I am among the "handful of Latinists" who read Cicero constantly and with pleasure, I am inclined to view the importance of Ciceronian oratory as self-evident. This book, however, is addressed to a wider public—to those who are not students of ancient rhetoric as well as to those who are. Therefore, the proposition that an understanding of Ciceronian persuasion is a piece of intellectual furniture well worth having requires some support.

The study of Cicero's social and political thought has often been justified, even among those who dismiss him as a thinker of slight depth and a politician of little weight, by the enormous influence his writings on these subjects had in antiquity and in later centuries. Less widely recognized, however, is the fact that Cicero's oratory was also extraordinarily influential not only in later ages but in the seminal period immediately following his death. The fall from favor of Ciceronian periodic style, even during the latter part of the orator's career, has misled many into presuming that the impact of Ciceronian oratory in the early years of the principate was negligible. But this is surely not the case. Like the philosophical works, the speeches of Cicero constituted an important part of the intellectual inheritance of the Roman elite in the first century B.C. One has only to glance at the pages of Livy to see how thoroughly the speeches were assimilated in the writings of an Augustan historian born several years after Cicero's consulship. It seems clear, then, that if we are to understand accurately the mass appeals on which Augustus and his supporters relied, we must explore the sources of those appeals in the late Republic and in the work of the acknowledged master of popular discourse during that period.

But it is not only the influence of Cicero's oratory on past ages that makes it worthy of our attention; Cicero's speeches have something to teach us about the art of persuasion in our own time. The rapid fall of totalitarian systems and their replacement by governments dependent on mass approval has, of late, cast a fierce light on the processes by which leaders create popular consensus and win widespread support. This has meant that rhetoric has once more become a subject of serious interest. Because Ciceronian oratory, like much of the most riveting speech making of the past decade, was an oratory of crisis and change, practiced under the ever-present threat of governmental and private violence, it provides, to use Livy's phrase, *exempli documenta:* that is, instructive instances of how rhetoric actually functions under such circumstances—its style, its modes of appeal, its strengths and weaknesses.

In the long-established democracies the progress of technologies of mass communication has led politicians to rely on new strategies in their efforts to influence their constituencies. The complex task of evaluating the verbal and nonverbal components of this new political rhetoric now occupies many of us: citizens, hoping to sort out truth from untruth and half-truth amidst a barrage of competing appeals; the mass media, alternately critical and uncritical purveyors of these messages; as well as political scientists and social historians. And in this enterprise, too, Ciceronian oratory has something to teach us. Ironically, the very difficulty of communication in the late Republic has given it much in common with the popular rhetoric of our own day. Cicero's need to sway a large, heterogeneous, and mostly unlettered and uneducated audience led him to exploit certain modes of persuasion that bear a striking similarity to those familiar in the present era. Chief among these is the orator's frequent recourse to rhetorical strategies that depend on integrating words with visual images—strategies, that is, that "represent" the real world to his audience in such a way as to seem to provide objective proof for the stated and unstated contentions of his speech.

Perhaps the ultimate value to the nonspecialist of studying Cicero's speeches lies in the fact that they provide a view of techniques common to rhetoric of all times and places being employed by a virtuoso performer. This does not mean that the reader ought to cast an uncritical eye on Ciceronian oratory, for even while admiring the skill with which the orator exploits commonplaces, creates semifictional personae, and balances logical and emotional appeals, the very act of analysis will sometimes lead us to condemn on an ethical basis what we applaud for its technical mastery. But even when it is recognized that Ciceronian rhetoric is, like all rhetoric, deeply flawed, we may yet see in it something humane and hopeful, for there we find as well the implicit assumptions that meaningful communication can take place between widely separated classes of society, that shared values and goals exist and may be articulated even within a deeply divided polity, and that the functions of government can be conducted through public debate rather than through violence.

The ideas for this book first took shape while I was engaged in writing a doctoral thesis exploring references to places in the early speeches of Cicero. As important as the freedom from other duties provided by concurrent fellowships from the American Academy in Rome and the Fulbright Foundation was the insight I gained into the interaction of text and ambiance by the opportunity I had to visit the Roman Forum frequently and study it intensively. I also profited from many conversations at the Academy with art historians, landscape architects, and architects, as well as with other classicists, and from the expertise of the senior scholars present during the year of my residence, especially Roger Hornsby, Lawrence Richardson, and William Harris. The book was completed during two leaves of absence from Boston University: the first, a one-semester leave for Junior Fellows provided by the Boston University Humanities Foundation, and the second, a year-long fellowship awarded by the Alexander von Humboldt-Stiftung. I am most grateful to Hildegard Temporini of Tübingen, who sponsored my work in Germany, as well as to Wolfgang and Martha Haase, whose kindness and friendship made my stay in Tübingen an especially pleasant one.

A number of my associates and friends have generously read and commented upon this work at various stages in its production. I extend my thanks to all of them, and especially to Elaine Fantham, Eleanor Leach, James May, John McManamon, and E. S. Ramage. I am also happy to acknowledge my debt to all of my colleagues at Boston University, particularly Donald Carne-Ross, Jeffrey Henderson, Meyer Reinhold, Michele Salzman, Stephen Scully, and Valerie Warrior, with whom I have had many stimulating discussions on various topics I have written about in these pages. I would like to acknowledge as well the publishers who have given me permission to make use of passages and ideas from three articles that have appeared in recent years: "Transforming the Visible," *Res* 6 (1983): 65–71; "The Masks of Rhetoric: Cicero's *Pro Roscio Amerino*," *Rhetorica* 3 (1985): 1–20; and "*Ars Dispositionis*: Cicero's Second Agrarian Speech," *Hermes* 116 (1988): 409–27. I have incorporated these earlier treatments in this book, albeit in substantially revised form.

The maps and plans in the book were drawn by James Timberlake and Jack Sullivan. Their contribution to this book goes beyond the illustrations alone, and I am very grateful to them both for their encouragement and interest, as well as for their fine drawings.

Finally, I would like to thank my husband, Rich, who has been a source of endless patience, support, and, perhaps most important, good humor during the writing of this book and during the two decades of our marriage. *Cui dono lepidum novum libellum? Tibi.*

Introduction:
Theory and Practice

The first [thing to notice] is that the motorcycle, so
described, is almost impossible to understand unless you
already know how one works. . . . The second is that the
observer is missing. . . . "You" aren't anywhere in the picture. Even the "operator" is a kind of personalityless robot
whose performance of a function on the machine is completely
mechanical. There are no real subjects in this description.
Only objects exist that are independent of any observer.

Robert Persig, *Zen and the Art
of Motorcycle Maintenance*

In the ancient Greek world the study of the art of persuasion sprang up
at almost the same time as the democratic forms of government that
made the ability to persuade large groups of one's fellow citizens,
whether in the courtroom or in the agora, crucial to political success.
The earliest handbooks of rhetoric are attributed to Corax and Tisias,
rhetors of the early fifth century B.C. who became teachers of forensic
oratory after the death of Hieron I had ushered in an era of democratic
government in Syracuse and other cities in eastern Sicily. Teachers of
oratory such as Gorgias of Leontini, who began arriving in Athens in
the latter half of the fifth century B.C., found the city filled with young
men eager to pay for instruction in the techniques of persuasion. The
kind of theoretical instruction offered by fifth- and fourth-century Sophists was mirrored in the handbooks of rhetoric written in the period,
now imperfectly preserved through the extant fragments, through their
incorporation in later works, and through the criticism leveled at them
by contemporary writers, especially Plato and Aristotle.[1]

---

1. For a survey of the early history of Greek rhetoric, see Kennedy, *Art of
Persuasion*, 26–124. For the rhetorical teaching of the Sophists and the handbooks attributed to them, see Guthrie, *Greek Philosophy*, 3:20, 44–54, 44–

By the Hellenistic period rhetorical theory had grown increasingly elaborate, related only tangentially to the progress of practical oratory. While Aristotle had accurately seen that the itinerant Sophists and rhetors of his time—and the handbooks that reflected their teaching— did not offer a rational and systematic exposition of the means whereby persuasion might be achieved, it should be kept in mind that the teachers and works he maligned were closely wedded to the world of everyday oratorical practice. These men knew the sorts of arguments and strategies that were successful and could teach them to those who were willing to pay. Aristotle, through his clarification and classification of rhetorical elements and strategies, succeeded in rationalizing the modes of persuasion to an extent never before achieved. But at the same time his treatise on the art of rhetoric was part of the process whereby rhetorical theory became divorced from rhetorical practice. Every theoretical description of an art is, by definition, divorced from the art it attempts to describe; but in the case of the *ars rhetorica* the theoretical tradition early on acquired an astonishing vitality of its own, frequently independent of the practical art that had first brought it into existence. So separate was rhetorical theory that its development, whether by philosophers or rhetoricians themselves, was hardly weakened by the shrinking of the role of deliberative and forensic oratory in the fourth and third centuries B.C. that was brought about by the demise of democratic systems in the Greek world. In fact, rhetorical theory flourished in the Hellenistic period, building an ever more complex superstructure upon the inheritance of the past.[2]

Unlike the Greeks, Roman orators for a very long time after the birth of the Republic (traditionally dated, like the overthrow of the Pisistratid tyranny at Athens, to 510 B.C.) seem not to have felt the need for formal instruction in the "art" of rhetoric. The old Roman system of education of the ruling class was based on a long period of apprenticeship in which a young man learned the arts of citizenship and governance by association with and observation of his father and his father's colleagues and

---

45 n. 4, 176–225. All translations in this and subsequent chapters are my own unless otherwise noted.

2. See Solmsen's survey of the development of ancient rhetorical theory, "The Aristotelian Tradition in Ancient Rhetoric." More recent discussions and bibliography dealing with Hellenistic rhetoric may be found in Kennedy, *Art of Persuasion*, 264–336, and *Art of Rhetoric*, 114–37; Wisse, *Ethos and Pathos*, 77–104.

friends as they went about the daily business of running the state. Although a Roman boy was under the control of his father for an extraordinarily long time—in theory until the latter's death—he was nevertheless expected to shoulder important public responsibilities while still in his teens, duties that often included service in the army as a junior officer and even the assumption of a major prosecution in the law courts.[3] Only in the second century B.C. did Greek-speaking visitors introduce into Rome the, by then, well-developed system of rhetorical training. It is unsurprising, therefore, that the rhetorical treatises that have come down to us in Latin were, for the most part, heavily dependent on the elaborate system of description and prescription already created by Greek rhetoricians.[4] If Roman practice was incorporated within the Greek theoretical system at all, it was only as an addition to a preexisting structure. Even when Cicero himself, the most experienced and successful of Roman orators, set out to create a new, more sophisticated description of rhetoric in the De oratore he ultimately failed to break free of the various organizations of the subject inherited from his Greek sources.

Their tendency to resort to excessive elaboration and subdivision, to assign only to one part of a speech techniques and strategies that in reality operate throughout, to assume implicitly that style can be separated from content, to ignore the question of how various techniques of persuasion function together as an ensemble, finally, their tendency to embalm rather than to enliven ancient oratory often make the rhetorical handbooks that have come down to us seem far removed from the stimulating world of ancient praxis. And yet this theoretical framework has been enormously influential and continues even today to determine to a great extent what we see when we look at an example of Roman oratory. The main outlines of the system found in the contemporary handbooks of Cicero's day, such as the Ad Herennium, can be summarized as follows. Three types of causes, listed here in descending order of importance within the rhetorical treatises, were identified—forensic (dealing with judicial decisions), deliberative (concerning public policy), and

---

3. See Clarke, Roman Mind, 1–7; Bonner, Education in Ancient Rome, 3–19.

4. The standard treatment of the development of persuasion in Rome is that of Kennedy, Art of Rhetoric. See also Clarke, Rhetoric at Rome; Leeman, Orationis Ratio. A good summary of the divisions of school rhetoric may be found in Leeman, 1:26–42.

epideictic (devoted to occasions on which individuals were praised or blamed). The duties or functions of the orator were summarized under the headings of Invention, Arrangement, Style, Memory, and Delivery. In theory the handbooks might have dealt with the application of the first three of these five categories to each of the three kinds of causes, but in practice the writers of the handbooks were chiefly interested in forensic oratory. The sections under Invention took up, among other subjects, the critical question of how the "status" of a case—that is, the basic issue involved and the overall strategy of defense (or prosecution)—was to be determined. Under the heading of Arrangement some treatises dealt with the divisions of a speech, although others subsumed this subject under Invention. Whether the subject appeared under Arrangement or Invention, its treatment included a great deal of material inherited from much earlier treatises in which the entire body of *rhetorica* had been organized under sections dealing with the chief parts of a forensic speech: the exordium, the narration, the proof, and the conclusion. To these four *partes* were sometimes added others, such as the division (following the narration) and the refutation (usually placed after the argument or proof). Discussions of style frequently included treatment of the three kinds of style (grand, middle, and plain), as well as a consideration of the "virtues" of an appropriate and well-wrought style. Briefer sections in the treatises dealt with the system of artificial memory used by the orator and the qualities of voice and movement that made for effective delivery.

One has only to look at a speech such as the *Pro Milone* to determine that it is possible to learn a good deal about Ciceronian oratory by analyzing it according to the system described above. Illustrated in the speech are many of the elements encountered in the *Ad Herennium* or Cicero's own *De inventione,* such as the clear and logical progression of the successive *partes,* the strategy found in the proem that is designed to remove the prejudice that existed against the unlikable defendant at the outset of the trial, and the defense against the accusation of murder, which makes twofold use of the status theory. In fact, reading the *Pro Milone,* or any other of Cicero's speeches, without the understanding of its formal framework that can be gleaned from the rhetorical handbooks may be compared to listening to the first movement of a symphony with no comprehension of sonata form. Or to being in the position of Cicero's audience for the *Pro Caelio,* to whom the orator remarks: "In [Caelius's speech] you saw not only his brilliance shine forth . . . but there was [in his speech], unless I am deceived by my goodwill towards him, a certain system, taught by liberal arts and refined by application and hard work" (45). Here Cicero assumes that any listener is able to recognize that a system or method (*ratio*) is being used in Caelius's speech but that the subtleties of its application and manipulation would escape those not trained in rhetoric.

Two interconnected problems soon become apparent, however, when we rely exclusively upon this kind of analysis. First of all, the pleasure taken in discovering the congruence between the structure found in a speech and that described in the rhetorical handbooks can lead one to forget that the recognition of a formal framework is not an end but a beginning. Just as the understanding of the conventions of ancient oral poetry is a necessary preliminary to literary analysis of the *Iliad* and the *Odyssey* (poems that often draw on, often transcend, the tradition from which they spring), in the same way, knowledge of the rhetorical structures and techniques encountered in the handbooks is but a beginning—the prerequisite to analyzing a particular articulation, which at once draws on and at the same time adds to this "language."[5] A second problem arises because this kind of formal analysis encourages one to see the speech as a static entity, a collection of parts, exacerbating a tendency already present in anyone who is reading a speech rather than witnessing its performance. It is as if the speech were an engine that we have become accustomed to describe not by considering it while functioning but by taking it apart, setting the pieces on the ground, and carefully examining each component, aided by the "parts manuals" furnished by antiquity.

These problems have not escaped notice. A number of leading scholars have taken pains to remind us that if we ever hope to understand ancient oratory, overall function must be considered as carefully as form. Thus an area of study that was at one time dominated by the desire to establish the application of theory to practice has turned increasingly to the "rhetoric of rhetoric"—that is, to the analysis of how the speeches would actually have convinced their audiences when given. The voices advocating this shift in emphasis are many. A. E. Douglas

---

5. Kennedy, *Art of Persuasion*, 5, compares early Greek oratory to oral poetry, stating how a speaker "used ancestors of the commonplaces of later oratory—the topics, the traditional examples, the maxims which he had heard and used before—in the same way that the oral poet used his devices." This was achieved, in this early period, "without conscious observance of rules." See the discussion of commonplaces below, pp. 252–54.

speaks disparagingly of unimaginative attempts "to see how far Cicero's speeches 'obey' the precepts of rhetorical theory rather than to see how far the theory is justified by the practice of the most successful exponents of practical oratory." [6] A. D. Leeman, in an article on the *Pro Murena*, affirms that his analysis "will transcend the purely rhetorical point of view, which is in itself too formal and sterile, and consider the speech as a document of progressive manipulation." [7] Wilfried Stroh compares the orator to an architect, stating that "as the architect creates an arrangement in space, so the orator does in time; and as the former arranges elements according to the requirements of a client, so the latter creates with regard to that which constitutes the goal of his speech: persuading the listener." [8] And C. J. Classen reiterates the notion that studies of individual aspects of the orations must be complemented by those which analyze every part of the speech in terms of its contribution to the persuasive strategy of the whole. [9]

Despite the enlightening work produced by these and other scholars, even recent studies of ancient speeches as "documents of progressive manipulation" have continued to depend almost exclusively on the primary categories of persuasive techniques set forth in the rhetorical handbooks and to depend as well on readings that contemplate the received texts in isolation, extracted from the circumstances of performance. It is my intention in the pages that follow to force rhetorical analysis into new paths by posing certain questions which I consider fundamental to the understanding of Ciceronian oratorical strategy yet which have been dealt with by ancient and modern rhetoricians either

6. "Intellectual Background," 98–99; see also 99 n. 13.
7. "Technique of Persuasion," 199.
8. *Taxis und Taktik,* 8–9: "Denn wie der Architekt im Raume, so ordnet der Redner in der Zeit; und wie jener nach den Bedürfnissen eines Auftraggebers disponiert, so baut dieser mit Rücksicht auf das, was den Zweck seiner Rede ausmacht: die Überzeugung des Hörers."
9. *Recht, Rhetorik, Politik,* 11–12. See also Neumeister, *Grundsätze der forensischen Rhetorik,* esp. 7–12. Notice should also be taken of recent works that achieve an understanding of Cicero's overall persuasive strategies by examining the speeches in the light of the three sources of persuasion defined in Aristotle's *Rhetoric: ēthos, logos,* and *pathos.* This Aristotelian division, adopted by Cicero in the *De oratore,* cuts across the artificial boundaries set up by most of the ancient rhetorical handbooks and allows an integrated analysis of all parts of the speech (see Solmsen, "Aristotle and Cicero on the Orator's Playing upon the Feelings"). For consideration of Ciceronian speeches based on these appeals, see, for instance, Craig, "Rational Argumentation"; May, *Trials of Character.*

peripherally or not at all: Can persuasion depend on the effect on an audience of the ambiance in which a speech takes place? If such an effect exists, how does the orator make use of it? What role might the representation of places and things play in oratory? Can the orator use references to monuments and places that the audience does not see in the same ways in which he manipulates their feelings about what is before their eyes? How does an orator respond to his audience's preconceptions of the physical world? How does his own representation of the physical world reorder, replace, or otherwise manipulate these preconceptions?[10]

I cannot claim that the sorts of passages that I will focus on in answering these questions have hitherto been ignored by scholars. In fact, they appear often in the work of historians, topographers, and art historians, usually as evidence supporting general statements about Roman attitudes. A danger exists, however, in the use of isolated extracts from the speeches as a source for "the Roman point of view." The practice of divorcing Ciceronian passages from their rhetorical context— while ignoring passages that may contradict those cited—has often resulted in the creation of a picture of Roman thought that is overly systematic and coherent at best. It is my belief that we must, first of all, read such passages as part of the rhetorical strategy of a particular speech and, second, analyze rather than ignore the inconcinnities that appear when passages from different speeches are compared. These inconcinnities are of great importance, for they alert us to the fact that the orator has adapted his representation of reality to suit his rhetorical goals. They are also a crucial part of any attempt to attain a more sophisticated understanding of a Roman weltanschauung, since the truth about the way the Romans saw their world is not a matter of "either/ or" but is found by identifying a spectrum of beliefs, and it is only the contradictions between speeches that allow us to establish the boundaries of that spectrum.

My consideration of the questions posed above takes the following form. In chapter 1 I shall indicate what theoretical role was assigned by Latin rhetorical theory to the representation of places in general and to ambiance in particular. Here I hope to make clear that although the techniques and strategies in which I am interested are not central to the description of rhetoric in any of these works—even in Cicero's own—

---

10. For the limited amount of recent work exploring the role of ambiance in Ciceronian rhetoric, see below, p. 35.

nevertheless, a sensitive reading of both ancient works of rhetorical theory and Cicero's political and philosophical treatises suggests that Roman praxis had made at least some inroads into the Greek theoretical tradition. Chapter 2 will show how in the case of the first and third *Catilinarians* ambiance was actually incorporated into a strategy of persuasion. The third chapter takes up the complex question of how descriptions of and allusion to unseen places and things can create an imaginary world in an audience's mind which may then be made to perform the same symbolic functions as do those things that an audience can actually see. The second half of the book looks at the question of the rhetorical representation of reality through a somewhat wider lens, describing how Cicero manipulates his audience's generic and ethnic images of the Roman and non-Roman world. Chapter 4 provides a necessary entree to this enterprise by exploring the sorts of preconceptions and prejudices about places a mass audience of Cicero's day would have been likely to have. The fifth chapter focuses on the "generic" locales of city and country, tracing Cicero's manipulation of his audience's images of both places in several speeches, while the sixth chapter demonstrates how ethnicity can provide a key to the creation of a psychological topography that supports the rhetorical aims of the orator. The close of the book considers the conclusions that can be drawn both about Cicero himself, as man and orator, and about his audience from the exploration of these little-considered aspects of ancient rhetorical practice.

It should be apparent that the kind of study I propose depends upon a reconstruction of various aspects of the performance that the text represents as taking place. But what faith can we put in the text as a guide to this performance? There is surely no reason to feel undue confidence that the extant text of the speech reproduces the words that were actually spoken in antiquity. Even if we exclude for the moment the speeches that we know were never delivered, or not delivered in anything resembling the form in which we now have them (e.g., the *Pro Milone*, the Second Action of the *Verrines*), we still have few reasons to trust the accuracy of the texts and several reasons to doubt it. Among the latter would be Cicero's desire to publish a more elegant and polished product than what was actually delivered, as well as the temptation he must have felt to make use of the hindsight he had acquired on political events when revising the speeches for publication. Scholars, especially German scholars, have labored long and hard in an attempt to separate the text of the original speeches from the form in which the speeches were published.[11] Much of this hard work, however, has in more recent years ground to a halt before one crucial realization: if Cicero—who published these speeches during his lifetime with the understanding that they would be read by individuals who were completely familiar with the circumstances that prevailed when they were given and even by many who were actually present when they were given—wrote the speeches in such a way as to maintain the illusion that they represented the text as delivered, how can we, who are separated from them by some two thousand years, presume to be able to distinguish—except in rare instances—what was added and what was elided, what was revised and what was left unchanged?

In spite of the fact that we cannot know the exact relationship of the written text to the speeches as delivered, nonetheless there exists a compelling reason for treating them as documents of persuasion: namely, there is evidence that perhaps the chief reason Cicero published the speeches was exactly this—that he wished them to serve as examples of practical rhetoric. They were intended to demonstrate to the student of oratory how Cicero had persuaded a particular audience at a particular time and place.[12] Classen's comment concerning the *Pro Milone*, which

11. Key arguments were first stated by Laurand, *Etudes*, 1:1–23, who maintained that, in general, the texts accurately reflect the speeches as given; and, on the other side, by Humbert, *Les plaidoyers écrits*, who thought that many of the speeches were composed of passages delivered at different times during the course of a trial or public meeting and passages added in redaction. A more sophisticated understanding of Cicero's rhetorical strategies has, in the case of many orations, led to a reassessment of passages that had hitherto been considered suspect. See the remarks of Classen, "Ciceros Rede für Caelius," 85–87, who after a careful analysis of the speech, concludes: "Every part has its function, every sentence is essential; and there is no need for the hypothesis that the individual parts came into this speech from different phases of composition" (86). See discussion and further bibliography in Kennedy, *Art of Rhetoric*, 176–77, 276–77; Stroh, *Taxis und Taktik*, 31–54. Quintilian (12.10.51) wrote in the first century A.D. that the published speech was nothing other than *monumentum actionis habitae*. Other ancient texts bearing directly on the question may be found in Humbert, *Les plaidoyers écrits*, 1–8.

12. For the contention that the main reason for publication was pedagogical, see Leeman, "Technique of Persuasion," 198–99, who asserts: "The fact remains that the only aim of an orator in a given case was to win over his audience, and a main reason for publication was to enable his young readers to study his means in achieving it"; Stroh, *Taxis und Taktik*, 21, 52–54. Cf. Cic. *Att.* 2.1.3: "I shall, however, send you some little speeches—both the ones you are asking for and several others in addition, since the things that we have writ-

we know to have been extensively revised after the failure of the original speech, puts the argument succinctly:

> Cicero published all of his speeches as practical examples of how one could achieve success in a certain situation, and [therefore] he gave them an appropriate form. . . . The published form of the *Miloniana* was also written with this purpose: that is, here too Cicero is concerned with "winning the case" and not with writing a speech according to the simplest pattern of rhetorical theory; for the most significant challenge to theory is in tailoring a speech to an individual case, rather than to any rigid pattern.[13]

Therefore, even if we can never know for sure whether the words of a Ciceronian oration were identical with those that the orator actually spoke, we can nevertheless feel assured that the text is a plausible recreation of the sort of speech that he gave (or would have given) on a particular occasion.

Beginning with the words of the text, then, I have attempted to reconstruct the circumstances of an original—even if, in some cases, hypothetical—performance. Here, I have paid particular attention to certain factors, extrinsic to the text, that would have affected the Roman audience's reaction to this performance. Admittedly, there are important circumstances affecting the reception of a speech that can never be recovered: the intonation, expression, and gestures of the orator; the appearance of the participants in the trial; the noise and excitement generated by the crowd of onlookers; the exact look of the buildings and the tribunals; the smell in the air; the heat and glare of the Italian sun beating down on those gathered in the Forum. It *is* possible, however, in the case of most of the orations, to draw on a wealth of information gathered in recent years by historians, archaeologists, art historians,

---

ten when influenced by the enthusiasm of the young please you also"; Quint. 12.10.53.

13. "Ciceros Kunst der Überredung," 185–86: "Cicero hat alle Reden als vorbildartige Beispiele dafür veröffentlicht, wie man in einer bestimmten Situation zum Erfolg kommen kann, und ihnen eine entsprechende Form gegeben (abgesehen von den jeweiligen programmatischen politischen Aussagen). Auch die veröffentlichte Fassung der *Miloniana* ist in dieser Absicht geschrieben, d.h. auch hier geht es Cicero um ein "vincere la causa" und nicht darum, eine Rede nach dem einfachsten Schema der Theorie zu verfassen; denn die wichtigste Forderung der Theorie ist es, eine Rede dem einzelnen Fall anzupassen und nicht einem starren Schema." Cf. Quint. 2.4.32, cautioning the orator to reject any argument, no matter how eloquently put (*quamlibet pulchra elocutio*), if it does not advance his cause (*nisi ad victoriam tendit*).

and other scholars in order to determine, for instance, where the orator and the audience stood when a speech was delivered; what the audience could see and how they might have felt about what they saw; what they would have known of various places and monuments mentioned by Cicero, and the sort of thoughts, images, and emotions that allusions to them might have conjured up. Thus it is only against a background of discussion of contextual matters that I undertake a detailed analysis of Cicero's rhetorical strategies and the role played by the representations of places and monuments within those strategies.

Those familiar with current trends in scholarship will recognize connections between the enterprise I have described and recent work in various fields of scholarly interest. While I have not made use of the technical vocabulary of semiotics, I share with semioticians certain presumptions; chief among them is the idea that both verbal and nonverbal signs are ubiquitous and that the study of how meaning is conveyed takes in a far wider field of signification than previously considered. In rhetoric, then, the process of persuasion must be examined not simply through interpretation of the text but through consideration of the text as a component in something that extends beyond it: the rhetorical performance, which is an instance of communication that makes use of more than words to convey meaning. I share with semioticians as well a special interest in the interpreter of signs and the "cultural codes" that determine the range of meanings available to the interpreter. Here, the semioticians' notion of the process whereby certain meanings are "blown up" in an interpreter's mind and others are "narcotized" is a useful one.[14] In the speeches we will find that from a wide range of meanings associated with the physical world Cicero carefully emphasizes some at the expense of others in order to support his overall rhetorical goals, and that this process often leads the orator to contradict in one speech the interpretations emphasized and deemphasized in other speeches, as well as leading him to create new interpretations of places and things that interact with those already available to his audience.[15]

14. Eco, *Semiotics and the Philosophy of Language*, 78–80.

15. An inquiry closely related to semiotic study of codes of interpretation is the *Rezeptionsästhetik* first introduced by Jauss. According to Jauss, the analysis of how a work conveyed meaning to any particular audience depends on the reference system of expectations of that audience. While I would disagree with Jauss as to the degree to which the "horizon of expectations" of Cicero's audience can be objectively formulated, nevertheless my own study takes for granted the need to analyze the audience's reception of Cicero's speeches within the his-

I must note, however, that certain basic attitudes separate this work from most semiotic studies. The first involves the assumption by most exponents of semiotics that sign systems are not "controlled." In *The Pursuit of Signs*, Jonathan Culler remarks:

> A whole tradition of thought treats man as essentially a thinking being, a conscious subject who endows objects around him with meaning. Indeed, we often think of the meaning of an expression as what the subject or speaker "has in mind." But as meaning is explained in terms of systems of signs— systems which the subject does not control—the subject is deprived of his role as source of meaning.[16]

My own work, by contrast, is in large part an effort to understand how Cicero attempts to draw on, add to, and, ultimately, to control a particular sign system (namely, the system of symbolic meanings that his audience associates with various places and monuments). Even in the case of locations that the audience perceived firsthand, I will show how an attempt was made by the orator—sometimes subtly, sometimes blatantly—to mediate the audience's interpretation of what they saw through the words of the speech. The order of presentation, the manner of description or allusion, the role played by places and things in various kinds of appeals, all are evidence of Cicero's attempt to manipulate the audience's images of the real world and their interpretation of those images. Essential to this study, then, is the idea of the orator as a conscious and controlling presence, whose rhetorical training and practical experience allow him (like the semiotician) to perceive consciously— and thus to exploit—the cultural codes that are unexamined by his audience.

It should also be kept in mind in assessing the relationship between this work and recent work in semiotics that a long-standing quarrel exists between rhetoric and semiotics regarding the very definition of the former. As competing philosophies of language, both attempt to describe the process of communication, although rhetoric tends to focus more steadily on the purposive generation of potentially meaningful signifiers, while semiotics is more concerned with the process by which a signifier becomes meaningful to an interpreter. As part of its attempt to supplant its more ancient rival, semiotics has rejected the definition of

---

torical and literary moment in which they occurred. See Jauss's "Literary History as a Challenge to Literary Theory."

16. *Pursuit of Signs*, 33–34.

rhetoric adopted by Aristotle, Cicero, Quintilian, and others, who saw in the *ars rhetorica* a study whose proper subject matter included all the means whereby a speaker might attempt to persuade an audience. While limiting rhetoric to only one of its five ancient divisions—namely, style—semiotics has gone on to claim for itself the task of analyzing signification in all its aspects.[17] Although in the present work I take note of the fact that important elements of Latin oratorical praxis were inadequately assimilated into ancient rhetorical theory, nevertheless my discussion assumes the validity of that broad definition of the scope of rhetoric first formulated in antiquity.

I would hope that a particularly close kinship might be discerned between this study and recent works that explore the representation of reality to mass audiences during the early principate. The latter are best exemplified by two books, both of which were based on lectures delivered for the Thomas Spencer Jerome Lecture Series at the University of Michigan: Paul Zanker's *The Power of Images in the Age of Augustus* and Claude Nicolet's *Space, Geography, and Politics in the Early Roman Empire* (originally published as *L'inventaire du monde: Géographie et politique aux origines de l'empire romain*). Surveying the wide range of images connected with the Augustan monarchy—including monuments, buildings, public rituals, and clothing—Zanker traces the development of a clear and consistent visual language that helped to create in the minds of Augustus's subjects a "new mythology of Rome."[18] Nicolet's particular interest is in geography and the process by which both the Roman people and their rulers evolved a conception of geographical space that allowed them to make sense of and administer a world empire. While Zanker is concerned chiefly, although not exclusively, with buildings and works of art, Nicolet devotes most of his attention to the representation of space found in two monuments that depended for their effect on texts as well as nonverbal symbols: the bronze tablets of the *Res gestae,* which stood before the Mausoleum of Augustus, and the great map of the world exhibited by Marcus Agrippa in the Campus

17. For the relationship between semiotics and rhetoric, see, for instance, Culler, *Pursuit of Signs,* 188–92. Culler points out that because it sees rhetoric as primarily concerned with metaphor and because it sees metaphor, in turn, as crucial to the creation of linguistic signs, semiotic theory rescues rhetoric from irrelevance, for it "asserts the responsibility and authenticity of rhetoric" and "grounds it in the perception of resemblances in experience, in intimations of essential qualities" (191).

18. Zanker, *Power of Images,* 4.

Martius, which was accompanied by explanatory *commentarii*. What Zanker and Nicolet have described is a "rhetorical" use of images, both actual and imaginary, which contributed to the development of a changed representation of the world in the minds of both rulers and ruled during the early principate. While both scholars look to the late Republic as a source of these images, Cicero's speeches have, for the most part, remained outside the scope of their studies. I believe that the present work will suggest that one of the chief sources of the later "rhetorical" manipulation of images in the early principate may be rhetoric itself.

CHAPTER ONE

Ambiance, Rhetoric, and the Meaning of Things

Nun machen wir die phantastische Annahme, Rom sei nicht
eine menschliche Wohnstätte, sondern ein psychisches Wesen
von ähnlich langer und reichhaltiger Vergangenheit, in dem
also nichts, was einmal zustande gekommen war, unterge-
gangen ist, in dem neben der letzten Entwicklungsphase auch
alle früheren noch fortbestehen.

Now let us consider a fantastic hypothesis: let us say that
Rome is not a human habitation, but rather a psychic entity
of similarly long and fruitful past, in which, however, nothing that existed has passed away and in which all earlier
phases of development still persist along with the last phase.

Freud, Das Unbehagen in der Kultur

AMBIANCE AND RHETORICAL THEORY

In the sixth book of the *Ab urbe condita* Livy tells of the trial for sedition of Manlius Capitolinus. Livy begins the narrative with the curious
statement that Manlius was at first saved from conviction because of
"the site" rather than because of his defense against the charges (6.20.5:
damnandi mora plebi non in causa sed in loco fuerit).[1] The trial took
place in the Campus Martius, and the historian states that here the defendant delivered a magnificent speech: after rehearsing his great deeds
and baring his breast to reveal the wounds he had suffered, he looked
up to the Capitoline and called on the gods to inspire the Roman people

1. Unless noted, all Latin and Greek quotes are drawn from Oxford Classical
Text editions. For the *De finibus,* J. N. Madvig's 1876 edition (reprint, Hildesheim, 1963) was used; for the *De legibus,* that of K. Ziegler (2d ed., Heidelberg,
1963).

with the same spirit they had given to him when he had defended that
place from the Gauls (6.20.8–9).

Livy had earlier prepared his readers for this appeal by noting that
when Manlius had first been thrown into prison, the people asked one
another whether they did not recall that night that had almost been
Rome's last; whether they could not see again the Gauls scaling the
Tarpeian Rock and Manlius, dripping with sweat and blood, as he had
been when he had saved (so it seemed) Jupiter himself from their enemies (6.17.4). Manlius's speech had such force that, in spite of strong
evidence of his guilt, the trial had to be adjourned by the prosecutors.
Livy explains that the tribunes realized that it would be hopeless to attempt to secure a conviction in a place where people could be visually
reminded of Manlius's glorious deeds (6.20.10: *nisi oculos quoque
hominum liberassent tanti memoria decoris, nunquam fore in praeoc-
cupatis beneficio animis vero crimini locum*). The trial was later recon-
vened in the Peteline Woods near the Flumentane Gate, from which
point the Capitol was said no longer to be visible, and there a guilty
verdict was wrung from the reluctant jurors.[2]

What does the story imply about the use of ambiance as an element
of persuasion? First, it seems clear that the effectiveness of Manlius's
appeal in the initial trial was not due simply to the sight of a place
(in this case, the Capitoline Hill) but depended as well on the gestures
and words that manipulated the audience's feelings about that sight.
The defendant, looking up from the place of the trial in the Campus
Martius, reminded his listeners of what he had done and begged
them to train their eyes on the Capitolium (the Temple of Jupiter
and its precinct) and the Citadel as they judged him (6.20.9: *orasse
singulos universosque ut Capitolium atque arcem intuentes*). Second,
mere verbal references to the associations of place do not function in
the same way, at least according to the story, since Manlius's appeals
proved insufficient to secure an acquittal once the venue of the trial
had been changed to the Forum Boarium. What is suggested by the
tale of Manlius, then, is a creative interaction of ambiance and *actio*
by which an orator might incorporate allusions to the visible environment into his speech in order to manipulate the response of his audience
to the speech.

2. The topographical information in the story is analyzed by Wiseman,
"Topography and Rhetoric."

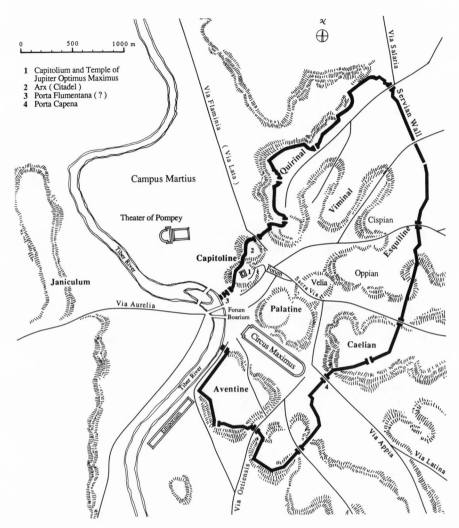

Fig. 1.   Republican Rome

This is not the only instance Livy gives us of a defendant exploiting the ambiance of a trial to his advantage. At the trial of Publius Horatius, who had killed his sister for mourning the death of one of the enemy Curiatii he had slain, the boy's father delivers a moving appeal within sight of the "Horatian Spears," the monument of Horatius's victory. Horatius's father, gesturing to the weapons his son had taken from the enemy, asks whether his audience could bear to see the young victor "beaten, tortured, and bound to the yoke" (1.26.10). He continues:

> Go ahead, lictor, bind the hands that, when armed but a little while ago, won dominion for Rome! Go ahead and veil the head of the liberator of this city; hang him from the barren tree! Beat him within the city walls—only let it be among the spears and armor of the enemy! Or flog him outside the walls— but let it be among the graves of the Curiatii! For where can you lead this young man in which the signs of his glorious achievements (*sua decora*) will not save him from so horrible a punishment?
>
> (1.26.10–11)

Livy states that the audience could not uphold Publius's conviction in the face of the "tears of his father" and the young man's extraordinary courage. Horatius was thus acquitted despite his legal culpability (1.26.12).[3]

Such striking illustrations would lead us to believe that this technique of persuasion might well have been a facet of Latin oratory as practiced both in Livy's time and earlier. This belief is strengthened by the fact that one of the most quoted passages in pre-Ciceronian oratory depends, at least in part, on an appeal to the visible. It is recorded that in a speech made a short time before his death Gaius Gracchus had asked: "Wretched as I am, where can I go? Where can I turn? To the Capitol? But it is soaked with my brother's blood. To my home? That I might see my mother—miserable, cast down, and in mourning?" That Cicero, Quintilian, and Julius Victor all quote the lines in connection with the

---

3. The story of the Horatii and Curiatii contains aetiologies for several land-marks of Augustan Rome: the graves of the fallen warriors, the trophy of spears, and the *tigillum sororium* ("Sister's Beam"). See Ogilvie, *Livy,* 113 (ad 1.25.14), 116 (ad 1.26.10), 117 (ad 1.26.13). On the process by which stories connected with such monuments were created, Wiseman, "Monuments and the Roman Annalists," 89, comments: "We cannot simply assume that accurate knowledge of the true nature of such monuments survived till the beginning of the Roman historiographical tradition—and the same may be said of such other 'documents' of early history as the tombs of the Horatii, the *tigillum sororium,* the statues of Horatius Cocles and Cloelia (or Valeria), the column of Minucius and the *busta Gallica.* The stories that accounted for them were part of the 'expansion of the past' (to borrow Badian's expressive phrase)—the elaboration into satisfying detailed 'history' of the meagre record of Rome's early past that was available to Fabius Pictor and Cincius Alimentus at the end of the third century."

discussion of effective gestures suggests that Gracchus must have raised his arms towards the Capitol when he spoke of it and that the passage preserves a memorable example of the effective combination of reference to ambiance and dramatic delivery.[4] The famous dilemma of Gracchus suggests as well that appeal to the visible environment was a facet of rhetorical training and practice long before Cicero's day. This thesis, however, receives little corroboration from the pages of the Latin rhetorical handbooks; explicit discussions of how an orator might exploit visible topography and monuments as a means of persuasion are nowhere to be found.[5] A number of references in such works to places that were *not* visible to the speaker's audience—a subject I shall examine in more detail in chapter 3—have at least an indirect bearing on the subject.

The description of places, for instance, is one aspect of "vivid description" (in Greek, usually termed *enargeia*, in Latin, often *illustratio*

4. Cic. *De or.* 3.214: "*Quo me miser conferam? Quo vertam? In Capitoliumne? At fratris sanguine madet. An domum? Matremne ut miseram lamentantem videam et abiectam?*" *Quae sic ab illo esse acta constabat oculis, voce, gestu, inimici ut lacrimas tenere non possent.* Cf. Quint. 11.3.115; Julius Victor in Halm, *Rhetores Latini minores,* 443; and "G. Gracchus" (XXIII: *Oratio extremis vitae diebus habita*) in Malcovati, *Fragmenta,* 1:196. On the form and the numerous examples of imitation of the passage in ancient times, see Bonnet, "Le dilemme de C. Gracchus."

5. In discussing the concept of *decorum,* Cicero notes that the style of a speaker must be adapted to the type of case at issue, the size and composition of the audience, the character and status of each speaker, and the occasion of and time allotted for the speech (*De or.* 3.210–11; *Or.* 123). In his discussion of the same concept (11.1.8: *quid deceat*) within an overall treatment of elements of style, Quintilian notes that the orator must consider the place where a speech is to take place (11.1.47): "It matters a great deal whether you are speaking in a public or private place, in one that is crowded or removed, in a foreign state or in your own, finally, in a military camp or in a forum: each place requires its own form and peculiar type of oratory (*suam quidque formam et proprium quendam modum eloquentiae*), since even in other realms of life it would not be suitable to do the same thing in the Forum, the Senate house, the Campus Martius, the theater, or at home; and many things that are not naturally blameworthy and sometimes are even absolutely required would be considered disgraceful if done in a place other than allowed by custom." None of this can be said to deal explicitly with the exploitation of ambiance as an aspect of *inventio,* although the implications are there, since, in the practice—if not the theory—of forensic and deliberative oratory, style (*elocutio*) can never be divorced from *inventio* (i.e., the strategy of persuasion employed in the speech). On this issue, see Neumeister, *Grundsätze der forensischen Rhetorik,* 33–34, 61–62 n. 7.

or *evidentia*), which was generally treated by the rhetorical handbooks under the heading of Style. Vivid description refers to a technique by which an orator created the illusion of sight through the use of concrete details of description. His aim was to induce his listener to envision a person, a thing, a scene, or an event in the mind's eye, thereby rendering it immediate and affecting. Subsumed under this technique was the description of places (sometimes termed *topographia* or *topothesia*).[6] The device seems in general to have been an important part of the orator's effort to arouse a strong emotional response in his audience, and the scenes given as examples of it are often those of high *pathos*, such as the depiction of the outrages to be expected when a city fell to a hostile army.[7] It might at first be supposed that this connection of detailed description with a pathetic appeal to an audience would have provided ancient rhetoricians with a basis for discussing the specific kinds of symbolic meanings attached to places and monuments, as well as ways in which these associations could most effectively be exploited. Such discussions would also, in turn, have revealed how an orator might draw on similar associations connected to aspects of the setting in which he delivered his speech. Unfortunately, no such discussions appear in the rhetorical handbooks of Cicero's day.[8]

Rhetorical treatises do note that description of places plays a role in two of the traditional divisions of a judicial speech, the *narratio* and the *argumentatio*. In sections dealing with the *narratio,* the orator is advised to consider carefully the place where an event occurred when describing that event. He is urged to review the physical characteristics of a place and its surroundings, as well as to consider such matters as "whether the place [was] sacred or profane, public or private, belonging to another or the property of him about whom one is speaking" (Cic. *Inv.*

6. See Quint. 4.2.63–65 (*evidentia, enargeia*), 123 (*rerum imago*); 6.2.32 (*enargeia*); 8.3.61–71 (*enargeia, evidentia, repraesentatio*); 9.2.40–44 (*hypotupōsis, topographia*); Her. 4.51 (*descriptio*), 63 (*effictio*), 68 (*demonstratio*). Zanker, "Enargeia," 298, states: "The rhetors, in their discussions of *ekphrasis,* see in *enargeia* the *aretē* of pictorial description." He notes that the Greek terms *ekphrasis* and *enargeia* are used by some authors "almost interchangeably." See *evidentia* in Lausberg, *Handbuch,* 1:399–407 (§§810–19), and further discussion below, pp. 89–102, 90 n. 3, 90–91 n. 4, 91 n. 5, 94 n. 11, 103 n. 26.

7. E.g., Her. 4.51; Quint. 8.3.67–70.

8. See below, esp. pp. 89–102, for further consideration of vivid description and its possible applications in rhetoric.

1.38) in devising an account that would appear credible to his audience.[9]

Before dealing with the importance of place to the *argumentatio*, or proof, a word of explanation is in order. Ancient rhetorical theory recognized different systems for classifying the kinds of arguments that would be of use to an orator faced with a variety of individual circumstances. Generally, the topoi, or sources of argument, were divided into those dealing with persons (*a persona*) and those dealing with matters, usually actions (*a re*). Among the topoi in the latter category were considerations of motive, place, time, means, and instrument. The arguments drawn from place were further broken down into those that concerned questions of fact, those that concerned questions of definition, and those that contributed to characterizing an action. It is obvious that these categories were derived from the method, primarily associated with the Hellenistic rhetorician Hermagoras, of determining the chief grounds of contention between two opponents, called *status* (or *stasis*) theory. Generally speaking, this theory posited three strategies of defense: that derived from the fact alleged ("He didn't kill the man"), that derived from the definition of what was done ("He killed him, but it was self-defense, not murder"), and that derived from the character of the action ("He had to murder him in order to save the Republic"). Here the same questions (*est? quid est? quale est?*) form the basis for determining the subcategories of arguments connected to place.[10]

The first of these categories (*est?*), which dealt with those arguments concerning place that would aid an orator in proving the facts, involved

9. Lausberg, *Handbuch*, 1:182–83 (§328), 210–11 (§§382–83). The grammarian Fortunatianus summarized the questions to be asked concerning the characteristics of place in the following way (*Ars rhet.* 2.3 = Halm, *Rhetores Latini minores*, 104):

> 1) aut naturalis, ut in mari, in monte, in campo;
> 2) aut positivus, ut in civitate; positivum quot modis consideramus? octo: a) publico, ut theatro, studio; b) privato, ut domo, villa; c) sacro, ut templo, adyto; d) religioso, ut mausoleo, sepulchro; e) infami, ut lupanari; f) intervallo, ut prope, longe; g) qualitate, ut contra, post, ante; h) quantitate, ut angusto, spatioso loco.

10. See Cic. *Inv.* 1.38; Quint. 5.10.37–41; Lausberg, *Handbuch*, 1:210–11 (§§382–83) for arguments involving place. For *status*, see Quint. 3.6.1–104; Kennedy, *Art of Persuasion*, 306–14; Lausberg, *Handbuch*, 1:64–129 (§§79–238); Wisse, *Ethos and Pathos*, 93–95. A fourth *status* involved a defense based on procedural matters, taking up such questions as whether the prosecutor had the right to prosecute the case or whether the proper court was hearing it.

the same aspects of *locus* that the rhetorical handbooks also specified as elements to be considered in creating a believable account in the *narratio*. In the *narratio*, however, the orator took pains simply to insure that the objective and subjective characteristics of a place did not contradict his description of what had occurred there. In the *argumentatio*, on the other hand, similar characteristics of place were to be considered with a view to supporting the contention that an event *must* have occurred in the way the orator had represented it. As an example of this mode of argumentation, the rhetorician Quintilian, writing in the first century A.D., refers to the *Pro Milone*. Here Cicero had argued that since the struggle between Clodius and Milo had occurred in the neighborhood of Clodius's estate and in a place in which Clodius and his retainers held the high ground, logic demanded that the audience conclude that it was Clodius who had ambushed Milo rather than vice versa.[11]

Considerations of place were sometimes relevant in questions of legal definition (*quid est?*), for the law could view the same action as criminal in one place and innocuous in another or could term an act one sort of crime when done in one place and a different crime when done elsewhere. An example that can be cited from Greek law concerned the rights of a husband whose wife committed adultery. If the husband came upon the offending couple *in flagrante delicto*, the law allowed him to kill the lover; if, however, he planned his revenge and carried it out later, he could be legally charged with murder. The fact that a husband's murder of a lover took place in the husband's own bedroom would therefore be the basis for the argument that his action had been unpremeditated and therefore could not be described as murder.[12] Again, the prosecutor of a man accused of robbery might argue that since a theft had taken place within a temple, the accused was guilty not merely of theft but of sacrilege.[13]

Under the final category mentioned above (*quale est?*) were subsumed those arguments connected to place that concerned the quality

11. Quintilian (5.10.37) is clearly referring to this passage (*Mil.* 53) when he states that Cicero carefully analyzed the characteristics of place in devising his argument in the *Pro Milone*.

12. The example is drawn from the situation described in Lysias's *On the Murder of Eratosthenes*. The prosecution in the case claimed that Eratosthenes had been killed at the hearth begging for mercy, which the defendant denied.

13. See Quint. 5.10.39. Cf. Arist. *Rhet.* 1.14.6 (1375a11–13), in which he notes that wrongdoing can be greater if done in a particular place; for instance, lying in a court of law.

of an action. Here the orator went beyond the mere legal definition of an act and attempted to use the place where an action occurred to characterize it, not only in terms of legality or illegality but according to extralegal standards of propriety (*decorum*) and justice. Thus a defendant might argue that an act was rightly (if not legally) done simply because it occurred in a particular place, while an accuser would hope to demonstrate that because of the place where it occurred, a particular action was especially blameworthy. After alluding briefly to arguments of this sort, Quintilian comments that arguments connected to place "are also effective in securing praise and blame" (5.10.41: *ad commendationem quoque et invidiam valet*). To illustrate this sort of appeal he cites two examples (5.10.41). The first, drawn from Ovid's *Metamorphoses,* reminds the reader both of Livy's description of Manlius's appeal before the Capitoline Hill and of his account of the appeal of Horatius's father before the "Horatian Spears." In the passage cited by Quintilian, Ajax argues his claim to the arms of Achilles by directing the gaze of his audience to the Greek ships that he had saved from burning and before which the dispute was being decided (*Met.* 13.1–6).

Quintilian's second example refers to the charge of Milo's prosecutors that the defendant had killed Clodius before the monuments of his ancestors (*Mil.* 17). Before looking more closely at this citation, it is worth nothing that Quintilian might well have pointed to several other kinds of exploitation of the associations of place to be found in the *Pro Milone.* In sections 83 and 84 of the speech Cicero speaks of the death of Clodius as the result of the *fortuna* of the Roman people and the will of the gods. He appeals to "the very hills and groves" of ancient Alba, which had been defiled when Clodius cleared large tracts of forested land; to Alba's "ruined altars," buried by Clodius's building projects; and to Jupiter of Mount Latiaris, whose lakes, forests, and enclosures had witnessed Clodius's crimes (85). This sacred landscape both ordained and witnessed Clodius's death. Cicero then declares that it was not by chance that Clodius had been killed near the shrine of the Bona Dea, whose rites he had earlier polluted; this goddess, too, had taken part in the divine retribution meted out to Clodius (86). It has already been noted that Cicero used the place where Clodius's death occurred to claim that Milo's act was self-defense rather than murder. In this passage the orator argues that even if Milo's act were to be described legally as murder, the very location where the incident took place showed that Milo had acted justly and as an instrument of divine vengeance in ridding the state of Clodius.

The *Pro Milone* not only provides this striking example of the use of place to characterize an action but includes as well an attempt to attack the validity of this same strategy of persuasion. Quintilian states (5.10.41) that Milo's accusers had charged that the defendant had killed Clodius on the Appian Way, among the monuments of his forebears. The topic must have furnished one of the chief sources of *pathos* for the prosecution, as it would have allowed the accusers to expatiate on the tragic irony of Clodius's demise on the road built by Appius Claudius Caecus and amidst the tombs of the Claudii that stood along that road. Its success with the audience and judges can be gathered from Cicero's need to refer to it three times in the speech he later published. In the exordium of the speech Cicero derides the notion that parricide is a greater crime when the victim is an ex-consul rather than an ordinary man, or that the death of Clodius was more cruel simply because it occurred among the monuments of his famous forebears (17). Again, a few lines later, he exclaims against the "great melodramas" (*quantas tragoedias*) called forth by the name of the Appian Way (18); and at the end of the argument (91) he once more speaks of "those who complain about the Appian Way," reproving them for their lack of concern for Rome itself. Although Quintilian finds it necessary to posit this strategy of "praise and blame" as a fourth category of arguments drawn from place, he seems actually to be referring to the emotional impact that could be derived from expanding on arguments of quality. Whether the technique should be classed under a separate heading or simply as an aspect of arguments of quality, it is clear that careful consideration of the physical aspects and psychological associations of a particular place was understood to provide the orator with opportunities for manipulating the feelings of his audience about actions that had occurred there.

It seems clear that a Roman orator was trained (*a*) to observe and describe concrete details of a place in order to provide his listeners with a vivid and moving description of a particular scene and the actions that occurred there, (*b*) to consider the objective and subjective characteristics of particular places in creating a convincing narration, (*c*) to draw on these same characteristics in claiming the inevitability of his version of events in the *argumentatio,* and (*d*) to use associations of specific places to manipulate the feelings of his audience. An orator trained and practiced in using these techniques to exploit the associations of places and monuments not visible to his audience would obviously be well equipped to draw on the characteristics of the place where he gave his speech as well, in order to amuse, convince, or arouse his listeners. It remains to be determined, however, whether the aims and effect of references to visible topography and monuments might have differed from the use made of verbal representations of places that were not visible to an audience. This question will be explored in more detail in chapter 3 through the analysis of the role played by Cicero's description of certain works of art, monuments, and topography in the fourth part of the Second Action against Verres.

It is worth noting that the use in persuasion of aspects of visible (as well as unseen) environments might well have been treated within a number of other rhetorical categories in addition to those mentioned above. For instance, the appeal to topography, statues, monuments, and the like could have been subsumed under the topic of "inartificial proof." Inartificial or nonartistic proof (*atekhnoi pisteis*) was that provided by direct evidence, such as documents, laws, and the testimony of witnesses, including that of slaves who had been examined under torture.[14] Although a variety of commonplaces existed to deal with such evidence, ancient rhetorical theory held that these kinds of proofs were "discovered" rather than "invented" by an orator. There are hints that Cicero might have seen the appeal to monuments and places as a form of inartificial proof. In the *Verrines,* the Temple of Castor—which would have been visible to the (hypothetical) audience—did not actually constitute direct evidence, since absolutely nothing could be deduced in support of Cicero's allegations against Verres simply by looking at it: in the first references to the temple (II.1.129–54) the monument functions merely as the visible focus of what is actually proved through argument, the testimony of witnesses, and the introduction of pertinent documents. And yet Cicero speaks of the temple as if it were, in fact, an inartificial proof, for it is not the gods Castor and Pollux but the building itself that is called a *testis* of the crime (II.1.154: *aedem Castoris testem tuorum furtorum*). This section of the speech ends with a statement that the eyes of the judges would be trained on the temple as they pronounced their verdict. A similar sort of conceit is also found in the *De imperio Cn. Pompei* (30–31). Here Cicero calls the entire Mediterranean world—Italy, Sicily, Africa, Gaul, Spain, "all shores and foreign lands and peoples, finally, all the sea, both in its whole expanse as well as in all its individual inlets and harbors"—to be "witnesses" (*testes*) to the virtue of Pompey.

14. Arist. *Rhet.* 1.2.2 (1355b35–39); 1.15.1–33 (1375a22–1377b12); Kennedy, *Aristotle,* 108–18.

Quintilian's allusion to the "praise and blame" that might be connected to specific places and things suggests that the topic could also
have been dealt with as an aspect of epideictic or demonstrative oratory
(and epideictic passages incorporated in deliberative and forensic
speeches). In a section of the *Institutio oratoria* devoted to the *genus
demonstrativum*, Quintilian states that an orator might on occasion be
called on to praise cities, public works (such as temples and walls), and
localities (3.7.26–27). And, turning to more general praise of places, we
also find that among the "externals" that the *Ad Herennium* lists as a
source of laudation and its opposite is "citizenship" (3.10: *civitas*).[15]
This idea of praising or censuring an individual by alluding to the positive or negative aspects of a place with which that person is connected
appears to be closely related to a crucial source of persuasion in forensic
oratory: the *probabile ex vita* argument, whereby an orator makes an
action attributed to an individual seem credible by placing it within a
general description of the mode of life of that person and the milieu in
which that life was lived.[16]

It must be acknowledged, however, that even if ancient rhetoricians
had explored all of these avenues in attempting to classify the role of
ambiance in persuasion, the Greek-derived structure of Latin rhetorical
treatises would have made it difficult to provide an adequate theoretical
description of the technique. Appeal to the visible milieu seems to have
played practically no role in ancient Greek rhetorical practice; it is
hardly surprising, therefore, that Greek rhetorical theory was ill suited
to its description.[17]

THE SPIRIT OF PLACE

While the material on ambiance gleaned from the rhetorical handbooks
is limited, certain passages from Cicero's later philosophical and rhetorical works shed additional light on the subject. Although the *De oratore*
does not refer explicitly to the use of the setting of a speech as a source
of persuasion, it is significant that the setting of the dialogue itself is

15. For further citations, see Lausberg, *Handbuch,* 1:133–35 (§§245.I;
247.1, 2) and 204–5 (§376.2, 3, 6, 7, 11).
16. Cic. *Inv.* 2.32–37; *Her.* 2.3–5.
17. See Pöschl, "Zur Einbeziehung anwesender Personen," 213–16, for the
negligible role played in Greek oratory by persons and objects present during a
speech.

made to play an important role in inspiring the conversation about oratory that takes place among Crassus, Antonius, and the others. At the beginning of the first book of the work (1.24–29), Cicero recounts how Q. Mucius Scaevola, Marcus Antonius, Gaius Cotta, and Publius Sulpicius assembled at Crassus's villa at Tusculum. On the second morning of the visit, the group is enjoying a pleasant walk when Scaevola suggests to Crassus that they "imitate Socrates as he appeared in the *Phaedrus*," for a spreading plane tree on Crassus's estate had reminded him of the plane tree of Plato's dialogue. It was this dialogue, says Scaevola, that had caused the tree to become famous, rather than the "little rill" that flowed beside the tree. He then declares that the rest Socrates had enjoyed "with his tough feet" ought even more readily be allowed to his own feet. Crassus agrees to the proposition, whereupon the entire group reclines under the plane tree.

Cicero had several reasons for beginning the *De oratore* in this way. On a purely artistic level, the vivid description of the scene introduces the characters and engages the interest of the reader in what they will say. The image of the plane tree with its cool shade and spreading branches and the realistic representation of the elegant conversation suggest the scene strongly to the reader's mind. Secondly, by his allusion to the scene of the Platonic dialogue, Cicero clearly hoped to signal that his own work, like the *Phaedrus*, would be of a philosophical character, far removed from the sterile prescriptions of the rhetorical textbooks.[18]

But one can go farther. The scene suggests as well that the experience of a *locus* can call to mind specific associations and that these associations, in turn, can move and inspire. The reader of the passage inevitably recalls the potent effect of the landscape on Socrates in the *Phaedrus:* how the fragrant plane tree, the clear, cold water, the breezes, the

---

18. See Cic. *Att.* 13.19.4 and *Fam.* 1.9.23 on the philosophic character of *De oratore*. While the connections between the *De oratore* and the *Phaedrus* are not limited to superficial allusions (Cicero, like Plato, wished to connect rhetoric with a kind of knowledge), there is much that is un-Platonic, even anti-Platonic, in Cicero's description of the ideal orator. For general background to Greek philosophic sources of the work, see Michel, *Rhétorique*, 80–149; Leeman and Pinkster, *De oratore*, 65–67 (for Cicero's allusions to Plato and their meaning); Guthrie, *Greek Philosophy*, 4:412–17; Solmsen, "Aristotle and Cicero on the Orator's Playing upon the Feelings" (for the Platonic vs. the Ciceronian view of the ideal orator). See Wisse, *Ethos and Pathos*, 151–52, for the Aristotelian mise-en-scène at the beginning of book 2, complementing Platonic parallels at the beginning of book 1.

music of the cicadas, and the lush grass provoke Socrates to stop and rest; how he warns Phaedrus, after calling the spot a "divine place" (238d: *theios . . . topos*), that he must not be surprised at the sort of speech he might deliver there; and how, after delivering a speech that he considers blasphemous, he feels himself prevented from leaving the place until he can substitute another, truer discourse. Plato had described Socrates, then, as drawing inspiration from the *locus* where he made his speech, reacting creatively and uncharacteristically—even mystically—to what he felt to be a sacred landscape.[19] Cicero not only alludes to this scene but depicts the characters in his own dialogue reacting to the associations of a similar setting. Crassus, as well as Scaevola, is affected by this atmosphere, for he is persuaded by the younger members of the group to do what he had never been known to do previously—deliver an extended disquisition on the nature and practice of oratory.

We should note, however, the degree to which Cicero has civilized and rationalized his topographical model. The characters in the *De oratore* do not, like Socrates and Phaedrus, wander in the countryside; they stroll around the manicured walks of Crassus's estate. When they are inspired to recline on the grass under the shady tree, they immediately send their slaves for cushions to sit on. Most important, Scaevola is depicted as drawing inspiration from the intellectual associations of the place rather than from the natural setting itself: the plane tree that he sees reminds him of the plane tree described by Plato, and the thought of that Greek plane tree is moving not simply because the tree was beautiful but because the dialogue that occurred under it was "divine."[20]

Cicero's emphasis here, at the beginning of his magnum opus con-

19. See Parry, "Landscape," 17: "The ambiance [of the *Phaedrus*] is one to suggest and reinforce that vision of natural truth with which Socrates wishes to counter Lysian rhetoric. Here the gods still live, who have no place in the sophistic milieu of the town"; and Walter, *Placeways*, 146–50.

20. In general, the urbane setting of the *De oratore* seems to guarantee the civility and predictability of the *locus*, while the Greek setting in nature contains hints of violence (the Orithyia legend) and unpredictability (the mystic power ascribed to the place). On the Ciceronian plane tree as a symbol of rhetoric itself, see Piderit and Harnecker, *De oratore* 38–39 (§19). See also the discussion of the "Marian oak" in *Leg.* 1.1–4. Cicero evidently hoped that his epic poem on Marius would give the Arpinate oak the same sort of eternal symbolic existence as the *Phaedrus* had given the plane tree of the dialogue.

cerning the nature of oratory, on the emotional response to the associations of setting suggests his consciousness of its importance in persuasion. In addition to this passage, statements that testify strongly—if indirectly—to the importance of this source of persuasion can be found in two of Cicero's philosophical works, the *De finibus* and the *De legibus*. The former, a discussion of the ethical philosophy of Antiochus, is set in the Athens of 79 B.C. Cicero depicts himself and his friends on an afternoon stroll from the house of Marcus Piso to the Academy. When they reach the walls of the Academy, Piso remarks:

> Naturane nobis hoc, inquit, datum dicam an errore quodam, ut, cum ea loca videamus, in quibus memoria dignos viros acceperimus multum esse versatos, magis moveamur, quam si quando eorum ipsorum aut facta audiamus aut scriptum aliquod legamus? . . . tanta vis admonitionis inest in locis; ut non sine causa ex iis memoriae ducta sit disciplina.
>
> (5.2)

> Is it inborn in us or produced by some trick that when we see the places in which we have heard that famous men performed great deeds, we are more moved than by hearing or reading of their exploits? . . . So great a power of suggestion resides in places that it is no wonder the Art of Memory is based on it.

The passage turns on the response each of the characters makes to various *loci*. When Piso looks on the grounds of the Academy he recalls Plato and his disciples, comparing the experience with the feelings he had when looking on the old Curia in Rome, a building that had always brought to his mind the great Romans of an earlier generation; Quintus's eye turns to the village of Colonos, recalling Sophocles and his depiction of Oedipus arriving at that place; Atticus predictably speaks of the many hours he has spent in the gardens of Epicurus; while Cicero tells of the impression left on him by his visit to the house of Pythagoras in Metapontum and refers to the hall in Athens in which Carneades used to sit. The youngest member of the group, Lucius Cicero, admits to walking along the beach where Demosthenes had practiced his speeches and to visiting the tomb of Pericles. Lucius ends by exclaiming that wherever they walked they encountered some reminder of the past (5.5: *quacumque enim ingredimur, in aliqua historia vestigium ponimus*).[21]

---

21. The phrase is especially difficult to translate, as the meaning of *historia* not only included all the kinds of associations mentioned by the characters in the dialogue (literary, philosophical, historical), but the Roman concept of the

This introductory scene ultimately abandons Piso's original question concerning the mysterious power of place and ends with Cicero's neat but unsatisfying statement that historical *loci* were useful in stirring young men like Lucius to emulate the great men of the past. We, however, may read another lesson in the text. The passage demonstrates the way in which places can stimulate the imagination, the memory, and the intellect. This power is not limited to Athens, for both the Curia Hostilia and the scenes of Pythagoras's activity in Italy are brought into the discussion. Clearly, both the places that possess this power and the particular associations called to mind by the places are as various as the temperaments and preoccupations of the individuals depicted.

In attempting to explain their response to particular milieux, however, several of the characters make use of the same verb: *movere*. Piso begins with the question of why people are more "moved" (*moveamur*) by seeing a place associated with famous men than by merely hearing or reading of their deeds. He goes on to declare that he himself is "moved" (*ego nunc moveor*). A few lines later, Quintus Cicero states that he is "greatly moved" (5.3: *commovit*), and his brother Marcus uses the word as well (5.4: *ego illa moveor exhedra*). The characters thus emphasize the emotional nature of their response to places. This, in turn, strongly suggests the importance of the phenomenon for Latin oratory, for in numerous passages from the rhetorical works Cicero asserts that the ability "to move" an audience was one of the three chief goals of rhetoric and that it was the possession of this ability that was the distinctive quality of the true orator.[22]

The *De legibus* provides a parallel to the passage discussed above.

---

past was quasi-religious as well. See Pöschl, "Die römische Auffassung der Geschichte." Note also that here *vestigium* refers to the marks of the present. In the passage from *De legibus* discussed below (pp. 31–33), it refers to the traces of the historical past; while in *In Verrem* II.4.107 the term refers to the signs of the ancient inhabitation of the gods of the Sicilian landscape.

22. On the pathetic appeal, see Solmsen, "Aristotle and Cicero on the Orator's Playing upon the Feelings," esp. 225–26; Schick, "Cicero and the Pathetic Appeal," 17–18; Michel, *Rhétorique*, 235–70; Wisse, *Ethos and Pathos*, 250–300; and *De or.* 1.17, 53, 60; 2.178, 215; *Brut.* 276, 279, 322; *Or.* 69, 128. For the three goals of oratory (*delectare, docere, movere*) see *De or.* 2.115, 128, 310; 3.104; *Or.* 69; *Brut.* 185, 276; *Opt. gen. or.* 3. Piso's comment concerning the "Art of Memory" will be explored further below (pp. 100–102).

Here Cicero, his brother Quintus, and Atticus take a walk in the Arpinate countryside, admiring its beauties.[23] At first it seems that Cicero's attachment to the place stems only from the natural charm of the landscape, but he soon reveals (almost confessionally) that he is especially moved by the associations called up by the place with his own family history.[24] Atticus, in turn, declares that he would thenceforth be particularly attached to the villa and to the very earth of the place, for it was here Cicero had been born. He continues:

> For we are in some strange way affected by the very places that carry the imprints (*vestigia*) of those whom we love or admire. My beloved Athens delights me not so much by the stunning monuments or the exquisite works of antiquity found there, but rather by recalling to my mind great men— where each one lived, where he used to sit and carry on disputations; why, I even enjoy looking on their graves.
>
> (2.4)

In depicting his own feelings about the scene of the dialogue, Cicero here testifies to the potent symbolism that had endowed, we might even say "inspirited," a *locus* with special meaning for him. In the case of Atticus, on the other hand, the passage demonstrates a process. At first, while admitting to the charms of the landscape (2.2: *ad requietem animi delectationemque . . . natura dominatur*), Atticus experiences no profound feelings about it. Only when the same place becomes connected in his mind to thoughts of his friend does it become a source of strong emotional attachment "from then on" (2.4: *posthac*). Further, he relates this process to his feelings about Athens, a city filled with constant reminders for him of the great men who once lived there.

Here again, as in the passages quoted from the *De oratore* and the *De finibus*, it is not chiefly "nature" that moves the participants in the dialogue but the association of particular landscapes with human history. There is a contrast implied between places that bear the spiritual imprint of the past, the "erlebte Welt" in Ernst Römisch's expressive

---

23. Römisch, "Mensch und Raum," draws on this passage in his discussion of the Roman sense of place. On differences between a modern appreciation of nature and Cicero's, see Davies, "Was Cicero Aware of Natural Beauty?"

24. 2.3: *si verum dicimus, haec est mea et huius fratris mei germana patria. Hinc enim orti stirpe antiquissima sumus, hic sacra, hic genus, hic maiorum multa vestigia. . . . Qua re inest nescio quid et latet in animo ac sensu meo, quo me plus hic locus fortasse delectet.*

phrase, and those that are devoid of human association, such as the wilderness.[25] No philosophical distinction, then, is to be drawn between city and country in this respect, for both are milieux pregnant with meaning. Further, Atticus's remarks about Athens (as well as the passage from the *De finibus*) make clear that a place outside the *imperium Romanum* was as likely as Arpinum to provoke emotional responses in the Romans depicted in the dialogues.[26]

Cicero does, however, make an important distinction between the strength of feeling generated by his place of birth and that felt for Rome, the *patria iuris*.[27] In section 2.5, after a rather dry explanation of the concept of dual citizenship, Cicero suddenly declares that the Republic must overshadow the land of one's birth in *caritas;* that to it we must consecrate our lives and for it we must even be willing to die. The orator concludes the passage with the statement that his native land was scarcely less pleasant to him (*dulcis . . . non multo secus*) than that other, greater homeland.

In spite of this passionate language, Cicero makes the basis for his connection to Rome a good deal less comprehensible than the basis for his weaker attachment to Arpinum;[28] but because he has used the same

25. For the phrase, see Römisch, "Umwelt und Atmosphäre," 128. Note that when Atticus thought that the landscape was actually wild, he could not understand Cicero's attachment to it (2.2: *nihil enim his in locis nisi saxa et montis cogitabam*). Cf. Lucas, *Greatest Problem,* 176–77: "The first time I saw the cloud-topped mountain ridges of Acroceraunia from the Adriatic, or the Leucadian Promontory white with sun and storm, or Hymettus, purpled with sunset, from the Saronic Sea, was something intenser even than poetry. But the same shapes and colours would not have seemed the same in New Zealand or the Rockies. Half their transfigured splendour came from the poetry of two thousand years before, or the memory of that other sunset on Hymettus when the hemlock was brought to Socrates." See also comments by Tuan, *Topophilia,* 93–95, 99–100.

26. As in the passage from the *De oratore* quoted above (pp. 26–28), Cicero here wishes to call to mind the scene of the *Phaedrus* while at the same time suggesting symbolically the differences between the two: Socrates had waded in the cool waters of the Ilissus; Atticus alludes to this scene but pronounces the water of the Fibrenus too cold to test—reminiscent of the reluctance of characters in the *De oratore* to recline directly on the grass.

27. See Salmon, "Cicero Romanus an Italicus anceps."

28. The text is, unfortunately, corrupt at the point at which Cicero indicates the fundamental difference between the two *patriae* (2.5: *Sed necesse est caritate eam praestare <e> qua rei publicae nomen universae civitati est . . .*). See, however, the similar passage in *De or.* 1.196: *Ac si nos, id quod maxime debet,*

terms of his feelings for Arpinum and of those he cherished for the Republic (*caritas/dulcis*), the distinction drawn is one of degree (*maior*) rather than of kind. The reader, therefore, may deduce the grounds for the greater from the lesser, and Cicero's attachment to Rome—the physical embodiment of the *res publica*—may be understood by examining the reasons for his attachment to his place of birth. Of the latter he had said to Atticus: "For in this place we [i.e., Cicero and his brother Quintus] sprang from a most ancient line; here are our holy rites, here our kindred, here the many reminders of our ancestors" (2.3: *Hinc enim orti stirpe antiquissima sumus, hic sacra, hic genus, hic maiorum multa vestigia*). These same concepts can be readily transferred from a familial to a communal context. The Romans, who traced their origin to the Latin founder Romulus and the Trojan Aeneas, also claimed to have sprung from ancient roots.[29] As Arpinum was the site of the *sacra privata* of Cicero's family, Rome held the *sacra publica* of the Roman people. And as the places of his native land moved in Cicero memories of his forebears, in Rome there were countless reminders of the semidivine ancestors who had changed Rome from a small and struggling state into a great one. The description in the *De legibus* of Cicero's emotional attachment to the places that spoke to him of his own history and identity thus reflects the deeper connection of the Romans to places in Rome of communal symbolic significance—places that spoke to them of their history as a people and of the meaning of the Republic.[30]

---

nostra patria delectat, cuius rei tanta est vis ac tanta natura, ut Ithacam illam in asperrimis saxulis tamquam nidulam adfixam sapientissimus vir immortalitati anteponeret, quo amore tandem inflammati esse debemus in eius modi patriam, quae una in omnibus terris domus est virtutis, imperi, dignitatis? ("And if our own native land delights us, which it certainly should—a thought that contains such power and natural force that Odysseus in all his wisdom preferred to immortality that Ithaca of his, affixed like a small nest amidst the most precipitous crags—with what passionate love, then, ought we to be fired towards a fatherland of this sort, one that is the sole terrestrial abode of virtue, dominion, and respect?"). Römisch, "Mensch und Raum," 227, comparing the vocabulary of the text with other Ciceronian passages, defines *caritas* as "die von Natur gegebene, gefühlsbetonte Verbundenheit, es ist die Liebe der Verwandten untereinander, die zugleich Verpflichtung umfasst."

29. E.g., Verg. *Aen.* 12.166: *Aeneas, Romanae stirpis origo.*

30. The feeling of this passage is so close to that found in the speech of Camillus on the meaning of the site of Rome in Livy 5.51–54 that direct Ciceronian influence on Livy seems probable. For stylistic parallels between Camillus's speech and Cicero, see Ogilvie, *Livy*, 743.

In one of the last speeches he delivered, the *Pro rege Deiotaro,* Cicero spoke of the oratorical inspiration he drew from such places of shared symbolic meaning. The oration was delivered *in camera* in 44 B.C. before Caesar, who had arrogated to himself as dictator all judicial power. In the speech Cicero complains of the difficulty of speaking within a private house, isolated from the people and scenes that had inspired him in the past (5). He then imagines the oration he would be capable of if he were allowed to speak in the Forum: "If only, Gaius Caesar, I were defending this case in the Forum, with you looking on and judging, what excitement I would draw from the assembled throng of the Roman people! . . . I would look on the Senate house; I would gaze upon the Forum; finally, I would call on heaven itself" (6).

The passage is strangely moving. In rhetorical terms it can be classed as a predictable ingredient in the successful *prooemium:* the plea for goodwill and sympathy based on the persona of the orator himself.[31] And yet it reads not so much as an appeal as a reminiscence. Cicero reminds Caesar—the other great public speaker of the age—of the oratorical power he had wielded in the past and complains that the changes the dictator has wrought have denied him two important sources of rhetorical effectiveness: first, the interaction between the orator and a vast popular audience, and, second, the setting in which that interaction took place. The passage illustrates Cicero's realization that great oratory, like great drama, demands both an audience and a stage.[32]

Ambiance appears to have played a key role in Ciceronian rhetoric.[33]

31. For appeal from the persona of the orator, see, for example, Cic. *Inv.* 1.22; *Her.* 1.8; Quint. 4.1.6–10.

32. Cf. the complaint of Secundus in Tacitus's *Dialogus de oratoribus* that contemporary oratory was vitiated by the fact that, unlike in an earlier generation, it had no great public stage on which it was practiced (39: "For the orator needs noise and applause, just like in a kind of theater. This was always the case for the ancient orators, when at the same time so many and such noble individuals crowded the Forum; when clients, as well, and fellow tribesmen and embassies sent from the towns and Italian representatives appeared in support of those on trial; and when in many trials the Roman people believed that their own interests were at stake").

33. In fact, a passage from the *Pro Plancio* suggests that Cicero was well known for his recourse to this strategy, for in the speech he refers to the prosecutor's fear that if the trial of Plancius were to coincide with the *ludi Romani,* Cicero would make a pathetic appeal for the defendant based on the sight of the sacred couches of the gods carried in procession through the Forum, just as he had on previous occasions (*Planc.* 83). Cf. Crassus's use of a Gallic shield hang-

The subject has received slight attention from modern commentators, although two scholars have at least pointed the way to further study. Victor Pöschl has examined Cicero's references to individuals present during his speeches. His work reveals a striking contrast between Cicero's practice and that of ancient Greek oratory, a contrast he attributes both to the emotional and flexible temperament of the Romans and to the idea that "consensus," or the perceptually expressed will of the majority, was understood by the Romans to be a barometer of truth.[34] Complementing Pöschl's analysis is a series of articles by Römisch that explore various aspects of the meaning of Cicero's references to place. In the first of these, the passage from the De legibus referred to above (2.1–8) provides a starting point for a meditation on the unique political-emotional-spiritual connection that bound the Romans to their environment. In later articles Römisch has cited a variety of passages from the speeches, the letters, and the philosophical and rhetorical essays as part of his examination of Ciceronian thought concerning places of symbolic (i.e., political, social, religious, or historical) significance.[35] The most recent of these articles has shown how Cicero's description of the scene outside the Temple of Concord in the fourth Catilinarian was transformed into a demonstration of the consensus omnium supporting the boni.[36]

While Pöschl and Römisch have thus identified a previously ignored aspect of Ciceronian persuasion, much concerning the orator's use of this technique remains unexplored. Even a brief survey demonstrates, first of all, that references to the visual milieu are of varying complexity. Certain passages are clearly of limited impact on the overall strategy of the speeches in which they occur. Allusions to familiar places, for instance, sometimes function as a kind of shorthand of characterization. The technique is familiar from a much-quoted passage in Plautus's Curculio (461–86) in which the choragus instructs the audience regarding the places where they may find a variety of individuals: perjurers can be

---

ing in front of a shop to ridicule his opponent (in De or. 2.266) and analysis of this passage in Perl, "Der Redner Helvius Mancia."

34. For comments and bibliography on the idea of Roman "collective morality," see Pöschl, "Zur Einbeziehung anwesender Personen," 216–18, 218 n. 21; Oehler, "Der consensus omnium."

35. See Römisch, "Umwelt und Atmosphäre"; "Mensch und Raum"; "Cicero."

36. Römisch, "Satis Praesidii."

found in the Comitium, liars and braggarts at the shrine of Venus Cloacina, rich spendthrifts and prostitutes *sub basilica*. The list goes on, mentioning many of the landmarks of the Republican Forum.[37] Cicero uses a similar technique in calling a certain Aebutius in the *Pro Caecina* "a fellow who hangs around the Regia" (14); or in the *Divinatio in Caecilium* in asking why Caecilius does not seek a defendant of his own class "near the Maenian column" (50); or in speaking of Naevius and his associates in the *Pro Quinctio* as individuals who can be found in "the Licinian [auction] halls" and at the entrance to the market (12; 25).

Other allusions to the visible milieu were intended simply to add vividness to abstract formulations. In the *Pro Roscio Amerino,* for instance, Cicero's claim that an unjust decision by the judges will unleash violence and anarchy is supported by his declaration that it is now up to the judges to prevent murders from being committed "here in the Forum, before the tribunal, . . . before your feet, judges, among the very benches of the court" (12). In the *Pro Quinctio* the orator attempts to impress his audience with the idea that the future of Roman justice hangs on the acquittal of Quinctius by declaring that either Truth will prevail or, driven from "this place," it will never again find anywhere to rest (5). Again, in the *Pro Sestio,* describing the destitution of public life after he had been forced into exile, Cicero asks: "Whom has the Curia missed more? Whom has the Forum more lamented? Whom have the very tribunals longed for as much? At my departure all became deserted, bitter, silent, full of tears and grief" (128). Through the use of this quasi-poetic anthropomorphism (a comparison with Daphnis's absence from the woodland comes inevitably to mind), Cicero no doubt hoped to heighten the *pathos* attached to the memory of his departure.

In many speeches, we find that Cicero makes powerful but relatively straightforward appeals to the religious and patriotic associations of the chief monuments visible from the Forum. Thus the fourth *Catilinarian* refers to the Curia, termed "the greatest haven of refuge for all peoples" (2: *summum auxilium omnium gentium*); the *De lege agraria* 1 speaks of the Arx, the "citadel of all peoples" (18: *arcem omnium gentium*); and, again in the fourth *Catilinarian,* Cicero declares that the Republic commends to the protection of the assembled senators "herself, the lives of all the citizens, the Arx and the Capitolium, the altars of the Penates,

37. Cf. *subbasilicanos* (Plaut. *Capt.* 815); *subrostrani* (Cic. *Fam.* 8.1.4); *canalicolae* (Fest. 40 L.); *forenses* (Livy 9.46.13).

that eternal fire of Vesta," and the temples and shrines of the gods, the walls and buildings of the city (18). Such passages are of great value in revealing to us the chief intellectual and emotional associations of the major monuments of the Capitoline and the Forum, and they can stand beside the great speech of Camillus in the fifth book of Livy's history or the depiction of Aeneas on the site of Rome in the eighth book of the *Aeneid* as evocations of the symbolic meanings attached to such places in the first century B.C.

Of greater interest in this work, however, is the process by which Cicero not only drew on the more accessible preexisting associations of monuments and topography but attempted to emphasize certain less obvious associations at the expense of others, as well as to create new meanings that would interact with preexisting associations to further his rhetorical aims.[38] The *Pro Scauro* provides a particularly clear example of this technique. In the speech, Cicero states that wherever he looked he found material for his defense of Scaurus (46: *quocumque non modo mens verum etiam oculi inciderunt*). He then connects each of a series of the most prominent monuments of the Forum with an event or idea redounding to the credit of the Scauri. The Curia calls to

---

38. The study I propose responds to the need to understand literature in the context of its historical reception. As Jauss argues, the effect of a new work of literature is felt by a reader "not only within the narrow horizons of his literary expectations but also within the wider horizon of his experience of life" ("Literary History as a Challenge to Literary Theory," 18). Of this interaction between the experience of literature and that of real life, Jauss writes: "The orientation of our experience by the creative capability of literature rests not only on its artistic character, which by virtue of a new form helps us surmount the mechanical process of everyday perception. . . . But the new form . . . can also make possible a new perception of things by forming the content of an experience which first appears in the form of literature. The relationship of literature and reader can be realized in the sensuous realm as stimulus to aesthetic perception as well as in the ethical realm as a stimulation to moral reflection" (37–38). (Cf. Jauss's *Towards an Aesthetic of Reception*, 41: "The horizon of expectations of literature distinguishes itself before the horizon of expectations of historical lived praxis in that it not only preserves actual experiences but also anticipates unrealized possibility, broadens the limited space of social behavior for new desires, claims, and goals, and thereby opens patterns of future experience.") Jauss speaks of two separate experiences: the experience of literature changes the subsequent perception of reality. In respect to the manipulation of visual stimuli, however, rhetoric is able to create a simultaneous process: the orator alters his listeners' sensual and moral perception while they are in the very act of perceiving.

mind the illustrious senatorial career of Scaurus's father (46); by his restoration of the Temple of Castor and Pollux, Scaurus's grandfather
seemed to have "established" (46: *constituisse*) the gods in the sight of
the jurors so that these deities might be able to intercede with them to
win the acquittal of his grandson; the Capitoline temple of Jupiter Optimus Maximus, Juno Regina, and Minerva called to mind the generosity of Scaurus's father and of Scaurus himself, who had made generous
gifts for its adornment (47); and the shrine of Vesta reminded the jurors
of the heroism of Lucius Caecilius Metellus, an ancestor of Scaurus's
mother, Caecilia Metella. As Pontifex Maximus, he had rescued the
Palladium—symbol of the well-being of the state—from the flames
that had threatened to destroy it when the shrine had caught fire in
241 B.C. (48).

In this section of the *Pro Scauro,* the manner in which Cicero uses the
visual milieu to manipulate the feelings of the audience towards his
client is relatively unambiguous.[39] In the case of two of Cicero's most
celebrated orations, the first and third *Catilinarians,* however, his use of
the associations of place is not so obvious; my analysis of the exploitation of setting in these works will therefore be the subject of the next
chapter.[40] This analysis must, of course, rely upon the received texts of
the speeches, and, as scholars have pointed out for generations, these
texts are not transcriptions but reflections—sometimes clear, sometimes
muddied—of the words actually spoken when the speeches were delivered.[41] It has often been argued that the *Catilinarians* in particular show
evidence of Cicero's desire in 60 B.C. to turn the speeches into apologiae
for his actions at the time of the conspiracy.[42] While it is probably cor-

39. For further discussion of this passage, see below, pp. 102–3 n. 25.

40. In spite of the existence of an extensive bibliography responding to the
manifold literary and rhetorical aspects of these speeches, no work has hitherto
attempted a systematic study of how appeal to ambiance actually functioned in
the overall strategy of each oration.

41. The speeches that we know to have been delivered form a continuum
between the *Oratio post reditum in senatu,* which was said to have been taken
down word for word, and the *Pro Milone,* which differed markedly from
the speech Cicero actually made in defense of Milo. On the relationship between the received texts and the original orations, see Humbert, *Les plaidoyers
écrits;* Laurand, *Etudes,* 1:1–23; Stroh, *Taxis und Taktik,* 31–54; and above,
pp. 8–9.

42. See, among others, Draheim, "Die ursprüngliche Form der katilinarischen Reden Ciceros"; Bornecque, *Les Catilinaires,* 145; Fuchs, "Eine Doppelfassung in Ciceros catilinarischen Reden"; Kennedy, *Art of Rhetoric,* 176–81.

rect to assume that certain lines might well have been added in redaction, those who have claimed to be able to identify numerous specific passages in each of the speeches that were not part of the originals have tended to ignore the importance of the excised portions to the thematic development of the whole. Nevertheless, I must here reiterate that any analysis of *actio*—that is, the speech as delivered—is to some extent theoretical. Thus the question that will be answered in the next chapter is, How do the transmitted texts of the first and third *Catilinarians* demonstrate the ways in which Cicero might have made use of the setting of the speeches to achieve his ends?

CHAPTER TWO

Transforming the Visible: *In Catilinam* 1 and 3

Nullus locus in [Roma] non religionum deorumque est plenus.

There is no place in Rome that is not filled with religious significance and with gods.

Livy 5.52.2

In August of 1963, Martin Luther King, Jr., began a now-famous oration with the following words: "Five score years ago, a great American, in whose symbolic shadow we stand today, signed the Emancipation Proclamation. . . . But one hundred years later, the Negro is still not free." The evocation of Abraham Lincoln was obvious to all present: in the diction of the opening phrase, in the allusion to the statue in the Lincoln Memorial, and in the explicit reference to the Emancipation Proclamation. If, two thousand years hence, we had no text of the Gettysburg Address, or were unsure where King stood when he spoke, or did not realize that the monument housed a huge statue of Lincoln, the rhetorical impact of the words might well be obscure. The phrase "five score years ago" would appear to be an inexplicable archaism, and the idea of the "symbolic shadow" of a "great American" might never be connected with the fact that King spoke in the actual shadow cast by the massive representation of the Great Emancipator.

The distance we are removed in time and place has obscured many of the associations that must have been immediately available to Cicero's audience. In a thoughtful analysis of the symbolism of the Marsyas statue in the Comitium of the Forum Romanum, F. Coarelli has spoken of ideas connected with a monument that "can easily escape a modern observer, yet were perfectly comprehensible to all at the time of their realization."[1] What is for us a recondite allusion to setting, extracted

1. Coarelli, *Il Foro Romano*, 2:90.

with some effort from the text, might well have been for Cicero's listeners immediately obvious. And an accomplished orator like Cicero would surely have avoided belaboring the obvious. In exploring this topic, therefore, we must keep in mind that Cicero's rhetorical instincts would frequently have counseled him to make connections between theme and setting subtle rather than patent, implicit rather than explicit. Furthermore, if we are to understand both the explicit and implicit allusions to places and monuments in the speeches, it is clear that we must go beyond analysis of the text in isolation and attempt to hear the speech as it was heard by its audience; we must try to understand, insofar as possible, the audience's reaction to what they heard in the context of what they saw. While certain elements of the topographical setting of the *Catilinarians* and the associations of that setting are irretrievably lost to us, much has been revealed through the work of Roman historians and archaeologists. We will begin, then, with the places where the speeches were delivered, focusing not only on their physical topography but also on their "metaphysical topography"—that is, the meaning these places would have held for a Roman audience in Cicero's time.

THE TEMPLE OF JUPITER STATOR

The first *Catilinarian* oration was delivered to the Senate in the Temple of Jupiter Stator, which was at the time surrounded by a large number of citizens, including a contingent of armed *equites*.[2] The building was located at the southeast end of the Forum valley on the elevated ground of the Velia at the base of the Palatine Hill.[3] In Roman, as in many an-

2. Cic. *Cat.* 2.12; Plut. *Cic.* 16.3; ps.-Cic. *Orat. pr. quam in exsil. iret* 24, in Orelli, Baiter, and Halm, *Opera*, 2:2.

3. While most scholars have until recently believed that the platform of peperino and travertine blocks uncovered just southeast of the Arch of Titus under the ruins of the medieval Turris Chartularia were the Flavian era remains of the Temple of Jupiter Stator, Coarelli (*Il Foro Romano*, 1:26–33) has cast doubt on that contention by arguing that the temple stood on the Sacra Via in the place now occupied by the so-called Temple of Romulus. Ongoing excavations in the Forum may soon resolve both the site of the temple and that of the Porta Mugonia. It is my belief that Coarelli's thesis cannot be sustained for the following reasons. (1) The two lists that make up the *Itinerarium*, a catalogue of the city from the fourth century A.D. that includes the *Curiosum* and the *Notitia*, both suggest that the Temple of Jupiter Stator stood at the beginning of the Sacra Via next to the Temple of Venus and Roma (see Jordan and Hülsen, *Topographie*,

cient religions, crossroads were sacred places, and the Temple of Jupiter Stator stood guard over a crossroads of great antiquity, sanctity, and strategic importance, formed by the meeting of the Sacra Via and the Clivus Palatinus. East of this point, the extension of the Sacred Way led out of the city through the Porta Capena and along the Via Appia; to the north the Velia descended towards the populous residential areas of the Subura; to the south the Clivus Palatinus led up the Palatine Hill, the ancient nucleus of Romulean Rome; and to the west the Sacra Via descended from this place, its beginning and highest point, past the monuments associated with the earliest days of the city—the house of the Vestal Virgins, the Temple of Vesta, and the Regia—down into the Forum proper.[4] Although its precise location remains a matter of debate, a review of the historical associations of the temple itself, as well as a general understanding of the topography and monuments of the

2:539–74). Coarelli discounts the idea that the lists reflect a topographical sequence by noting that in one the Basilica Nova and the Basilica Aemili Pauli are named together, although they did not stand next to each other (*Curiosum: Basilicam Novam et Pauli*). This combination, however, is the only departure from a clear topographical sequence, and it is obviously done for the sake of convenience of notation. Furthermore, Coarelli's contention that since the authors of the catalogues located the monument in the region of the Temple of Peace, it must have stood north of the Sacra Via is not persuasive, since the authors did not hesitate to violate strict regional divisions in a number of other cases. For instance, they have included the Basilica Aemilia in Region IV, in spite of the fact that it stood in the Forum Romanum. (2) Coarelli's argument that the silence of the lists concerning the "Temple of Romulus" requires us to identify it with the Temple of Jupiter Stator is not compelling, since the lists also neglect to mention a much more important monument and one that dominated the entire area, the Arch of Titus. (3) A comparison of Livy 1.12.1–8, Dion. Hal. 2.43.1–5, and Ov. *Tr.* 3.1.31–32 suggests that the location of Romulus's vow and, therefore, of the temple was within the Palatine *pomerium* rather than outside it, but Coarelli's new siting of the temple would put it outside the line of the ancient *pomerium*. (4) The identification of the Temple of Jupiter Stator with the "Temple of Romulus" contradicts two ancient sources: Plutarch (*Rom.* 18.7) states that the Romans drove the Sabines from the place of Romulus's vow back to the Regia and the Temple of Vesta; this can hardly refer to the extremely limited distance between the "Temple of Romulus" and the termination of the Sacra Via at the Regia. Ovid's statement in *Tr.* 3.1.31–32 that the Temple of Jupiter Stator is to the right as one proceeds up the Sacra Via is equally at odds with Coarelli's hypothesis.

4. This is what Varro (*LL* 5.47) and Festus (372 L.) define as the "popular" definition of the Sacra Via.

area, allows us to reconstruct the kinds of emotional and intellectual meanings this place would have held for Cicero's audience.[5]

The stories that were connected with the foundation of the Temple of Jupiter Stator in Cicero's time are preserved in the histories of Livy and Dionysius of Halicarnassus.[6] Both Augustan historians trace the vowing of the temple to a battle in the war with the Sabines that followed the forcible abduction of the Sabine women by the Romans. And in both accounts of this battle the reader can discern the joining of two important aetiological narratives, one explaining the location and name of the Temple of Jupiter Stator on the elevated ground at the southeast end of the Forum valley, and the other accounting for the Lacus Curtius at the opposite end of the Forum.

In the opening of his account of the battle, Livy describes how the Sabines rushed down into the Forum from the Capitoline citadel, which they had seized through the treachery of Tarpeia. In the Forum they met the Romans, led by Romulus, who had poured forth from their walled settlement on the Palatine. During the battle the Roman champion Hostilius falls, and the tide of the struggle suddenly turns. Romulus is swept by his retreating troops back to the "old gate of the Palatine" (i.e., the Porta Mugonia), where he addresses a prayer to Jupiter, reminding him that it was with his divine assent that he had first founded the city "here on the Palatine" (1.12.4). He goes on to ask the god to "drive the enemy back at least from this spot" (1.12.5) and to stay the flight of the Romans, promising that he will dedicate a temple to Jupiter Stator to serve as a reminder that the city had been saved by divine intervention. He then announces to his men that Jupiter Optimus Maximus commanded them to renew the battle, and he rushes to the forefront of his troops.

This event, which the reader expects to be followed immediately by a description of the success of the Romans in driving the enemy back across the Forum, is instead succeeded by an account of the fortunes of the Sabine champion, Mettius Curtius. At a point when the reader assumes that Romulus and his men, inspired by Jupiter Stator, have already forced the enemy back from the Porta, Curtius is depicted "not

---

5. For a survey of ancient sources on the temple, see Platner and Ashby, *Topographical Dictionary*, 303–4; for more recent bibliography, see Nash, *Pictorial Dictionary*, 1:534; Coarelli, *Il Foro Romano*, 1:26–33.

6. The variants in the two accounts indicate the historians drew on different annalistic sources. On sources, see Ogilvie, *Livy*, 75–78. The later narrative of Plutarch (*Rom.* 18.2–7) agrees closely with that of Dionysius.

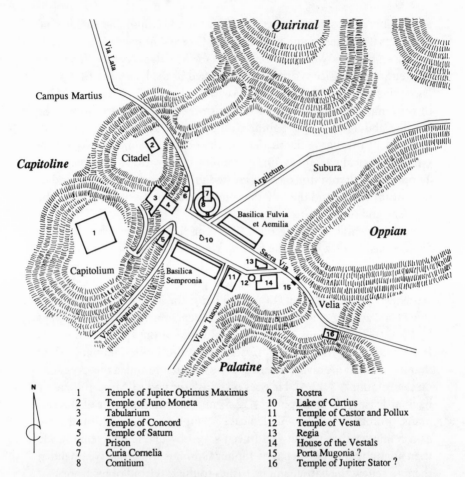

Fig. 2.   The Center of Republican Rome, showing the Capitoline Hill, the Velia, and the Forum valley. The plan illustrates the positions of key monuments as they might have existed in 63 B.C.

1	Temple of Jupiter Optimus Maximus	9	Rostra
2	Temple of Juno Moneta	10	Lake of Curtius
3	Tabularium	11	Temple of Castor and Pollux
4	Temple of Concord	12	Temple of Vesta
5	Temple of Saturn	13	Regia
6	Prison	14	House of the Vestals
7	Curia Cornelia	15	Porta Mugonia ?
8	Comitium	16	Temple of Jupiter Stator ?

far from the gate of the Palatine" (1.12.8), taunting the Romans as cowardly and already defeated. Spurred by Curtius's challenges, Romulus leads a charge against the enemy, whereupon the Sabines retreat. Curtius is plunged by his horse into the marsh at the opposite end of the Forum but soon emerges to renew the battle. By his wedding of these two narratives Livy encourages the reader to see the same series of events from two different points of view: in the first part of the narrative the Roman flight to the Porta is attributed to the fall of their champion

Hostilius, and the Roman recovery depends on Romulus's leadership and his prayer to Jupiter Stator; in the succeeding episode, however, the Romans appear to have been driven back to the Porta by the onslaught of Curtius and are moved to counterattack by Romulus, who has been aroused by Curtius's taunts.

Dionysius's account of the battle (2.42.1–43.5) also appears to be a conjunction of the same episodes, although the order of the two has been reversed.[7] In the first, Mettius Curtius, commanding the Sabine center, drives the Romans back to the gates of the city but is himself forced back when Romulus abandons command of the right wing to aid his retreating troops in the center (2.42.3). This account ends with Curtius's escape from the swamp. In the episode that follows, Romulus is wounded on the head by a stone and carried inside the walls. The Romans are forced to retreat, pursued "even up to the city" (2.43.2: *achri tēs poleōs*), until Romulus, recovered from his wound, again leads his men out and turns the tide of battle. It is now the Sabines who are forced to retreat, a maneuver in which they are hampered by the pursuit of the Romans, who attack from the high ground (2.43.4). While Dionysius makes no mention of Romulus's vow in this description of the battle, in a later passage he reports that because the god had heard his prayers and caused his routed troops to stand and fight, Romulus inaugurated a temple to Jupiter Stator near the Porta Mugonia (2.50.3).

The Temple of Jupiter Stator, then, was associated with Rome's first great military crisis. The flight that carried Romulus and his men to the Porta Mugonia was the turning point in a battle in which the very survival of Romulus's new city was to be decided. At the outset of the battle the Romans had been forced to abandon the rest of Rome to their enemies, and they controlled only the ancient core of the city within the Palatine walls. It was back to these walls, within the *pomerium,* or sacred boundary, of the Palatine city, that the Sabines had driven the Romans at the critical moment of Romulus's appeal to Jupiter. From this point no further retreat was possible, for if the Sabines had succeeded in breaching the Porta, the city would have been lost. The moment is dramatically akin to the night attack on the Capitoline by the Gauls when the Arx alone was held by a remnant of defenders against the enemy. And just as the sight of the Arx evoked the memory of Manlius, who

---

7. In addition, Dionysius describes two separate Sabine battles, whereas Livy compresses the action into a single dramatic narrative.

had prevented the final victory of the Gauls, the Temple of Jupiter Stator served as a testament to the leadership and heroism of Romulus, who had saved the newly founded city at a moment of profound danger.

The accounts of Livy and Dionysius also show that the continuance of Rome was not only the work of human resolve; central to the meaning of the story that the Romans associated with the temple was the belief that the salvation of the city at this time was owed to the direct intervention of Jupiter on Rome's behalf. This divine intervention is to be seen in two ways. In Livy's narrative, Romulus appeals to Jupiter in his capacity as Stator or "Stayer" to halt both the attack of the Sabine enemy (1.12.5: *hinc saltem arce hostes*) and the flight of the Romans (1.12.5: *deme terrorem Romanis fugamque foedam siste*). This latter interpretation of the meaning of the cult title of the god is the more common of the two and reappears in a second story in Livy connected with the temple (10.36.4–12).[8] Here the historian states that in 296 B.C., when M. Atilius Regulus was hard-pressed in a battle against the Samnites at Luceria, he vowed a temple to Jupiter Stator if the god would stay the flight of the Roman troops. Immediately thereafter the Romans halted their retreat, turned, and routed the enemy. Explaining why the same temple at the foot of the Palatine was twice vowed, Livy adds that Romulus had inaugurated only a *fanum,* or consecrated area, while the building itself was erected by the state subsequent to Atilius's vow (10.37.14–16). From these accounts it is clear that Cicero's audience would have seen Jupiter Stator as a god of battle who acted on behalf of Rome in moments of grave military crisis. He was both a divine protector who repulsed the attacks of Rome's enemies and a heavenly ally who brought victory by inspiring Roman troops to overcome their panic and fear.[9]

The senators who assembled to hear Cicero's speech would have felt Romulus's presence in this place in yet another way. Not only did the site evoke the memory of Romulus in his role as military leader, but it also recalled his actions as founder, for this area was closely associated with the Palatine Hill and the city that had been founded there by Ro-

8. Cf. Dion. Hal. 2.50.3; Plut. *Rom.* 18.7; August. *De civ. d.* 3.13; Flor. 1.1.13.

9. See Fears, "Cult of Jupiter," 48–52; Goar, *State Religion,* 36–45. Cf. *CIL* VI.434, 435 for Roman inscriptions to Jupiter Stator. For dedications to Stator outside of Rome see *CIL* III.895 (Dacia), 1089 (Apulum); VIII.17674 (Numidia); IX.3923, 3949 (Alba Fucens), 4534 (Nursia); X.5904 (Anagnia).

mulus. First of all, the site constituted the chief topographical link between the Forum valley and the Palatine, since the saddle of the Velia formed a natural ramp leading up the hill. Here was the easiest access to the Palatine, the point at which the earliest herdsmen would have driven their cattle up into the archaic settlement. In fact, Varro (*LL* 5.164) states that the name of the Porta Mugonia, the gate that stood immediately by the Temple of Jupiter Stator, came from *mugire* and referred to the lowing of the cattle that had once been herded along this path.[10]

In addition to being the easiest point of access to the Palatine, the site of the Temple of Jupiter Stator was also the most ancient and solemn area of approach to the hill. The Romans believed that the colonial founding rites practiced in their own times had been initiated by Romulus when he founded the city of Rome.[11] According to these rites the founder used a bronze plow to mark out the *pomerium,* the sacred boundary, of the new city. The walls of the city followed the circuit thus created, while the gates were indicated by lifting the plow in certain places along the line of this circuit. The Porta Mugonia, which appears in all the ancient references as the monument most closely associated both topographically and notionally with the Temple of Jupiter Stator, was one of the three gates believed to have been created by Romulus when, by this rite, he founded the Palatine city.[12] Further, it was in this place, according to Ovid, that Romulus had initiated these rites by burying the burnt offerings made on behalf of the new city and by beginning the sacred furrow.[13] It is for this reason that Livy depicts Romulus,

10. For the Porta Mugonia, see Platner and Ashby, *Topographical Dictionary,* 410; Ogilvie, *Livy,* 77–78 (ad 1.12.3); Luck, *Tristia,* 2:165–66 (ad *Tr.* 3.1.31); Tac. *Ann.* 12.24; Ziegler, "Palatium," 25, calls this the *Haupttor* of the Palatine and the only one accessible in Ovid's time.

11. For founding rites, see Salmon, *Roman Colonization,* 24, 168 n. 27; Rykwert, *Idea of a Town,* 27–71. For ancient sources on the founding of Rome, see Lugli, *Fontes,* 1:7–36.

12. Tacitus (*Ann.* 12.24) states that Romulus established the *pomerium* of the early city by plowing a furrow around the base of the hill, and mentions three points in the circuit: the Hercules altar in the Forum Boarium, the altar of Consus in the Circus Maximus, and the Temple of the Lares in this area of the Velia.

13. Cf. Ov. *Tr.* 3.1.31–32 (*"Porta est" ait "ista Palati,/ hic Stator, hoc primum condita Roma loco est"*) and Ov. *Fast.* 4.821–26 (description of the founding ritual). Although Ovid does not use the name, his description of the pit in which the offerings were placed and the altar then erected on the spot

when he vows the temple to Jupiter Stator, reminding Jupiter that "here on the Palatine, commanded by your birds, I laid the first foundations of the city" (1.12.3–7: *Iuppiter, tuis, inquit, iussus avibus hic in Palatio prima urbi fundamenta ieci*).

The immediate area of the temple would have contained a number of other visible monuments (in addition to the Porta) connected with this act of foundation. The line of the archaic *pomerium* of the Palatine, followed by the celebrants of the Lupercalia, would probably have been marked by stone *cippi*.[14] Ovid (*Fast.* 4.821–25) refers to an altar set up here by Romulus during the ritual founding of the city to mark the place where the first fruits had been buried. Unless this altar was one of those that had fallen to ruin and been restored by Augustus, it would no doubt have been visible in Cicero's day. Finally, in this area stood a temple to the Lares, the indwelling spirits of the city of Rome, as well as one to the Di Penates, the household gods carried by Aeneas from Troy. Both of these monuments were associated with divine sanction for and protection of the city from its earliest existence.[15]

---

corresponds with that of the shrine of "Roma Quadrata" in Festus (310, 312 L.). Festus, however, locates this shrine *ante templum Apollinis*. This shrine has sometimes been identified as a *mundus Palatii* corresponding to a *mundus* in the area of the Comitium. The sources, however, are contradictory and confused. See Plut. *Rom.* 11.1–2; Fest. 124–26, 144–47 L.; Varro ap. Macr. 1.16.18; Serv. ad *Aen.* 3.134. For discussion, see Magdelain, "Le pomerium archaïque"; Weinstock, "Mundus patet"; Fowler, "Mundus patet"; Verzar, "L'umbilicus urbis"; Catalano, "Aspetti spaziali," 452–66; Rykwert, *Idea of a Town*, 117–26, 129; Platner and Ashby, *Topographical Dictionary*, 346–48; Coarelli, *Il Foro Romano*, 1:207–26.

14. Scullard, *Festivals*, 76–78.

15. According to Ovid (*Fast.* 6.791–94), the feast of the Lares temple and that of Jupiter Stator were on the same day, June 27, a chronological association that seems to reflect their topographical association. Solinus (1.21–24) speaks of a Lares temple *in summa sacra via*. It is possible that this is the same monument Tacitus speaks of as one of the points on the Romulean *pomerium* (*Ann.* 12.24). See also Obseq. 41; Cic. *Nat.d.* 3.63; Pliny *HN* 2.16; *CIL* VI.456; Platner and Ashby, *Topographical Dictionary*, 314–15; Coarelli, *Il Foro Romano*, 1:34–38. For the Temple of the Penates, see Castagnoli, "Il tempio dei Penati"; Lugli, *Monumenti minori*, 165–92; Varro *LL* 5.54; Livy 45.16.5; Obseq. 13; Solin. 1.22. Both temples, restored by Augustus, received specific mention in the *Res gestae* (19). See also Ov. *Fast.* 5.129: *praestitibus Laribus;* Cic. *Sull.* 86: *di patrii ac penates, qui huic urbi atque huic rei publicae praesidetis.* On the Lares and Penates in Roman religion, see Latte, *Römische Religionsgeschichte*, 89–

If one were to think of Romulus's foundation on the Palatine in terms of a house, the site of the Temple of Jupiter Stator was the *janua*, the sacred entrance, to that house. Or, to draw a different analogy, the associated monuments of the temple and the Porta Mugonia formed the "Propylaeum" of the Palatine. It was on this strategic site that the Palatine "began" in a topographical, religious, and ceremonial sense. And in this place Cicero could assume that images of the foundation of Rome by Romulus and of the great battle later fought against the Sabines to protect the city were particularly vivid in the minds of his audience.

THE FIRST *CATILINARIAN:* *MUNITISSIMUS LOCUS*

At the very outset of the first *Catilinarian* Cicero draws attention to the setting in which the speech takes place.[16] The orator begins the proem

---

94, 108; for belief in the Trojan origin of the Penates, see Bömer, *Rom und Troja;* Alföldi, *Die trojanischen Urahnen der Römer.*

16. The bibliography on all aspects of the conspiracy is large. For relatively recent work, see Criniti, *Bibliografia.* Mitchell, *Cicero,* 219–40, provides an excellent account of the speeches and their political background. Even a cursory reading reveals that Cicero had two principal aims in the speech and that these two were somewhat at odds. His first goal was to induce Catiline to leave Rome, thereby declaring himself in open rebellion against the state. Since the consul was unwilling to put the question of Catiline's exile to a vote in the Senate— whether due to lack of support or to the questionable legality of such a measure—he had to convince Catiline that it was in his interest to depart. In the speech, therefore, he argues that Catiline's continued presence in Rome was to no purpose, since, he, Cicero, was in firm control of the city (note, in this regard, images of Catiline as watched, beset, surrounded: 1: *constrictam;* 6: *obsessus; oculi et aures . . . speculabuntur atque custodient; teneris undique;* 7: *circumclusum*). Cicero also hoped to convince those who refused to take seriously the danger represented by Catiline that strong and concerted action was politically required, legally sanctioned, and morally justified. The orator's litany of his enemy's actions and plans, therefore, is intended as a demonstration of the increasingly bold attempts by Catiline to seize power. The listener is led to understand that although the consul had thus far restrained Catiline, the latter's continued presence in Rome would be disastrous for the state. The dual strategy is masterfully carried through and successfully avoids the appearance of self-contradiction. On the one hand, it must have persuaded Catiline that his plans in Rome were hopelessly compromised by the loose tongues of his coconspirators; and on the other, it would surely have convinced many of the disbelievers

with a riveting series of challenges to Catiline that move from a wider to an ever narrower focus on the prevailing ambiance. After referring to the armed guards who have stood night watch on the Palatine, the fear that has gripped the people, and the loyal citizens who have gathered outside the temple, he asks Catiline whether "the fact that the Senate has met in this well-fortified place (*munitissimus locus*) has disturbed" him (1). The passage culminates with an allusion to the "faces and expressions" of the senators who sit within the temple. In a later passage, Cicero goes on to describe in more detail the scene inside the building. Here he recalls how upon Catiline's entrance none of those assembled greeted him but rather shrank away in fear, and how when he took his seat, the benches around him immediately emptied (16). The mute hostility and dread displayed by the senators both here and at the moment when Cicero orders Catiline from the city (20–21) is contrasted with the raucously expressed sentiments of the citizens who surround the building (21). These men, according to Cicero, have scarcely been restrained from physically attacking Catiline and eagerly await the opportunity to escort him to the city gates.

These allusions to the highly charged ambiance within and without the temple were intended by Cicero to focus the attention of his listeners on the crisis that was being played out before their eyes. Everything they saw and heard around them became a perceptible demonstration of Cicero's contentions: that Catiline had paralyzed the city with fear; that the masses, the *equites,* and the Senate itself were united in their opposition to the conspirators; that the consul's prudent action had thus far allowed the city to be preserved from harm; and that the crisis had deepened to the point that firm and courageous action was now imperative. Most of all, such scenes become a visible sign of Catiline's alienation from the city and its inhabitants, an isolation so complete that now the very light and air of Rome could no longer hold any pleasure for him.[17]

In addition to describing the general milieu in which the speech was taking place, Cicero twice addresses Jupiter Stator, the deity to whom the building was dedicated and whose statue would have dominated the

---

and fence sitters that Catiline was now embarked on a violent revolutionary course that must be opposed.

17. See 13 (*delectare*); 15 (*potestne tibi haec lux . . . aut huius caeli spiritus esse iucundus*). For further discussion of Cicero's effectiveness in describing the complete isolation of Catiline from his physical environment, see Römisch, "Cicero," 50–52; "Umwelt und Atmosphäre," 125.

inside of the temple (11, 33). Cicero could be sure that these references to the god would call up a number of associations in the minds of his listeners, especially when we note that these references are embedded in a text that makes constant use of metaphors drawn from war and personal combat.[18] For instance, the defenders of the state congratulate themselves on avoiding Catiline's "weapons," while the final decree of the Senate is termed a "sword hidden in its sheath" (2, 4). In section 15 Cicero uses a dueling metaphor to describe his escape from Catiline's attacks "by, as it were, a slight swerve of the body" and goes on to refer to "the dagger" that has "so many times . . . been wrested from [Catiline's] hand" or "by chance slipped from [his] grasp" (16). Since the primary understanding of Jupiter's role as Stator appears to have been as a divine "steadier" in the heat of combat who brought victory through stemming panic and flight, it seems clear that the orator's allusions to the temple and its god, when set within a pattern of references to metaphorical combat, would have led his listeners to feel that the struggle with Catiline and his followers could already be seen as a war, and that in this war the forces of the *boni* were encouraged, protected, and supported by the god of battles in whose temple they met.[19]

But allusions to the temple and to Jupiter Stator would have called up other, even more specific, associations, and these were also prepared for by Cicero's development throughout the speech of images of Catiline and his followers. Clearly, one of Cicero's chief aims in the first *Catilinarian* was to induce his audience to see Catiline not only as a pernicious citizen (3: *civem perniciosum*)—a traitor deserving of exile—but

18. Actual military preparations included the establishment of Manlius's camp in Etruria (7), the attempt upon Praeneste (8), the military plans formulated in Laeca's house (8–10), the planned joining of Manlius's and Catiline's forces (23), and the sending of the military standard of the revolutionaries (the legionary eagle of Marius) to Forum Aurelium (24). According to Cicero, violence within the city included past and present plans for the massacre of leaders of the *optimates* (7, 15), indiscriminate murder and arson (9, 12), assassination attempts on Cicero's life (9, 11, 32), and constant disruption of public business (32).

19. The importance of Stator's functions arises from the crucial role played by the psychological element in ancient warfare. This is illustrated in Caesar's accounts of the battle of Pharsalus (*B.civ.* 3.88–95) and of the Sambre (*B.Gall.* 2.19–27). See also Watson, *Roman Soldier,* 117–29; Adcock, *Roman Art of War,* 21–22, 83–84, 109–10, 118–19. For the development of imagery drawn from gladiatorial and military conflict in the *Pro Sestio,* see Fantham, *Republican Latin Imagery,* 128–32.

as a *hostis* whose plans and actions had thrust him outside the pale of citizenship and the legal protection that accompanied that status.[20] At various points, therefore, within the overall pattern of military metaphors noted above, the orator exploits the concept of Catiline as an enemy leader from without who has managed to penetrate the walls of the city.[21] Early in the speech the consul declares: "Why, you see the general and commander of this enemy within the walls, and even within the Senate" (5: *eorum autem castrorum imperatorem ducemque hostium intra moenia atque adeo in senatu videtis*); and similar diction is repeated when the *patria* remonstrates with Cicero for allowing the future leader (*ducem*) and general (*imperatorem*) of a war against the state (*bellum*) to leave the city (27). When the orator says to Catiline, *exire ex urbe iubet consul hostem* (13: "The consul orders the enemy to leave the city"), the syntax and diction of the phrase make clear that the orator is encouraging his listeners to see Catiline as the enemy chief (*hostis*) who has breached the city walls, while the consul assumes the role of military commander and defender of the city (*consul*), the "togate general" engaged in a duel to the death with the leader of the enemy forces to see which of the two will carry off the *spolia opima*.[22]

This theme of "the enemy within" is reinforced as well by the orator's oft-repeated allusions to the walls themselves. These begin with the passage cited above (5), in which Cicero exclaims that the enemy general has not only succeeded in entering within the city walls but has even dared to appear inside the Senate. Two subsequent references (10, 19) emphasize the extreme personal danger posed to the consul by his opponent's presence within Rome. In section 32, however, the image of the city wall is a vital one in generalizing the cause. Here Cicero commands

20. Note Cicero's citation of precedents for summary execution of revolutionary citizens (3–4, 27–28) and his statement that *numquam in hac urbe qui a republica defecerunt civium iura tenuerunt* (28). The contrast between *civis* and *hostis* first appears at the beginning of the speech (3: *civem perniciosum quam acerbissimum hostem*), but here it had been implied that Catiline fit into the former category. For the legal and political background of the term, see Hellegouarc'h, *Le vocabulaire latin;* Jal, "Hostis (publicus)."

21. These images are interwoven with those that depict Catiline as a scourge that has arisen from inside the state (see 11, 30: *pestis rei publicae;* 12: *sentina rei publicae;* and 17–18, in which Catiline is compared to a householder hated by his slaves and a son hated by his parents).

22. For Cicero as *dux togatus*, see *Cat.* 2.28 (*uno togato duce et imperatore*), 3.15, 23; *Sull.* 85; *Har. resp.* 49 (*togatum domestici belli exstinctorem*); and Nicolet, "Consul togatus," 240–45.

the conspirators to depart and, in so doing, imagines the walls of the city as a physical and moral boundary between patriots and traitors, between good men and evil, between *boni* and *improbi*. The injunction that Catiline's followers be separated "from us" by the city wall is prefaced by the remark that this was a demand that Cicero had made many times before. It is not to be doubted, then, that this same theme was one that had been exploited in many previous speeches of Cicero's consular year and had become familiar to his audience.[23]

Such passages prepared Cicero's audience to make an obvious connection between past and present. By the end of the speech, when the orator appeals in prayer to Jupiter Stator, his listeners would surely have felt the special relevance to their own situation of the circumstances under which the temple had been founded. In the early days of the city its loyal defenders had been forced to confront an enemy who had treacherously breached the city walls. Now Cicero's audience too was confronted with an enemy who threatened them from inside the walls. From their foothold within the city the Sabines had launched their attacks throughout the Forum. Catiline and his coconspirators had also created panic and violence throughout the city: they had planned attacks in the Comitium (7, 15, 32), disturbed the tribunals of the judges (32), and threatened "the temples, buildings, and walls of the city and the lives of its citizens" (12). Like their forebears, the *boni* had now been driven back by the fierce attacks of the enemy to the *munitissimus locus* at the foot of the Palatine. The senators in Cicero's audience are thus encouraged by the orator to see Catiline and his followers in the role of the Sabine *hostes* while identifying themselves with the hard-pressed defenders of the Palatine settlement who had been inspired by the will of the god.

In this scenario Cicero himself implicitly assumes the role of Romulus, for he solicits the aid of Jupiter Stator from the very spot where the founder had prayed for the intercession of the same god at a moment of similarly grave danger to the continued existence of the city. The sonorous and moving prayer that concludes the speech is surely intended by Cicero as a verbal echo of that of Romulus, and the orator's diction is markedly similar to that used later by Livy in depicting the vow made by the founder. "But you, O father of gods and men, repulse the enemy at least from this place" (1.12.4–5: *At tu, pater deum hominumque,*

23. The danger posed by the enemy within is reiterated in other extant speeches from this year: *Cat.* 2.4, 17, 27; *Rab. per.* 33; *Leg. agr.* 2.102.

hinc saltem arce hostes), Romulus prays at the turning point in the battle. "You, Jupiter, will repulse [them] from the buildings and walls of the city and . . . punish the enemies of the state" (33: *Tu, Iuppiter . . . a tectis urbis ac moenibus . . . arcebis et . . . hostis patriae . . . mactabis*) is Cicero's prayer at the end of the first *Catilinarian*. We shall see that this role of *alter Romulus* (or, in the sarcastic phrase of one of his enemies, "the Romulus from Arpinum") was one the orator would attempt to play throughout the Catilinarian crisis.[24]

The strategy of the speech, then, encouraged a connection in the listener's mind between the traditional story of the temple's founding and the present crisis; but a closer look at the passages addressed to Jupiter Stator shows that Cicero is suggesting as well a broader understanding of Jupiter's role. In the first of these passages, which immediately follows Cicero's command that Catiline depart and thereby "purge" the city, the orator gives thanks to all the gods and especially to Jupiter Stator, whom he calls "the most ancient guardian of this city" (11: *antiquissimo custodi huius urbis*), because the citizens had so often avoided "such a foul, horrid, and destructive bane" (11: *tam taetram, tam horribilem tamque infestam rei publicae pestem*). While the reference to Jupiter Stator as the city's "most ancient guardian" could be understood as an allusion to the god's action in inspiring the Romans during the battle with the Sabines, it seems to hint at a different and more general understanding of his function. Further, the appeal to Jupiter Stator to save the city from what is termed a "plague" or "curse" suggests that his sphere of action extends beyond that normally associated with a god of battles.[25]

The second and more extended reference to Jupiter Stator, already cited for its implicit exploitation of the connection between past and present, makes clear what was only hinted at in the earlier passage. Here Cicero had said:

24. Cf., for example, Cicero's equation of himself with Romulus in *Cat.* 3.2 (*profecto, quoniam illum qui hanc urbem condidit ad deos immortalis benivolentia famaque sustulimus, esse apud vos posterosque vestros in honore debebit is qui eandem hanc urbem conditam amplificatamque servavit*) and criticism of his assumption of the role in ps.-Sall. *Inv. in Cic.* 7: *Oro te, Romule Arpinas, qui egregia tua virtute omnis Paulos, Fabios, Scipiones superasti, quem tandem locum in civitate obtines?*

25. For Catiline and his followers as a *pestis*, see 11 and 30; for Catiline as bringing *pestem*, see 2 and 33.

Tu, Iuppiter, qui isdem quibus haec urbs auspiciis a Romulo es constitutus, quem Statorem huius urbis atque imperi vere nominamus, hunc et huius socios a tuis ceterisque templis, a tectis urbis ac moenibus, a vita fortunisque civium omnium arcebis et homines bonorum inimicos, hostis patriae, latrones Italiae scelerum foedere inter se ac nefaria societate coniunctos aeternis suppliciis vivos mortuosque mactabis.

(33)

You, Jupiter, who were established by the same auspices as those by which Romulus established the city, whom we rightly call the Stator of this city and its *imperium,* may you repel this man and his companions from your temple and from the other temples, from the buildings and walls of the city, from the lives and fortunes of all the citizens; and may you visit with everlasting punishments—both while they are living and after they are dead—these opponents of good men, enemies of the fatherland, brigands of Italy, who are now joined in criminal society and evil confederation.

The text begins with two striking and surprising locutions. First, Jupiter is addressed as "Stator of this city and its *imperium.*" Here Cicero has transformed the meaning of the cult title, as Stator can in this case no longer be understood simply as "Stayer." Cicero's phrase looks to the root meaning of the word: Jupiter Stator becomes Jupiter "the stabilizer," "the one who makes the city stand." Cicero emphasizes this reinterpretation by inverting the normal word order of the verb so that *constitutus* (also derived from the root *stare*) appears as close as possible to the word Stator.

Second, Cicero states that Jupiter as Stator was established by Romulus (*constitutus*) "by the same auspices" (*isdem auspiciis*) as those by which the city was established. If one thinks of the meaning of the temple only in connection with the battle fought against the Sabines, the statement is unintelligible. The traditional stories depicting the *auspicia urbis condendae,* while varying in other details, are unvarying in chronology: the taking of auspices by Romulus (and, in vain, by Remus) is always presented as the first and determinant act in the establishment of the city.[26] On the other hand, the auspices taken by Romulus that estab-

26. The sources are collected in Lugli, *Fontes* 1:23–26. Skutsch, *Annals of Ennius,* 221–23, 225–27, believes that the earliest version of the auspice taking placed Remus on the so-called Remoria, a spur on the southeast corner of the Aventine once known as Murcus, and Romulus *in alto . . . Aventino.* When the Murcus and Aventine later merged, the story was altered to retain the image of the twins on opposite hills. For Romulus on the Aventine, see Ennius 1.80–81 in Cic. *Div.* 1.107 and Arn. 4.3. Servius seems to know both this version (ad

lished the *templum* (or, according to Livy, the *fanum*) of Jupiter Stator came only later in the history of the city, after the battle with the Sabines.

There is clearly something amiss in the way the passage has been interpreted. When Cicero says, *Tu, Iuppiter qui . . . es constitutus, quem Statorem . . . vere nominamus,* it has been assumed that this should be understood as "Tu, Iuppiter Stator, cuius templum constitutum est."[27] If, however, we take Cicero at his word, it is Jupiter who was "established" by Romulus at the moment of the foundation, not his *templum.* This use of the verb with a personal subject is in no way unusual; and the use of the verb *constituere* in connection with both the personal (*tu*) and the inanimate (*urbs*) in the same sentence is an example of zeugma, a figure often used by Cicero.[28] Cicero here implies that in the augural signs granted to Romulus more was signified than simply divine sanction for the establishment of the city. Cicero interprets these first auspices as a covenant between Romulus and Jupiter, according to which the god both assented to the foundation of Rome and assumed the role of Stator, that is, establisher and protector, of the new city. The orator thus joins conceptually and chronologically the two chief associations of the location where the speech was delivered: the founding here of the

---

Aen 3.46) and the version that placed Romulus on the Palatine (ad *Aen* 6.779). The later version became standard (see the list of sources in Pease, *De divinatione,* 293). Curiously, it was not the *site* of the new city—always agreed to be the Palatine—that was to be determined by augury but the honor of its founding and naming (Livy 1.6.4: *legerent qui nomen novae urbi daret, qui conditam imperio regeret*).

27. E.g., Haury, *Orationes in Catilinam,* 88: "Ecart chronologique insignifiant entre la fondation de Rome et le voeu du temple pendant le combat contre les Sabins"; Goar, *State Religion,* 36: "In his striving after solemnity Cicero has greatly exaggerated the age of the temple in which he is addressing the meeting of the Senate"; Richter, *Ciceros catilinarische Reden,* 48: "*eisdem auspiciis*— ungenau: denn der von Romulus im Sabinerkrieg gelobte Tempel wurde erst viel später im J. 294 erbaut, aber der Platz war doch schon geweiht gewesen"; Halm, *Ciceros Reden gegen L. Sergius Catilina,* 50: "*isdem auspiciis,* mit rhetorischer Übertreibung, da das Heiligthum erst im Sabinerkrieg von Romulus gelobt (Livy 1.12) und der eigentliche Tempel viel später erbaut worden ist."

28. Kühner and Stegmann, *Grammatik* (2:565–66), note the following examples of zeugma in Cicero: *Att.* 10.4.4 (*conflictati*); *Tusc.* 2.57 (*missa*), 4.64 (*accidit*), 5.66 (*alebatur*), 5.87 (*corrupta*); *Cat.* 3.24 (*redundavit*); *Mil.* 3 (*denuntiant*); *Fin.* 2.88 (*fruitur*).

Palatine city by Romulus and the subsequent dedication of a temple in this place to Jupiter Stator.

On a philosophical level, this reinterpretation of Jupiter Stator's role constitutes a significant broadening of the sphere in which the god was *praesens* (i.e., both present and efficacious). His function as a god of battles in stemming the attack on the Palatine city and emboldening the Roman troops becomes an expression of his larger role—as *Stator urbis atque imperii* or, in the language of the earlier passage, *antiquissimus custos urbis* (11). Römisch has shown that a parallel approach can be found in the *Pro Milone*. Here, Jupiter Latiaris, the Latin god of the Alban hills, is seen not only as the avenger of Clodius's sacrilege within his own space but as the guardian of Rome's destiny;[29] similarly, in the first *Catilinarian*, Jupiter Stator is no longer restricted in his sphere but has become the protector of the city itself and its *imperium*.[30] This sense is strengthened by the diction of the address to Jupiter, for the orator's appeal to the god to protect the city and its citizens uses the ritual terms *arcere*, meaning "to keep the *profani* at a distance," and *mactare*, referring to destruction that is dedicated to or ordained by a divinity.[31] The *templum* of the god, then, is not to be thought of as simply the consecrated area on the Velia but extends to the entire area within the walls. The conspirators' crimes are a profanation of this *templum*, and Cicero proclaims that Jupiter himself will avenge them.

It is not likely that this interpretation of the cult title of the god was in the popular consciousness at the time of the speech; it is unclear, however, whether Cicero was actually the originator of the

29. Römisch, "Umwelt und Atmosphäre," 119–20: "Jupiter Latiaris, in dem höchsten Heiligtum der Latiner, dem auch Roms Magistrate Verehrung zollen, wird angerufen. . . . Clodius hat sein Gebiet ebenfalls geschändet. . . . Doch ist das Eingreifen der Götter zwar Reaktion auf die ihnen widerfahrene Kränkung, aber nicht nur das. Es ist zugleich Ausdruck der *cura immortalium*, der göttlichen Fürsorge für das Schicksal Roms."

30. For evidence of other correspondences between the philosophical works and the speeches, see Heibges, "Cicero—A Hypocrite in Religion?" who points out that by far the most frequently invoked god is Jupiter, in his guise as "the all-pervading deity" of the Stoics (306); Bruwaene, *La théologie de Cicéron*, 246; Heibges, "Religion and Rhetoric."

31. See Ogilvie, *Livy*, 78 (on Livy 1.12.4, Romulus's vow during the Sabine battle). Other parallel uses cited by Ogilvie: Hor. *Carm.* 3.1.1; Ov. *Fast.* 6.482; Tac. *Hist.* 5.8; Luc. 5.139. For *mactare* (and *macte*), see *The Oxford Latin Dictionary;* Cato *Agr.* 132.1, 2; 134.2, 3, 4; Non. 341–42 (Müller).

concept.[32] A similar interpretation later appears in Seneca's *De beneficiis,* where the philosopher states that the term Stator did not derive, "as the historians relate," from the fact that Jupiter had halted the flight of the Roman troops, but because "all things exist by his beneficence, he is the establisher and stabilizer [of all]" (4.7.1: *et Iovem . . . Statorem, qui non, ut historici tradiderunt, ex eo, quod post votum susceptum acies Romanorum fugientium stetit, sed quod stant beneficio eius omnia, stator stabilitorque est*). The passage, which testifies to the syncretism of all aspects of the chief god, echoes a section of the *De legibus* (2.28) in which Cicero states that all virtues were rightly held divine, including things to be hoped for such as Salus, Honor, Ops, and Victoria, as well as cult titles of Jupiter such as Invictus and Stator. The assertion of the unity of divine functions would seem to point to a Stoic source for this interpretation. If this is the case, then the manipulation of the ideas found in the speech is an example of the orator's effort not only to abstract general principles from individual instances (a constant feature of Ciceronian rhetoric), but also to make use of philosophical tenets as part of this process of abstraction.

The degree to which these associations were accessible to Cicero's audience is witnessed by a passage from a later speech by an imitator of Cicero. The speech, entitled *Oratio pridie quam in exsilium iret,*[33] alludes to the first *Catilinarian,* attempting at the moment of Cicero's exile—his greatest failure—to recall the moment of his greatest triumph. In section 24 the author (assuming the persona of Cicero) addresses Jupiter in the following words:

> teque, Iuppiter Stator, quem vere huius imperii statorem maiores nostri nominaverunt, cuius in templo hostilem impetum Catilinae reppuli a muris, cuius templum a Romulo victis Sabinis in Palatii radice cum Victoria est collacatum, oro atque obsecro.

> I beg and beseech you, Jupiter Stator, whom our ancestors have rightly called the establisher of this *imperium,* in whose temple I repelled from the walls Catiline's hostile attack, and whose temple was established with that of Victoria at the root of the Palatine by Romulus after the Sabines had been defeated.

32. Pariente, "Stator," argues that this was the original, archaic meaning of the cult title, subsequently forgotten and reinterpreted.
33. Orelli, Baiter, and Halm, *Opera,* 2:2.

The passage functions as a gloss on the earlier speech, for here the associations implicit in the first *Catilinarian* become clumsily explicit. The author alludes both to Jupiter Stator's role in the general, "philosophical" sense as guarantor of Roman *imperium* and to his role as "Stayer" in the battle against the Sabines. The analogy between Cicero and Romulus is also made more explicit by the allusion to Cicero's success in driving the enemy "away from the walls" (*reppuli a muris*). If the author of this speech had been inspired only by the historical situation of the first *Catilinarian,* he would hardly have claimed that Cicero had repelled Catiline and his followers from the walls, since Catiline had been within the Temple of Jupiter Stator when the speech was delivered. It is only in reaction to the rhetoric of Cicero's oration that the author is led to make this analogy.

It was Cicero himself who summoned the Senate to meet in the Temple of Jupiter Stator. The claim that it was security alone that prompted the decision is weak, as temples on the Palatine itself or the Temple of Castor would have served this purpose better. In choosing the Temple of Jupiter Stator, Cicero was chiefly concerned not with the *reality* of security but with the *perception* of security. Even if the Temple of Jupiter Stator was not necessarily the strongest defensive point in which to hold the meeting, it was the temple whose associations made it most clearly *munitissimus:* it was the monument guarding the chief approach to the Palatine, the site of the earliest foundation of Rome; it was thought to be the spot where Jupiter had repelled the Sabine enemy and thereby saved the newly created city; and, through the reinterpretation of the cult title carried out by Cicero's rhetoric, it could be made to symbolize the divine protection of Jupiter for the city as a whole.

In this place the orator could assume that his audience might be particularly receptive to the themes he would inevitably play on that day, whether Catiline were present or not. Here would be an especially potent symbolic *locus* from which he might expound upon the gravity of the danger that threatened them from within the walls and to rally all patriotic Romans to the divinely supported defense of the embattled city. And in this place, closely connected both with the founding of the city by Romulus and his defense of it in the battle against the Sabines, Cicero could foster his own "Romulean" role as political, moral, and spiritual leader of Rome in its hour of crisis.

ROSTRA AND COMITIUM:
THE CENTER OF THE CENTER

In a recent book, E. V. Walter has described the various aspects of place in the following way:

> The concept of expressive space means the subjective dimension of located experience. Expressive reality refers to what people feel and think and imagine, just as perceptual reality signifies things they perceive, and cognitive reality, things they understand. A place is a concrete milieu and an expressive universe within specific social and physical boundaries, with a location in physical space and time and an identity.[34]

There are many indications that, for the Romans, Rome was an "expressive universe" of extraordinary richness. The physical environment of the city in Cicero's day constituted then, as now, a nexus between present and past, and, to the Roman, the past was of inestimable importance. "Not to know what happened before you were born is always to remain a child. For what is a person's life if it is not woven into the lives of those who came before by the memory of things past?" Cicero writes in the *Orator*.[35] Roman religious ritual lovingly preserved in incomprehensible detail antique words and actions; noble Roman houses were adorned with the realistic busts of the dead, who thereby commanded the daily notice of the living; and Roman history was an almost unbroken sigh of regret for the men and institutions that had gone before. The stimuli that sparked the remembrance of the past were, in large part, the statues, temples, graves, altars, and countless other monuments that graced the city, each carrying its story and its special significance.

This quality of historical allusiveness connected with places and monuments is perhaps best illustrated by Vergil's depiction of Aeneas's visit to Rome in the eighth book of the *Aeneid,* where even in the settlement of that archaic time the hero continually finds himself discovering some vestige of a lost past. Vergil, from the perspective of the first century B.C., looks on the Forum Boarium, the Capitoline, the Roman Forum, and the Palatine of Augustan Rome and creates in these places the image of the proto-Rome of Aeneas's host, King Evander. But the poet's imagination carries him back still farther, for Evander recalls for his guest the story of Hercules' visit and his battle with the monster

34. Walter, *Placeways,* 143.
35. *Or.* 120: *Nescire autem quid ante quam natus sis acciderit, id est semper esse puerum. Quid enim est aetas hominis, nisi ea memoria rerum veterum cum superiorum aetate contexitur?*

Cacus on the Palatine. The ruined walls of the Capitoline lead the king
to speak of an even more distant Golden Age, when Saturn himself had
ruled from the Capitolium. Nor, according to Evander, was Saturn the
first inhabitant of the place, for he had found on the site of Rome a
rough and uncultivated society of rustics and shepherds, people sprung
from the trunks of trees, whom the god had civilized and to whom he
had given laws.[36]

There was perhaps no place in ancient Rome more intricate and mul-
tilayered in terms of its "expressive energy" than the place from which
Cicero delivered the third *Catilinarian*. Unlike the modern city, stretch-
ing out before the Victor Emmanuel monument, or the medieval city,
huddled beside the curve in the Tiber, or even the imperial city, which
proceeded north in the great measured steps of the imperial fora, Republican Rome faced south from the Capitoline, towards the Forum Romanum, the gathering place of the crowded city, the great drawing
room of Rome. The Comitium-Rostra complex, in turn, constituted the
nerve center of the Forum valley. Here was the scene of political rallies,
voting assemblies, judicial business, social intercourse, and, not infre-
quently, sectarian violence. Here religious rituals were enacted and
omens reported, ambassadors were received, funeral laudations pronounced. From this place news of war and peace and of other great
events affecting the state was announced to the people. From here the
very times of the day had been marked.[37] Dionysius of Halicarnassus,
referring to the area of the Rostra and the adjoining Lapis Niger, termed
it "the chief part of the Forum"; while Pliny the Elder called the Rostra

---

36. Cf. Freud's reference to Rome as a "psychisches Wesen" in *Das Unbehagen in der Kultur;* see above, p. 15.

37. Pliny (*HN* 7.212–15), quoting Varro, states that the first sundial in Rome
was set up on a column by the Rostra (in 263 B.C.) by M'. Valerius Messala;
that Q. Marcius Philippus later erected a more accurate one beside it; and that
these were replaced in 159 B.C. by Sc. Nasica's water clock, which probably
stood in one of the basilicas (*sub tecto*) near the Comitium. Before the First
Punic War it had been the duty of an attendant of the consuls to announce the
middle and end of the day by noting when the sun appeared between the Rostra
and the Graecostasis and when it appeared between the Carcer and the Maenian
column (Pliny *HN* 7.212; Varro *LL* 6.5, 89). During this period the Comitium—extending from the Curia on the north to the Rostra on the south—
served as a giant sundial. Coarelli observes (*Il Foro Romano,* 1:140): "Non solo
lo spazio del Comizio, un templum, come è noto, ma anche il tempo, che il
passaggio del sole su di esso provedeva a scandire, ne resultava in un certo modo
sacralizzato, e in sintonia con le varie funzioni che nella piazza si svolgevano."

"the most visible place" in the city.[38] Before discussing in more detail the subjective aspects of this place for Cicero's audience, we will review first its architecture and topography.

The Rostra and Comitium of Cicero's day would have reflected a series of architectural changes extending back to the earliest days of Rome. Although the Comitium was eventually transformed into a circular area bounded by a platform that was mounted by steps from within, the earliest form of the monument (which Coarelli dates to the beginning of the sixth century B.C.) was probably a square, marked out by palings and extending symmetrically in front of the archaic Curia Hostilia.[39] The hypothesis that the archaic Comitium took this form arises both from archaeological data and from evidence that, from the earliest period, the Comitium was a *templum*, a square marked out by the augur and—at least in the case of the first Curia and Comitium— inaugurated with reference to the cardinal points of the compass.[40] The

38. Dion. Hal. 1.87.2 (tomb of Faustulus); 3.1.2 (tomb of Hostilius); 5.25.2 (statue of Horatius Cocles). Pliny *HN* 34.24: *quam oculatissimo loco, eaque est in rostris.* Cf. Pliny *HN* 34.26, where the statues of Pythagoras and Alcibiades that stood *in cornibus comitii* fulfilled Pythian Apollo's command that statues of "the bravest and wisest of the Greeks" be erected *celebri loco.*

39. My discussion of this material is chiefly indebted to the review of the archaeological and literary evidence for the area undertaken by Coarelli (*Il Foro Romano,* 1:119–226; 2:11–59, 87–166). Drawing on recent work, Coarelli's analysis is not only in accordance with the majority of the evidence but possesses a beautiful simplicity. A starting point for any study of the Republican Rostra-Comitium complex is the interpretation of Boni's excavation of the area by Gjerstad, "Il Comizio romano." For further bibliography, see Nash, *Pictorial Dictionary,* 1:287 (Comitium); 2:272 (Rostra). It seems highly likely that the Comitium after the third century B.C. was a circular structure similar to that of Roman colonies such as Alba Fucens and Cosa. (For the implications of the latter in interpreting the form of the Roman Comitium, see Richardson's "Cosa and Rome.") The hypothesis of a square Comitium in archaic times, proposed in the nineteenth century by Detlefsen, "De Comitio romano," and further explored by Hülsen, "Das Comitium," is now accepted by Coarelli (*Il Foro Romano,* 1:138–48).

40. The question of the *templum,* although exhaustively discussed, continues to be unresolved, as the ancient citations are often ambiguous, often mutually contradictory. Questions center on (*a*) the nature and topography of the place of augury; (*b*) the definition of the epiphanous space created by the augur; (*c*) the definition of boundaries when the inauguration of a space (rather than an action) takes place. The majority of the evidence suggests that a *templum* "on the ground" (Varro *LL* 7.6–10) was rectilinear and, in archaic times, oriented according to the cardinal points of the compass. See the discussions of Nissen,

first speaker's platform, created in approximately 500 B.C. and associated with the foundation of the Republic, stood almost directly south
of the Curia, across the space of the Comitium. It also was rectilinear in
shape and oriented on a north-south, east-west axis. In the fourth century the Comitium was enlarged, and in 338 B.C. the speaker's platform
received the ship beaks (*rostra*) captured by Maenius in the naval victory
against the Antiates that gave it its name.[41] The area was completely
rebuilt in the third century B.C., when the Comitium took the circular
shape it retained until the transformation of the entire northern end of
the Forum by Julius Caesar. The Rostra, perhaps 12 Roman feet (3.5 m)
in height, would have formed a segment within the southern arc of the
circular platform of the Republican Comitium.[42]

In a passage from the *De finibus* (5.2), part of which was quoted in
chapter 1 of this study, Marcus Piso speaks with nostalgia of the Curia
Hostilia as it existed before 80 B.C. Cicero's audience at the time of the
Catilinarian conspiracy would, like Piso, have carried in their minds
two images of the area where they were assembled, that of the present
and that which existed before the many changes in the Forum wrought
by Sulla.[43] The Curia Hostilia (after this period sometimes called the
Curia Cornelia) had been enlarged to accommodate the new senators
added by the dictator. This enlargement, in turn, resulted in the trunca-
tion of part of the circle of the Comitium. The Comitium of Cicero's
day, then, was a relatively restricted space that stood in the northeast
corner of the Forum valley, in roughly the area that now extends between the Curia Julia on the east, the Arch of Septimius Severus on the
west, the church of SS. Luca e Martina on the north, and the Sacra Via
on the south.

The Sullan building program resulted not only in the shrinking of the
space of the Comitium but also in the displacement of statues and the
covering over of certain shrines by the new pavement. The statues of

---

Templum; Weinstock, "Templum"; Torelli, "Un templum augurale"; Coarelli,
Il Foro Romano, 1:100–103; 2.126–29. On the square or rectangle as a symbolic division of space, see Tuan, *Topophilia,* 32–34, 37–38, 153, 160–68.

41. Livy 8.14.12.

42. For the height of the Rostra, see Taylor, *Voting Assemblies,* 45. Cf. Richardson's estimate of Pompeian tribunals as between three and four feet high
with surface area between sixteen and eighteen square feet in "Tribunals of the
Praetors of Rome," 221.

43. The standard analysis remains that of van Deman, "The Sullan Forum."

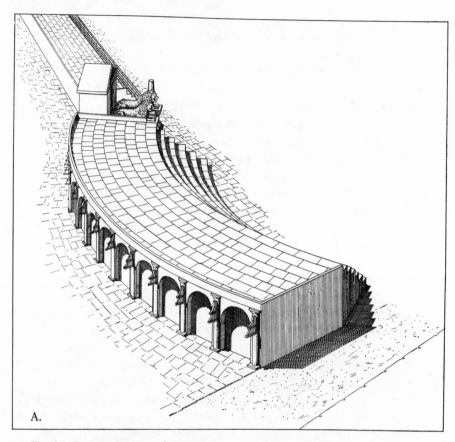

A.

Fig. 3.   Rostra, Curia, and Comitium.

A.   Reconstruction of the Rostra. Adjacent to the Rostra and shown with *aediculum* and pair of lions is the area of the Lapis Niger, the site of a shrine thought to mark the *heroon* of Romulus. (From Gjerstad, "Il Comizio romano," 143.)

B.   Reconstruction of the area of the Curia and the Comitium prior to changes made by L. Cornelius Sulla (81–79 B.C.). The plan shows the hypothetical positions of the praetorian tribunals and the Rostra. (Adapted from Coarelli, *Il Foro Romano*, 2.23.)

C.   Schematic plan of the relationship of Sulla's new Curia (Curia Cornelia) to the older Curia Hostilia, with hypotheses regarding the locations of the following monuments: (1) statue of Attus Navius; (2) Ruminal fig tree; (3) wolf; (4) statue of Marsyas; (5) puteal (wellhead); (6) Maenian column; (7) statue of Pythagoras; (8) statue of Alcibiades; (9) tabula Valeria; (10) bench of the tribune of the people. (Adapted from Coarelli, *Il Foro Romano*, 2:120.)

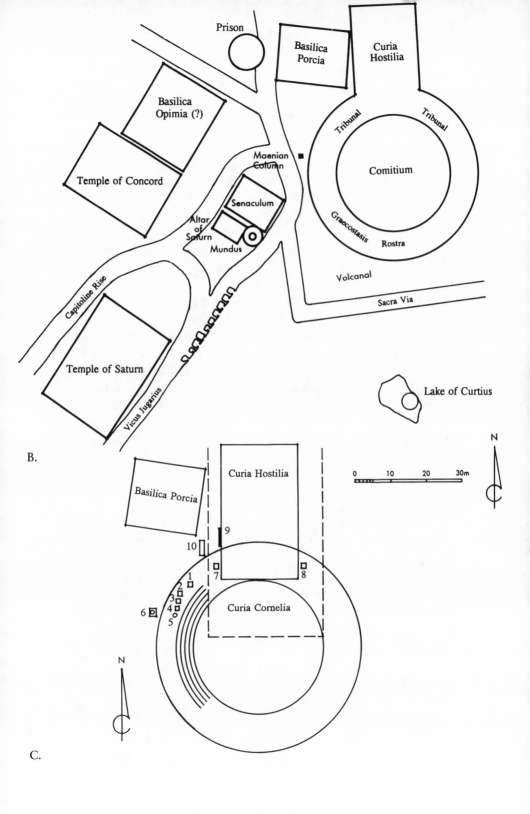

Prison

Basilica
Porcia

Curia
Hostilia

Basilica
Opimia (?)

Tribunal

Tribunal

Temple of Concord

Maenian
Column

Comitium

Senaculum

Altar
of
Saturn

Mundus

Graecostasis

Rostra

Capitoline Rise

Volcanal

Sacra Via

Temple of Saturn

Vicus Jugarius

Lake of Curtius

N

B.

Curia Hostilia

0   10   20   30m

Basilica Porcia

9

10

7

1

2

8

3

4

6

5

Curia Cornelia

N

C.

Pythagoras and Alcibiades that had stood *in cornibus comitii* ("on the 'horns' of the Comitium") were at this time removed,[44] while the site of the shrine to Stata Mater was paved over, necessitating the transfer of the cult from the Forum to the city neighborhoods.[45] The Sullan era architects were faced with a problem when contemplating the renovation of the space between the Rostra and the Graecostasis, which for centuries had been the site of an altar, a cone-shaped monument, and a *cippus* with an archaic inscription thought to date to the sixth century B.C.[46] This area was evidently of such sanctity that its shrine could not simply be secularized or moved; it therefore remained a sacred area, probably covered at this time by the black stone paving known as the Lapis Niger.

Not only was the front of the Rostra (that is, the side facing the Forum) adorned with the beaks from Maenius's naval victory, but the Rostra and the Comitium supported a bewildering number of other monuments and statues. We read, for instance, that a rostrated column dedicated to Maenius stood between the Comitium and the Carcer (Prison), and another such column in the Comitium held a statue of Gaius Duilius, the first Roman to win a naval victory over Carthage, in 260 B.C.;[47] that statues of Horatius Cocles, Hostus Hostilius, and Hermodorus of Ephesus also stood in the Comitium;[48] that a bronze *aedi-*

44. Pliny *HN* 34.26.

45. Fest. 416 L.

46. Palmer, *The King and the Comitium,* 51–53, believes the *cippus* under the Lapis Niger refers to the *rex sacrorum* and is a prohibition against pollution of the sacred grove of the Comitium, while others (e.g., Dumézil, "Remarques sur la stèle archaïque") interpret *recei* as referring to an actual king of the late monarchical period. The latter hypothesis is strongly supported by the new chronology of the earliest levels of the Comitium (see Coarelli, *Il Foro Romano,* 1:127–30; Castagnoli, "Per la cronologia dei monumenti del Comizio"). On the site, see also Lugli, *Roma antica,* 115–31, and *Monumenti minori,* 1–27.

47. For the Maenian column, see Pliny *HN* 7.60, 34.20; Cic. *Clu.* 39; *Div. Caec.* 50; ps.-Asc. ad loc.; Cic. *Sest.* 18; schol. Bob. ad loc.; *Sest.* 124; schol. Bob. ad loc.; Porphyr. ad Hor. *Sat.* 1.3.21; ps.-Acr. ad Hor. *Sat.* 1.3.21; Symmachus *Ep.* 5.54.3. For Duilius's column, see Pliny *HN* 34.20; Serv. ad G. 3.29; Quint. 1.7.12. For the inscription under this column, see the Loeb Classical Library edition entitled *Remains of Old Latin,* vol. 4, ed. E. H. Warmington (Cambridge, Mass., 1979), 128–29.

48. Horatius: Livy 2.10.12; Plut. *Publ.* 16.7; Dion. Hal. 5.25.2; Aul. Gell. 4.5.1–7; Pliny *HN* 34.22; *De vir. illus.* 11.2. Hostilius: Dion. Hal 3.1; Fest.

cula to Concordia adorned the Graecostasis and that statues of Pythagoras and Alcibiades stood *in cornibus comitii* (all three of which were displaced by the Sullan building program);[49] and that a wellhead in the Comitium marked the place where the miraculous razor and whetstone of Attus Navius, an augur during the monarchy of Tarquinius Priscus, were buried.[50] A statue of this same Navius stood before the Curia until both Curia and statue were destroyed in the funeral pyre for Clodius in 52 B.C.[51] The fig tree of Attus Navius, enclosed by a bronze fence, grew in the Comitium, as did a cypress that was thought to be coeval with the city.[52] In the Volcanal, adjacent to the Comitium, grew a lotus tree, and here was said to have been a bronze statue of Romulus with quadriga.[53]

---

184 L. Pliny (*HN* 34.21) states that a statue of Hermodorus of Ephesus, interpreter of the laws of the Twelve Tables, stood *in comitio*. Some sources relate that the Twelve Tables themselves were engraved on bronze (or ivory) tablets and affixed to the Rostra (Diod. Sic. 12.26.1; Dion. Hal. 10.57; Justin. *Digest* 1.2.2.4).

49. On the *aedicula* to Concordia, see Livy 9.46.6; Pliny *HN* 33.19. On Pythagoras and Alcibiades, see Plut. *Num.* 8.10 and Pliny *HN* 34.26, who relate that the Delphic oracle had instructed the Romans to erect statues of the wisest and the bravest of the Greeks. Statues were sometimes removed from the crowded area of the Comitium, the Forum, and the Rostra to make way for others (Pliny *HN* 34.30; Cic. *Phil.* 9.4).

50. Puteals marked places struck by lightning. For the story of Navius, see Cic. *Div.* 1.31–33; *Rep.* 2.36; *Leg.* 2.33; Dion. Hal. 3.71.1–5; Livy 1.36.3–5.

51. Pliny *HN* 34.21; Dion. Hal. 3.71.5; Livy 1.36.5.

52. For the cypress, see Pliny *HN* 16.236; fig: Dion. Hal. 3.71.5; Pliny *HN* 15.77. Most sources (e.g., Plut. *Rom.* 4; Serv. ad *Aen.* 8.90; Livy 1.4.5; Fest. 332–33 L.) indicate that the *ficus Ruminalis* stood near the Lupercal on the southwest side of the Palatine slope. Pliny (*HN* 15.77) reports that a fig tree associated with the augur Navius stood in the Comitium and that this tree commemorated the Ruminal fig. Near it was a statue group depicting Romulus, Remus, and the wolf. It is unclear from the passage whether or not Pliny believed Navius's tree was the Ruminal fig, magically transplanted. Tacitus (*Ann.* 13.58) speaks of the Ruminal fig as located in the Comitium in his day.

53. Lotus: Pliny *HN* 16.236. For the statue of Romulus, see Dion. Hal. 2.54.2. According to Festus (370 L.) the Volcanal also held the grave and statue of a *ludius* killed by lightning. See below, n. 87. The location of the Volcanal remains unclear. Festus (370 L.) locates its *supra Comitium*, which was also the site of the Graecostasis, according to Pliny (*HN* 33.19); Dionysius of Halicarnassus (2.50.2) describes it as *mikron hyperanestēkoti tēs agoras*. For a discussion of finds, see Castagnoli, "Per la cronologia dei monumenti del Comizio," 189, with n. 13. For sources, see Coarelli, *Il Foro Romano*, 1:161–

On or near the Rostra itself stood statues of Camillus (*in rostris*) and of the satyr Marsyas, symbol of plebeian *libertas;* statues of Hercules and of three Sibyls were said to be *iuxta rostra,*[54] and either a single stone lion or a pair of lions stood next to the Rostra above the monuments of the Lapis Niger.[55] The Rostra also held statues of ambassadors who had been killed in the service of the state, including the four ambassadors treacherously killed at Fidenae in 434 B.C. and Gnaeus Octavius, who also died while on an embassy.[56]

The audience facing the Rostra would have seen the speaker, then, flanked by such statues and monuments and against the backdrop of the enlarged Curia of Sulla. To the east stood the Basilica Aemilia; to the west, behind Sulla's Tabularium, rose the twin heights of the Capitoline Hill: the Capitolium, which included the sacred precinct of Jupiter Optimus Maximus, and the Arx, the most prominent building of which was the Temple of Juno Moneta.[57] At the time of the third *Catilinarian,*

78, who identifies it with the Rostra itself, and Platner and Ashby, *Topographical Dictionary,* 583–84.

54. For Hercules, see Pliny *HN* 34.93; for Camillus, see 34.23 (*sine tunica*); for the Sibyls, 34.22. Livy (8.13.9) speaks of the erection in 338 B.C. of equestrian statues of Maenius and Camillus *in foro,* but Eutropius (2.7) locates them *in rostris.*

55. Cf. Dion. Hal. 1.87.2 (lion over the tomb of Faustulus) and ps.-Acr. ad Hor. *Epod.* 16.13 (two lions over the tomb of Romulus).

56. Livy 4.17.6; Pliny *HN* 34.23; Cic. *Phil.* 9.4 (who indicates that the statues of the ambassadors to Fidenae had been removed from the Rostra during his lifetime). Pliny (*HN* 34.24) speaks of a Publius Junius and a Titus Coruncanius, also killed on embassy. Cicero, proposing the erection of a statue of Servius Sulpicius Rufus, who had died of natural causes on a state mission to Antony, declares that if such a statue were set up on the Rostra, the memory of his embassy would be immortal (*Phil.* 9.10). In 80 B.C. an equestrian statue of Sulla was also reportedly *pro rostris* or *in rostris,* but this monument might well have been removed in the years after the dictator's death (App. *B.civ.* 1.11.97; Cic. *Phil.* 9.13; Vell. Pat. 2.61.3; Suet. *Iul. Caes.* 75.4; Cass. Dio 42.18; and see Crawford, *Coinage,* 1.397, no. 381.1a; 2, plate XLVIII, no. 22, for numismatic representation of this statue). Equestrian statues were rare in the Forum in the early period (Livy 8.13.9), and Sulla, Pompey, and Caesar were apparently the only men voted equestrian statues near the Rostra in the late Republic (Vell. Pat. 2.61.3).

57. Pliny reports that two colossal statues stood on the Capitolium, one of Apollo (erected by M. Lucullus in 73 B.C. and said to have been forty-five feet

the numbers of those who gathered in the Forum to hear the consul would have been huge. They would have filled the open spaces in front of the Rostra and crowded the porches of the temples. Describing a similar scene in the fourth *Catilinarian,* Cicero declared to the senators gathered in the Temple of Concord: "Everyone is present, men of all orders, all classes, all ages. The Forum is full, the temples around the Forum are full, all the entrances and grounds of this temple are full" (14).

We now take up a question more important to our purposes than any involving the physical aspects of the Rostra-Comitium—namely, What was the meaning of this place for Cicero's audience? To answer this question we must discuss some of the separate strains that contributed to the perception of this complex space; but, in so doing, it should be kept in mind that a Roman of Cicero's day would not have been accustomed to thinking in terms of discrete divisions between, for instance, the "political," the "historical," and the "religious." As has often been pointed out, these concepts—which we are accustomed to rationalize into distinct aspects of experience—were overlapping and interwoven in the Roman consciousness.

A great number of the activities that went on in the Comitium and on the Rostra during the many centuries of their existence were judicial in nature.[58] The high platform surrounding the floor of the Comitium had long been the site of the tribunal of the urban praetor and of the *praetor peregrinus* as well. Here were the benches of the tribunes, who were ready to use their power to protect from summary judgment those who appealed to them. The tribunal of the Rostra had also been used as

---

high) and another of Jupiter. He states that the latter, erected by the consul Sp. Carvilius after his victory over the Samnites in 293 B.C., was so huge that it could be seen from the Temple of Jupiter Latiaris on the Alban Mount, ten miles from Rome (*HN* 34.39–43). The statue is nowhere else mentioned; Livy (10.46.14–16) speaks only of a temple to Fors Fortuna erected from the spoils. If Pliny's report is accurate, this Jupiter figure must have loomed over Cicero's audience in the Forum. For a discussion of the type, see Richardson, "Early Roman Sculpture," 92–96.

58. See Gioffredi, "I tribunali del Foro"; Johnson, *Roman Tribunal;* Richardson, "Tribunals of the Praetors of Rome." Richardson provides some thought-provoking hypotheses, although I cannot agree with his theory that before the fourth century B.C. the Rostra stood before the doors of the Curia.

a court of final appeal: the tribal assembly was summoned here in order to hear the arguments of defense and prosecution and then to decide by their votes the guilt or innocence of the accused.[59] In spite of the transfer in the second and first centuries of some of the judicial functions once carried on in the area, the Rostra-Comitium area continued to be a focus of many of the activities surrounding litigation. Several of the standing courts would have been set up in or near the Comitium, and, even after the judicial *comitia* no longer voted in the Comitium, the public meetings or *contiones* that preceded the voting continued to be convened at the Rostra.[60] It is also to be remembered that many of the judges and jurors who sat at the tribunals of the permanent *quaestiones* were the same men who gathered in the Curia. The area of the Comitium and that near the Rostra must have been continually alive with the legal hubbub produced by praetors and judges, defense lawyers and prosecutors, mourning-clad defendants soliciting sympathy and support, accusers and their adherents, witnesses, lictors, and scribes. Surely, then, one of the more important meanings attached to the Comitium in general and the Rostra in particular for Cicero's audience would have stemmed from its function as a *locus iustitiae*.

As its name shows, the Comitium had originally been the chief meeting place of the voting assemblies of the people. In the early days of the Republic both the Comitia Curiata and the Comitia Tributa used the enclosed space of the Comitium to vote on certain magisterial candidates and on legislative and judicial proceedings. The Comitia Curiata

59. For procedure in judicial *comitia*, see Taylor, *Voting Assemblies*, passim; Hall, "Voting Procedure"; Botsford, *Roman Assemblies* 317–29; Staveley, *Greek and Roman Voting*, 121–74; Greenidge, *Legal Procedure of Cicero's Time*, 338–66.

60. Horace (*Sat.* 1.6.119–21; and ps.-Acr. ad loc.), apparently drawing on a Republican tradition, speaks of the area near the statue of Marsyas as a place where legal business was typically conducted. Evidence of the proximity of certain tribunals to the Rostra is provided by Cicero's statement (*Q.fr.* 2.3.6) that his defense of Calpurnius Bestia on the charge of *ambitus* took place *in foro medio* and by Asconius's testimony (ad *Mil.* 35) that the trial of Milo occurred within sight and hearing of Pompey, who sat in the *pronaos* of the Temple of Saturn (*ad aerarium*). Richardson, "Tribunals of the Praetors of Rome," 224–27, believes that two of the tribunals of the permanent *quaestiones* were to be found on the Rostra and two in the Comitium. See Gruen, *Roman Politics*, for the century-long development of the permanent *quaestiones* that eventually replaced the judicial *comitia*. The end point in this process is reached with the Sullan reorganization. On judicial *contiones*, see Taylor, *Voting Assemblies*, 19.

continued to meet here, although by the late Republic its functions had withered to the purely formal, and the members of the Curiae no longer met individually but were represented by thirty lictors. In the second century B.C., lack of space forced the tribal assemblies to abandon the Comitium and instead to assemble to cast their votes in the open area on the Forum side of the Rostra. The Rostra continued to serve until the end of the Republic, however, as the chief platform for directing the voting of these assemblies.[61] All that was required by the change from Comitium to Forum was that the magistrate overseeing the proceedings would have turned to face the Forum rather than the Curia.[62] When a vote was taken, the tribes would then have filed up, either to the Rostra or, perhaps, to a slightly lower wooden structure attached to the Rostra, in order to record their decisions.

The fact that the voting assemblies once met in the Comitium leads us to consider another aspect of this space. In archaic Rome all "political" actions required divine sanction. For this reason the magistrates were strictly bound by religious constraints governing the time and place of assemblies (which could be held only between sunrise and sunset and had to be convened within a *templum*) and were required to take the auspices to determine the will of the gods before convening such *comitia*.[63] The use of the Comitium and of the Rostra, then, as settings for the conduct of state business was intimately tied to their sacral character, for the status of these spaces as inaugurated *templa* guaranteed divine approval and protection of the political activities that went on there.[64] The Comitium was also the scene of a number of religious rites and ceremonies whose roots went back to archaic Rome: the Salian priests danced in the Comitium on March 19 (the Armilustrium) during the purification of the sacred shields; here the *rex sacrorum* enacted the

61. Most legislative and certain magisterial elections continued to be directed from the Rostra until Caesar's time; in addition, orators addressing the meetings (*contiones*) that preceded electoral assemblies would have spoken from the Rostra.

62. Cicero (*Amic.* 96) and Varro (*RR* 1.2.9) state that C. Licinius Crassus (tr. pl. 145 B.C.) was the first to lead the people from the Comitium out into the Forum. That Cicero and Varro were referring to voting assemblies is convincingly demonstrated by Taylor, *Voting Assemblies*, 23–25. See also Coarelli, *Il Foro Romano*, 2:157–58.

63. The tribal assemblies that were convened by the tribunes of the people, who were not religiously authorized to take the auspices, were an exception to this rule.

64. Cic. *Vat.* 24, *Rep.* 2.31; Livy 8.14.12.

rites of the Regifugium; and, according to R. E. A. Palmer, the Comitium was also the scene of the ritual combat between inhabitants of the neighborhoods of the Sacra Via and of the Subura that was connected with the celebration of the October Horse.[65] The perceived sanctity of the place was further reinforced by the presence of the Volcanal and, immediately next to the Rostra, of the sacred area of the Lapis Niger under which was thought to be the *heroon* of Romulus (or, according to some sources, the grave of the shepherd Faustulus or of Hostus Hostilius).[66] As noted, the refusal on the part of the Sullan era architects to secularize or transfer the sanctuary must have stemmed from a belief in its special holiness and inviolability.[67]

This space was also sanctified in the Roman mind by tradition, for here had been enacted momentous events in the history of the state. Some of these would have been summoned to mind by the statues that crowded upon the platform, but many links between this place and the past found their memorials only in the stories and legends learned by

65. Salii: see Varro *LL* 5.85; Palmer, *The King and the Comitium*, 4 with n. 25; Scullard, *Festivals*, 93; *Fasti Praen.* March 19. Regifugium: Fest. 346–47 L.; Plut. *Quaest. Rom.* 63; Palmer, *The King and the Comitium*, 5; Scullard, *Festivals*, 81–82. Ritual battle of the October Horse: Fest. 190 L.; Scullard, *Festivals*, 193–94; Palmer, *The King and the Comitium*, 9.

66. Romulus: Hor. *Epod.* 16.13 (*ossa Quirini*); ps.-Acr. ad loc. (*aiunt in Rostris Romulum sepultum esse*); Porph. ad loc. (*post rostra*); Fest. 184 L. Hostus Hostilius: Dion. Hal. 3.1.2. Faustulus: Dion. Hal. 1.87.2; Fest. 184 L.

67. Cf. Livy's account (5.54.7) of the building of the Temple of Jupiter Optimus Maximus, when the shrines of Terminus and Juventas could not be displaced without endangering the *fortuna* of the city.

The Comitium was also the place of judgment and punishment of certain offenses that involved religious pollution (see Palmer, *The King and the Comitium*). Livy, for instance, recounts how a man who had been convicted of adultery with a Vestal had been scourged to death in the Comitium. The choice of the Comitium as the place for such punishments was probably not because of its proximity to the Carcer (although the scourging of lower-class criminals took place nearby at the Maenian column); rather, because certain crimes were thought to pollute the city and to alienate the gods, the criminal was considered *sacer*, or one whose punishment was devoted to the god as atonement. The consecrated space of the Comitium was therefore an appropriate setting for what was in essence a sacrificial offering. The same reasoning applies to the earlier practice of staging gladiatorial games within the Comitium, for originally the participants in such games were probably considered sacred offerings. See Livy 22.57.3 (scourging of adulterer), 24.20.6 (execution of deserters), 25.7.14 (scourging of hostages), 27.36.8 (gladiatorial show); *Per.* 55 (deserters scourged to death in Comitium).

generations of Romans. While a detailed knowledge of history would have been the possession only of the few, certain events were surely known by all. Those that looked on the Curia Hostilia knew how the tyrant Tarquin had cruelly thrown the rightful king, Tullus Hostilius, down its steps. They would have heard of the struggles that took place at the Rostra between Marcus Manlius Capitolinus and the dictator Cornelius Cossus, or between the dictator L. Papirius Cursor and his master of the horse, Q. Fabius Maximus Rullianus.[68] Here the great Scipio Africanus, conqueror of Hannibal, had defended himself against the charges of the Papirii, then retired to the temples on the Capitoline, followed by the entire crowd that had witnessed his speech.[69] Of more recent and sinister memory were the scenes acted out here during and subsequent to the turbulent tribuneships of the Gracchi. It is reported that during the period of the civil wars Marius and Cinna had begun the gruesome tradition of displaying the heads of their victims on the Rostra, a practice adopted by Sulla a few years later. (On Caesar's Rostra, the head and hands of the murdered Cicero would be displayed by Antony in 43 B.C.) Sulla had probably used the Rostra to post the lists of the proscribed and here he had presided over the auctioning of their goods.[70] The place, then, would have inspired both the horror associated with the violence of the recent past and the unique and quasi-religious reverence felt by the Romans for the distant past.

The place from which Cicero delivered the third *Catilinarian* constituted the point of topographical intersection between the Curia and Comitium, on one hand, and the Forum, on the other. It was, therefore, in a political, social, and psychological sense, the focal point of interaction between the *principes,* who met in the Senate and Comitium, and the *populus,* who assembled in the Forum proper. While in the early Republic the Rostra would have been primarily the *locus* from which the magistrates of the state commanded, directed, informed, bullied, or appeased the populace, by the second century B.C. the initiative had shifted, and the Rostra became the principal scene of tribunician challenges to the status quo. Here reformers and demagogues such as the Gracchi, Saturninus, and Glaucia had questioned senatorial competence and authority and had even succeeded at times in transferring to popu-

68. Livy 8.33.9–10.
69. Livy 38.51.12.
70. App. *B.civ.* 1.8.71; Flor. 2.9.14; Livy *Per.* 80; Oros. 5.19.23; Vell. Pat. 2.19.1; App. *B.civ.* 1.10.94; Plut. *Sull.* 33.

lar vote questions of policy long kept strictly within senatorial control. This significant change in the public interaction between Senate and people was symbolized by the story that Gaius Gracchus had been the first orator to turn his back on the Curia and the senators assembled in the Comitium in order to face the masses gathered in the Forum.[71] Whether the anecdote is true or merely ben trovato, it marks the transformation of the Rostra into a *locus popularis*. Henceforth, even young nobles (at least in the early stages of their careers) might be expected to make popular noises in their speeches here.[72] Cicero, in his first consular speech delivered from the Rostra, felt compelled to couch his objections to an agrarian bill in the rhetoric of the opposition: he argued that the true interests of the people rested in continuing prosperity, stability, and peace and that he—as legally, even divinely, appointed guardian of these blessings—was truly a *consul popularis*.[73]

If the scene of the first *Catilinarian* was particularly evocative to the senators who heard the speech of the glorious legends of Romulean Rome, the scene of the third *Catilinarian* was surely inhabited by the *genius* of Republican Rome. The Rostra was in symbol and in reality the center of the postmonarchical state, and if Romulus was evoked here, it was in the guise of the deified founder Quirinus, whose *heroon* stood beside the speaker's platform.[74] In this place, consecrated by religion and history, a magistrate of the late Republic could no longer depend on respect for his *auctoritas* to bend the masses to his desires, for the demagogues of the late Republic had accustomed their audiences to expect the orators who addressed them here to define all issues in terms of the libertarian catchwords and slogans of the day. In the best of times, the best of orators might successfully induce his audience to equate their own interests with the welfare of the state; in the worst of times, all persuasion yielded to violence. It was to be expected, then, that a Ciceronian speech delivered from the Rostra before an assembly of the people would be markedly different from one delivered before the Sen-

---

71. It is necessary to distinguish here between C. Licinius Crassus's action, in assembling the voting *comitia* in the Forum, and that of Gracchus, who, I believe, was the first to turn towards the people rather than towards the *principes* in giving an address from the Rostra (Plut. *C.Gracch.* 5.4). Cf. Polyb. 6.16.5 on the power of the tribunate. See above, p. 71 n. 62.

72. Gruen, *Last Generation of the Republic*, 24–28, 180–89.

73. *Leg. agr.* 2.9. See Seager, "*Popularis*," and Hellegouarc'h, *Le vocabulaire latin*, 518–41.

74. See above, p. 72 n. 66.

ate, and that the "popular" content and themes of such an oration might be supported by the rhetorical exploitation of this ambiance.

THE THIRD *CATILINARIAN:*
URBS AMISSA, URBS RESTITUTA

Like an overture, the carefully crafted opening lines of the third *Catilinarian* sound the major themes that are to be played upon throughout the speech:

> Rem publicam, Quirites,
>
> vitamque omnium vestrum,
> bona, fortunas, coniuges liberosque vestros
> atque hoc domicilium clarissimi imperi,
> fortunatissimam pulcherrimamque urbem
>
> hodierno die
>
> deorum immortalium summo erga vos amore
> laboribus, consiliis, periculis meis
> e flamma atque ferro ac paene ex faucibus fati
> ereptam et vobis conservatam ac restitutam
>
> videtis.

As shown by the manner in which it has been printed above, this first sentence is composed of two parts, divided in the middle by the phrase *hodierno die*. While the break is easily recognized, the sentence as a whole is knit together by the repetition throughout of the endings *-am/-em/-um* (e.g., *rem, publicam, vitam, omnium, vestrum, domicilium, urbem, immortalium, ereptam, conservatam, restitutam*); by symmetrical construction, in which two pairs of phrases stand on either side of *hodierno die;* and by the suspension of the verb governing the long list of accusatives (*videtis*) until the final word.

The sentence begins, significantly, with the word *rem publicam*, then goes on to define the elements that constitute the state for the audience: the first phrase speaks of the lives, property, and families of the listeners, while the second phrase, whose weighty superlatives force the speaker to slow and ultimately to halt, refers to "this abode of the most glorious empire, this most fortunate and beautiful city."[75] It is a momentous be-

---

75. For the sentiment and tenor of such passages, cf. John of Gaunt's speech in *Richard II*, act 2, scene 1, lines 40–41: "This royal throne of kings, this sceptered isle,/ This earth of majesty, this seat of Mars."

ginning. To those of his listeners who believed that the threatened coup might have brought an amelioration of their condition, accomplished at the price of the lives of a few *optimates,* Cicero declares that, in fact, all that was of value to them—their lives and property and even the continued existence of the city itself—had hung in the balance at this time. The second part of the sentence begins by defining the agency through which the as-yet-unspoken event, affecting the citizens and their city, has occurred: what has happened has taken place because of the "love of the immortal gods" for the audience and because of the exertions, plans, and risks of the orator.[76] The final phrases of the sentence build to a climax. Cicero defines the danger that had threatened—fire, sword, and a mysterious *fatum*—then triumphantly declares the Republic now "snatched," "preserved," and "restored" from that danger. In this last phrase the central placement of *vobis* (picking up the earlier *vestrum/vestros* in the first part and *vos* in the second) emphasizes that all has been done in the interests of the audience.

The sentence as a whole is governed by the verb *videtis:* the people are told that on this day they "see . . . the city saved and restored." The use of the verb is significant, for throughout the oration as a whole Cicero continually emphasizes the importance of the visual and perceptible. This thematic development supports the avowed purpose of the third *Catilinarian,* which was to inform the people of the incontrovertible evidence (the so-called inartificial proofs) that had at long last been secured concerning the conspiracy. Throughout Cicero's account of how this evidence had been obtained and of what it consisted he never ceases to emphasize the objective and perceptible nature of these proofs: he begins with the statement that he will reveal to the people what had earlier been "made clear," "laid open," and "disclosed" to the Senate, promising to show his audience "how manifold and how obvious" (3: *quam manifesta*) this evidence was; he states that his hope had always been that all would be able to see the crime "with their eyes" (4) and rejoices that at last the gods had brought it about that all could be "made plain to both Senate and people" (4: *manifesto*); he recounts that

76. The use of *amor* of the gods' goodwill towards humans is unusual. In spite of his statement in *Part. or.* 88 that *caritas* usually describes our love for gods, parents, and country, Cicero frequently uses *amor,* especially in speeches of this period, of patriotic love of the *patria* or *res publica* (*Verr.* II.2.117; *Prov. cons.* 23; *Flac.* 96, 103; *Sest.* 12, 49; *Dom.* 103; *Cat.* 4.15; *Sull.* 87; *Leg. agr.* 1.26).

the force of the crime thus "detected and revealed" (11: *manifesti atque deprehensi*) had completely unnerved the usually haughty Lentulus; and he speaks of how these "most definite . . . proofs and signs of crime, writing tablets, seals, handwriting, and finally, the confession of each accused man" were supported by even more certain signs of guilt on the part of the conspirators, namely, their "blushes, glances, expressions, and their silence" (13). At the end of the first half of the speech he declares that no robbery in a private house had ever been so plainly proved (17: *manifesto comprehensa*) as had the present conspiracy against the state.

It seems clear, then, that the orator's triumphant declaration at the beginning of the speech—that the audience could now see their city "saved and restored"—signaled his intent to make the city itself an integral part of the perceptible proof that formed the chief subject matter of the oration. The sight of the city rising up around them is to be a sign to his audience of Cicero's great victory over the conspirators: that he had crushed them "without slaughter, without bloodshed, without an army, and without a battle" (23) and that he had "preserved both city and citizens whole and unharmed" (25). The difficulty of this strategy consisted in the very fact that the city was indeed "whole and unharmed" and appeared no different than it would have if the conspiracy had never existed.[77] In order to make the unchanged aspect of the city meaningful to his audience, then, Cicero must impress on their minds the indelible image of the city as it might have been had the conspiracy succeeded.

Cicero accomplishes this rhetorical aim by continually referring in the speech to the horrors to be envisioned if the city were to succumb to a hostile attack. Elements of such a description were part of the stock-in-trade of an orator of Cicero's time, for the "captured city" topos was a commonplace of ancient oratory.[78] Cicero's embroidery on this theme

77. Ceausescu, "Altera Roma," 88–89, believes that Octavian faced the same problem in his attempt to paint himself as a new Romulus and second founder of Rome. Asks Ceausescu: "De quelle manière avait-il [i.e., Octavian] fondé de nouveau Rome, puisque la ville n'avait pas été détruite?" The answer, he believes, is to be found in Octavian's claim to have saved Rome from Antony, a man who could be represented as having planned to transfer the seat of empire to the East.

78. Cf. Quint. 8.3.67–70; *Her.* 4.12, 51; Plut. *Sull.* 14.2–5 (Sulla's capture of Athens); Hom. *Il.* 9.590–94; Dio Chrys. 32.89; Sall. *Cat.* 51.9; and Paul, "*Urbs Capta.*"

was a mixture of the real and the imagined: Catiline's actual plans for arson and murder were supported by images familiar from the rhetorical topos, and the orator's report of the evidence seized from the conspirators serves as the starting point for references to limitless destruction and indiscriminate murder. In the passage from the exordium quoted above, Cicero had spoken of the "fire and sword" from which the city had been rescued, and a few lines later he pictures fire "placed under and all around" the buildings and walls of the city, and the conspirators' swords at the very necks of the citizens (2–3). In another passage the orator declares that Volturcius had testified before the Senate that the conspiracy included a plan to fire the city in all its parts, to massacre the populace, and even to intercept and cut down outside the walls those who attempted to flee (8).[79] The audience is then told of the disagreement between Lentulus and Cethegus as to when "the slaughter and the burning of the city" (10) should commence. Yet another reference to "the burning of the city" is made in connection with L. Cassius, who is pictured as overseeing the planned arson (14). Cicero also carefully quotes the language of the *supplicatio* decreed in his name by the Senate. In it the consul is thanked for having "freed the city from fire and the citizens from slaughter" (15).

Such images culminate in a section that occurs towards the end of the speech. Here Cicero compares the aims of the conspirators with those of past instigators of civil strife. In the past, men did not wish that the Republic cease to exist, but rather that they should be the chief men in it. They did not desire to burn down the city, says Cicero, but wished that they might flourish in it (25). Only in this "war," which the orator calls the greatest and cruelest in human memory, have the opponents of the state held the opinion that any who were able to be safe while the city was intact should be considered their enemies. The section ends with Cicero's declaration that while the enemy had supposed that only that part of the city that fire was unable to destroy would remain, *he* had preserved the city and the citizens intact and unharmed (25). The hyperbole of this passage would have been supported by images of recent bloodshed and destruction still fresh in the audience's minds. When Cicero declares that Catiline would have exceeded past instigators of civil war in cruelty, he speaks to an audience who had themselves lived

---

79. This was apparently standard procedure in warfare (see Cic. *Rosc. Am.* 151).

through the horrors of the struggle between Marius and Sulla, and reminds them of the days when the Forum was strewn with "heaps of corpses" and "flowed with the blood of citizens" (24).[80]

Cicero further reinforces these images of destruction and murder by references to prophecy, omen, and the concept of an evil destiny that had threatened the city. The word *fatum* is introduced in the opening lines when Cicero declares the city to have been "snatched from the jaws of fate," and the same term reappears in the Gauls' account to the Senate of Lentulus's conversation with them. Lentulus had at that time told them that, according to the soothsayers, that very year would prove "fateful" for the destruction of the city and its *imperium* since it was the tenth since the acquittal of the Vestals and the twentieth since the burning of the Capitolium (9). The omens of 65 B.C., when a number of monuments on the Capitol had been struck by lightning, are also mentioned. The soothsayers from Etruria had reported at that time the imminent danger of "murder, fire, the destruction of the laws, civil war, and the fall of the whole city and its *imperium*" (19).

Cicero's emphasis on the danger through which the city had passed was calculated not only to induce his audience to see their surroundings with new eyes; it also represented a celebration of his own actions at this time. The greater the peril in which Rome had stood, the more exalted ought to be the status of the man who had saved the city. It has already been noted that, in the opening line of the speech, Cicero had declared that the citizens now saw the Republic "snatched" (*ereptam*) from imminent danger, "saved" (*conservatam*), and "restored" (*restitutam*). The last of these participles, *restitutam*, means literally "having been caused to stand again," and its conjunction with *conservatam* joins the idea of the salvation of the state with its restoration or reestablishment. While in this sentence Cicero states that the "saving and restitution" of the city has occurred both through the love of the gods and through his own "exertions, plans, and dangers," in the following lines he expands only on the latter theme. Here the happiness of the present day is compared with that on the day on which the city was founded, thereby reinforcing the suggestion contained in the joining of *servatam* and *restitutam* that this day was to be looked upon as a kind of refoundation. Not only are the founding of the city by Romulus and the saving of it by Cicero presented as commensurate events, but the consul seems

80. Cf. *Rosc. Am.* 11–12, 154.

to have surpassed the deified hero, since Romulus had founded a city of uncertain future, while Cicero had saved one that had grown great (2: *hanc urbem conditam amplificatamque servavit*).[81]

Cicero's subsequent allusions in the speech to Romulus and to the foundation of Rome are, at least in part, attempts to keep this comparison of founder and "refounder" alive. We note, in this regard, that the orator twice more repeats the phrase *hanc urbem condidit*, by which he had referred to Romulus in the exordium (2). In his announcement of the *supplicatio* decreed in his honor he states that it was the first such public thanksgiving made on behalf of a private citizen "since the city was founded" (15). The phrase is again used in the description of the objects on the Capitol struck by lightning (19: *et tactus etiam ille qui hanc urbem condidit Romulus*). In this second passage Cicero's use of *etiam* marks the importance ascribed to the statue of Romulus above those listed previously, in spite of the fact that the destruction of a statue of Jupiter is the ostensible basis for alluding to the event at all; and the phrase *hanc urbem condidit* again points to a notional connection between the events of the present and the time of the foundation of the city.[82]

Cicero's aim in all this is clear: to make it appear that Rome had passed through a crisis so grave that its salvation was a new beginning and its unchanged aspect was a testament to Cicero, its savior and "refounder." Not only is Romulus invoked in this strategy, but we may assume that the image of Camillus, whose statue stood on the Rostra, was also meant to suggest itself. Camillus had saved Rome after the Gauls had burnt most of the city and murdered those left outside the walls of the Arx; Cicero, as he repeatedly asserts, had not only rescued the city but had done so before any bloodshed or destruction could occur. According to Livy, Camillus was hailed for his deeds as "Romulus," "the father of his country," and "a second founder of the city" (5.49.7: *Romulus ac parens patriae conditorque alter urbis*); in the third *Catilinarian* Cicero too wished his audience to see him as *pater patriae* (an honor later voted him by the Senate), *conditor alter urbis,* and *alter Romulus.*

---

81. The theme of the restitution of the city became a common one in later orators. See, for example, Ramage, "Velleius Paterculus," 266–71.

82. Cicero emphasizes the role of the single founder, the sole *pater patriae,* by excluding any mention of Remus, although the sculptural group that was destroyed portrayed the wolf with both of the twins. See Cic. *Div.* 1.20 (*parvos Mavortis semine natos*); Obseq. 60 (122: *lupam Remi et Romuli fulmine ictam*).

SIGNUM JOVIS

This, even in the self-aggrandizing world of the Roman Republic, was surely going too far, and Cicero was not so enamored of his own success as not to have known it. While the orator wished to establish his own claims in unmasking and crippling the conspiracy, he knew that it was necessary to put those claims within a larger context—one that would, without diminishing his stature as savior of the Republic, make his role a more acceptable one. One of Cicero's rhetorical aims in the speech, then, was to present all that had happened as an expression of the will of the gods. In the development of this theme the manipulation of the symbolism of what the audience saw before their eyes was again to be crucial.

While, in general, the scene that greeted the audience who assembled for the third *Catilinarian* was a familiar one, yet in at least one respect a perceptible change had taken place. Cicero had seen to it that a new statue of Jupiter would that morning be set up on a high column within the Capitolium so as to be visible to the audience that stood in the Forum below. The section of the speech in which Cicero first alludes to the statue begins with the statement that all that he had done had been planned and foreseen by the immortal gods, and that this was proved by the fact that the gods had lately been *praesentes* (18) in the city in such a way that one "could almost see them with one's eyes." Cicero then speaks of the omens that had recently occurred: the lights and flames seen in the night sky, the various incidents of lightning and earthquake, and, most important, the signs of the year 65 B.C., when various monuments on the Capitol, including a statue of Jupiter, had been struck by lightning. At that time soothsayers had advised that another statue of Jupiter, larger than the one that had been destroyed, should be made and placed on the Capitolium.[83]

What Cicero wanted his audience to think and feel when they saw this statue becomes clearer when we note the meaning that had been attributed to the other signs and omens of 65 B.C. Among the objects destroyed by lightning were statues of gods and heroes, the bronze table of the Laws, and the statue group of Romulus, Remus, and the wolf. The soothsayers stated that these events signified the onset of murder, arson, the destruction of the laws, civil war, and the fall of the city and its *imperium* (19). It is evident, then, that the lightning was not inter-

83. On the statue and its location see Cic. *Div.* 1.21 and 2.46.

preted as a sign of divine displeasure with the city. Rather, the method of the soothsayers was to read the physical as an analogue for the conceptual. Just as lightning had struck the Capitol, destructive plans that would strike at the heart of the city were being formed; as the Capitolium had been ravaged by fire, so the plans would include an attack by fire on Rome; and as the physical monument of the Laws had been destroyed, in the future the conceptual laws would be overturned. By objectifying the peril in which the city stood Jupiter had made perceptible that which was hitherto hidden and thereby made it possible for those who saw and understood the signs to take action to prevent the fulfillment of the evil.

Just as these visible signs were seen as a divine "objectification" of the danger that threatened to destroy the city, Cicero presents the new statue of Jupiter as a human attempt to objectify the means by which the city might be saved. He states that the soothsayers, after declaring that supplicatory games in honor of the gods should be inaugurated and that a larger statue of Jupiter should be erected on the Capitolium, made the following statement:

> ac se sperare dixerunt, si illud signum quod videtis solis ortum et forum curiamque conspiceret, fore ut ea consilia quae clam essent inita contra salutem urbis atque imperi inlustrarentur ut a senatu populoque Romano perspici possent.
>
> (20)

> They said that they hoped that if the statue that you see were to look on the rising sun and the Forum and the Curia, that those plots that had been secretly formulated against the welfare of the city and its *imperium* would become evident to the Senate and the people.

The meaning of the passage is carried both by its diction and syntax. After *dixerunt* three phrases occur, the first ending with *conspiceret,* the second with *inlustrarentur,* the third with *perspici possent.* Each of these phrases turns on the concept of the visible and what is represented by the visible. The statue (*signum*), which can be seen by the audience, is a sign (*signum*) of Jupiter, who is unseen.[84] The "gaze" of the statue, looking towards the rising sun that floods the Forum with light, is a symbol of the divine illumination (*inlustrarentur*) of what has been concealed. The statue looks down on the Forum and the Curia; in a parallel position (albeit in chiastic order) in the third phrase of the sentence are the

---

84. For discussion of the term *signum* in the speech, see Ferry, "Art of Cicero," 203.

groups symbolized by these two *loci:* the Senate and the people of Rome. The intended collocation of object and place, then, is an attempt to concretize the relationship between the divine and the human that will allow the city to be saved. The hoped-for result of this relationship will be that Jupiter Optimus Maximus will cause the plots that have hitherto been hidden to be revealed and made plain to the Senate and the people.[85]

At first the assertion by Cicero that if the visual field of the statue would include the Forum and Curia, then the people and Senate might be saved from disaster by divine intervention appears to be a rather crude attempt to manipulate the religious credibility of his audience. However, the relative complexity of Cicero's intent becomes clearer when we compare his handling of the material with the traditional interpretation given a similar event, preserved in an account of Aulus Gellius (4.5.1–7).[86] Gellius reports that when the statue of Horatius Cocles in the Comitium was struck by lightning Etruscan soothsayers were summoned to interpret the event and to advise the Romans what action ought to be undertaken. Out of enmity to Rome, the soothsayers said that the statue should be reerected in a low place where the sun, cut off by the shadow of surrounding buildings, would never strike it (*sol . . . numquam illustraret*). The plot of the soothsayers was eventually exposed, and it was found that the statue was actually meant to be relocated in a high place (*in locum editum*), where, presumably, the sun would always illuminate it. When these instructions were carried out the interests of the Republic prospered (*ex quo res bene ac prospere populo Romano cessit*).[87]

85. In the same passage in which he alludes to the associations developed by Cicero in the first *Catilinarian,* the author of the *Oratio pridie quam in exsilium iret* (Orelli, Baiter, and Halm, *Opera,* 2:2) refers to this passage in the third *Catilinarian:* in section 24 he calls on Jupiter, Juno, Minerva, and all the gods "who dwell in their appointed abode upon the Capitoline rock, on a lofty hill within the city, not only so that you are able to look upon the entire city, but so that you are able, in truth, to look after the whole state" (*qui excellenti tumulo civitatis sedem Capitolii in saxo incolitis constitutam, ut non solum cunctam intueri, sed etiam tueri possitis civitatem*).

86. Gellius states that his story was derived from the first book of Verrius Flaccus's *Rerum memoria dignarum* and was found as well in the eleventh book of the Annales Maximi.

87. Vitruvius (1.7.1) speaks of the importance of erecting the temples to the chief gods of a city in a high place where they might look upon as much of the city walls as possible. Cf. Plutarch (*Cam.* 42.4), who tells of the erection of the

In the case of the statue of Cocles, what is implied is a kind of sympathetic magic whereby the placement of the statue itself served to determine whether benefit or harm would come to the state. Cicero, on the other hand, speaks of the decision to erect the statue of Jupiter as an attempt to emblematize topographically the relationship between the divine and the human that will bring about the salvation of the city.[88] This action is not a binding of divine forces but rather a supplication of the gods. It is "hoped" (20: *sperare*) that the physical relationship between the statue, on one side, and the Curia and the Forum, on the other, will reflect the true relationship between the god and his people. Only if Jupiter assents to this relationship, may the citizens be assured that he will exercise his power to "bend" (19) the destructive fate that impends.

The intent to erect the statue, then, is presented by Cicero as an appeal to the gods, and the erection of the statue in itself could neither guarantee nor prove that the city was divinely protected. But in the chronological coincidence of the carrying through of this intention and the revelation of the conspiracy the statue takes on a new significance. Cicero asks whether it was not obvious that all had occurred by the will of Jupiter Optimus Maximus when it happened that the conspirators and witnesses had been led through the Forum to the Temple of Concord, where they disclosed the details of the conspiracy, at precisely the same time that the new statue of Jupiter had been set up overlooking the Forum and the Curia (21). The fact that Jupiter had caused the conspiracy to be made known on the day his statue was placed on the Capitolium was evidence that it was he who had actually brought about the

---

Temple of Concord by Camillus following the bitter class struggles of the fourth century. The intention of the architects was to place the building so that it might "face the Forum and the Curia," doubtlessly hoping that the spirit of Concord would embrace the spaces commanded by the temple. A similar motif is found in Festus (370 L.), who tells of a *ludius* (chariot driver?), killed by lightning in the Circus, who was buried on the Janiculum. Later, prodigies were interpreted by the soothsayers that caused the Senate to relocate his grave in the Volcanal and there to erect a statue of the deceased on a column. See also *Verr.* II.1.7, in which Cicero speaks of Verres' profanation of holy places and his hiding away in darkness of statues of the gods (*simulacraque deorum . . . iacent in tenebris ab isto retrusa atque abdita*).

88. Cf. *Verr.* II.5.186: *vosque, omnium rerum forensium, consiliorum maximorum, legum iudiciorumque arbitri et testes celeberrimo in loco populi Romani locati, Castor et Pollux.*

revelation of the plot. The sight of the statue, therefore, becomes visual evidence that "all that we see and especially this city is guided by the will and power of the immortal gods" (21).

This interpretation by Cicero of the meaning of the statue is accompanied by a reinterpretation of his own role in what had occurred. The consul once again summons up the image of the urban landscape— "even the temples and shrines of the gods"—threatened by destruction (22: *non solum vestris domiciliis atque tectis, sed etiam deorum templis atque delubris*), an image introduced at the beginning of the speech (2: *toti urbi, templis delubris, tectis ac moenibus*). In the exordium, however, Cicero had claimed that he himself had put out the fire threatening the city, had turned away the daggers from the necks of the citizens, and had been responsible for illuminating and revealing the details of the plot (3: *inlustrata, patefacta, comperta sunt per me*). By the end of the speech, however, the focus has shifted. Jupiter rather than Cicero is said to have turned aside the fire threatening the city, and the conspirators' plans have been "illuminated and revealed" (21: *inlustrata et patefacta*) not simply through the vigilance of the consul but by means of divine intervention.

The orator, in fact, emphatically and explicitly refuses credit for saving the city, declaring that if he himself were to claim that he had foiled the conspiracy, he ought not to be endured. Pointing to the statue on the Capitol, he declares, *ille, ille Iuppiter restitit; ille Capitolium, ille haec templa, ille cunctam urbem, ille vos omnis salvos esse voluit* (22). In the passage the demonstrative *ille* is repeated twice at the beginning of the second sentence and six times in all. Over and over again Cicero demands that the audience direct their attention to the monument that has been rhetorically transformed into evidence of the protection of Jupiter for Rome and the relationship between the god and his people. The result of that relationship has been the manifestation of the conspiracy, which Cicero now asserts has occurred by divine, not human, will. It has been Jupiter, not Cicero, who has protected "the Capitol, these temples, and the whole city" (22). Here, the sequence of topography pictures the protecting power of the god extending from his preserve on the Capitoline Hill to the temples of the gods visible to the audience in the Forum, to the whole of Rome, rising up beyond the boundaries of the Forum valley. Since the entire city, according to Cicero, owed its continued existence to the gods, not only does the statue on the Capitolium become a reminder of the divine patronage of Rome; all that the audience sees (21: *omnia quae videmus*) becomes such a reminder.

This change in interpretation, although couched in self-effacing terms, provides Cicero with no less exalted a role than that which he had earlier claimed. At first the unmasking of the conspiracy appeared to be a testament to his own unstinting labor, his vigilance, and his courage, but by the end of the speech he claims that his actions were guided by divine wisdom, and he presents himself as an instrument of Jupiter. While, for the modern reader, there is little to choose between the two assertions in terms of self-advertisement, Cicero would surely have felt the distinction was an important one to make. By indicating that his own actions stemmed from the gods' desire to preserve the city and, in turn, that this desire on the gods' part arose from their love of the Roman people (1: *summo erga vos amore*) Cicero gave his listeners a powerful motivation to accept his interpretation of events: to honor him was to affirm the divinely sanctioned status of themselves and their city. Further, if his audience accepted the orator's claim that his actions had been guided by the gods, then the fulfillment of the demand made at the end of the speech for their undying honor and respect was not simply a debt of gratitude but a religious imperative involving their *pietas*.

Thus a series of changes in the listeners' perception of the meaning of what they see around them plays a central role in the speech. Cicero first makes his audience aware of the extreme danger through which the city has passed. Its unchanged appearance is not to be taken for granted but is a special circumstance requiring explanation and interpretation. At the beginning of the speech Cicero makes the emergence of the city from peril the equivalent of a rebirth, thereby celebrating his own role as savior, refounder, and *alter Romulus*. Later in the speech, however, the orator asserts that the revelation of the conspiracy has been chiefly the work of the gods, and he enlarges on this theme through the meaning given the new statue of Jupiter set up on the Capitol.

By the end of the speech, then, we have arrived at the same conclusions as in the first *Catilinarian:* that Rome is a unique foundation, "guided by the will and power of the immortal gods" (21); that opposition to Catiline is inseparable from a belief in this unique sanction of Rome and her mission; and that Cicero's own leadership of the opposition to Catiline expressed his role as an instrument of divine will. The rhetorical course traveled in order to arrive at these conclusions, however, has differed in the two speeches, just as the audience and setting of the speeches have differed. In fact, the most striking conclusion of our analysis is that the ideas Cicero used to bridge the gap between the specifics of each rhetorical situation and the general patriotic and religious conceptions referred to above were not just supported by the ambiance of each speech but were *determined* by it. In both speeches, the welfare of Rome is made dependent on the special connection between the chief god and the city. In the first speech, however, delivered in the shadow of the Palatine Hill, Cicero had spoken of this connection as a kind of covenant between Jupiter and Romulus made at the city's inception, while in the speech delivered from the Rostra, Cicero announces to the people of Rome that the saving of the city has been accomplished through "the great love of the gods for you" (1). In the first speech, delivered to the Senate within the Temple of Jupiter Stator, the *principes* of the state are described as the chief targets of Catiline's murderous plans, and it is they who, like the early Romans of the Palatine city, must force the enemy back from the walls. In the later speech Cicero emphasizes that in the great battle that has been won with the help of the gods the lives of all and even the existence of the city itself had hung in the balance. Finally, in the first *Catilinarian* Jupiter Stator is referred to as the most ancient protector of Rome, and it is he who is invoked from his temple to protect Rome from the conspirators; in the rhetoric of the third *Catilinarian*, Jupiter Optimus Maximus, whose statue had recently been erected on the Capitolium, is restored to his traditional role as the supreme guardian of the city.

CHAPTER THREE

Signa and Signifiers:
A World Created

Tanta vis admonitionis inest in locis; ut non sine causa ex iis
memoriae ducta sit disciplina.

So great a power of suggestion resides in places that it is no
wonder the Art of Memory is based on it.

Cicero, *De finibus* 5.2

Any reader of Cicero's speeches, even one unfamiliar with the Roman
political system, is quick to note that the orator constantly requires his
audience—whether senators, jurors, or ordinary citizens—to direct
their imaginations beyond the walls of the city of Rome. Not only are
the speeches delivered on behalf of provincial governors characterized
by frequent references to Roman allies and provinces, but many other
Ciceronian orations are similarly filled with allusions to every corner of
Italy and the Mediterranean world. The deliberative speeches *De imperio Cn. Pompei* and *De provinciis consularibus* are only the most conspicuous of many that could be cited in this regard. The *Pro Balbo,* for
instance, in which the orator defended an individual whose legal right
to Roman citizenship was challenged, contains frequent references to
the western Mediterranean, from which the Spaniard Balbus had come;
similarly, in his defense of the claim to citizenship made by the poet
Archias, Cicero had numerous occasions to speak of the eastern Mediterranean. A wide range of allusions to places both outside of and
within Italy is found in the *De lege agraria* 2, and in the *Pro Milone*
Cicero speaks of various locales, most notably the Appian Way and the
place where a fatal altercation between Clodius and Milo occurred.
Such examples might be multiplied almost endlessly, but it is not my
intention to produce a catalogue of passages in which "the world" figured in Ciceronian rhetoric. Since the ways in which Cicero made use of
references to places and monuments were scarcely less numerous than
the ways he used metaphorical language, for instance, a catalogue of the

form and intent of these passages would surely be as dull as the lists of figures of thought and speech in the ancient rhetorical handbooks that it would inevitably resemble. More important, such a catalogue could be created only by divorcing, to a large extent, the passages within it from consideration of the overall strategies of persuasion in the speeches in which they occurred. Insight into a wide range of stylistic variation would be achieved, therefore, at the expense of our ability to understand the more complex and subtle ways the passages in question contributed to persuasion. Thus this chapter will be restricted to the description of certain statues, monuments, and topography within a single text, the fourth part of the Second Action against Verres. I have chosen this particular work because it is one that offers striking analogies in the realm of places that Cicero described to the kinds of references to places actually visible to the audience considered in the last chapter.

RHETORICAL THEORY: *ENARGEIA* AND MEMORY

As has been noted in chapter 1, Latin rhetorical handbooks have a number of things to say on the subject of references to places and monuments that were not part of the visible milieu.[1] We have seen that these works speak of the importance of considering the subjective and objective qualities of places when crafting a believable narration or a compelling argument. Quintilian's comment that "praise and blame" (5.10.41: *commendationem . . . et invidiam*) could be derived from the qualities of a place also suggests that the Roman orator was encouraged to consider various aspects of places in making emotional appeals, although Quintilian goes into little detail in explaining exactly how this technique was to be carried out.[2]

Of practical use to the orator who intended to speak at length about a place or monument neither seen by nor familiar to his audience was

1. See above, pp. 19–25.
2. As mentioned in chapter 1 (pp. 23–24), Quintilian gives two examples of such "praise and blame" connected to place (5.10.41), referring to a passage spoken by Ajax in Ovid's *Metamorphoses* (13.5–6) and to the charge of Milo's prosecutors in the *Pro Milone* (17, 18, 91). Also, according to the rhetorical concept of "decorum" or "propriety," the place where a speech was delivered was to be included among the considerations determining the style of a speech. Cf. Quint. 11.1.46–47 and similar remarks in Cic. *De or.* 3.210–11; *Or.* 123 (although Cicero does not refer specifically to place). See above, p. 19 n. 5.

the material in the rhetorical handbooks referring to a particular kind of description in which the speaker was advised to use concrete details in order to create a "visual image" in the minds of his listeners. As mentioned in chapter 1, the technique can be found under a variety of names, and it is often identified with *ekphrasis, enargeia, hypotypōsis, diatypōsis, evidentia, repraesentatio, illustratio, demonstratio, descriptio,* and *sub oculos subiectio.* Further, it is subsumed under a number of theoretical categories, including techniques of the narration and of the peroration, aspects of ornate style, and figures of thought.[3] It seems clear from this proliferation of terms and categories of treatment that Latin rhetoricians and orators well understood the importance of using this kind of description but were unsure how to define it precisely and how to integrate it into the received structure of rhetorical theory. Concerning one point, however, there is no ambiguity. The successful employment of *evidentia* (to settle on one of the terms) caused the listener to picture what was described with "the eyes of the mind" (Quint. 8.3.62). The subject matter of such descriptions can be found listed in later rhetorical treatises, for the technique became one of the standard exercises (*progymnasmata*) of the oratorical schools of the Empire.[4]

3. Lausberg, who notes the importance of using *enargeia* (or *evidentia*) in the narration of a speech, categorizes it in the following way (*Handbuch,* 1:13–16): *Evidentia* is one of five figures of thought appealing to the emotions. Both figures of thought and figures of speech are subdivisions of ornamentation, which (along with clarity and Latinity) is a stylistic virtue. The stylistic virtues are, in turn, an aspect of style (*elocutio*), the third of the five divisions of rhetoric. For a summary of ancient citations, see Lausberg, *Handbuch,* 1:399–407 (§§810–19). In Latin, see esp. *Her.* 2.49; 4.68; Cic. *Part. or.* 20; *De or.* 3.202; *Inv.* 1.104, 107; 2.78; *Or.* 139; Quint. 4.2.63; 6.2.32; 8.3.61–71; 9.2.40–44. Some sources define *topographia* as the description of a geographical location, and *topothesia* as the description of an imaginary place (Lausberg, *Handbuch,* 1:406–7, §819).

4. For terms used in Quintilian and *Ad Herennium,* see above, p. 20 n. 6. As mentioned in chapter 1, Zanker ("Enargeia," 298) states that *enargeia* and *ekphrasis* are often used almost interchangeably, although he defines *enargeia* as a heightened form of *ekphrasis* or description. (See also Krieger, *Ekphrasis,* 7 n. 8: "In this broad assignment of its function, ekphrasis would seem to overlap, almost totally, the rhetorically encouraged virtue of *enargeia,* which is also defined as vivid description addressed to the inner eye.") The distinction between a more (*enargeia*) or less (*ekphrasis*) "ocular" description, barely perceptible in Greek texts, disappears amidst the profusion of terms found in Latin texts. I have, for the most part, avoided using the term *ekphrasis* as an equivalent for Latin *evidentia* or *illustratio* in this chapter since (*a*) many scholars understand

Subjects for vivid description included places (*topoi*), times/seasons (*chronoi*), persons (*prosōpa*), occasions/celebrations (*panēgyreis*), events (*pragmata*), and, most familiar from poetry, statues and other artistic representations (*agalmata, eikones*). As was the case with earlier treatment of the technique, however, no clear theoretical understanding of vivid description is to be found in the *progymnasmata* of the later Empire, and only its emphasis on "visualization" separated it from other, closely related, rhetorical techniques, such as narration or characterization.[5]

Before dealing in more detail with the way *evidentia* was to be used in oratory, it is revealing first to consider the technique in light of the dominant ideas concerning perception and imagination in Cicero's day. While theories about these aspects of the mind varied among the major

---

it to refer only to its later meaning—i.e., the literary description of a work of art (see Krieger, *Ekphrasis*, 7–8, on the narrowing of the term to include only objects from the plastic arts); and (*b*) the term does not seem to have been current in Cicero's own time (see Zanker, "Enargeia," 305). For primary sources on *ekphrasis*, see Spengel, *Rhetores Graeci*, 2:16–17 (Hermogenes), 46–49 (Aphthonius), 118–20 (Aelius Theon); 3:251 (Georgios Choeroboscus), 491–93 (Nicolaus the Sophist). See also Downey, "Ekphrasis," esp. cols. 921–30; Norden, *Kunstprosa*, 1:285–86; Lausberg, *Handbuch*, 1:399–407 (§§810–19); Friedländer, *Johannes von Gaza*, 1–103; Zanker, "Enargeia"; Krieger, *Ekphrasis*. Norden's list of subjects of *ekphraseis* in Silver Age Latin prose includes "sunrises and sunsets, the calm sea and a pleasant journey, a grove, a charming house, especially a villa (temple, church) or painting, a city, a lovely girl, a splendid animal" or "horrid caves, the ocean and its terrors, . . . storm and shipwreck, torments, murder."

5. Since vivid description was understood to include the description of actions and events as well as of objects and people, no clear distinction can be drawn between it and narration. See the discussion of description as an aspect of narration in Genette, "Boundaries of Narrative," 5–8. Theoretical discussions of both *enargeia* and *evidentia* seem to combine the idea of stimulating an audience to visualize what is described (a potentially static tableau) with the idea of "actualization" (moving tableaux). See the discussion of the related technique of *energeia* in Arist. *Rhet.* 3.11.1–4 (1411b22–1412a9), where he speaks of bringing things "before the eyes" by the use of striking, often metaphorical, diction; and in Steiner, *Colors of Rhetoric*, 10–11. Cf. Krieger's discussion of the implications of *ekphrasis*, which—according to his definition—ultimately embraces "every attempt, within an art of words, to work toward the illusion that it is performing a task we usually associate with an art of natural signs" (*Ekphrasis*, 9). For Krieger the most fascinating but impenetrable aspect of *ekphrasis* consists in its attempt to force language into denying its temporality and creating a kind of stasis.

philosophical schools, a notion shared among them was that the mind was capable of receiving impressions in much the same way that soft wax receives the impression of a sealing stone.[6] But much controversy revolved around the question of exactly what sort of mental impressions arose from various sources. Cicero addresses the topic in the *Academica*. In this dialogue, he depicts Lucullus speaking on behalf of the philosophy of Antiochus, who had abandoned the Skepticism of Carneades and claimed to have returned to the position of the so-called Old Academy. Lucullus states that it is possible for an individual to arrive at knowledge of what is true by means of the information received through the senses, and he bases this assertion on the idea that we can distinguish "true presentations" to the senses (*visa vera*) from "illusionary" or "false images" (*visiones inanes*) by means of the "clarity" (*perspicuitas*) of the former. These true presentations, which arise from actually existing objects, can be "grasped" by the mind and form the basis both for memory and for accurate judgment.[7] Cicero, defending the Skeptical position of the "New Academy" of Carneades, argues that false sensory data are, in fact, often indistinguishable from true. For instance, the dreamer, while dreaming, is aware of no mark that distinguishes the images he or she "sees" from what is real. Cicero goes on

6. For the metaphor, see Plato *Tht.* 191c–d; Arist. *Mem.* 450a31; Theophr. *De sens.* 52; Sext. Emp. *Math.* 7.228. Hellenistic theories of sense perception can be divided into three groups. (1) According to the intromission theory of the Epicureans, thin films of atoms (*eidōla/simulacra*), produced continuously by every object, travel from an object to the eyes of an observer. These films are then capable of entering through the eyes and creating an image (*phantasia*) of the object in the mind of the observer. (2) The extramission theory associated with Euclid and the mathematicians assumed that sight depends on visual rays sent out from the eyes and falling on the surfaces of objects. (3) The "mediumistic" theory, associated with the Stoics, stated that sight occurs when a visual *pneuma* (a mixture of air and fire) originating within the eye causes the air between observer and object to be stretched taut in the shape of a cone. The cone of stretched air, the base of which is constituted by the observed object, then carries back to the eye the aspect of that object.

7. For Stoic theories of sense perception, see Hahm, "Early Hellenistic Theories of Vision"; von Staden, "The Stoic Theory of Perception"; Long, *Hellenistic Philosophy,* 123–31, and *Problems,* 91; Watson, *Stoic Theory of Knowledge,* 34–37. While judgment of the validity of various sense impressions is seen by the Stoics as volitional, nevertheless the clear and perspicuous presentation "virtually seizes us by the hair, dragging us off into assent" (Sext. Emp. *Math.* 7.257). For Aristotelian theories of perception, see Modrak, *Aristotle: The Power of Perception.*

to maintain that although it is impossible to distinguish absolutely whether sensory data are true or false, we may judge—and therefore act—on the basis of probable truth or falsity. He compares this process to a sea voyage. At the beginning of a voyage, the traveler aims at a certain destination and makes informed judgments on the basis of available evidence but cannot know for certain what the course of the voyage will actually be (2.100). Similarly, the careful application of rational judgment to the data provided by the senses can help us to make decisions concerning probable truth and falsity, although absolute certainty remains beyond our powers of discrimination.[8] Lucullus had not only argued that true and false images could be distinguished; he had also contended that only a true, "graspable" presentation (*phantasia kataléptikē*) arising from actual objects was available to memory.[9] Cicero takes issue with this statement as well, asserting that both images that have their origin in real objects and those that are merely illusory could be impressed upon the mind and thus made available to memory.

Although Cicero does not explicitly confront the question of what kind of impression images created through *evidentia* might make on the mind, it is clear from the *Academica* that, from the point of view of the audience, such images would be classified as "false" (*visiones inanes*) rather than "true" (*visa vera*), and therefore comparable to the impressions of dreams, hallucination, or the imagination.[10] If we follow Ci-

---

8. For Skeptical criticism of the Stoic account of perception, see especially von Staden, "The Stoic Theory of Perception," 112–27; Long, *Hellenistic Philosophy*, 90–97, 128–29.

9. For the *phantasia kataléptikē*, the "cognitive presentation" of the Stoics, see, for example, Sandbach, "Phantasia Kataleptike"; von Staden, "The Stoic Theory of Perception," 97–99; Long, *Hellenistic Philosophy*, 126–31; Long and Sedley, *Hellenistic Philosophers*, 1:241–53.

10. "False" images include (a) those that have no counterpart in the real world, such as that of a unicorn; (b) those that appear to be presentations of objects that are not actually available to the senses at the time perceived, such as the image of an existing object seen in a dream or in a hallucination; and (c) images of reality that do not accurately represent reality, such as a straight stick that appears bent in water. Cf. definitions of *imago* in Julius Victor (Halm, *Rhetores Latini minores*, 339.33–36: *Ab imagine; est autem imago, cum ipsi aliquid simile effingimus, quamvis non sit in rerum natura, ut Marcus Tullius in Verrem: nam sicut Scyllam, inquit, nautis infestam accepimus*) and Macrobius (*Sat.* 4.5.9: *et imago, quae est a simili pars tertia, idonea est movendis affectibus. ea fit cum aut forma corporis absentis describitur, aut omnino quae nulla est fingitur*), cited by Schrijvers, "Invention, imagination et théorie des émotions," 401.

cero's (rather than Lucullus's) arguments in the dialogue, we may suppose that verbally induced images, like other illusionary images, could potentially be indistinguishable from the actual in the impressions that they leave on the mind and, therefore, in their availability to processes of memory and feeling. This supposition is reinforced by the similarity of vocabulary used in passages dealing with the two kinds of impressions. When Lucullus argues that the "real" object creates an image that can be distinguished from the illusory, the terms he uses to describe the special, distinguishing characteristic of the real are "clarity" and "perspicuity."[11] Even a philosophical Skeptic like Cicero, who argues in the dialogue that this apparent clarity could not serve as an unshakable criterion of the real, does not attempt to deny the affective power on the mind of the clear and perspicuous presentation. When we turn from philosophy to rhetorical theory, we find that it is precisely this quality of "perspicuity" that is the chief characteristic of vivid description: *evidentia* involves a mode of verbal expression that produces a clear, "visual" impression on the listener through "the eyes of the mind." It seems reasonable to infer, then, that ancient orators who, like Cicero, were familiar with both Greek philosophical and rhetorical theory might have seen in the technique of *evidentia* a verbal counterpart to the sensory reception of clear and striking images. While no one could claim that a listener might mistake the mental image created by verbal description for the visual experience of an existing object or objects, the use of the concept of clarity or *enargeia* to describe both *visiones* hints at the belief that these two avenues to the memory and emotions had a similarly potent effect.

11. *Enargeia* (cf. Cic. *Acad.* 2.17: *enargeia/perspicuitas/evidentia*) was defined by Epicurus as the quality of clarity in a sense impression that allows us to trust its reliability (*Ep. Hdt.* 52). The Stoics argued that the "cognitive presentation" (*phantasia kataleptikē*) could be distinguished from other presentations by the fact that it is "striking" (*plēktikē:* Sext. Emp. *Math.* 7.257, 258, 403) and "evident" (*enargēs:* Sext. Emp. *Math.* 7.257, 403). Apparent clarity was, for the Skeptics, one—but only one—of the criteria that might lead one to conclude that a sense impression was probably—but not absolutely—true (cf. Long, *Hellenistic Philosophy*, 96–98). Zanker, "Enargeia," 308–10, traces the use of *enargeia* by the philosophers, particularly Epicurus, for whom it is the "indispensible condition for those sense impressions (*phantasiai*) which alone can be trusted as evidence for the external properties of the senses." He suggests that Hellenistic literary critics borrowed the term from contemporary philosophical writings, especially Epicurean texts, where the connection between *enargeia* and sight is emphasized.

Of the connection of such verbally produced images with the emotions the ancient rhetoricians had little doubt.[12] In a passage introduced by the statement that it was his intention to reveal to his readers the hidden secrets of his art (6.2.25), Quintilian asserts that in order to stir the emotions of others an orator must first be moved himself (6.2.27). He then explains how the orator may learn to generate feelings in himself:

> There exist those things that the Greeks call *phantasiai* and that we term *visiones*, by means of which the images of absent things are represented in our minds in such a way that we seem to see them with our eyes as if they were actually present.[13] Whoever is extremely responsive to these (6.2.30: *has . . . bene conceperit*) will have the greatest power over the emotions. . . . In fact, we may acquire this power easily if we desire it.[14] When our minds

12. See, for example, *Her.* 2.49 (*decimus locus*); 4.51, 69; Cic. *Inv.* 1.104 (*decimus locus*); *De or.* 3.202; Quint. 6.2.32–34; 8.3.61–71; [Longinus] *On the Sublime* 15.1.

13. As von Staden ("The Stoic Theory of Perception," 127 n. 11) remarks, "*Phantasia* . . . is a translator's nightmare." According to Lee, Plato believed *phantasia* to be "nothing less than the master-concept for our entire perceptual relation with the physical world" ("The Sense of an Object," 46). For Aristotle *phantasia* refers to a process or "movement" (*kinēsis*) by which images are presented to the mind. On the one hand, it is related to perception (*aisthēsis*), since all *phantasmata* originate in sense perception; on the other, it is related to judgment (*hypolēpsis*), which relies on it in forming opinions. It is, however, identical with neither perception nor judgment. (For Aristotelian *phantasia*, see, for instance, Most, "Seming and Being," 27–30, 32 n. 30; Rees, "Aristotle's Treatment of *phantasia*"; Engmann, "Imagination"; Schofield, "Aristotle on the Imagination"; Watson, "*Phantasia* in Aristotle," and *Phantasia*, 14–37; Modrak, *Aristotle: The Power of Perception*, passim.) Epicurus used the same word to describe an aspect of the mechanics of perception—the creation of an image in the mind by the reception through the eyes of successions of *eidōla* (Epicurus *Ep. Hdt.* 49.6–50.4). The Stoics usually defined *phantasia* as the presentation in the psyche of an observed object, frequently (but not always—see Sext. Emp. *Math.* 8.56–57 [*SVF* 2:29, no. 88]) reserving *emphasis, phantastikon,* and *phantasma* for images of nonexisting objects or objects not present at the time of perception (*SVF* 2:21–22 [nos. 54, 55], 24 [no. 61]). For the Stoic *phantasia katalēptikē*, the clear and striking presentation virtually demanding assent, see above, p. 93 n. 9. For citations of ancient evidence, translation, and commentary, see Long, *Hellenistic Philosophers*, 1:72–90; 2:75–93. See Watson, *Phantasia*, for a clear and useful review of evidence on *phantasia* from Plato to the Greek Neoplatonists.

14. Quintilian here makes clear the difference between poetic *phantasia*, through which the poet is emotionally transported and is thereby able to depict vividly scenes beyond the realm of reality, and rhetorical *phantasia*, which—

are unoccupied and open to empty wishes and daydreams, the images about which I am speaking appear, so that we seem to be making a journey or sailing or fighting or addressing the people or spending riches we do not actually possess, and it seems to us that we are not thinking these things but acting. Why shall we not make practical use of this defect of our minds? Suppose that I am complaining that a man has been killed; shall I not keep before my eyes everything that well might actually have occurred? . . . Will not the blood, the pallor, the terrible groan, and finally the death rattle of the victim reside in my mind? From this follows *enargeia*, which Cicero calls *illustratio* and *evidentia*, by which things seem not so much to be said as to be shown; and our emotions are aroused no differently than if we were actually present at an event.

(6.2.29–32)

Quintilian begins with the assumption that false images (i.e., *visiones inanes,* which do not come from an object actually available to the senses at the moment they are perceived) often exist in the mind, although he makes no attempt to explain exactly how these images originate. In the ordinary person these simply occur when the mind is at rest (*inter otia*). The orator, however, can train himself to produce particular images in order to bring about the emotional response that accompanies them. When he hopes to arouse sympathy in his audience for a murdered man he will first create that emotion in himself by imagining in vivid detail the scene of a pathetic and brutal attack. Quintilian does not say that he will think of what he knows *did* happen but, rather, will summon up a "believable" scenario for the murder (6.2.31: *quae in re praesenti accidisse credibile est*). So far, Quintilian is speaking only of the orator and the process by which he could summon remembered images to his own mind. Then, however, he makes a crucial intellectual leap by connecting this process, which takes place within the mind of the orator, with his use of verbal descriptions in order to stimulate visualizations in the minds of his audience. The reader of the passage is therefore led to see the entire process as a connected sequence: the

---

although rousing the emotions of the orator—is a rationally controlled exercise. One has the sense that, for Cicero and Quintilian, the successful orator can never be so moved by emotion that he does not constantly observe himself and the effect he is having on his audience. See Russell, *Criticism in Antiquity,* 108–10, and Schrijvers, "Invention, imagination et théorie des émotions," for differences between poetic and rhetorical *phantasia* implied by Quintilian and discussed by the author of *On the Sublime* (15.1–12).

speaker first summons images from his memory, where they are stored; if the orator is skillful and imaginative, these stimulate the particular emotional response that he had hoped to create in himself; the orator then, through vivid description, stimulates corresponding *visiones* in the minds of his audience; and these, in turn, produce a seemingly inevitable emotional reaction in the listeners. The process by which the mind of the orator is moved and that by which his audience is moved is, in essence, the same. A particular image (*visio*), summoned to mind, sets in motion a predictable emotional response (*pathos*).[15] The difference lies chiefly in the control exercised by the orator, who—through conscious exercise of the imagination—creates the vision and, seemingly, is able to transmit it in words to his listeners, who then passively receive it.

Much of this appears fairly peculiar to the modern reader, and yet those aspects of the theoretical discussion of *evidentia* that appear most strange to us are perhaps most revealing of differences between Cicero's audience and ourselves. Implicit in these discussions of the images derived from experience of real objects is the idea that such images were able to produce a cohering and lasting physical impact on the mind by means of the eyes, as if the persisting image produced from staring several moments at a dark shape on a white ground were not a fleeting illusion but a lasting impression that could be retained by the mind and reproduced from memory. Even those *phantasiai* that manifestly originate within the mind, as in daydreams or sleep, were usually conceived of as pictures preserved by memory from previous sensory experience.[16] This made mental images that had no corresponding existence in the real world somewhat difficult to explain, but a number of theories were evolved to deal with the problem; no explicit attempt was made, however, to explain the perceptual mechanics of *evidentia*, by which the orator, through words, produced images not previously perceived in the

15. Cf. [Longinus] *On the Sublime* 15.1–2, where the process is understood in exactly the same way: "For the term Imagination (*phantasia*) is applied in general to an idea which enters the mind from any source and engenders speech, but the word has now come to be used predominantly of passages where, *inspired by strong emotion (enthousiasmou kai pathous) you seem to see what you describe and bring it vividly before the eyes of the audience*" (trans. W. H. Fyfe, Loeb Classical Library edition of Longinus [Cambridge, Mass., 1953]; italics added).

16. See, for example, Arist. *De insomn.* 460b1–8; 461b22–23 (images in dreams are the residue of actual sense impressions).

minds of those he addressed.[17] Most striking in the ancients' attempts to wrestle with such problems is their tendency to describe much of what goes on in the human mind as the creation or remembrance of coherent, retrievable pictorial images rather than as a manipulation of abstractions.[18]

It is also to be observed that the accounts of *evidentia* or *enargeia* found in ancient sources assume an extraordinary degree of correspondence between words and images. The effect in such descriptions of

17. Aristotle (*De insomn.* 461a15–25) describes how the confusion (through illness, for instance) of movements in the mind can produce monstrous and distorted images. For the Stoics as well, altered states (madness, illness, drunkenness) explained the propagation of certain kinds of false images in the mind. The Epicureans, with their intromissionist theory of perception, explained the ability to conceive of false images (in the sense of those mental images that did not correspond to any previous sensory perception of an actual object) by our reception of flimsy, composite films created by the accidental adhering of *eidōla* from different objects (Lucr. 4.722–55). Quintilian's statement (8.3.64) that those who hear ekphrastic description imagine details beyond those specified by the orator suggests that each listener, stimulated by the words of the orator, creates images out of his or her previously existing store of remembered *phantasiai*. The emphasis in rhetorical *ekphrasis* on realism (e.g., Quint. 8.3.70; [Longinus] *On the Sublime* 15.8) also suggests that the orator's descriptions were meant to summon scenes with which all were familiar, whether from their own experience or from dramatic or artistic representations. The description of a captured city, for instance—a standard ekphrastic topic (*Her.* 4.51; Quint. 8.3.67–70)—would probably have summoned to the minds of an audience images from well-known paintings. Cf. Jos. Addison, *The Spectator*, no. 416, 27 June 1712: "When I say the ideas we receive from statues, descriptions or suchlike occasions, are the same that were actually once in our view, it must not be understood that we had once seen the very place, action, or person, that are carved or described. It is sufficient that we have seen places, persons, or actions in general which bear a resemblance, or at least some remote analogy, with what we find represented; since it is in the power of the imagination, when it is once stocked with particular ideas, to enlarge, compound, and vary them at her own pleasure."

18. Cf. Arist. *De an.* 3.8 (432a7–11), trans. W. S. Hett, Loeb Classical Library edition: "No one could ever learn or understand anything without the exercise of perception, so even when we think speculatively we must have some mental picture of which to think; for mental images (*phantasmata*) are similar to objects perceived except that they are without matter." Cf. L. Wittgenstein, *Philosophical Investigations* no. 396, trans. G. E. M. Anscombe (New York, 1953), 120: "It is no more necessary to the understanding of a proposition that one should imagine anything in connexion with it, than that one should make a sketch from it."

words *as* words, each freighted with emotional resonance for the listener, is scarcely acknowledged by ancient rhetorical theorists. Only in Quintilian (8.3.64) is there any recognition that the words of description, once filtered through the individual consciousness of the listeners, might stimulate different images, thoughts, and emotions in the mind of each individual. The supposition is rather that the words of the description are irrelevant except for their efficacy in creating for the listeners a mental picture of what is described; and, further, that essentially the same mental picture would be present in the mind of each listener. Without embarking on a full-scale review of the implications of *evidentia* for the *ut pictura poesis* thesis, we may simply note that these assumptions by ancient rhetoricians about the way vivid description worked in the minds of an audience suggest that ancient, nonliterate society may well have possessed powers of pictorial visualization much greater and more intense than our own.[19]

Of what use was *evidentia* to the ancient orator? The material in the rhetorical textbooks emphasizing the effectiveness of the technique in rousing the emotions of an audience is useful, considering the crucial role played by emotional appeals in Ciceronian oratory, and yet unsatisfying, when we compare it with the complexity of Cicero's use in the *Catilinarians* of images the audience actually had before their eyes.[20] As has been demonstrated, when Cicero directed his listeners to consider the cult statue of the Temple of Jupiter Stator in the first *Catilinarian* or the statue of Jupiter Optimus Maximus on the Capitolium in the third speech, in each case he aimed not simply at a straightforward appeal to the emotional impact of what the audience saw but at a complex series of thoughts and feelings dependent both on what he said and on what was before their eyes. This leads us to consider whether rhetorical theory might not suggest a more subtle and far-ranging employment of

19. Cf. Yates, *Art of Memory*, 4: "Ancient memories . . . could depend on faculties of intense visual memorization which we have lost." There is an extensive bibliography on the relationship between verbal description and visual representation. See, for instance, Mitchell, *Iconology* (with full bibliography on the *ut pictura poesis* question); Brilliant, *Visual Narratives*, 73–76; Steiner, *Colors of Rhetoric*, esp. 1–69; Leach, *Rhetoric of Space*, esp. 3–24.

20. The idea that such passages were emotionally powerful is extremely important, since it was Cicero's belief that of the three offices of oratory—to teach, to delight, to move—it was the third on which the success of a speech ultimately depended (see Cic. *De or.* 1.17, 53, 60; 2.115, 178, 215; *Or.* 128; *Brut.* 276, 279, 322).

the technique, analogous to strategies of persuasion observed in Cicero's exploitation of the visible milieu.

I believe that ancient rhetorical theory does indeed point the way to a broader use of vivid description through what it has to say about the art of memory. In the passage from the *De finibus* quoted in chapter 1, the experience of seeing a sequence of memorable places, each with vivid and moving associations for Cicero and his friends, had caused Piso to exclaim at "how great a power of association resides in places" (5.2: *tanta vis admonitionis inest in locis*) and to recall that upon this fact depended the system of artificial memory (*memoriae . . . disciplina*). According to this system, which was believed to have been created by the poet Simonides (the same poet, it should be remembered, who was also reputed to have called poetry "speaking painting"), an orator was taught to recall the various ideas or even words for his speech by associating them with images of things (*imagines*) and to remember the order of these ideas by picturing the images in various *loci* or backgrounds.[21] The *imagines* were compared to letters, the *loci* to writing tablets, and the latter were meant to be impressed on the mind in an unvarying sequence and reused on different occasions with a variety of images. The *Ad Herennium* suggests that the orator choose these backgrounds in locations that will not be confusing because of the coming and going of large numbers of people (3.31). Furthermore, they must be distinct, one from the other, and neither too close together nor too far apart, neither too bright nor too dim (3.31–32). The axially and hierarchically ordered rooms of the Roman atrium house, memorized in a fixed order, made an excellent series of mental *loci*. The *Ad Herennium* also notes that these backgrounds did not all have to be memorized through actual experience, since "thought" (3.32: *cogitatio*) could provide an endless supply of suitable places.

What are the implications of this system of artificial memory for the use of *evidentia*? First, training in the *ars memoriae* not only accustomed the orator to create "visual" pictures in his mind but taught him to associate abstract ideas with these pictures. As Frances Yates has pointed out, "The word 'mnemotechnics' hardly conveys what the artificial memory of Cicero may have been like, as it moved among the

21. For Simonides's statement, see Plut. *Mor.* 346f (cf. 17f; 58b). On the art of memory, see Quint. 11.2.1–51; Cic. *De or.* 2.351–60; *Her.* 3.28–40; Lausburg, *Handbuch*, 1:525–27 (§§1083–90); Yates, *Art of Memory*, 1–49; Caplan, "Memoria"; Kennedy, *Art of Rhetoric*, 123–26.

buildings of ancient Rome, *seeing* the places, *seeing* the images stored on the places, with a piercing inner vision which immediately brought to his lips the thoughts and words of his speech."[22] And, just as Quintilian had connected the orator's practice of visualizing a scene in order to rouse his own emotions with that same orator's effort to induce his audience also to visualize emotionally charged scenes, so it seems likely that, in this instance as well, a speaker would realize that a technique he had employed as part of the private propaedeutic of speech making could also be used to manipulate the thoughts and feelings of his audience. Thus Cicero may well have understood that the mnemonic technique by which he impressed ideas on his own mind could be employed to impress concepts on the minds of his listeners.[23] The first step in this process would be to create a series of distinct and memorable settings in the minds of his listeners. This he could do in the same way he himself had learned to keep in mind "backgrounds": either by direct visual experience or by the creation in the mind's eye of vivid images of various locations. On the one hand, he could make use of the familiar monuments and buildings visible to the audience in the Forum, leading them to connect with these *loci* symbolic values supporting his rhetorical goals. We have seen how in the *Pro Scauro,* for instance, Cicero directed the attention of his audience to the key monuments of the Forum and tied to each a meaning relevant to the status and character of the accused. On the other hand, the orator could induce his audience to imagine a *locus* through his employment of vivid description. This *locus* and the images created within it could then be used by the orator not simply to elicit an emotional reaction but at the same time to trigger associations with various larger and more complex ideas. The *ars memoriae,* therefore, is able to provide us with the theoretical link between the use of *evidentia* to create emotionally potent images in the minds of listeners and the much more far-reaching use of the same technique to attach symbolic values to those images. At the same time, through its implicit acknowledgment that both imagination and experience are effective ways of impressing *loci* on the mind, the *ars memoriae* points to a theoretical connection between the kinds of meanings developed by Cicero

22. *Art of Memory,* 4.

23. Speaking of artistic representation of memory images, Yates writes (*Art of Memory,* 81): "For when people were being taught to practice the formation of images for remembering, it is difficult to suppose that such inner images might not sometimes have found their way into outer expression."

for elements of the visible milieu and those meanings tied to places and things merely described to an audience.

This hypothesis, of course, leaves many questions unresolved. If the orator were to follow the suggestions in the rhetorical handbooks, we assume that he would (a) attempt to engage his own emotions in treating the subject matter of his speech by means of imaginative reconstructions of events; (b) stimulate visualizations in his audience through vivid description; (c) impress ideas and their sequence on his own mind through memorization of a large number of images set within various loci; and also, perhaps, (d) attempt to impress image-filled memory loci on the minds of his audience, either by the manipulation of actual visual milieux or by vivid descriptions. But would the images that aroused the orator's own emotions (a) be identical with those he hoped to produce in the minds of his audience through vivid description (b)?[24] Would either of these be identical with the loci and images he kept in mind to remember what he wished to say and when (c)? And what was the relationship between these memory loci (c) and those he created in the minds of his audience (d)?[25]

24. Yates, *Art of Memory,* 86, commenting upon the artificial memory techniques used by Renaissance preachers, notes that "the similitude spoken in the sermon is not strictly speaking the similitude used in artificial memory. For the memory image is invisible, and remains hidden within the memory of its user, where, however, it can become the hidden generator of externalized imagery."

25. The orator's need to avoid confusion by minimizing the number of images kept in mind suggests that a great deal of overlap would have had to exist in the use to which images were put. To return once more to the *Pro Scauro,* when Cicero wished to stimulate within himself feelings of pity for the danger in which his client, Aemilius Scaurus, stood, he might have pictured to himself the outstanding deeds and character attributed to various of the Scauri (cf. Antonius's description of exactly this process in *De or.* 2.194–95). It would, in turn, advance his case to mention some of these same events to the audience as well, since a celebration of Scaurian dignity, generosity, and bravery would serve to attach the audience to the defendant. Furthermore, his mention of these events could be calculated to have a greater impact if it took the form of a vivid description of memorable scenes that stimulated striking images in the minds of the audience. The images that originated in the mind of the orator would thus form the basis for those he hoped to create in the minds of his listeners. Since certain of these images—for instance, that of Lucius Metellus saving the Palladium from the burning shrine of Vesta—could be associated with monuments visible in the Forum, Cicero could memorize these places in a fixed order and connect with them *imagines* he wished to describe, as well as broader concepts to which the *imagines* were wedded. These private memory loci and their con-

I hope that we may begin to explore some of these problems through an analysis of *In Verrem* II.4, but, whatever the answers to specific questions may be, a general principle ought here to be affirmed: namely, that this technique, like any technique of Ciceronian oratory, was not an end in itself but was a means to an end. Ignoring this principle has led many to classify vivid description in oratory merely as an ornament of style and to analyze its rhetorical use in the same way one would analyze the use of *enargeia* or *ekphrasis* in poetry.[26] Whether or not the source of the technique lay in poetry, its aims in rhetorical texts were not the same as in poetry. The stylistic beauty or affective power of a descriptive passage in a deliberative or forensic speech and the emotion it must have engendered in those who heard it were never, in themselves, the raison

---

nection with various associative ideas could then, in turn, form the basis for the external structure of this section of the speech.

If this habit of mnemonic visualization was as important a part of the orator's training as we have assumed, it seems probable that it would have been reflected in other literary works as well as in speeches. Perhaps the "associative" itinerary of Athens in Cicero's *De finibus* (5.2) and the poetic itinerary of the center of Rome in the *Tristia* (3.1.27–74) of Ovid, the most rhetorical of Augustan poets, provide evidence of the adaptation of rhetorical training and technique to nonrhetorical uses.

26. Most modern discussions of *ekphrasis* focus on its long poetic history and its frequent use as an epideictic technique in imperial school and public rhetoric, and there is a corresponding tendency to interpret its use in Ciceronian oratory in terms either of poetry or of epideictic. Norden (*Kunstprosa*, 1:285), for instance, agrees with Rohde's interpretation of ekphrastic passages in rhetoric as motivated by a desire to imitate and "compete with" ekphrastic passages in Hellenistic poetry. A similar conception of the ornamental function of description in classical rhetoric appears in the more recent study of Genette, "Boundaries of Narrative" (6). A useful corrective to this emphasis on techniques of style is found in Brink's discussion of differences between poetry and rhetoric in "Cicero's *Orator* and Horace's *Ars Poetica.*" Brink (99–100) points out that the concept of *flectere*, missing from poetry, is always related in rhetoric to a practical purpose. See also Neumeister, *Grundsätze der forensischen Rhetorik*, 156–92, for the impossibility of separating "style" from the practical goals of persuasion in forensic and deliberative rhetoric. In "Ekphrasis and the Theme of Artistic Failure," 136 n. 5, Leach warns that "although imitation within the declamatory schools is a token of the admiration with which *ekphrasis* in poetry was regarded, it should not be taken to indicate that the purposes of the poets and orators were precisely the same." Leach's intent is to rescue poetic *ekphrasis* from misinterpretation, but the same sentiment should also be applied to rhetorical *ekphrasis*.

d'être of such a passage. Rather, vivid description in Ciceronian oratory was always part of an overall strategy meant to lead an audience to a predictable emotional and intellectual stance vis-à-vis the particular subject at issue before them, whether their role was as jurors, voters, or simply members of the body politic. Before analyzing the description of places and things in the text of *In Verrem* II.4, therefore, it will be useful to consider the chief factors that informed Cicero's rhetorical strategy in the work.

THE RHETORICAL CHALLENGE OF *IN VERREM* II.4 ("DE SIGNIS")

The fourth part of the Second Action against Verres was devoted to a discussion of the statues and monuments stolen by Verres during the latter's tenure as praetor in Sicily. The most obvious rhetorical goal of the speech was to arouse the indignation of the Roman audience at the revelation of Verres' plundering of these works of art. Since many of the works had been removed from temples of the gods, one would assume that no great eloquence would have been required on Cicero's part. The reader of Republican and Augustan literature is often led to envision a society particularly susceptible to the emotional impact connected with such works. One need only think, for instance, of the Roman belief in the numinous power of places and of man-made and natural objects; of the reverence accorded the statues of gods and heroes, especially those of great antiquity, adorning the city's temples and public places; of the significance to the Roman citizen of the many monuments erected to commemorate great leaders and signal events in the city's history; or of the private observances devoted to objects placed in family shrines and *sacraria*.

It is necessary, however, to draw certain distinctions among objects of this kind. It is surely true that statues and monuments long familiar to a Roman audience, woven over the decades into the very fabric of the city, would have acquired a complex and powerful set of associations. The familiar landmarks of the Comitium and the Forum in particular not only shaped the poetic itinerary of a Plautus or an Ovid but constituted a source of cognitive and emotional orientation for every citizen of Rome. Allusions to these were part of the stock-in-trade of the Roman orator, who would frequently have attempted to connect the arguments, ideas, and themes of his speeches with visual symbols he knew to be rich in patriotic and religious meaning for his audience. In addition, certain monuments were held in special reverence and were thought to be directly connected with the continuing welfare of the city, such as those struck by lightning or spoken of in oracles.

It is nevertheless clear that special significance could not have attached to every statue and monument, as their very number would have precluded such a possibility. In book 34 of his *Naturalis historia* Pliny the Elder provides us with an impressive catalogue of statues that stood in the city at various times (34.1–93). The antiquarian reports that during one theatrical show the theater supported three thousand statues (34.36) and that large numbers of statues sometimes were ordered removed from the Forum, apparently due to their abundance there (34.30–31). Thus, while certain Roman monuments acquired a powerful symbolic significance closely identified with the function and meaning of the place where they stood, the importance of others must have been relatively inconsequential. It can be assumed, for instance, that the statues erected to honor still-living generals and politicians would, in many cases, have been held in less awe than those of gods and heroes. Cicero refers in the *Verrines* to the many statues of Verres erected in Rome, ostensibly "by the people of Sicily as a whole" (II.2.154). The orator expresses little surprise that a politician of no great repute should have been the subject of so many honorary monuments. His only objection to the statues is that the money for these works had been extorted from the Sicilians rather than willingly donated. If such an extensive visual propaganda campaign could have been mounted by a relatively minor figure like Verres, it may be assumed that men of much greater reputation, power, and ambition would have been even more widely represented, and that the commonness of these honorary statues would have dulled their impact.[27]

If many of the statues and monuments commissioned by the Senate or by private individuals and visible daily to Roman citizens lacked enduring symbolic significance, what of those that had been seized from conquered states? The plunder of precious objects of all sorts had ac-

27. Cassiodorus (*Var.* 7.15; cf. 7.13) reports that by his time—the sixth century A.D.—Rome had a "duplicate population" of stone and bronze. Plutarch (*Cat. Mai.* 19) recalls an anecdote revealing that in the time of Cato the Elder many statues were dedicated to individuals of limited fame. When certain prominent but controversial figures died or fell from favor, their statues were subject to official removal or unsanctioned destruction by their opponents (see, for instance, Suet. *Iul. Caes.* 75.4 for statues of Sulla and Pompey overturned by the populace; and *Verr.* II.2.158 for destruction of Verres' statues in Sicily).

companied Rome's military progress throughout the Italian peninsula and across the Mediterranean. In the Italian phase of this expansion, the practice of *evocatio* and the building of temples dedicated to the divinities of the conquered suggest that the Romans in many cases perceived the gods and heroes of Italians, Etruscans, and south Italian Greeks as either identical with their own gods or worthy of incorporation into their expanding pantheon. This would lead us to assume that the plundered statues, at least of divinities, would have been treated by the Romans with reverence and a sense of religious awe. However, as Rome's victims became more alien and more numerous, religious scruples governing the treatment of such objects must have eroded. The victories over Syracuse, Carthage, and especially Corinth would have resulted in a flood of statues entering Rome and Italy.[28] By Cicero's day the Roman public had become used to seeing the most precious and sacred works of Greek art exhibited in the games and shows held by the aediles and other magistrates and carried in the triumphs of victorious generals.[29] Statues that formed part of the booty plundered from a conquered city might later be dedicated in Roman temples or public places, or they might be kept privately by the former *imperator* to grace his own villas or those of his friends. On the one hand, the practice of public exhibition and donation might be taken as evidence of the interest of the Roman public in objects of this sort and of their effectiveness as tools of propaganda, reminding the viewer of a greater or lesser victory of Roman arms and of the piety, courage, and patriotic generosity of the leader who had won it. On the other hand, such statues, displayed in large numbers and out of their original (usually religious) context, would have been stripped of much of their emotional and symbolic impact.

The objection might be raised that Verres was not the military conqueror of the places where he exercised magisterial power and that we must distinguish the Romans' cavalier attitude towards objects plun-

28. For Greek artwork imported to Rome, see Pape, *Griechische Kunstwerke aus Kriegsbeute*. Ancient sources are collected and translated in Pollitt, *Art of Rome*, 22–95.

29. See *Verr.* II.1.57 (triumphal exhibition of P. Servilius); 4.6 (aedileship of C. Claudius Pulcher), 126 (statues and ornaments in the Temple of Felicitas, the Temple of Fortuna, the Porticus Metelli, the villas of Verres' friends, and the shows of aediles), 133 (shows in the aedileships of L. Crassus, Q. Scaevola, G. Claudius).

dered from hostile states in time of war from their attitude towards the confiscated goods of allies, client states, and provinces.[30] In fact, in one passage Cicero indicates that the Romans believed that sacred objects were "deconsecrated" by falling victim to Roman arms: speaking of Marcellus's actions after the fall of Syracuse, Cicero states that "through his famous victory he had rendered all things profane" (II.4.122).[31] This was indeed an ingenious method of exculpating Roman actions that could otherwise be viewed as sacrilege, and from a legalistic point of view one could in fact argue that the statues and monuments removed by Verres ought not be compared with those seized in war, since Verres' plunder, unlike war booty, was viewed as sacred and therefore still protected by religious scruples. But as regards the perception of the objects themselves, the treatment of war booty would have had a profound effect on how the Romans responded to all such objects. The Roman public, accustomed to viewing hundreds of statues and works of art exhibited in triumphs and during festivals or donated to the state, would hardly have made fine distinctions among the supposedly "deconsecrated" statues seized from hostile states and those still sacred works bought or borrowed by Romans traveling abroad or illegally extorted from friendly states.[32]

30. Even judged by the much wider latitude given the military commander, Verres' actions were of questionable legality, since most historians agree that, with the exception of a certain fixed portion of the booty allotted to the general (*manubiae*), the booty seized in war was the property of the state. See Shatzman, "The Roman General's Authority."

31. The orator goes on to contend that by Verres' day the same objects had once again become *sacra* and *religiosa* due to the long period of peace that had since elapsed and the loyalty to Rome exhibited by the Syracusans throughout that time. The lack of logical or emotional force in such a distinction can be seen in the fact that Cicero himself disregards it when he praises Mummius for plundering only "profane" objects in Messana and refusing to touch those that had been consecrated (II.4.4).

32. If Cicero had praised without reservation the plundering—even in war—of works similar to those Verres had stolen, it would have tended to undermine his attempt to make Verres' theft of such statues an outrage to religious sensibility. Therefore, understanding the dangerous ground on which he was treading, Cicero emphasizes the pious restraint and generosity supposedly exercised by men like Scipio Aemilianus, Mummius, Marcellus, and others. In addition, he underlines the fact that such men had chosen to contribute to the state the works of art they had removed from conquered cities, while Verres, after appropriating such objects illegally, had kept them for himself and his friends. See

For most of Cicero's audience, admiration for works of art was not based on their religious or symbolic significance but would have derived from the precious materials of which they were composed, from their rarity, from the cleverness of artistic conception embodied in them, or from the beauty of their craftsmanship.[33] If the Roman public responded to displays of artwork enthusiastically, it was an enthusiasm little to be distinguished in many instances from that shown for exhibitions of exotic animals also shipped to Rome for games and festivals. And, as in the case of such animals, jaded sensibilities would have required ever-increasing numbers and rarity in order to guarantee a successful reception. It was only when statues or monuments had long stood within the city that they gradually acquired a new meaning for the Roman viewer, interwoven of associations connected with the origin, subject matter, and appearance of the statue, the circumstances of its arrival in Rome, and the "history" of the statue in its new location.

A passage from the *Verrines* (II.1.58–59) well illustrates the difference between the response of the Romans, who saw these works abstracted from the surroundings that had given them meaning, and the response of those from whom the statues had been taken. Cicero speaks of the display in the Forum and Comitium of a number of statues plundered by Verres from the Greek communities in the East. While the orator leaves us to imagine the Romans taking in the scene, mentioning only the enthusiasm of the upper classes for possessing such works, he describes in vivid detail the reaction of the ambassadors from Asia and Achaea who happened to be in the city serving on deputations. The orator relates how these men stood in the Forum, tearfully venerating the images of the gods stolen from their temples.[34]

Verr. II.1.55 (L. Scipio, L. Paulus); 1.57 (P. Servilius); 1.55; 4.129 (T. Quintius Flamininus); 1.11; 2.3, 86–87; 4.73, 93, 97; 5.124 (Scipio Aemilianus); 1.55; 3.9; 4.4 (L. Mummius); 1.11; 2.4, 50; 4.115, 120–23, 130; 5.84 (M. Marcellus); 4.6 (C. Claudius Pulcher); 4.133 (L. Crassus, Q. Scaevola, C. Claudius Pulcher).

33. Herbert I. Schiller, "Pitchers at an Exhibition," *Nation*, 10 July 1989, 56: "The art object . . . abstracted from its social and historical context . . . becomes merely a product itself—lovely, perhaps, but without meaning or connection."

34. For the weakness or lack of interest exhibited by Roman patrons in protecting their provincial clients, see Brunt, "Patronage and Politics in the 'Verrines,'" esp. 273–78. As Brunt points out, the Sicilians' Roman patrons were

Cicero also would have realized that he could not with impunity display an extravagant admiration for such works of art, since a certain public philistinism was always in vogue in ancient Rome. Just as in other speeches the orator is careful not to show too deep a knowledge of literature or philosophy, in his attack on Verres he continually affects ignorance of Greek art and artists. This seems a bit startling, considering the growing sophistication of the first century B.C. and the fact that Verres was a product of his time whose interest in the collection of Greek art was shared by many of his class, including Cicero himself. The astute Roman politician, however, carefully separated his private pursuits and inclinations from his public persona.[35] Thus Cicero claims in the *Verrines* to have little aesthetic judgment (II.4.94). He calls himself and his audience *idiotae* (II.4.4) and *rudes* (II.2.87) in the field of Greek art and is quick to deny that he places any great value on objects of this sort (II.4.13). In an elaborate little charade, he affects not to know for certain the names of artists such as Praxiteles, Myron, and Polyclitus, who had created the statues stolen from a certain Gaius Heius of Messana (II.4.4–5). It is also interesting to note that in several passages describing the pain caused to the Sicilians by Verres' depredations Cicero feels he must carefully explain to his audience the religious reverence felt by the Greeks for the works of art inherited from their ancestors (II.4.132); and he mentions that even statues of their enemies were held in honor and protected by religious scruples (II.2.158–59). Further, Cicero remarks in the most condescending of tones that the Greeks unfortunately took an excessive delight in statues, paintings, and works of this sort (II.4.124, 132–34), objects that, he claims, he

---

unable to prevent the prorogation of Verres' governorship, despite evidence of abuses.

35. Cicero's "real" attitude towards art is an extremely complex matter in which *ars gratia artis* played a relatively small role. See *Fam.* 7.23.2; *Att.* 1.1.5, 1.3.2, 1.4.3, 1.6.2, 1.8.2, 1.9.2, 1.10.3, 1.11.3. Scholars continue to debate the question: Showerman, "Cicero's Appreciation of Greek Art"; Desmouliez, "Sur l'interpretation du 'De Signis'"; Michel, *Rhétorique,* 298–327; Pollitt, *Art of Rome,* 76–79. Recently a number of scholars have begun to explore the importance of the art collection in the creation of an image of the collector. The persona thus created could be called neither strictly public nor strictly private but would share in both realms. See, for instance, Wocjik, *La Villa dei Papiri;* the review of Wocjik by Leach; and Leen, "Cicero and the Rhetoric of Art," on the "rhetorical" considerations underlying the choice of sculpture for Cicero's Tusculan villa.

and his audience viewed as trifles. It was in recognition of this fact, Cicero goes on, that the *maiores* had adopted the practice of allowing conquered peoples to retain many of the works in which they took such delight—this as a kind of solace for the loss of their independence (II.4.124, 134).

Against this background of arrogance, abuse, indifference, and hypocrisy, the rhetorical problem confronting Cicero in discussing Verres' theft of the statues and other precious objects was not primarily a legal one. There was no difficulty in proving that Verres was guilty of the crimes with which he was charged; this had, after all, been accomplished in the first part of the trial. Rather the problem was to make Verres' guilt matter. Cicero needed to invest these objects, which were not even visible to the audience and had originally been the property of subject states, with a meaning that could make their loss a matter of deep concern to a Roman audience. The orator himself articulates this challenge in a passage of the *Divinatio in Caecilium*. In questioning Caecilius's ability to take on the prosecution of so complex a case, he asks: "Do you believe that you are able to accomplish the thing that is most critical when dealing with a defendant of this sort, that is, to make the libidinous, criminal, and cruel things he has done seem as painful and unjust to these men who merely hear of them as they seemed to those who experienced them?" (38).

THE RHETORICAL SOLUTION

The raw material of the fourth speech of the Second Action was the extraordinarily long and potentially tedious inventory of stolen and extorted objects revealed by the witnesses and documents introduced in the First Action. For the speech to be successful Cicero had to transform this catalogue into a logically compelling and emotionally gripping narrative with both a comprehensible overall form and a cohesiveness among its parts. He accomplishes these aims in a variety of ways, one of which is to knit the work together structurally through a geographical progression, in which he surveys the crimes committed by Verres on the island in a variety of cities, beginning with Messana and culminating in an account of events in Syracuse. Further, he links the individual accounts thematically through the development of a number of repeated ideas and images—most prominently, the comparison of the tyrannical Verres with other, noble Romans who had exercised power in Sicily. In order to invest the references to each individual crime with interest for his audience, Cicero relies on the same method as that exploited in poetic catalogues from Homer to Vergil: the expansion of factual material through incorporation of suggestive detail. In many cases this consists only of a few words or phrases concerning the object stolen or the individual or community from which it was taken; but at certain points within the list Cicero extends the account of an object or objects into a longer discussion with a beginning, middle, and end. Within these discussions, the rhetorical technique he constantly exploits is that of *evidentia* or vivid description, whereby what is narrated not only enters the minds of the audience but seems to be present "in the eyes and vision of all" (*Div. Caec.* 27: *in oculis conspectuque omnium*).

In the fourth *Verrine* four of these extended narratives are of special interest, as they illustrate important aspects of the persuasive strategy pursued in the work as a whole. Each of these narratives focuses on a particular object or group of objects. These are the statues appropriated from Gaius Heius of Messana (II.4.3–28); the candelabrum that Verres tricked Antiochus, crown prince of Syria, into surrendering (II.4.60–71); the statue of Diana extorted from Segesta (II.4.72–83); and the statue of Ceres taken from Henna (II.4.105–15). It is the form of these episodes and the meaning assigned by Cicero to the works of art described within them that I wish to discuss.[36]

THE STATUES OF HEIUS OF MESSANA

Cicero begins this account with a sentence typical of the opening of the narrative section of a speech: "Gaius Heius is a Mamertine, and as all who have experience of Messana willingly admit, he is the most honored man in all respects in that state" (II.4.3: *C. Heius est Mamertinus—omnes hoc mihi qui Messanam accesserunt facile concedunt—omnibus rebus illa in civitate ornatissimus*).[37] He then, however, shifts to an unusual tack, focusing on a description of place. He states that

36. Fuhrmann, "Tecniche narrative," discusses these and other episodes in the *Verrines,* analyzing the role Cicero, as narrator, assumes. He divides the narratives analyzed into three groups: (1) those in which Verres commits an assault that meets with no resistance, (2) those in which Verres' assault is futilely resisted, and (3) those in which Verres makes an attempt but is successfully repulsed.

37. Cf. *Rosc. Am.* 15: *Sex. Roscius, pater huiusce, municeps Amerinus fuit, cum genere et nobilitate et pecunia non modo sui municipi verum etiam eius vicinitatis facile primus; Caecin.* 10: *M. Fulcinius fuit, recuperatores, e munici-*

Heius possessed the finest and best-known house in Messana. Before Verres' advent the house had constituted one of the chief beauties of the town, but now that the house had been stripped bare, the town could take pride only in its situation, walls, and harbor. In this way the orator orients his audience to the setting of what has occurred: the town of Messana, which is the first place the traveler encounters in crossing from the Italian mainland into Sicily, will be the beginning of Cicero's verbal journey throughout the island, cataloguing the crimes committed by the defendant.

Once he has oriented his audience to the town as a whole and the importance within it of Heius and his house, he then reveals that there is a room within the house especially visited and admired, the family shrine. This shrine he describes as an "extremely ancient place" (*sacrarium ... perantiquum*), handed down from Heius's ancestors. The audience then learns the source of its renown: within the *sacrarium* stood four statues of exceptional beauty—a marble Cupid, an impressive bronze Hercules placed opposite the Cupid (both of which stood behind small altars), and two charming bronze statues of maidens carrying baskets on their heads. Cicero also names the sculptors of the works (albeit with a show of difficulty), giving special attention to the Cupid of Praxiteles. A similar sculpture by the same artist, he states, was the property of the town of Thespiae in Boeotia; when Mummius captured this town he took away all the "profane" statues (II.4.4: *profana ... signa*) but left the Cupid untouched because it had been consecrated. Cicero also notes approvingly that the very statue belonging to Heius had earlier been borrowed and subsequently returned by Gaius Claudius Pulcher at the time of his celebrated aedileship.

In this opening section of the account of Verres' crime (II.4.3–7), Cicero has made use of a familiar narrative technique: "There is a town and within the town is a house and within the house is a room . . ." and so on. Not only does this serve to acquaint the audience with the general setting of the events that will be described, but by suspending mention of the statues it invests them with greater mystery and importance. It should be noted as well that when Cicero does go on actually to describe the statues, he is careful to incorporate in the description both the reason for their renown among outsiders and their value to Heius. Even

---

pio Tarquiniensi; qui et domi suae cum primis honestus existimatus est et Romae argentariam non ignobilem fecit.

idiotae—Verres' term for ordinary Romans like Cicero and his audience (II.4.4–5)—were able to take pleasure in viewing such strikingly beautiful works; for Heius, however, they were not only magnificent statues but sacred objects handed down from his ancestors and worshipped as reverently by himself and his family as the town of Thespiae worshipped the consecrated statues Mummius had piously refused to plunder.

In the second part of the narrative (II.4.8–14) Cicero goes on to confront the contention of the defense that Verres had bought rather than extorted the works from Heius. The charge is rebutted both by evidence (in which Cicero cites the law forbidding such purchases and the accounts stating that Verres had supposedly purchased the statues for an absurdly low sum) and by the argument from probability (depending on Cicero's contention that it was not credible that Heius would give up the statues at all, much less for such a price). In this section Cicero, who claims to place little value on the statues himself, impresses upon the audience both their high value on the open market and their special meaning for Heius.

In the third and longest part of the narrative (II.4.15–28) Cicero explains why the town of Messana had decreed an official eulogy of Verres and why that eulogy had been delivered at the trial by none other than Gaius Heius himself.[38] His rebuttal of the eulogy is achieved through a twofold strategy. First, he attacks the city itself. We learn that during Verres' governorship Messana had become the center of his criminal activities and had been rewarded for its assistance by exemption from the burdens it normally owed the Roman state. The official eulogy, according to Cicero, was part of a criminal quid pro quo by which Verres and the town profited while many Sicilians and the interests of the Roman state as a whole suffered. This discussion of the town also allows Cicero to remind his audience of two other grave charges expanded on in other parts of the Second Action: namely, that Verres had been derelict in the continuing war against the pirates and that he had illegally executed innocent people, including a Roman citizen who was crucified at Messana.

38. The matter of official eulogies was clearly an important one, for Cicero confronts the issue at two critical points, the beginning and the end of the oration: he attempts at the outset (II.4.19–25) to vitiate the praise of Verres decreed by Messana, while at the end of the work he includes a lengthy explanation of the motivation and attitude of the inhabitants of Syracuse, supposedly the only other city that had voted a eulogy (II.4.137–44).

Cicero also attempts to discredit the eulogy decreed by Messana through a discussion of the circumstances under which Heius came to deliver it. In the course of this explanation he depicts Heius as a man of high character who, by delivering the eulogy, had carried out the official duties required of him as the chief citizen of Messana, but had refused to falsify the account of his personal dealings with Verres (II.4.16). Throughout, Cicero primarily uses references to Heius's feelings about the statues to reveal Heius's character to his audience. The objects taken by Verres are seen by Heius as "holy things" (II.4.17: *sacra*) handed down from his forebears and as "the household gods of his ancestors" (II.4.17: *deos penatis . . . patrios*). He humbly acquiesces in the loss of what are merely precious works of art, but—referring to the marble Cupid and the bronze Hercules—he demands that the "images of the gods" (II.4.18: *deorum simulacra*) be returned. In this way Cicero establishes Heius's spiritual communion with the Roman senators who sat on the jury and who would have understood implicitly the familial piety that motivated Heius. The orator also draws in clear outlines the ethical opposition between Verres, a man with no shame, no sense of piety, and no fear (II.4.18: *pudor/religio/metus*), who has not hesitated to rob from his host's *sacrarium* the images of the gods, and Heius, whose sense of *religio* has led him both to fulfill the odious duties required of him in praising Verres (II.4.16: *de religione sua ac dignitate*) and to demand the restitution of the paternal gods he piously worships (II.4.18: *quia religioni suae . . . in dis patriis repetendis . . . proximus fuit*).

In this narrative, the description of Heius's stolen statues has provided the focus for the passage as a whole. The statues—and that of Cupid in particular—constitute the visual images that will ultimately symbolize the ideas, arguments, and themes of the entire narrative. The audience is first prepared to anticipate eagerly the reference to the statues and then to visualize them through Cicero's description. They are then led by the orator to attach to that visualization a stream of ideas associated with the story of the theft of the statues—ideas concerning Verres' greed, Heius's nobility and piety, and the criminal complicity of the town of Messana.

THE CANDELABRUM OF ANTIOCHUS OF SYRIA

In this narrative Cicero recounts how Verres tricked the prince of Syria into surrendering to him a variety of precious objects, including a magnificent candelabrum that was to be dedicated to Jupiter Optimus Maximus as soon as his Capitoline temple in Rome, burned in the fire of 83 B.C., was completed. The story of the uneven battle of wits between the crafty Verres and the naive, if not fatuous, young prince depends for its initial effect on Cicero's statement of the singular importance of the event in the catalogue of Verres' crimes (II.4.60) and on his detailed account of the accoutrements at the dinners given by Verres for the prince and by the prince for Verres. In recounting the latter occasion the orator refers to the quantity of silver plate and the jewel-encrusted gold cups set on the table. He mentions in particular a wine ladle, sculpted out of a single huge gem, with a handle of gold (II.4.62), and he goes on to describe the reaction of Verres, who, like a greedy child, had picked up and fondled each object.

The predictable outcome of the inflaming of Verres' greed for the works is then interrupted as Cicero begins anew, introducing the following section of the narrative with the statement that the story of what then occurred was known throughout the world (II.4.64). The previous description of precious objects now appears as but a prelude to the mention of the real treasure possessed by Antiochus. This is the great lamp stand intended as a gift from the Syrian throne to the restored Temple of Jupiter Optimus Maximus, an object "of marvelous workmanship" and "fashioned from the most precious stones" (II.4.64). Verres, having heard that Antiochus had the candelabrum in his possession, begs the prince to allow him merely to view it. As in the case of the statues of Heius, Cicero emphasizes the mystery, beauty, and importance of the object in his narrative. The lamp stand is not meant to be viewed before its dedication and is therefore sent to Verres carefully shrouded (II.4.65: *involutum quam occultissime*). The scene when the object arrives is then vividly played out for the audience: the removal of the wrappings, the shout of astonished delight from Verres, the exquisite beauty and stunning size of the work. Verres, of course, will not allow the candelabrum to be returned to the prince, and the next section of the story recounts the dismay of the young man and his public proclamation of the theft. Again, as in the case of Heius, the rightful owner of the work states that the loss of other precious objects had not greatly disturbed him. His outrage stems from the theft of the candelabrum, which he considers as already consecrated to the god by intent; he then publicly declares before all those assembled in the forum that he "gave, donated, offered, and consecrated the work to Jupiter Optimus Maximus" (II.4.67).

In the concluding sections of the account (II.4.67–71) Cicero guides
the response of his audience to the story he has just told. Here the orator
leaves nothing to chance in the interpretation of the meaning of the candelabrum and its theft by Verres. He had introduced the narrative with
the statement that this one action by Verres would not simply demonstrate his greed but would be an act in which all crimes were contained,
since in it the gods were violated, the reputation and authority of the
Roman people were impaired, the duties of hospitality betrayed, and
friendly kings and the nations under their power alienated from Rome
(II.4.60). In the narrative itself Cicero emphasizes the injustice done the
young man, but the final passages expand on the harm done the interests of the Roman state by the theft. The orator argues that the crime
committed against Antiochus, the representative of a rich and powerful
kingdom, will be seen as an outstanding example of the pattern of abuse
now typical of Roman magistrates in their treatment of subject and allied states. The incident will not only result in the besmirching of the
name of the Roman people but will soon cause independent states to
alter their intention of sending generous gifts to adorn the Capitolium
(II.4.68). He then calls on Quintus Catulus, the restorer of the Temple
of Jupiter Optimus Maximus and one of the judges at Verres' trial, to
take thought for the temple that will consecrate the memory of his name
forever (II.4.69–70). The final passage of the account focuses exclusively on the impiety of Verres' action. Cicero argues that in taking the
candelabrum Verres has stolen not from Antiochus but from Jupiter
himself. Could anything, Cicero asks, be sacred or holy to a man who
would commit such a crime (II.4.71)? The orator then fits the incident
into a larger pattern of sacrilege by stating that it was the gods themselves who were claiming restitution at the trial—not only Roman Jupiter, but all those other divinities of Asia and Greece whose sanctuaries
Verres had plundered (II.4.71).

The rhetorical exploitation of the symbolism of the lamp stand
hardly needs fuller explanation, as its meaning has been explicitly developed and stated by Cicero.[39] The theft of the object by Verres plays an
important part both in *In Verrem* II.4 and in Cicero's overall develop-

39. This is true in the case of many of the objects referred to in the speech
(cf. II.4.93, in which the symbolic meanings attributed to a statue of Apollo are
somewhat clumsily catalogued). One may compare the technique used in this
early oration with the more subtle treatment of the statue of Jupiter in the third
Catilinarian.

ment of the image of the defendant as a tyrant whose behavior is typical of all tyrants. Not only has Cicero used this and other narratives to illustrate that Verres possessed the stereotypical traits of the tyrant— greed, lust, cruelty, and impiety; he has also attempted in this story to suggest that Verres' career fit into a pattern typical of the tyrannical personality. In the stereotypical narrative of this kind the tyrant is a man of large capacities who becomes corrupted through the exercise of power.[40] The turning point in his career is usually an act of great criminality, after which point he is depicted as a bestial figure, hated by all and devoid of redeeming characteristics. At the end of the Antiochus narrative, which occurs in almost the exact center of the speech as a whole, Cicero states that "once [Verres] had conceived this horrible crime, thereafter he considered nothing in all of Sicily to be either holy or sacred; for three years he therefore conducted himself in that province as if he believed that he had declared war not only on men but even on the gods" (II.4.72).[41] It is at this point, then, that Cicero wished his audience to mark the degeneration of Verres into the archetypal tyrant, a man like the cruel despots who had ruled in Sicily before the Romans, a *contemptor deorum hominumque*.[42]

DIANA OF SEGESTA

Immediately after the statement quoted above, Cicero recounts the story of the theft of the statue of Diana from the town of Segesta (II.4.72–83). "Segesta," says Cicero, "is an extremely ancient foundation in Sicily . . . which they say was founded by Aeneas after he fled from Troy

40. For the stereotype of the tyrant, see Dunkle, "The Rhetorical Tyrant," and "The Greek Tyrant"; and Vasaly, "Personality and Power," 215–21. Cf. *Her.* 2.49; Cic. *Inv.* 1.102. Plutarch (*Sull.* 30.5) questions whether the evil traits exhibited by the tyrant are a manifestation of his inborn character or whether they express a character that has been corrupted by power.

41. Cf. *Verr.* II.1.6: *Multa enim et in deos et in homines impie nefarieque commisit;* 5.188: *ceteros item deos deasque omnis . . . quorum templis et religionibus iste . . . bellum sacrilegum semper impiumque habuit indictum.*

42. The phrase is Augustan. See Livy 3.57.2; Verg. *Aen.* 7.648: *contemptor divum* (describing Mezentius). For Sicilian tyrants, see Grimal, "Cicéron et les tyrans de Sicile." For comparison of Verres with rulers such as Phalaris or Dionysius, see *Verr.* II.4.73, 123: *taetrior hic tyrannus Syracusanis . . . quam quisquam superiorum;* 5.145: *Versabatur in Sicilia . . . non Dionysius ille nec Phalaris, tulit enim illa quondam insula multos et crudeles tyrannos, sed quoddam novum monstrum.*

and arrived in these parts" (II.4.72). This beginning thus emphasizes the legendary connection of the town with Rome. The importance of this connection to the theft of the statue becomes clearer as the story unfolds. The orator relates how the statue had been removed from the town when it was plundered by the Carthaginians. Such was the beauty and sanctity of the work, however, that even this enemy people devoutly worshipped it (II.4.72). Many years later, when Carthage fell to Scipio Aemilianus, the great general set about returning many of the works plundered over the centuries by the Carthaginians, including the Diana of Segesta, which was then reerected with an inscription honoring Scipio. When Verres, called now by Cicero "the enemy of all that is holy and sacred" (II.4.75), sees the statue he is driven almost mad with desire to possess it. After recounting the intimidation that finally compels the Segestans to give up the statue, Cicero describes the chaotic scene of Diana's removal. The women and girls of the town rush to accompany the goddess out of their land, anointing her with unguents, covering her with flowers, and burning spices and incense throughout the journey.

In this narrative Cicero leads his audience to see the meaning of the statue not only in religious terms; it is also a monument to Scipio's victory and a symbol of Roman rule. In refusing at first to part with the statue, the Segestans appeal to its *summa religio* (II.4.75) and to the fact that the statue was "the property of the Roman people," since Scipio had placed it there as a "memorial of the victory of the Roman people" (II.4.75). Again, after Verres had taken the statue, Cicero claims that the anger of the Segestans was roused not only because of the sacrilege committed (II.4.78: *religiones . . . violatas*) but also because Verres had destroyed "the glory of the great deeds, the memory of the bravery, and the token of the victory of Publius Africanus, the most gallant of men" (II.4.78).

What follows next is an appeal by Cicero to Publius Scipio Nasica to defend the reputation of his famous ancestor, since, as the orator remarks, "it is a custom handed down from our ancestors for each to defend the memorials of his forebears" (II.4.79). This digression, if such it can be called, is of crucial importance not only to the analysis of the meaning assigned the statue of Diana but to the understanding of Cicero's strategy in the *Verrines* in general. Throughout the corpus Cicero rarely depends entirely on an appeal based on abstract justice or on the audience's disinterested sympathy for the Sicilians; rather, considerations of justice are interwoven with appeals to self-interest. On many occasions he attempts to demonstrate that corrupt administration such as that exercised by Verres was detrimental to the aims of the governing class. In the short run, it had blackened the reputation of the upper classes and had endangered the senatorial monopoly on the jury system; in the long run it could result in the loss of *imperium* itself.[43] Even in the case of the removal of the statue of Diana from Segesta one can see a form of the argument from self-interest, since—as has been noted— Cicero has been careful to present the statue not only as a religious object but as a symbol of Roman power and hegemony.[44]

In the address to Scipio Nasica, however, the statue comes to stand not for Roman power alone but for an ideal in the exercise of that power. Here Cicero first appeals to Nasica—a supporter of Verres— asking him who there will be to guard the "monuments and tokens of Scipio's gallantry" (II.4.80: *monumenta atque indicia virtutis*) if not his descendants. The orator goes on to answer his own question, for he declares that Scipio's reputation is not truly the property of one family, or even of the Roman aristocracy, but of all Romans, and especially "new men" like himself, who were united to Scipio not by birth but by sharing with him the virtues that had made Rome great. Among these virtues Cicero mentions justice, diligence, self-control, the protection of the wretched, and the hatred of the wicked (II.4.81: *aequitate, industria, temperantia, defensione miserorum, odio improborum*). This "kinship" of virtue (II.4.81: *cognatio studiorum et artium*), claims Cicero, is as strong as any relationship of blood or marriage.

The *Verrines* thus create two opposed images of imperial government. On the one hand, Cicero gives ample evidence of the naked exploitation exemplified by Verres' public career, the ineluctable rights of the conqueror over the conquered, the power that "makes all things profane" (II.4.122), to use the orator's phrase. On the other hand, Cicero sets up an ideal no different from that which Vergil would later articulate in the sixth book of the *Aeneid* (851–53: *tu regere imperio populos, Romane, memento/ hae tibi erunt artes, pacisque imponere morem,/ parcere subjectis et debellare superbos*). Using the image—but surely not the reality—of past heroes of the Republic as exempla, Cicero points to the supposed religious scrupulosity of a Mummius, the restraint, generosity, and *humanitas* of a Marcellus, and the generosity

43. See below, pp. 211–12.
44. Thus the Roman governor could not allow the statues of Verres to be overturned, as it was an affront not simply to an individual but to Roman power (II.2.158–60).

of a Scipio Aemilianus as a justification for Roman rule.[45] Even this appeal is not purely altruistic, for just as Scipio Nasica Corculum (the great-great-grandfather of Scipio Nasica, to whom Cicero addresses this appeal) had once argued for the preservation of Carthage not out of consideration for Carthage itself but from his desire to preserve the best in the Roman character, so Cicero's argument for just treatment of the provinces and allies is, in part, an effort to halt Roman corruption for Rome's own sake.[46] Nevertheless, Cicero's vision is clearly one in which the interests of both ruler and ruled are served. The statue of Diana that Scipio had returned to Segesta becomes, in Cicero's account, a monument to this ideal of mutual advantage, in which the subject peoples are allowed to become "as prosperous and as splendid as possible" (II.4.134: *ut imperio nostro quam ornatissimi florentissimique essent*).

CERES OF HENNA

The fourth extended narrative in the speech (II.4.105–15) has often been the subject of stylistic analysis.[47] It is couched in terms so poetic

45. L. Mummius: II.1.55; 3.9; 4.4; M. Marcellus: II.1.11; 2.4, 50; 4.115, 120–23, 130; 5.84; Scipio Aemilianus: II.1.11; 2.3, 86–87; 4.73, 93, 97; 5.124. Aemilianus asks the Sicilians to consider the fact that they had prospered under the *mansuetudo* of Roman rule, having suffered under earlier Sicilian tyrants like Phalaris (II.4.73: *monumentum et domesticae crudelitatis et nostrae mansuetudinis*). If, however, Roman rulers like Verres merely recreated the cruelty of the tyrant's rule, what loyalty could be demanded from this naturally loyal people (II.5.115: *illam clementiam mansuetudinemque nostri imperii in tantam crudelitatem inhumanitatemque esse conversam*)?

46. P. Cornelius Sc. Nasica Corculum (cos. 162, 155 B.C.), opposing the blind hostility of Cato towards Carthage, ended each speech with a statement that Carthage ought to be preserved. See App. *Lib.* 69; Plut. *Cat. Mai.* 27.1–2; Scullard, *Roman Politics*, 242–43; RE4¹(1900):1497–1501 ("Cornelius" no. 353). Corculum is praised several times by Cicero (*Brut.* 79, 212; *Tusc.* 1.18). Cicero's addressee was consul in 52 B.C. See RE3¹(1897):1224–28 ("Caecilius" no. 99). There is perhaps some irony in Cicero's lecture to Nasica concerning the real significance of the tokens of Scipio Aemilianus. Scipio Nasica later set up statues of his famous ancestors in many places in the city, including the Capitolium. Cicero complains to Atticus (*Att.* 6.1.17) that the statue of Nasica's great-grandfather had the caption "censor"—an office the man never held. Further, the statue of P. Cornelius Scipio Serapio bore the features of Scipio Aemilianus, an embarrassing blunder that Cicero attributes to Nasica's shocking ignorance.

47. Recently, see Romano, "Cicerone e il ratto di Proserpina"; Römisch, "Cicero," 43–47, and "Ovid," 173–74; Hinds, "An Allusion in the Literary

that Cicero twice apologizes for including material of this sort. "Forgive me," he says at the outset, "if I seem to delve into and trace somewhat too deeply this account of religious significance" (II.4.105: *memoriam religionis*). He begins his story not with a theft or extortion perpetrated by Verres but with the statement that the entire island of Sicily was believed to be sacred to the goddess Ceres.[48] Cicero then relates how Proserpina was thought to have been carried off from a wood near Henna by Dis, the god of the underworld, whereupon the distraught Ceres lit her torches from fiery Aetna as she set out in quest of her daughter. Topography and mythology become one in Cicero's description of Henna. The town, rising on a lofty plateau in the very center of Sicily, is believed to be the sacred birthplace and dwelling of the goddess. Like Delphi in Greece, the region is called the *umbilicus* of the island and is isolated from the surrounding countryside by lakes, woodlands, and precipitous cliffs. It is seen by Cicero as a kind of *locus amoenus,* watered by "eternal springs" and surrounded by flowers that bloom in all seasons with never-ending fecundity. Here the god of the underworld had suddenly appeared from "a bottomless cave" and had snatched the maiden Proserpina, plunging with her beneath the earth at a spot near Syracuse where a lake had subsequently appeared. The place itself, says Cicero, seemed to confirm the myths about it, as it was marked by the very signs (*vestigia*) of the gods.[49] He ends this section of the narrative with several proofs of the universal reverence with which the shrine of Ceres of Henna had always been regarded, citing the fact that the Romans, when long ago instructed by the Sibylline Books to worship "the most ancient Ceres," had sent ambassadors to this place (II.4.108).

In the second part of the narrative Cicero describes how Verres had removed from her shrine at Henna the oldest and most sacred cult image of Ceres—a bronze statue of moderate size and outstanding workmanship, depicting the goddess with the torches that lit her way as she

---

Tradition." The passage is also mentioned by Seneca the Elder (*Suas.* 2.19) and frequently by Quintilian (4.2.19, 3.13; 9.4.127; 11.3.164).

48. Part of Cicero's strategy consisted in undermining the connections between Verres and the powerful cult in northwestern Sicily of Venus Erycina— which Verres had apparently fostered—by emphasizing the symbolism of the cult of Ceres of Henna. On Verres' exploitation of the cult of Venus, see von Albrecht, "Cicero und die Götter Siziliens"; della Corte, "Conflitto di culti"; Martorana, "La Venus di Verre."

49. II.4.107.

searched for her daughter (II.4.109). Unable to take away as well two
very large statues of Ceres and Triptolemus that stood in front of the
shrine, Verres had also carried off an extraordinarily beautiful (II.4.110:
pulcherrime factum) statue of Victory that had stood in the right hand
of the goddess. Following his account of this theft, Cicero describes the
reaction of the Sicilians to this shocking act. As in previous narratives,
the orator denies that consideration of monetary loss was the principal
complaint of those whose goods had been plundered. He claims that the
Sicilians would have endured in silence all other outrages against them;
the theft of the Ceres of Henna, however, was a sacrilege that could not
be borne, for the city was deemed by its inhabitants to be the "shrine"
of Ceres; the citizens, her priests (II.4.111). Cicero describes the terror
felt by the Sicilians at the desecration of their most sacred temple and
tells of the emptiness of the countryside, which had been abandoned by
the farmers. The whole land, he claims, had become deserted, uncultivated, and neglected after this outrage (II.4.114).

Cicero's treatment of this narrative, as he twice confesses, has de-
parted markedly from "the everyday way of speaking" and "the custom
of the law courts" (II.4.109). Why does the orator give this story such
prominence, distinguishing it both in style and in content from others?
The answer to this question turns, in part, on the connection of this
section of the speech with Cicero's attempt throughout the *Verrines* to
characterize the defendant as a tyrant. The orator's manipulation of this
stereotype is especially apt here, since the Sicilian tyrants were famous
in antiquity for their cruelty—a fact that Cicero pointedly alludes to at
the conclusion of the speech (II.5.143–45). One element of this commonplace characterization has already been noted in the story of Antiochus—that is, the notion that a turning point exists in the career of the
tyrant after which his character sinks rapidly into ruin—and other elements drawn from the stereotype recur throughout Cicero's indictment
of Verres: he is cruel, governed by whims rather than reason, greedy for
wealth as well as for power.

There is, moreover, one aspect of the stereotype of the tyrant of ancient drama, rhetoric, and historiography that functions as a kind of
emblem for the depravity of his character: his sexual *libido,* the objects
of which are usually women and children, the most vulnerable members
of society.[50] The theme of Verres' sexual depravity, therefore, is a crucial

50. Cf. Livy's account of the rousing of the tyrannical Appius Claudius's
desire for Verginia (3.44.2). For sexual libido as an analogue for the obsessive

element in the *Verrines,* and a particularly memorable treatment of this theme occurs in the first part of the Second Action, where Cicero relates the story of the defendant's attempt upon a young virgin in Lampsacus (II.1.63–85). Accounts of actual outrages perpetrated against women are not prominent in the fourth part of the Second Action, however, and Cicero alludes only briefly in his litany of Verres' crimes in Syracuse to "the violation of married women" (II.4.116).

The theme is exploited in *In Verrem* II.4 not through reference to the *actual* rape of women but through reference to Verres' assaults upon the *images* of women and female divinities. In the narrative concerning Heius of Messana, for example, two of the four statues taken by Verres are described by Cicero as "not large but of extraordinary charm, with the appearance and clothing of virgins" (II.4.5: *virginali habitu atque vestitu*). These, like the marble Cupid, will end up in "the house of a panderer and amidst the customs of a prostitute" (II.4.7). The robed statue of Diana of Segesta is said to be "quite large and tall, but nevertheless, for all its magnitude, its age and appearance were that of a virgin" (II.4.74: *aetas atque habitus virginalis*), and it is noted that no Segestan, whether free or slave, was willing "to lay hands upon it" (II.4.77: *attingere*), so that foreigners had to be found to take the statue from the town.[51] And in Syracuse, Verres is accused of plundering the beautiful paintings and exquisite doors from the Temple of Minerva, thereby "transferring the embellishments of the virgin Minerva to the house of a prostitute" (II.4.123: *ornamenta Minervae virginis in meretriciam domum*). Cicero could hardly have illustrated and summarized this aspect of the defendant's character more memorably than by de-

---

desire for power, see Vasaly, "Personality and Power," 219–20. Here the rhetorical manipulation of the stereotype of the tyrant overlaps with another commonplace evident throughout the *Verrines:* the "captured city" topos. Verres' progress throughout the eastern Mediterranean and Sicily has been like that of a marauding enemy. In fact, Cicero declares that Syracuse had not been dealt with as ruthlessly when it had actually fallen to Marcellus in the Second Punic War as it has been treated under Verres (II.4.115). In this topos one of the greatest fears exploited is that concerning the sexual threat posed by the enemy to women and children. Cf. above, p. 77 n. 78 ("captured city" topos) and pp. 117 nn. 40, 42, 120 n. 45 (stereotype of tyrant). Cf. *Her.* 2.49, in which the author states that the seventh commonplace for arousing an audience's emotions comes from showing that an act is "a horrible crime, cruel, impious, and tyrannical, such as the assaulting of women."

51. Cf. Ter. *Hec.* 135–36; Catull. 67.20: *non illam vir prior attigerat.*

scribing Verres' violent seizure of the image of the goddess most sacred to all Sicily—an account introduced by the story of Pluto's violent abduction of Proserpina from the very place where Verres had perpetrated his crime.

Quintilian (4.3.12–13) terms the passage in this speech dealing with the praise of Sicily and the rape of Proserpina a "digression" (*egressus/ egressio*). The use of this term is surely accurate if it signifies that the passage in question does nothing to advance the logical argument of the case or to prove objective truth or falsity; it is inaccurate, however, if the term "digression" is used to imply that this passage is not crucial to the strategy of persuasion within the speech. Not only does the narrative dealing with the statue of Ceres fit into the pattern Cicero has created of Verres' assaults upon innocent young girls and women; symbolically it goes farther. In it Cicero had declared that to the Sicilians Verres had become a second Orcus (II.4.111: *alter Orcus*) who had stolen away not Proserpina but Ceres herself from their midst. Just as the legend tells how the mourning of the goddess of grain for her absent daughter brought the devastation of crops, so Cicero declares that Verres' theft of the Ceres statue had resulted in general desolation and the abandonment of the rich Sicilian fields. It seems clear that in this elaborate and poetic account the orator not only intended to impress upon the minds of his audience a further instance of Verres' outrages against the innocent; at the same time—and intimately connected with the images created by the narrative—he wished them to read in the story an allegory for Verres' rape of Sicily itself.

NARRATIVE FORM AND RHETORICAL INTENT

The extraordinary length of the Second Action of the *Verrines* made it impossible for Cicero to structure the speech in the ordinary way, that is, by dividing the whole into proem, narration, argument, and peroration.[52] He therefore divided the speech as a whole into five parts that

52. It is generally assumed that the length (as well as the elaborate style) of the Second Action betrays the fact that it was a speech written for publication rather than for delivery. (See, for instance, Fuhrmann, "Tecniche narrative," 41–42.) I believe, however, that the Second Action accurately represents the kind of speech that might actually have been made in a complex trial when a single orator presented the case for the prosecution.

focused on the periods in Verres' public career and the places where he had held power (II.1: magisterial offices exercised in Gaul, Asia, and Greece prior to his praetorship, his tenure as urban praetor in Rome) and on the general categories of crime perpetrated by the defendant as governor of Sicily (II.2: abuses of judicial power; II.3: crimes committed in the purchase and taxation of grain; II.4: plundering of precious objects throughout Sicily; II.5: dereliction of duty as military commander, cruel and tyrannical behavior exhibited towards Sicilians and Roman citizens in the province). Even the five individual parts of the Second Action each contained such an extensive body of material that no listener (or reader) could have been expected to assimilate it if it had been presented according to the rhetorical rules governing *dispositio,* for the bewildering amount of data that Cicero would have been obliged to cover in the narration of each would surely have been forgotten or confused by the time he returned to it in the argument and peroration. Thus in the fourth part of the Second Action Cicero organizes his account of Verres' theft of precious objects through reference to a sequence of places within Sicily, as well as to the types of objects stolen, giving shape and form to this catalogue by turning many of the crimes discussed into miniature dramas with a beginning, middle, and end.[53]

In three of the four narratives studied above, Cicero begins by setting the story within a particular topographical or geographical framework, which itself plays a role in manipulating the feelings of the audience about the account that follows. In the case of Segesta, Cicero refers to its legendary founding by Aeneas, stating that the connection between the Segestans and the Romans was not only one of "continual friendship and alliance" but also one of blood relationship (II.4.72: *perpetua societate atque amicitia, verum etiam cognatione*). The topographical and geographical introduction to the narrative set in Henna emphasizes the religious centrality and sanctity of the place, a sanctity that, according to Cicero, had long been recognized by Romans as well as Sicilians. In dealing with the theft of the statues belonging to Heius of Messana, Cicero is prevented from beginning the narrative by celebrating the religious or political connections of the town with Rome, since the Messanans had seen fit to decree a eulogy of Verres. Cicero's introduction

53. Cicero alludes to the difficulty of a complete enumeration of Verres' crimes and to his method of choosing illustrative *indicia* and *exempla* (II.4.49, 57).

serves, however, to inform the audience that Heius's house had long been the chief dwelling within the city and had served as a showplace not only for Messanans and other Sicilians but for Roman visitors as well.

Having oriented his audience to the setting of the action, Cicero goes on in each of the episodes to recount a story in which an object or group of objects is taken by Verres from its rightful owner. In each narrative the object or objects stolen become the "visual" center of the story, for the statues of Heius, the lamp stand of Antiochus, the statue of Diana of Segesta, and that of Ceres of Henna are all described in some detail. By impressing the image of the artwork on the minds of his audience and retailing the events that lead to its loss, Cicero recreates a context for the stolen object or group. While he sometimes speaks of the extreme devotion of the Sicilians to their possessions in condescending, even—to put it more precisely—"patronizing" terms, the vividness and narrative power of the stories must have seduced the audience into seeing the objects through the eyes of those from whom they had been taken.

But this is not all Cicero wished to accomplish within the narratives, for it is through his statements about the feelings and actions of the Sicilians vis-à-vis their stolen possessions that their characters are revealed. For Heius, the statues in his *sacrarium* are made to seem an expression of his piety towards the ancestors from whom he had inherited them, a sentiment with which a Roman audience could strongly empathize. The young prince of Syria reveals his exceptional piety towards the chief god of the Roman state and his loyalty to that state through his intention to dedicate to Capitoline Jupiter the precious lamp stand described in the narrative, and Cicero's description of his reaction to the loss of the object focuses on these same admirable traits. The community of Segesta is shown by Cicero to view the statue of Diana not simply as the focus of their communal devotion to the goddess. The honor in which they hold the statue and their pain at its loss, Cicero claims, also bespeak the citizens' admiration and respect for Scipio Aemilianus, who had returned the statue to them from Carthage and to whom the pedestal on which the statue stood had been inscribed (II.4.82). Both the statue and its pedestal (subsequently removed by Verres) are signs of the relationship that formerly existed between Segesta and Rome, a relationship characterized by generosity on the part of the conquerors and loyalty on the part of the conquered. For the people of Henna and for all Sicilians the statue of Ceres is a sign that the island is a unique place, whose pious inhabitants have been blessed by the goddess with the gift of abundant grain. This piety towards Ceres is presented as part of what the Romans owed their divinities, for Cicero claims that the Ceres of the Sicilians had always been an object of Roman worship. *Religio [non] aliena* (II.4.114) are the words the orator uses in affirming the universal sanctity of Hennan Ceres. In fact, the phrase aptly describes Cicero's strategy throughout, since in each of the accounts he has led his audience to connect the setting, the symbolism of the object or group stolen, and the feelings of the complainants about the object or objects with unambiguously Roman religious and patriotic sentiments.

Although I have termed these narratives "miniature dramas," they do not, in fact, conclude in the way either a drama or a literary narrative usually ends, for there is nothing in the episodes that corresponds to a denouement. Rather, after the introductory and narrative sections of each, Cicero combines a kind of argument and peroration. Such a strategy is predictable, given the fact that the orator, unlike the dramatist, must avoid the sense of closure and recovered equilibrium provided by the dramatic denouement. He strives, instead, to convince his audience at the end of each narrative of the justice of his position, to rouse them to emotional engagement with this position, and to make them eager to hear another example of the accused's misdeeds.

In three of the four episodes discussed in this chapter Cicero has created for his audience a visual image of an artwork or a group of works by placing it within a topographical or geographical framework and then carefully describing it. The image created through this combination of *topographia* (description of place) and *enargeia* or *evidentia* (vivid description) is then tied by the orator to various associations and ideas, for in each case Cicero has attempted to create a binding link in the minds of the audience between the visually imagined object and the meaning he has assigned to it. As noted at the beginning of this chapter, this technique might well have been related to the system of mnemonic training current in Cicero's time, as well as to Cicero's own understanding of the rhetorical possibilities of *evidentia*. In a lengthy and complex work like the fourth *Verrine,* Cicero's strategy of connecting a variety of symbolic meanings with objects that he has carefully described for his audience, placed within a topographical setting, and subordinated to an overall geographical progression might have reflected the process he himself went through in creating for himself a visually imagined structure for the speech. This same structure was then adapted to impress the material and its meaning on the minds of his audience. The objection might be raised that in examples from the ancient mnemonic system the train of thought linking idea and object had no inherent meaning, while the associations used by Cicero in the fourth *Verrine* are never a fortuitous graft of idea on image but are sensitively and imaginatively linked in order to create specific rhetorical effects. The answer to this objection is the presumption that Cicero (or his teachers) must have realized that in order to be of use in persuading an audience the techniques of artificial memory had to be altered so as always to involve the association of a *locus* with an idea that advanced the speaker's case. In the language of the rhetorical textbooks, *In Verrem* II.4 suggests that certain aspects of *memoria* (the mnemonic system) and *elocutio* (vivid description) could be adapted to serve the needs of *inventio* and *dispositio*.

THE SEEN AND THE UNSEEN

In chapter 1 I raised the question of whether the way Cicero exploited visible monuments and topography as a source of persuasion was similar to the way he made use of what was merely described to his audience. Our study has shown that, in both cases, Cicero's constant endeavor was to connect things and places with religious and patriotic themes. As regards the *invention* of arguments, then, there seems to be little difference between the meanings assigned to the visible and those assigned to things described.[54] But what of the comparative effect on an audience of the two techniques of persuasion? Was Livy correct in depicting Manlius's speech at his first trial as making a much stronger impression on his audience than the speech he delivered at his second trial, simply because the first speech was able to draw on what the audience could actually see? The question bears, at least in part, on the relative impact of what is seen and what is heard or read, a topic about which scholars have long debated. On one side stand those who argue the priority of the verbal over the visual, supporting their position by emphasizing the direct access to the imagination secured by words over images. "Words," wrote Joseph Addison, "when well chosen, have so great force in them that a description often gives us more lively ideas

54. This conclusion accords well with the implications of Quintilian's use of examples drawn both from the visible (Ajax before the ships) and from the nonvisible (Clodius's death before the monuments of his ancestors) in his discussion of the exploitation of place as a source of "praise and blame" (5.10.41).

than the sight of things themselves. The reader finds a scene drawn in stronger colours, and painted more to the life in his imagination, by the help of words, than by an actual survey of the scene which they describe."[55] On the other side are those who argue the superiority of visual images over words by emphasizing the undeniable impact of the sensual. As Leonardo da Vinci observed, "What a difference there is between imagining a light while the eye is in darkness and seeing it in actuality!"[56]

The dichotomy posited here between what is seen and what is imagined is, however, a somewhat misleading one. What neither Addison nor Leonardo acknowledges is that seeing itself cannot exist without imagination and that the act of sight, even at its most "mechanical," is an act of interpretation.[57] Further, a study of Cicero's references to the visual environment shows that, in fact, such references frequently depend for their success upon an audience's imaginative reconstruction of an event. Consider, for instance, an extended section of *In Verrem* II.1 in which Cicero refers to the Temple of Castor and Pollux (129–54). His recital of a plot by Verres to defraud a young heir contains a number of vivid descriptions, including the tour of the temple by Verres, in which he and his henchmen attempt to fabricate the need for repairs, and the account of the letting of a contract for a vast sum in order to accomplish the absurd task of taking down and reerecting the columns, which were supposedly out of plumb. The audience, who—if the Second Action had gone forward—would have been able to see the temple during this narrative, was meant to envision the scenes that had taken place during Verres' praetorship. The temple itself would have served as a kind of prop, a starting point for a leap of the imagination—similar, but not identical, to the kind of imaginative leap required of the audience by the description of an event that had occurred in a place not visible to them.

The difference between the two modes of persuasion is not to be found, therefore, in the presence or absence of an imaginative response on the part of an audience. Perhaps the real difference lies in the fact

55. *The Spectator*, no. 416, 27 June 1712.
56. Leonardo da Vinci, "Paragone: Of Poetry and Painting," in *Treatise on Painting*, ed. A. P. McMahon (Princeton, 1956) 1 (Text): 14.
57. Mitchell, *Iconology*, 118: "When we try to postulate a foundation experience of 'pure' vision, a merely mechanical process uncontaminated by imagination, purpose, or desire, we invariably rediscover one of the few maxims on which Gombrich and Nelson Goodman agree: 'The innocent eye is blind.'"

that when Cicero alluded to the meaning of the visual ambiance he did not begin with a "clean slate"—by which I mean that the places and things that Cicero's audience saw before them had already set in motion a variety of imaginative, emotional, and rational responses even before he had begun to speak. The orator could draw on these responses, guide them, and add new meanings to those that had existed previously, but his invention was partly circumscribed by the associations available in the setting in which he and his audience found themselves. The purely verbally constructed environment, on the other hand, placed fewer restrictions on the orator's invention. In it he was able to create a world adapted only to his rhetorical goals. He could not, however, fully reproduce through description the sensual impact of the visual on an audience. In the passage cited above, in which Cicero revealed the wrongdoings committed by Verres that were associated with the Temple of Castor and Pollux, the fact that the audience would have been able to gaze on "the scene of the crime" while listening to the account would have added much to its affective power. Thus what the visual milieu lost in rhetorical control it gained in direct sensual impact; and what the vividly described environment lost in immediacy it gained in the opportunity it gave the orator to introduce only those "visual" elements he wished, and in the precise sequence in which he determined that they would be most persuasive.

CHAPTER FOUR

Ēthos and Locus:
Ancient Perspectives

We have now seen how Cicero exploited specific monuments and topography in order to manipulate the thoughts, emotions, and perceptions of his audience. The examples cited have demonstrated how, both through allusion to what would have been visible to his audience and through description of what could not be seen by them, Cicero attempted to shape his listeners' images of concrete reality so as to allow him to graft to those images associations useful to his overall rhetorical goals. A more general aspect of Cicero's representation of reality remains to be explored: namely, the orator's depiction of certain geographical, ethnic, and cultural milieux. As will become clear in the chapters that follow, Cicero's representation of various places was a means of defining for his audience the character (*ēthos*) of individuals associated with those places.

In looking at the orator's exploitation of these more general representations of reality we should keep in mind that the image of the world that Cicero presented to his audience was, in essence, a verbal construct and that he was free to manipulate this construct in any way that suited him.[1] To be successful he was bound by only two constraints: first, the

---

1. Cf. Cic. *De or.* 1.70: "For the poet is closely related to the orator: the poet is somewhat more constrained in rhythm, although freer in his use of words, and is the companion and almost the equal of the orator in many kinds of ornamentation. In this, however, they are surely identical: they do not circumscribe or limit by any boundaries their right to use their skill and ability to roam

images he created of the world had to further his rhetorical goals; and, second, he needed to make it appear to his audience that these images were an accurate reflection of reality. In this latter requirement, the orator parts company from the poet, the novelist, and the dramatist, for audiences allow the writer of fiction to create a world they know to be unreal, if only this world be compelling and internally coherent. But the world created by an orator must possess both internal and external consistency. Whether or not it is actually true, it must always *appear* to be true in order to be rhetorically successful. Cicero endeavored, therefore, to speak about the world in such a way as to echo ideas about places that he knew his audience already held, whether consciously or unconsciously. The beliefs, prejudices, impressions, and perceptions of his audience—often confused, frequently mutually contradictory—formed the raw material out of which he fashioned his images of reality.[2] Before looking at the way in which Cicero wedded images of place (*locus*) with assumptions about character (*ēthos*) in various speeches, therefore, something should be said about this "raw material"—about the various conceptions about *locus* that would have influenced the content and reception of oratory on this subject in the late Republic. How did the Romans see themselves, their city, and its place in the Mediterranean world? What opinions would Romans of Cicero's day have had about why Greeks or Gauls or Sicilians were the way they were (or, more precisely, the way the Romans believed they were)? What might they have presumed the influence of geography or environment or race was on an individual's character? What was their stereotype of the mountain dweller or the lowland farmer? Did they suppose that good men could be produced in bad places, or bad men in good places? What, finally,

---

wherever they wish" (*Est enim finitimus oratori poeta, numeris astrictior paulo, verborum autem licentia liberior, multis vero ornandi generibus socius ac paene par; in hoc quidem certe prope idem, nullis ut terminis circumscribat aut definiat ius suum, quo minus ei liceat eadem illa facultate et copia vagari qua velit*); Quint. 8.3.70 (on the impression of reality as the key to effective description). See the discussion of the relationship between poetry and rhetoric in Lausberg, *Handbuch*, 1:41–44 (§§34–36). On epideictic and epideictic aspects of forensic and deliberative oratory, see Lausberg, *Handbuch*, 1:129–32 (§§239–42).

2. While it was possible for the orator to introduce into a popular oration ideas not consonant with prevailing opinion, thereby "teaching" (*docere*) in addition to "moving" (*movere*) and "entertaining" (*delectare*) his audience, the task was recognized by Cicero as an extraordinarily difficult one (*Top.* 73).

was the "horizon of expectations" that affected the ancient audience's interpretation of and reaction to Cicero's representation of reality in these speeches?[3]

CULTURAL MYTHOLOGY

Comparative mythology demonstrates that a common feature of the belief system of many primitive cultures is the assumption by each that it constitutes the physical and spiritual center of the world.[4] For each culture, the world outside the home ground is viewed as a series of concentric rings in which one's own habitation occupies the center, while people and places lose reality (or, at least, everyday reality) as one travels outward from the center. Those areas on the outermost fringes become the setting of mythological and legendary events in which the normal rules governing life in the central community are suspended. Reflections of this point of view in ancient Greek mythology abound, including the designation of Delphi as the "navel of the world" and tales of monsters, magical events, and alien deities occupying the distant places to which only heroes ventured.[5]

There is no doubt that the Romans of Cicero's day saw themselves as living in the center of the world. This centrality, however, was not expressed in terms of a traditional mythology, for the Greek-derived myth of Rome's founding put the city on the fringes of the world.[6] Ethnocen-

---

3. For discussion of the "horizon of expectations" see Jauss, "Literary History as a Challenge to Literary Theory," and *Towards an Aesthetic of Reception;* and above, p. 37 n. 38.

4. Tuan, *Topophilia,* esp. 30–44, 59–91; Eliade, *Cosmos and History,* 12–17, and *Images and Symbols,* esp. 37–56; Rykwert, *Idea of a Town,* 163–87.

5. One thinks in this regard of the folktale preserved in the *Odyssey* in which it is foretold that Odysseus will one day embark on a journey carrying an oar over his shoulder. When he arrives at a place where none can identify this object, there he is to plant the oar. The same story can be found in different forms in a variety of cultures, representing the understanding that by long journeying one arrives at places so exotic that the most recognizable objects of everyday life cease to have meaning. See Hansen, "Odysseus' Last Journey."

6. It is somewhat misleading to distinguish mythic from "scientific" geography, since the two were little distinguished in antiquity. While Eratosthenes rejected as fabulous Homer's account of both the places Odysseus visited and the events that occurred in these settings, many other ancient scholars (Strabo, Polybius, Posidonius) believed Homer referred to places in the real world, and disputed about which locations he intended as settings for his adventures

tricity could nevertheless be reinforced in other ways. Italy was, after all, a temperate land that did not suffer from the extremes of temperature found in the frozen north or the sunburnt south. If it was not actually situated in the center of the inhabited world (thought to stretch from Portugal to the Indian Ganges), still Italy occupied the geographical center of the Mediterranean, and Rome stood at the center of the Italian peninsula.[7] But it was political perception rather than climate or geography that most powerfully reinforced the idea of Roman centrality.[8] By the first century B.C. the victories of Pompey in the East and, later, Caesar in the West gave birth to the fiction that "the whole world" had succumbed to Roman arms and that this domination had been divinely ordained.[9] The political center of the subjugated world was the area contained within the *pomerium,* or sacred boundary, of the city of Rome.[10]

(Strabo 1.2.3–40, chaps. 16–47). Odysseus's journey to the "far west" was generally thought to have taken the hero to Italy. Augustan poets elaborated on this picture by describing Italy as an ideal land in which Saturn had reigned during the Golden Age (cf. Verg. *G.* 2.136–76; Prop. 3.22.17–42; Canter, "Praise of Italy"; Geffcken, "Saturnia Tellus"). For nonpoetic treatments of Italy that nevertheless speak of it in ideal terms see, for instance, Pliny *HN* 3.38–42; Strabo 6.4.1, chap. 286; 5.3.1, chap. 228; Varro *RR* 1.2.3–7. On the Aeneas story, see Alföldi, *Die trojanischen Urahnen der Römer;* Bömer, *Rom und Troja;* Horsfall, "Aeneas Legend."

7. On the site of Rome: Cic. *Rep.* 2.5–11 (but see also Cic. *Leg. agr.* 2.96). The fact that Rome was situated in a latitude of temperate climate was incorporated into the mythology of Italy as the ideal Saturnian land (Pliny *HN* 37.201; Strabo 6.4.1, chap. 286; cf. Cic. *Rep.* 6.21).

8. On Rome's sense of the justice and inevitability of its world empire, see Cic. *Phil.* 6.19: [*populum Romanum*] *di immortales omnibus gentibus imperare voluerunt; Har. resp.* 19. The most famous articulations are Augustan: Livy 5.51–54; Verg. *Aen.* 1.257–96, 6.847–53; Hor. *Carm.* 4.15.13–16.

9. The idea of world empire is frequent in Cicero's speeches: *Imp. Pomp.* 53; *Mur.* 22; *Cat.* 3.26, 4.11; *Sull.* 33; *Leg. agr.* 1.18; *Red. sen.* 2; *Mil.* 90; *Phil.* 6.19; *Prov. cons.* 33–34. For Caesar's contribution, see *Prov. cons.* 32–35; *Balb.* 64. For Pompey, see, for example, *Sest.* 67; *Balb.* 16; *Imp. Pomp.* passim. On the growth of the idea of Rome as a world city, dominating the *oikoumenē,* see Vogt, *Orbis,* 151–98. For discussion of the sources and the development of the topos, as well as further bibliography, see Nicolet, *Space, Geography, and Politics,* 29–56.

10. The intimate relationship between the space of the core and that of the periphery that it dominated was expressed by the fact that the *pomerium* could be extended whenever the boundary of *imperium* had been extended. On the

Along with this belief that Rome stood at the center of a world-embracing empire, there is evidence to suggest that by the first century B.C. the Romans had wedded a religious aspect to the notion of political domination. Perhaps the best illustration of the notion is found in a passage from Livy. In the speech of Camillus that ends the fifth book of the *Ab urbe condita* the Augustan historian portrays Camillus as arguing against the proposal to move the Roman people to Veii after the Gallic sack of Rome. The hero declares that there was no place in Rome that was not "filled with religious meaning and with gods" (5.52.2) and that the solemn rites of sacrifice were fixed in place no less than in time.[11] He asks how the obligations of religion—the prayers, sacrifices, cults, and festivals in honor of the gods—could possibly be met in any place other than Rome. Were the priests to journey back from Veii to the ruined site of Rome in order to perform the sacred rituals? Or would they attempt to perform these rites in the new city? Neither, says Camillus, would be possible. The sacred banquet of Jupiter could not take place elsewhere than on the Capitolium, nor could Vesta's fire and the shields of Mars, holy objects as old and even older than the city itself, be worshipped in any other place. Camillus argues that explicitly religious ceremonies could not take place outside of Rome without sacrilege, and that the political activities of the state would be tainted as well. How, he asks, could the auspices be taken unless within the *pomerium*? And how could the *comitia* meet anywhere but in their customary places?

In this passage the sanctity connected in the public mind with the

---

extensions of the *pomerium,* see the discussion and recent bibliography in Boatwright, "The Pomerial Extension of Augustus"; Poe, "The Secular Games, the Aventine, and the Pomerium." For ancient sources, see Lugli, *Fontes,* 2:115–31. At the center of Rome stood the Forum Romanum. Within the Forum Romanum, which could be thought of as the center of the center, was placed the Golden Milestone, the spot from which all roads, real and imaginary, spread out to the corners of the Empire. See Platner and Ashby, *Topographical Dictionary,* s.v. "Milliarium aureum," 342. Although the monument was Augustan (20 B.C.), the perception that all roads led to (and from) Rome predated the monument.

11. Ogilvie, *Livy,* 741–43, believes that the idea of Rome's special destiny developed during the Social War (91–87 B.C.), in response to the challenge posed by the rebellious Italians, who had set up Corfinium (renamed Italia) as the new capital of Italy. Note that the city was not itself referred to as *sacra* in spite of its divine sanction. (See comments of Scully, "Cities in Italy's Golden Age," esp. 74–75.)

most sacred places of the city is extended to include the city as a whole, and the physical environment of Rome is seen as an instantiation of its meaning, its mission, and its destiny. At the end of the speech Livy has Camillus declare that whereas it might be possible to transfer the virtue of the Roman people to Veii, the *fortuna* of the Romans was inextricably tied to the fortune of the place where Rome now stood (5.54.6). Camillus then reminds his audience that when the Capitoline was being cleared to prepare for the building of the Temple of Jupiter Optimus Maximus, a human head had been found there. Further, it was discovered that two shrines, those of Juventas and of Terminus, could not be moved. These omens were interpreted as signs of the sanctity and immutability of the city and of its future greatness. For Livy, then, an inseparable bond existed between the meaning of the state, on one hand, and the city of Rome as a physical entity, on the other. Rome had been instituted and guided by the gods, and its growing power and astounding military success were believed to be derived not only from the virtue of its citizens or even from heavenly support for Roman arms but from a divinely ordained fate attached to the very site of the city.

Complementary to the Romans' belief that they inhabited "the center place" was their belief that those who lived on the fringes of the Roman world were different from themselves. Although sophisticated Romans of the first century B.C. no longer believed that the old tales learned from Greek mythology represented a true description of places on the fringes of the *imperium Romanum,* nevertheless the perception endured that there existed in these distant places a world disparate from that of their own experience. This sense was reinforced by the works of various travelers and ethnographers, whose accounts emphasized the most striking and unusual features of foreign places and the aspects of these places that differed most radically from the experience of their readers.[12] As will be seen, political propaganda also had a role to play in making the geographically removed seem alien and often threatening. Nor should we forget that the actual experience of the Romans was a source of conceptions about the strangeness of people from distant places. By the late Republic, Rome was a city of perhaps a million inhabitants, a heterogeneous mix of nationalities from throughout the Empire. The unfamil-

12. Cf. Strabo 1.2.29, chap. 36: "Those peculiarities of each individual country that are in some way strange and unexpected are the ones that are most generally known and manifest to everyone."

iar appearance and strange habits of this great mass of foreigners—visitors, diplomats, teachers, merchants, litigants, charlatans, freedmen, and slaves—gave rise to vivid impressions of the character of various ethnic groups and the nature of the lands from which they came. Given the xenophobia of what was originally a conservative, agrarian society, the resentment of Romans and Italians who had to endure the bitter spectacle of foreign freedmen rising to positions of wealth and influence, and the Roman need to justify the enslavement of vast numbers of individuals from every corner of the Mediterranean world, it is little wonder that the literature recording the Romans' impressions of foreign inhabitants of the city was filled with hostility and prejudice.[13]

Cultural ethnocentricity provided the orator of ancient Rome—as it has provided orators in every culture—with a familiar topos: "them and us." By exploiting the negative side of this topos, the Roman orator might easily convince his Roman audience that distant peoples were barbarous, monstrous, implacably hostile, or morally inferior. "Our" interests, crucial to the preservation of the whole *imperium,* must therefore take precedence over "theirs," which were by definition parochial

---

13. It has been demonstrated, however, that Roman hostility to foreigners was not based on color prejudice. (See especially Snowden, *Blacks in Antiquity,* 169–95, and Thompson, *Romans and Blacks,* with accompanying bibliography.) For general discussion and bibliography, see also Balsdon, *Romans and Aliens,* esp. 30–71, 214–59. Foreigners (that is, non-Italians) probably constituted as much as three-quarters of the population of Rome in Cicero's day (Brunt, *Italian Manpower,* 376–88; Balsdon, *Romans and Aliens,* 12–16). Hopkins, *Conquerors and Slaves,* 7–8, estimates that more than two million enslaved alien peasants were transported to Italy between 80 and 8 B.C. For xenophobic descriptions of Rome's foreign population, see Sen. *Cons. ad Helv.* 6.2–3; Juv. 3.60–125; 6.511–626; Martial 7.30; Luc. *Phar.* 7.535–43. On Jewish, Syrian, and Egyptian enclaves in Rome, see Balsdon, *Romans and Aliens,* 16; la Piana, "Foreign Groups in Rome"; Grant, *The Jews in the Roman World;* Leon, *The Jews of Ancient Rome;* Reinhold, *Diaspora,* 121–26. The drafting of men into the armies that fought the internal and external battles of the last century of the Republic, as well as the intense economic activity of this period, would have meant that many Italians and Romans of Cicero's day would have had firsthand experience of the provinces. Interest in and assumptions about the non-Roman world would also have been stimulated by the institution of the triumph (in which prisoners, booty, and paintings of foreign scenes were displayed) and by the exhibitions of exotic animals in the games and festivals (see the comments of Rawson, *Intellectual Life,* 257–58).

and marginal; and "our" assessment of justice, objective and rational, was superior to "theirs," which could be presented as idiosyncratic or the product of the flawed thinking of an inferior ethnic group.[14] As will be shown, it is easy to point to a variety of examples in Cicero's rhetoric in which he exploits this tendency to dehumanize the foreign. In fact, the same strategy could be and was used even against places little removed from Rome. Sallust reports that the orator himself, native of a Latin town not sixty miles from Rome, was called by Catiline a "resident alien" of the city of Rome.[15]

The same thinking that viewed the periphery or the distant as a place of negative extremes, however, could also see such places as the location of positive environments, for both dystopian and utopian communities were thought to exist in places that were far removed. In Greek mythology, the Isles of the Blessed were believed to be located in the far west, and in the lands of the distant south the gods took their pleasure, passing their days feasting with the Aethiopians. Although some Romans of Cicero's day may have questioned the existence of a paradise beyond the Pillars of Hercules, still it was possible for a Roman orator not only to demonize the alien but to idealize it as well. When it suited his purpose, he could create an image of the world outside of his audience's everyday experience as a better one, in which the negative aspects of

14. The literature on Roman imperialism is vast. See, for instance, Harris, *War and Imperialism;* Hammond, "Ancient Imperialism"; Morgan, *"Imperium sine finibus"*; Garnsey and Whittaker, *Imperialism;* Badian, *Roman Imperialism,* esp. 1–15; Sherwin-White, *Roman Foreign Policy;* Vogt, *Orbis;* Balsdon, *Romans and Aliens,* 1–17; Gruen, *Hellenistic World,* 1:273–87; Werner, "Das Problem des Imperialismus." On Cicero in particular, see Vogt, *Ciceros Glaube an Rom;* Guite, "Cicero's Attitude to the Greeks"; Izzo, "Cicero and Political Expediency"; Smethurst, "Cicero and Roman Imperial Policy"; Neuhauser, *Patronus und Orator,* 12; Trouard, *Cicero's Attitude towards the Greeks;* Meyer, "Cicero und das Reich."

15. Sall. *Cat.* 31. We learn from the *Pro Sulla* that Lucius Manlius Torquatus, as prosecutor of Sulla (the dictator's nephew), had referred to Cicero as a "foreign king" (22: *peregrinum regem*). When asked what was meant by the word "foreign," Torquatus supposedly responded: "I mean that you are from a [Italian] *municipium*" (22). Cicero rebukes Torquatus by referring to leaders such as Cato the Censor, Tiberius Coruncanius, Manius Curius, and Gaius Marius, who had also come from municipal backgrounds (23–25). If this hostility to Italians seems surprising, it may be less so when it is recalled that the Social War, in which much of Italy had risen against Roman domination, was a vivid memory in the minds of Cicero's contemporaries.

Roman life had no place. Caesar and Tacitus, for instance, found in the Germans virtues that the Romans had long since lost.[16] Positive stereotypes of inhabitants of the unsophisticated outposts of empire could also support an orator's attempt to rouse the sympathy of his audience (so long as they could indulge in this emotion without compromising their own interests), since litigants from such places could readily be cast in the role of simple and humble supplicants, naive about the ways of the world and pitiably dependent on Roman protection and good faith.

Closely related to positive and negative images of the spatially removed were those that related to chronological distance, an idea that can best be understood in reference to ancient conceptions of anthropology. Stated simply, the Greco-Roman world was capable of viewing human history both as an ascent and as a decline. On the one hand, human life on earth was envisioned as a progress in which the gradual creation of law, politics, and the other arts of urban civilization (including rhetoric) had raised human beings from the bestiality of the animals to a level that reflected the divine spark of rationality that separated them from the lower orders.[17] On the other hand, the span of history was interpreted, at least in a moral sense, as a great slide downward. This view was often articulated metaphorically through the Myth of the Ages, in which an original Golden Age had degenerated into one of Silver, the Age of Silver had passed to Bronze, and, at last, the Age of Bronze had given way to the present, a debased Age of Iron. According to this conception, the primitive past was an Edenic period in which natural justice prevailed and the earth poured forth her bounty without the need for plowing or planting. Material "progress" in the form of technological advance was seen not as progress at all but as corruption

16. See the discussion of Pliny and Tacitus in Sherwin-White, *Racial Prejudice,* 33–61. See also, for example, Diod. Sic. 3.17.4, 18.2 (on Ichthyophages); 5.21.5 (on British simplicity); Megasthenes in Strabo 15.1.53, chap. 709 (on Indians); or Pliny *HN* 6.84–91, who pictured the people of Taprobane as an uncivilized and innocent race living in a state of happiness and harmony. For primitivism in general, see Dodds, *Ancient Concept of Progress,* 13–17.

17. Greek myth is replete with "culture givers," most prominently Prometheus and Hercules. Cicero pictured the first civilizer as either a philosopher or an orator-philosopher (cf. *Inv.* 1.2–3; *Tusc.* 5.5). For the civilizing power of *logos* and humans' unique possession of it, see Cic. *De or.* 1.33; Isoc. *Nicocles* 5–6; *Antid.* 253–54, 293–94; *Paneg.* 48–50; Xen. *Mem.* 4.3.11–12.

and degeneration.[18] A compromise between these two opposing views depicted the intermediate stage of the life of the small agricultural community as an ideal, a brief hiatus of human contentment between a savage past and a decadent future.[19]

A powerful link could be forged between conceptions tied to separation in time and the positive and negative ideas we have shown to have been associated with spatial separation. Far-removed regions inhabited by primitive societies similar to those believed to have existed in the distant past could be viewed negatively: these were places that were frozen in time, the barbaric abode of people still less than fully human. Or these same places could also be presented as constituting ideal locations, happily untouched by the degeneration of a modern age. The attractiveness of the latter conception was enhanced by the prevailing Roman view of their own history as a decline from simple individual virtue and social harmony. The Romans saw their preimperial past as an ideal in which the great upheavals that convulsed their world had yet to occur. While Roman historians and poets saw fit to praise the fact of empire—the victory of Roman arms was, after all, evidence of heaven's approval of the Roman people—these same writers could not but see the destructive changes wrought by military success. The destabilizing effect of such features of Roman expansion as the influx of wealth and its accumulation in the hands of a few, the change from small subsistence to

18. On ancient anthropologies, see Rose, "Sophocles' *Philoctetes*"; Cole, *Democritus;* Robin, "Sur la conception épicurienne du progrès"; Guthrie, *In the Beginning*, 80–94; Dodds, *Ancient Concept of Progress,* esp. 1–25, in which he speaks of the tension between ideas of progress and the "two great antiprogressive myths" of the Lost Paradise and Eternal Recurrence (3).

19. In Lucretius (and, it is to be assumed, in Epicurus as well) humans ascend, without benefit of divine guidance, from barbarism to the creation of cities and political institutions, and yet a kind of semiprimitive ideal is reached at an intermediate stage, *before* the full attainment of civilization. (See Blickman, "Lucretius, Epicurus, and Prehistory"; Fredouille, "Lucrèce et le 'double progrès contrastant'"; Perelli, "La storia dell' umanità nel V libro di Lucrezio.") If there are hints of primitivism in Lucretius's seemingly rationalist and materialist anthropology, there are likewise hints of the presence of the savage in Vergil's Saturnian Golden Age. (See Moorton, "The Innocence of Italy"; and Guthrie, *In the Beginning,* 98, who notes that Vergil depicts *pre*-Saturnian Italy as inhabited by a rough and savage race.) Guthrie, *Greek Philosophy,* 3:135–47 and 135 n. 1, terms this the "social compact" stage in the Sophistic conception of evolution.

large-scale, slave-based agriculture, the transformation of Italian small holders into professional soldiers or dispossessed urban dwellers, and especially, the agonizing cycle of civil wars of the last century of the Republic were recurring themes in Roman literature. Such problems reinforced the Roman tendency to idealize the past, especially that time in the middle Republic when the city had not yet succumbed to foreign influences and the typical Roman citizen-soldier was, at least in popular belief, an honest, hardworking farmer. At the same time, current problems also disposed the Romans to idealize those people and places that they believed most closely approximated that period in their past.[20]

NATURE AND NURTURE: HIPPOCRATIC MEDICINE

Growing knowledge of the diversity of cultures and mores in the wider world had provided a strong stimulus to ancient Greek philosophical speculation concerning the nature of humankind, for it was travelers' accounts of places in which customs differed radically from those familiar to the Greeks that had led thinkers to question the existence of moral absolutes and to attempt to define the relative roles of custom and nature (*nomos* and *physis*) in human societies. Although it is beyond the scope of this work to enter in detail into the complex subject of philosophical positions concerning the Greek attitude to the "*barbaroi*," we may note that, on the one hand, absolutists like Plato and Aristotle had subscribed to the idea that an ethnic group could by nature be inferior or superior to others and had argued on this basis that the enslavement of the inferior (barbarians) by the superior (Greeks) could be justified;[21] on the other hand, a variety of philosophers believed that human nature was essentially one and attributed the diversity of ethical norms observed among different peoples to factors such as culture and education

20. On late Republican and early imperial nostalgia for an idealized past, see Gruen, *Hellenistic World,* 1:274–78; Köstermann, "Das Problem des römischen Dekadenz"; Pöschl, "Die römische Auffasung der Geschichte"; Knoche, *Vom Selbstverständnis der Römer.* On the justice of Rome's early, as opposed to later, dealings with foreign peoples, see Cic. *Off.* 2.26–29; *Rep.* 3.41.

21. It should be kept in mind that Plato's and Aristotle's statements bearing on this subject vary a good deal according to context. See, for instance, discussion of key passages in Baldry, *Unity of Mankind,* 72–101.

rather than nature. This latter view, in turn, encouraged doubts about whether slavery of foreign populations could be justified.[22]

Among the first group of thinkers to attempt to formulate empirical responses to the same issues that stimulated debate among the philosophers was the fifth-century school of medicine that grew up around Hippocrates of Cos. On Airs, Waters, Places, one of the works that has come down to us under the name (if not the pen) of the great founder of rational medicine, attempted to advise the peripatetic medical practitioners of its day on the physical and psychological effects of environment. Climate, water supply, and topography were each considered by the author with a view to allowing the doctor to predict the weaknesses and strengths of groups who lived in a variety of physical settings.

While this effort to establish a rational basis for endemic disease is laudable and worthy of Hippocrates himself, the execution as found in On Airs, Waters, Places leaves much for the modern to criticize. Although generalizing theories are presented as if based on direct observation of diverse populations, what passes for factual observations is actually composed of confused and often contradictory remarks drawn from a variety of sources. But the very diversity of the kind of materials found in this medical tract of the fifth century B.C. provides a useful example of some of the factors influencing description of lands and places not only at this early date but persisting even in Cicero's time.[23]

22. See the discussion and bibliography in Guthrie, Greek Philosophy, 3:152–63; Baldry, Unity of Mankind, 52–101. Cf. the peroration to Cicero's sixth Philippic (19): "It is not right for the Roman people, whom the immortal gods wished to rule all races, to be slaves. We have arrived at the final crisis; that which is to be decided is freedom. You must either conquer, citizens—which you doubtlessly will do, through your loyalty and unanimity—or do anything rather than be slaves. Other nations are able to tolerate slavery, but freedom is the special possession of the Roman people."

23. A useful introduction to this Hippocratic treatise is Levine, Hippocrates, 128–50. While a number of medical writers influential in the late Republic touched on the subject of the health of diverse populations, unlike the author of On Airs, Waters, Places, they limit their remarks to the explanation of physical, rather than mental or emotional, characteristics. On the relation of place to disease and mortality: Asclepiades of Prusa believed all bodies to be made of the same particles but also noted the varying effects of climate (Diels, Doxographi Graeci, 443–44), and his anti-Empiric bias was apparently behind the assertion that differing patients and places necessitated differing treatments (Rawson, Intellectual Life, 174); Varro (RR 1.4.5, 12.2), demonstrating his familiarity with Hippocrates, noted that earth, water, and air were all capable of sending out pestilential vapors; and Vitruvius (1.1.10) noted the connection of environmen-

In several passages the author appears to have been strongly influenced by a combination of mythology and the accounts of wonders retailed by travelers and ethnographers. His description of the women belonging to the Scythian tribe of the Sauromatae (17) seems to be derived from tales of the Amazons (although the term is never used).[24] Before marriage these women are said to ride, hunt, and engage in battle just like men. Further, the author's statement that mothers cauterized the right breast of their daughters so that all the strength of that side of their bodies would flow into their muscles corresponds to the etymology usually given for the term Amazon (that is, "without breast"). Similarly, the work's extensive description of Asia doubtlessly drew on descriptions of the Golden Age, for the author paints it as a quasi-mythical land in which flora, fauna, and humans grow larger and more beautiful than elsewhere, and boundless fecundity characterizes both wild and cultivated land. The assertion that this region is "closest to spring" in character (12) is a clear echo of the "eternal spring" of the Golden Age. Although the inhabitants are said to be well nourished, handsome, large, and gentle, there exists one drawback to this quasi-perfect environment: the unchanging mildness of the environment causes the Asians to lack courage, endurance, industry, and high spirit, for "pleasure governs all" (12).

In the summary of the comparison of Europeans and Asians the hypothesis of environmental determinism thinly veils a traditional ethnic stereotype distinguishing the Greeks from the peoples who inhabited the lands farther east. The author claims that change and extremes of climate account for the courage and spirit of the Europeans, while the lack of violent climatic change in Asia leads to stagnation and weakness. He then bolsters his argument by making use of the kind of political propaganda that must have been common during the period of the Persian wars and would later be identified with the idea of Panhellenism, a movement that combined calls for Greek unity with hostility to the non-Greeks of the eastern Mediterranean.[25] The autocratic political systems of the Asians, he states, reinforced their native tendencies to

---

tal factors (climate, wind, water sources) with physical health. Such material is discussed and evaluated with great acuity by Rawson, 170–84.

24. Cf. Hdt. 4.110; Diod. Sic. 2.45.1–46.6; 3.52.1–53.3.

25. The concept is found in Gorgias and Lysias but is most closely identified with Isocrates. See Haarhoff, *Stranger at the Gate,* 60–71; Kessler, *Isokrates;* Dobesch, *Der panhellenische Gedanke;* Baldry, *Unity of Mankind,* 66–72.

weakness and cowardice, while the autonomous systems of the Greeks reinforced their natural courage and independence (cf. 16; 23).

Some of the above material seems to derive not only from ethnic stereotypes of Greeks and Asians but also from the author's desire to contribute to the *nomos-physis* controversy. He is interested, for instance, in describing how custom can serve either to reinforce or to overcome natural tendencies in the case of Asian political institutions: he notes that the autocratic governments under which the Asians lived contributed to their weakness (16); that bravery and endurance could, however, be produced through law, even in those in whom these qualities did not exist by nature (24); and that free Asians, whether Greek or non-Greek, were courageous and warlike (16). Furthermore, in describing a race known as the "Longheads," he gives his readers an example of how nature can be changed by custom. This tribe, according to the author, had developed the habit of wrapping the heads of their babies in order to elongate the skull while still malleable. He goes on to affirm that, after a period of time, nature itself reinforced custom by producing babies that were long-headed from birth.

The importance of a work such as *On Airs, Waters, Places* to the development of later rhetorical topoi can be seen in a number of its features. Above all, the author establishes the crucial connection between *ēthos* and *locus,* that is, between the way people look, think, and act and their physical environment. Here, then, was a powerful strategy by which the orator could establish probability (*to eikos*) in arguing for the behavior or character of various persons in a case. By describing the place where an individual came from, he could at the same time claim to be establishing the character of that individual.

The treatise not only establishes this principle, but, thanks to the confused logic of its author, it provides both specific positive and specific negative probabilities for a variety of locations. At the outset (12), lack of climatic change is presented as ideal in terms of creation of physical well-being, for the unchanging temperateness of their land had made the people of Asia handsome, well nourished, and free from excessive passion (although this climate is also responsible for their unwarlike temperament). In later passages in the treatise, however, lack of climatic change is asserted to be the reason for physical as well as mental debilitation, and the author states that those whose land is rich, soft, well watered, and blessed by a favorable climate are themselves fleshy, ill-articulated, and overly "moist" (24). Description of the Europeans, who live in an environment of frequent climatic change and fierce extremes

of cold and heat, is generally favorable and emphasizes the positive attributes of courage and independence of spirit. Other passages, however, speak of the violence, wildness, and unsociability to which this
environment also gives rise. An orator, searching here for characteristics
of various regions, might well find ample material either for praise or
for blame. It is to be noted in particular that in this work one sees one
of the first extant articulations of the stereotypical ethnic and political
differences between East and West (cast in the form of comparisons of
Asia and Europe), a usefully fluid and imprecise topos as far as the objects of praise and censure are concerned.[26] Although the author of *On
Airs, Waters, Places* was primarily intent on emphasizing the differences
between Greeks and Asians, the ideas within the work could easily be
adapted to castigate Asian Greeks at the expense of mainlanders or,
later, to explain the negative qualities of the Greeks themselves, who
were often viewed through Roman eyes as sharing the corruption attributed to peoples of the East.

ETHNOGRAPHY, POLITICS, AND PHILOSOPHY

As mentioned above, ethnographical writing was an important source
of Roman images of places and peoples, at least among the educated
classes. The genre dates back at least to the sixth century B.C., by which
time the rapid expansion of Greek trade and colonization had made the
wider world a subject of keen interest.[27] The earliest Greek descriptions
of "foreign places" ranged from the purely informational accounts of
early navigators (*periploi*) and the credulous reporting of wonders associated with distant lands, to the more searching ethnographical material in the work of Ionian logographers and the ethnographical
"digressions" (if such they may be termed) in the works of historians

26. For a wide-ranging discussion of both the rhetoric and the reality of the
"East vs. West" topos, see Carratelli, "Europa ed Asia." For the topos "North
and South" (usually cast as a comparison between Scythians and Ethiopians),
see Snowden, *Blacks in Antiquity,* 169–75, who notes that characteristic differences between the two groups are normally attributed by Greek and Roman
writers to environmental differences.

27. Seminal works in the study of the ethnographical tradition are Norden,
Die germanische Urgeschichte; Trüdinger, "Studien zur Geschichte der
griechisch-römischen Ethnographie." Thomas, *Lands and Peoples,* 1–5, provides a useful summary of the genre. For a valuable overview of geography and
ethnography in the late Republic, see Rawson, *Intellectual Life,* 250–66.

such as Herodotus. The eastern campaigns of Alexander gave rise to a
second wave of interest in geography and ethnography, and, as A. Dihle
points out, this Hellenistic material was strongly influenced by the incli-
nation to ascertain the rational causes of observed phenomena. Dihle
notes that those who wrote of foreign places in these times—officers,
diplomats, and travelers—couched their observations within the context of general aetiological theories. Further, he asserts that "the public
for whom these men composed their observations demanded an anthro-
pological, geophysical, moral or historical arrangement of new information."[28]

The aetiologies advanced by Hellenistic authors to explain their data
are difficult to recover from the later works in which they are incorporated. They may in general, however, be divided into two groups: those
theories (like that of the author of *On Airs, Waters, Places*) that emphasized the direct effect on the human constitution of "climate"—by
which the ancients meant such things as distance from the sun, moist-
ness or dryness in a location, or the characteristics of a particular band
of latitude; and, on the other hand, those theories that assumed that the
psychological and physical characteristics of individuals, as well as the
level of civilization achieved by particular ethnic groups, could be explained by the combined effect of customs, traditions, and practices.
These customs, traditions, and practices, in turn, were thought to be
determined by a variety of environmental factors—including geography, climate, exposure to other cultures, and, especially, the means
available in a certain location for sustaining life.[29] This latter viewpoint
is well represented in the pages of Diodorus Siculus, who begins his universal history with a rationalizing anthropology that attributes human
progress to a process of trial and error, spurred by the necessity of maintaining life and facilitated by humans' possession of "hands, speech,
and acuity of mind."[30] For Diodorus (and certain of his Hellenistic
sources), the explanation for the astounding diversity of human mores

28. "Zur hellenistischen Ethnographie," 209: "Verlangt das Publikum, für
das sie ihre Berichte abfassen, nach anthropologischer, geophysikalischer, mo-
ralischer oder geschichtlicher Einordnung der neuen Informationen."
29. Dihle, "Zur hellenistischen Ethnographie," 216, contrasts the point of
view of figures such as Megasthenes and Agatharchides, who explained ethnic
traits by reference to custom and custom by reference to general environment,
with that of figures such as Posidonius, who is criticized by Strabo (2.3.7, chaps.
102–3) for his reliance in ethnography on the idea of climatic zones.
30. 1.8.9.

could be found in the natural drive of humans to use whatever means exist in a particular location in order to sustain life.[31]

Earlier Hellenistic ethnography, an exclusively Greek science, was reflected in both Greek and Latin literature of Cicero's day. By the late Republic, the categories, if not the contents, of ethnographical discussions were fixed: the authors of such excursuses invariably alluded to aspects of the physical environment of a particular ethnic group (including physical geography, climate, crops, raw materials) as well as to their social institutions (including political, religious, and military groupings). A review of ethnographical passages in several works of the period reveals the kinds of assumptions about the connection between ethnic groups and their habitation that would have been widespread at the time.

The short ethnographical account of Africa in Sallust's *Bellum Jugurthinum* (17–19) is, unfortunately, of limited use here, as the author hardly goes beyond the bare facts that he has received from his Carthaginian source and does not encourage the reader to analyze the reasons for the character traits and institutions he ascribes to the Africans. He presents a picture of a North Africa inhabited by mixed races: according to Sallust, the nomadic and savage Gaetulians, a people without customs, laws, or rulers, had intermarried with the Medes, a race who had come to western Europe with the army of Hercules, to produce the "Numidians" of his own day.[32]

---

31. See 1.8.1–10 (anthropology and discovery of language), 43.1 (Egyptians' discovery of edible foods); 2.38.2 (repetition of 1.8.9 in description of India); 3.10.6 (nature guides animals to survive), 15.7 (adaptation through necessity), 19.2 (house building), 49.5 (development of military skills). Diodorus also takes note of the effect of climate on health and body type (2.48.8; 3.34.8; 5.19.3), although only once does he explain mental ability in terms of the direct influence of climate (2.36.1: Indian skill in the arts is explained by the purity of the air and the quality of the drinking water). This theory of chance discovery, however, does not prevent the author from constantly reproducing his sources' euhemeristic or mythical accounts of the contributions of various culture givers (Hercules, Dionysus, Hermes, etc.) to human progress.

32. See Scanlon, *The Influence of Thucydides,* ad loc., who compares Sallust's ethnography with Thucydides' digression on Sicilian antiquities (6.1–5), noting the shared pragmatic desire on the part of the two authors to acquaint their readers with information that will orient them in preparation for the description of the military campaign to follow. (Cf. Polyb. 3.36.8; 5.21.4–9; Cic. *De or.* 2.63; *Or.* 66.) Paul, *Historical Commentary,* 71–72, in analyzing Sallust's excursus, agrees with Tacitus's description of such passages as an attempt to

Ethnographical passages in the *Geography* of Strabo, however, are more revealing and merit consideration because although this work was not available to Roman readers during his lifetime, it drew on many other earlier and contemporary sources that would have been well known to the educated classes of Cicero's day. A review of the ethnographical material in the *Geography* leads the reader to conclude that for Strabo differences between ethnic groups were primarily the result of cultural, economic, and geographical circumstances rather than due to the inborn traits of various peoples.[33] When Strabo speaks of the Turdetani of Baetica (Cordoba), for instance, he notes that they were the cleverest and most civilized of the Iberians in his own time but were formerly the most brutish (3.1.6, 3.2.4–15). Likewise, the wildness of the mountain-dwelling Lusitanians is not, according to the author, due to any inherent defect but is explained by their "remoteness" (*ektopismon*), which has prevented the growth of communal organization (*to koinōnikon*) and civilization (*to philanthrōpon*) (3.3.8). Although it is true that Strabo often has recourse to stereotypical descriptions of ethnic groups—the Iberians, for example, are dour and malicious; the Celts, passionate and fickle; and the Western barbarians in general are cruel—he implies that the passage from savagery to civilization may be made by all. This passage is initiated through contact with Greco-Roman city-states and leads, in places where geography has been suitable, to the creation of stable agriculture, private property, law, and, the ultimate sign of civilized life, large urban centers. Where land was not suitable for settled agriculture, however, the inhabitants were apparently doomed to a life of savagery.[34]

The employment of ethnography in the writings of Julius Caesar is a more complex matter than in Strabo's *Geography*, for with the *Bellum Gallicum* we encounter the exploitation of seemingly objective ethnographical material in support of a cleverly disguised but nonetheless tendentious account of history—the first Latin example of what might be

---

"entertain and refresh" the reader (cf. Tac. *Ann.* 4.33: *situs gentium . . . retinent ac redintegrant legentium animos*). See also Syme, *Sallust*, 153, 192–95.

33. See especially Strabo's criticism of Posidonius (2.3.7–8 chaps. 102–3). See also Sherwin-White, *Racial Prejudice*, esp. 12–13.

34. For agriculture as the sine qua non of civilization, see Guthrie, *In the Beginning*, 95–98, and *Greeks and Their Gods*, 285–87. Cf. Caes. *B.Gall.* 5.14.

called a consciously "rhetorical" ethnography. It is chiefly in those sections of the work in which the author hoped to justify a controversial military policy that he has recourse to stereotypes of the barbarians as cruel, arrogant, faithless, or given to passionate anger. For instance, in the first book of the *Bellum Gallicum* Caesar creates a picture of the German Ariovistus and his followers as cruel and savage barbarians in order to cast his campaign against them in the form of a moral tale in which Roman arms are used "to spare the conquered and vanquish the proud" (Verg. *Aen.* 6.853).[35] Such sections stand in marked contrast to the author's overall portrayal of the barbarian struggle against Roman arms as motivated primarily by a noble desire for *libertas*.[36]

For the most part, Caesar's explanation for the differences in customs and temperaments among barbarians recalls that of Strabo. The least civilized and most savage tribes are those farthest from Greco-Roman trade and settlements. The Gauls were formerly fiercer and more savage than the Germans, but the nearness of the Roman provinces and their exposure to the amenities of civilization had made them soft (6.24).[37] Caesar's admiration for the fortitude of his enemies is clear, and he notes several times that the tribes who were least civilized were also his bravest and most formidable foes. In addition to simple geographical isolation as an explanation for the relative degree of civilization or savagery among ethnic groups, Caesar points to the desire of the barbarians themselves to preserve their way of life. The Germans are the hardiest and bravest of peoples not only because they are farthest removed from the luxury goods of the civilized world but also because they actively reject them as emasculating (4.2).

In rare instances Caesar departs from the idea that the chief ethnic differences between barbarian tribes are to be explained by their isola-

---

35. Ariovistus is described chiefly through the complaints of the Gallic tribes whom he has dominated: the German is said to exercise his power "haughtily and cruelly" (1.31: *superbe et crudeliter imperare*); he is "savage, fierce, rash" (1.31: *hominem . . . barbarum, iracundum, temerarium*); and the tribes live in fear of his "cruelty" (1.32: *crudelitatem . . . horrerent*) and "tortures" (1.32: *omnes cruciatus*). Caesar concludes that such "wild and savage men" (1.33: *homines feros ac barbaros*) posed a threat to Roman territory, and he must therefore pursue this war, even though it takes him beyond the confines of the Roman province. (See Sherwin-White, *Racial Prejudice,* 13–15.)

36. *B.Gall.* 3.10; 5.27, 29, 54; 7.1, 76.

37. Cf. *B.Gall.* 1.1, 36; 4.3; 5.14.

tion from or contact with civilizing influences.[38] In his account of the revolt of all Gaul under the leadership of Vercingetorix, the author describes how the Aedui, formerly closely allied with the Romans, were drawn into the rebellion. He states that some were influenced by avarice, others by anger and "by the rashness that is especially engendered in the [Gallic] race" (7.42: *impellit alios avaritia alios iracundia et temeritas, quae maxime illi hominum generi est innata*). The fickleness and mental mobility of the Gauls—seen in their most insidious dimensions in the depiction of the Gauls' perfidy and faithlessness to their commitments, in a less threatening guise in their tendency to hopelessness and loss of spirit when faced with adversity—are frequently alluded to and are treated by the author as inherent traits rather than products of culture.[39]

We might take note as well of a curious statement in Caesar's account of the Suebi, the largest and most bellicose of the German tribes. Describing the group's rough and uncivilized life, which is chiefly devoted to hunting and warfare, Caesar remarks that the reasons for the Suebians' great physical strength and huge stature (4.1: *vires . . . et immani corporum magnitudine*) were to be found in their food (consisting of milk, cheese, cattle, and the flesh of hunted animals), their daily exercise in hunting or warfare, and the "freedom of their life" (4.1: *libertate vitae*). In explanation of this last Caesar notes that from boyhood the Suebians are not schooled in duty or discipline and do nothing at all that they do not wish to do (4.1: *nullo officio aut disciplina adsuefacti nihil omnino contra voluntatem faciant*). It is clear to any reader of the *Bellum Gallicum* that Caesar ascribed the triumph of Roman arms in Gaul not only to his own good fortune and ability but in large part to the discipline and fidelity to duty of those who served under him. The work illustrates time and again how the gravest of perils could be over-

38. In spite of his acceptance of slavery and of the idea of the natural inferiority of the barbarians to the Greeks, Xenophon had made the same observation, stating that the "most barbarous" barbarians are those "farthest removed from the customs of the Greeks" (*An.* 5.4.34). For primitivist assertions that barbarian society was corrupted by contact with the Greco-Roman world, see Cic. *Tusc.* 5.90; Strabo 7.3.7, chaps. 300–301; Justin. *Epit.* 2.2; Dio Chrys. 6.25.

39. *B.Gall.* 2.1 (*mobilitate et levitate*); 3.8 (*Gallorum subita et repentina consilia*), 19 (willingness to begin a war but lack of steadfastness in defeat); 4.5 (prey to rumors). This same *mobilitas* may be implied in Caesar's observation that the Gauls were especially quick-witted and adept at imitating other cultures (7.22).

come by an army schooled in the belief that the individual must be willing to sacrifice his own desires and interests to those of the group as a
whole. It is striking, therefore, to note that in this passage Caesar argues
that it is the absence of this very *disciplina* and sense of *officium* that
allowed the individual to grow most powerful, at least in a physical
sense.

Caesar's accounts of the Gauls and the Germans, his analysis of their
motives and intentions, and his interpretation of the character of the
tribes in the areas in which he operated must have reached a large popular audience, for the *Bellum Gallicum,* even if its contents were not
identical with the dispatches sent back to the Senate from Gaul, surely
reflected the tone and content of those dispatches. And Caesar was well
aware that it would be his account of events in such dispatches that
would ultimately form the basis for reports to the populace about the
course of events in the war, for speeches by his adherents celebrating his
deeds, and for proclamations of public thanksgivings to be celebrated in
honor of his victories. His exploitation of ethnographical material,
then, was directed to both Senate and people and was meant not simply
to inform but to persuade as well.[40] This observation leads us to consider, at least briefly, the role that characterization of non-Roman
groups played in Roman politics in general.

When Roman orators appeared before the people to speak on behalf
of declaring war against a foreign state or granting a military command
to an individual they would have combined considerations of expediency with those of justice, since fetial law demanded that the Roman
state act only in a just cause.[41] Those who favored a declaration of war,
therefore, would have needed to prove that the state in question was
guilty of wrongdoing against Rome or her allies, while those opposed
could argue that Roman honor or *fides* to an ally did not require military intervention. Both those attacking and those defending a declaration of war against a foreign state would have supported their interpretation of events by fitting particular incidents into a pattern of past
actions—a pattern that, in turn, would have been explained through

40. On Caesar's ethnography, see Beckmann, *Geographie;* Klotz, "Geographie."
41. See "fetiales" in *RE* 12(1909):2259–65; Harris, *War and Imperialism,*
166–75; Cic. *Off.* 1.36–38. Although by the late Republic fetial law would
have lacked any actual "motive power"—as Badian has noted (*Roman Imperialism,* 11–12)—the necessity to give lip service to claims of justice would have
endured.

assumptions about the character and temperament of the people in question. The underlying motives for urging declarations of war were many and in most cases must have outnumbered those inclining speakers towards advocating restraint. Actual fear of a perceived threat, the insatiable desire of the upper classes for military command and glory, and the efficacy of a campaign against an external enemy in suppressing internal faction are but a few of the former. Given the constant engagement of Roman armies throughout the Mediterranean, the citizens of Republican Rome doubtlessly proved a receptive audience for a barrage of indictments lodged against foreign peoples for their supposed duplicity, ferocity, barbarism, and impiety.[42]

Arguments concerning the character and intentions of Rome's allies, provinces, friends, and enemies not only figured in the conduct of foreign policy but at the same time played an essential role in internal political struggles, also fought out before the eyes of Roman voters. Vilification of a foreign people could serve as part of an overall strategy in which one's political opponents were themselves identified with an external enemy. Octavian's propaganda against Antony's governance of the eastern provinces provides the most conspicuous example of such a strategy, the precedent for which was surely the claims of Alexander's enemies that he had become more Asian than Greek.[43] On the other hand, internal political considerations might also prompt a man to defend the character of a foreign people. Roman politicians would frequently have attempted to increase their own prestige by acting on behalf of their foreign *clientela,* and the power of a leader was greatly enhanced if, as patron, he were able to procure citizenship for a subjugated or allied people. Political enmity might also influence a politician's

42. For a summary of Roman stereotypes of specific ethnic groups, see Balsdon, *Romans and Aliens,* 30–71. Some military operations were initiated by a Roman governor or by the Senate without action by the Comitia Centuriata. It is unclear from the ancient evidence how often, in Cicero's day, appeal was made to the voters for a formal declaration of war; a speech such as the *De imperio Pompei,* however, shows that there would indeed be opportunities for public debates (*contiones*) concerning projected military action.

43. Alexander's opponents attempted to rouse their fellow Greeks to rebellion by claiming that the Macedonian king had succumbed to the model of Persian satrapy. See Haarhoff, *Stranger at the Gate,* 80–84; Badian, "Agis III"; Borza, "The End of Agis' Revolt," esp. 233–35. On the other hand, anti-Persianism was exploited by Isocrates in support of Philip. See Bringmann, *Studien,* 96–102; Dobesch, *Der panhellenische Gedanke;* Cloché, *Isocrate,* 57–127; Kessler, *Isokrates,* 45–80.

support of foreign peoples. We learn, for instance, that Cato accused
Caesar of outraging the rights of innocent Germans and argued that he
should be bound and handed over to them for his violations of fetial
law.[44] Of the role of characterization of non-Romans in the arena of the
law courts more will be said in the next chapter.

Finally, some mention should be made of attitudes identified with the
philosophical schools dominant in late Republican Rome: Stoicism and
Epicureanism. While it cannot be claimed that these schools would have
had a direct influence on the opinions of the masses, they might well
have had an indirect effect, for a combination of philosophical and advanced rhetorical training played a role in the education of the leading
politicians of Cicero's day, and such men would surely have made use of
philosophical tenets—albeit disguising them well—whenever these
ideas were useful in furthering their positions.[45] In spite of the gap that
separated the two philosophies, there existed an underlying similarity
of belief between them.[46] Both schools were cosmopolitan in outlook
and addressed themselves to the question of the happiness of the individual through assumptions about human nature at all times and in all
cultures. Epicurean physiology recognized no essential differences between one person and another and assumed that culture, not nature, lay
at the heart of perceived differences between peoples. Lucretius, chief
Roman exponent of Epicureanism in the late Republic, does not acknowledge racial differences as a determining factor in the pursuit of
happiness in *De rerum natura*. Similarly, Stoic philosophy taught that
all people were alike, united by the divine spark of rationality that they
shared. Although Stoicism countenanced the enslavement of individuals, it did not do so on the assumption that enslaved races were by na-

44. For discussion of this event, see Gelzer, *Caesar,* 131, with n. 2.
45. Cf. Cic. *Para.* 2: *nos ea philosophia plus utimur, quae peperit dicendi
copiam et in qua dicuntur ea quae non multum discrepent ab opinione populari.*
46. See Baldry, *Unity of Mankind,* esp. 141–203; Verbeke, "Le stoïcisme,
une philosophie sans frontières." For a general account of Greek philosophers
in Rome in Cicero's day, see Rawson, *Intellectual Life,* 282–97. For the Stoic
idea of the world conceived as a single city, see Bréguet, "Urbi et orbi," 150–51.
For Stoic anthropology, see references to Posidonius in Seneca's *Ninetieth Let-
ter.* It is, in general, impossible to make assumptions about what sort of specific
connections would be made between *ēthos* and *locus* by individual Stoic or Epicurean writers. Strabo, for instance, shows affinities with Epicurean ethnographical theories and criticizes Posidonius. See Dihle, "Zur hellenistischen Ethnographie," 216.

ture intended for such a fate. Rather, Stoics saw no reason to support the elimination of slavery, since they believed that only moral enslavement to vice could undermine the happiness of the truly wise person.

The foregoing, while not an exhaustive survey of the complex body of ideas about the relationship between *ēthos* and *locus* prevalent in the late Republic, may serve as an introduction to ancient thinking on the subject. It is important to keep in mind that, in most cases, we can only speculate about the degree to which the concepts discussed above actually influenced popular belief, since this survey is, first, dependent on the vagaries of literary survival and, second, skewed by the fact that both the authors and the intended audience of most of the sources that have survived were restricted to a small, well-educated upper class. Gravestones, inscriptions, and dedications may tell us of the numbers of foreigners in Rome or of the popularity of foreign cults, but little survives to speak to us of the way in which the common man and woman looked at the world and the people in it. If Rome possessed drama comparable to Greek Old Comedy or tragedy, with its frequent allusions to barbarians, our task would be made easier.[47] Roman comedy, however, derives from a period generations removed from that of Cicero and, furthermore, is adapted from Greek New Comedy. Its value in predicting the sentiments and beliefs of citizens in the late Republic is therefore limited.

A similar problem presents itself when we turn to rhetorical handbooks as a source of Roman ideas about other peoples and places, for these works, like Roman comedy, constituted a hybrid genre, as much dependent on Hellenistic Greek sources as on contributions from Roman writers.[48] Latin rhetorical handbooks did indeed advise the orator

47. Long, *Barbarians in Greek Comedy*; Bacon, *Barbarians in Greek Tragedy*.

48. For citations of ancient rhetorical works, see Lausberg, *Handbuch*, 1:204–6 (§§376.2, 3, 6, 7, 11), covering arguments based on characterization of a person (*argumenta a persona*), which include consideration of *natio* (*nam et gentibus proprii mores sunt, nec idem in barbaro, Romano, Graeco probabile est*), *patria, educatio et disciplina, habitus,* and *studia* (*nam rusticus, forensis, negotiator, miles, navigator, medicus aliud atque aliud efficiunt*); and 133–34 (§§245.I, 247.1, 2), covering epideictic and epideictic elements in forensic and deliberative rhetoric, in which praise or blame of an individual includes consideration of *genus* and *patria*. For the related topic of praise of places or cities, see 1:135 (§247.1, 2). On descriptions and encomia of cities, see also Classen, *Die Stadt*, esp. 4–5.

to use considerations of race, nationality, city-state, education, and habits of life to characterize individuals either positively or negatively. But when we turn from such general admonitions to the exceedingly rare specific examples, we find passages such as that in Cicero's *De inventione* noting that distinctions of race would lead one to consider whether a person "[was] a Greek or a barbarian," and distinctions of birthplace would raise the question of "whether one [was] an Athenian or a Spartan."[49]

This state of affairs leaves us extraordinarily dependent on the extant speeches themselves as a reflection of everyday thought in the late Republic, for of all the literary works that we have inherited from this period rhetoric alone depended for its success on the belief of the many. Concerning this subject Cicero wrote that "both those who make legal judgments and those who make moral judgments are completely guided by [the opinion of the crowd]" (*Top.* 73: *vulgi opinio mutari vix potest ad eamque omnia dirigunt et qui iudicant et qui existimant*).[50] This is not to say that a one-to-one correspondence exists between the conceptions found in the speeches of Cicero and the opinions held by most Roman citizens. Cicero's oratorical success, however, allows us to assume that in the speeches we find a storehouse of ideas and beliefs that were both understandable and credible to the Roman public at the time at which they were delivered.

---

49. *Inv.* 1.35. For the general question of *ēthos* in rhetorical theory, see Kennedy, *Art of Rhetoric*, 100–101, 222–23; Vasaly, "Masks of Rhetoric," 1–4; May, *Trials of Character*, 1–12; Wisse, *Ethos and Pathos*.

50. Cf. Quint. 12.10.53: *Cum vero iudex detur aut populus aut ex populo, laturique sint sententiam indocti saepius atque interim rustici, omnia quae ad obtinendum quod intendimus, prodesse credemus adhibenda sunt.*

CHAPTER FIVE

Place and Commonplace: Country and City

There is hardly a topic in Latin literature that appears more frequently or in a greater variety of guises than that of the contrast between the mores of the country and those of the city. Roman writers of all periods seemed never to tire of praising the simple, honest existence of the farmer and pastoralist while bewailing the growing corruption of city life.[1] Although this chorus of praise for the country resounds often, it is not without a countertheme; there appears almost as frequently in Latin literature extravagant praise for the city of Rome.[2] In examining the way in which Cicero exploits general representations of place, we might therefore begin by tracing the orator's variations on this familiar topic of country and city. Two orations are of particular interest, as they illustrate the sharp contrasts to be found in the works of an orator trained to argue *in utramque partem*, that is, on either side of an issue. In one of Cicero's earliest speeches, the *Pro Roscio Amerino*, the strategy of persuasion depends to a great extent on a positive appraisal of the country and a negative one of the city; while in the *Pro Caelio*—a witty, sophisticated oration from a later period in the orator's career—the assessments of the two milieux are implicitly reversed.

1. For a survey of ancient citations on the subject, see Bléry, *Rusticité et urbanité;* Kier, *De laudibus vitae rusticae.*
2. See Classen, *Die Stadt.* For an overview of ancient attitudes to city and country, see Ramage, *Urbanitas.*

THE HONEST FARMER

The *Pro Roscio* was a crucial oration in the political and rhetorical career of the young Cicero.[3] The defendant in the case was a property owner from the town of Ameria who had been falsely accused of the murder of his father. This sensational charge would in itself have attracted a great deal of public attention to the trial, but vastly increasing its notoriety was the fact that this was the first capital case heard before a jury for some years. Sulla, who had seized power following his victory in the civil wars, was attempting in 80 B.C. to return the state to a constitutional system after several years of government by terror and intimidation. The trial was no doubt intended as a showcase of the new order, in which strict legal procedure resulting in severe punishments would replace the violence and anarchy of the recent past. Sulla had not yet, however, allowed the reins of power to slip from his hands; at the time of the trial he held the offices of both dictator and consul. How he intended to use the power of these offices remained to be tested. Cicero's difficulties in planning a defense for Roscius were heightened by the fact that behind the charge, nominally lodged by the professional prosecutor Erucius, stood two of Roscius's fellow townsmen and a freedman of Sulla himself, Lucius Cornelius Chrysogonus.

After an introduction establishing the great difficulties against which he contended (1–14) and a narration revealing the plot against his client that had been set in motion by the latter's enemies (15–29), Cicero begins the argument of the speech (35–142) by dividing his case into three parts: first, the charge brought by Erucius; second, the "boldness" of the attack on Sextus Roscius mounted by T. Roscius Magnus and T. Roscius Capito (henceforth, Magnus and Capito); and, third, the political power of Chrysogonus, on which the success of the plot depended. Cicero then proceeds to take up each of these topics, beginning with a defense of his client on the charge itself. At the outset of this defense he declares that it is incumbent upon a prosecutor who would prove a man guilty of parricide to show that the accused possessed the abandoned habits and depraved character that alone could make so heinous and astounding a crime credible. Cicero calls the potential parricide a man of "unparalleled boldness, . . . savage character, a fierce disposition, and

3. For rhetorical and structural analyses of the speech see Solmsen, "Cicero's First Speeches"; della Morte, *Studi;* Stroh, *Taxis und Taktik,* 55–79 (with bibliography, 309). For the role of the speech in Cicero's political career, see Mitchell, *Cicero,* 52–92. For Cicero's later pride in the speech: *Off.* 2.51.

a life completely given over to vice and crime"(38). Was his client a bold cutthroat, accustomed to committing murder? he asks. Was he a debauched pleasure seeker, overwhelmed by debt? Hardly. In fact, says Cicero, his client owed no one money, and, so far from being a pleasure seeker, he scarcely ever went out to dinner parties, as the prosecutor himself had admitted. At this point Cicero sounds the theme that will dominate the following sections of the argument: "How could unbridled desires (*cupiditates*) exist in someone who was always in the country, occupied with the cultivation of his land?" (39). They could not, he declares, since rustic life "is especially separated from desires and joined to dutifulness" (39: *quae vita maxime disiuncta a cupiditate et cum officio coniuncta est*).

Here, in both his rebuttal to Erucius's attack and his arguments for Roscius's innocence, Cicero makes use of the *probabile ex vita* argument.[4] On the one hand, he calls on Erucius to demonstrate that Roscius was the kind of person capable of parricide, while, on the other, he proclaims that he will show that Roscius's background, moral character, and habits of life made his guilt impossible. Ironically, it appears that the specific tack Cicero pursued here had been furnished in part by the prosecutor himself. The latter had claimed that Roscius had murdered his father because the older man had intended to disinherit his son; and, in attempting to fabricate both a motive for this intended change in the elder Roscius's will and proof of the father's dislike for the son, Erucius had apparently spoken several times of the accused as "savage and boorish" (cf. 39, 42, 74: *ferum atque agrestem*) and had pointed out to the audience that the father had "relegated" (44: *relegatio atque amandatio*) his son to the family estates in Ameria rather than allowing the son to live with him at Rome. As will be seen, these ill-conceived remarks by the prosecutor provided Cicero with a golden opportunity. By agreeing to the prosecutor's characterization of Roscius as a rustic he could convince his audience that his client was incapable of committing the crime with which he was charged.

As if Roman farmers as a class had been attacked by Erucius, Cicero turns his defense of Roscius into an extended and spirited defense of the value of rural life itself. He begins by reminding his listeners of the sentiments of *patres familias*, especially men "of [Roscius's] class from the

---

4. See Cic. *Inv.* 2.32–37; *Her.* 2.5. For the importance of this aspect of persuasion in Roman oratory as practiced, in contrast both to rhetorical theory and to ancient Greek practice, see Stroh, *Taxis und Taktik,* 251–55.

country towns" (43: *illius ordinis ex municipiis rusticanis*). These men, according to the orator, were eager for their sons to supervise their estates, just as Roscius had done for his father. Far from being a punishment, says Cicero, such an action demonstrated a father's respect and affection for his son (44). There is, no doubt, a thinly veiled note of condescension in Cicero's description of these old-fashioned farmers, whose lives would have had little connection with the urban preoccupations of most of the audience. It should be remembered, however, that the senators on the jury were tied to such men as friends and clients; they stayed in their houses when traveling through the countryside and expected their votes when important issues were being decided at Rome. Indeed, the jury Cicero addressed was composed of a landed elite who in many cases could trace their roots to this same municipal nobility. That they were enrolled in rural rather than urban tribes was not simply an example of ancient gerrymandering; it expressed the fact that the roots of the Roman senatorial class were planted in the country, not the city. Although such men surely disdained the actual work of the farm and had their estates managed by slave overseers, they nevertheless clung tenaciously to the image of themselves as country gentlemen. They would therefore have been reluctant to appear to condemn the supposed sentiments of these municipal landowners.[5] The section ends with Cicero's assertion that by showing disdain for rural life Erucius had spoken against "the natural order of things, the normal habits of individuals, and the commonly held beliefs of men" (45).

The following section of the speech develops this contention, for Cicero states that because it had been Erucius's lot to be of uncertain parentage, he could hardly know how fathers felt and behaved towards their children (46). The orator suggests that a man like the prosecutor had to learn such facts from literature rather than from experience. He then refers to a play of Caecilius in which, like the elder Roscius, a father kept one son, Eutychus, in the country and one, Chaerestratus, in the city. The orator asks his audience if they believed that this fictional father valued his country son any less than he did his city son. Although the particular play Cicero cites is no longer extant, his reference to it leads to the surmise that in the play (in contrast to the reversal of expectations of behavior that characterizes a play like Terence's *Adelphi*) the

5. For the prestige of land ownership in the late Republic, see Heitland, *Agricola*, 154–55, 157; White, *Roman Farming*, 11–12, 50–52, 335–36; Cossarini, "Il prestigio dell' agricoltura in Sallustio e Cicerone."

stereotypically virtuous actions of a country son were played out against the mischievous conduct of a city son.[6]

By alluding to this play, ostensibly in order to support his defense of rural life, Cicero hoped to encourage his audience to see Roscius as possessing the traits of a "typical rustic" like Eutychus.[7] It should be remembered, however, that the "typical rustic" of drama does not appear in only one guise. Rather, two contrasting types appear. The old rustic is a distinctly disagreeable character, a descendant of such figures in Greek Old Comedy as Strepsiades, the crude and irritable countryman of Aristophanes' *Clouds*.[8] The type is also illustrated by Menander's Knemon, the antisocial farmer of the *Dyskolos*. Perhaps most familiar is the hard-bitten Demea of Terence's *Adelphi*. Here, this cynical old farmer describes himself to his urbane brother as "rustic, harsh, gloomy, stern and tenacious" (*Ad.* 866: *agresti', saevo', tristi', parcu', truculentus, tenax*), and he specifically attributes these traits to the hard life he has endured on the farm. No doubt this was the sort of persona Erucius wished the jury to ascribe to the defendant. He would have encouraged them to think of Roscius as a man like the gloomy and unsympathetic old boors of drama whose downfall at the end of a play excited laughter rather than pity.

The young rustic of ancient comedy shared a number of traits with his older counterpart, for they both were depicted as unsophisticated, conspicuously out of place and ill at ease in the city, and completely

6. The play here referred to is the *Hypobolimaeus* of Caecilius Statius. Warmington, in the Loeb Classical Library edition of the *Remains of Old Latin* (Cambridge, Mass., 1935), 1:494–501, believes that Cicero has interchanged the names of the two characters, but there is no strong evidence for this, and although Cicero sometimes feigns doubt or ignorance in literary matters, he does not give misinformation. Caecilius's model seems to have been the *Hybolimaios ē Agroikos* of Menander (Edmonds, *Fragments*, vol. 3B.740–47, frags. 481–96). The extant fragments are insufficient to reconstruct the plot of the play, but see the suggestions of Webster, *Menander*, 100–101.

7. A summary of stereotypical rustic traits appears in Bléry, *Rusticité et urbanité*, 4–38. For positive descriptions, see Kier, *De laudibus vitae rusticae*.

8. The theme was a popular one, as there is evidence for plays entitled *Agroikos* (or *Geōrgos*) from Old, Middle, and New Comedy: e.g., Old: Aristophanes (*Geōrgoi*); Middle: Anaxilas, Antiphanes, Augeas (*Agroikos*), Anaxandrides (*Agroikoi*), Timocles (*Geōrgos*); New: Menander (*Geōrgos*), Philemon (*Agroikos*). See Edmonds, *Fragments*, indices (1: 1004–12, Old Comedy; 2: 652–67, Middle Comedy; 3B: 1217–26, New Comedy). A good analysis of Knemon's character is found in Ramage, "City and Country."

unequipped to deal with the complexities of the urban milieu.[9] In other ways, however, the young rustic (no doubt distinguished from the old rustic by hair color and mask) is quite a different creature.[10] Gorgias, the young farmer in Menander's *Dyskolos,* may be taken as the typical young rustic. He is straightforward, hardworking, slow to anger, and displays intelligence in country matters. By comparing Roscius to Eutychus, the young rustic in Caecilius's play, Cicero encouraged his audience to identify him with such attractive and sympathetic characters. The orator is much aided in this attempt by the fact that the case revolved around Roscius's relationship with his father. The audience was therefore inclined to picture Roscius, like Eutychus, in the role of the country son.

Cicero does not restrict the development of this image of his client to this part of the speech alone. Throughout the oration the audience is frequently encouraged to see the defendant as a typical *rusticus bonus.* For instance, the orator states that Roscius was completely devoted to agricultural pursuits and that he was, in fact, quite clever within his own metier (49). This preoccupation with the affairs of the farm was, of course, an important part of the character of the *rusticus,* as was the intelligence he demonstrated in rural matters. Cicero not only refers to Roscius's wit within his own milieu; he vividly describes his client's utter helplessness when he is driven from the farm to the city (cf. 27, 88). This kind of incompetence in urban affairs is yet another feature of the typical rustic. Perhaps most important in establishing Roscius's rustic character—and in distinguishing it from the unattractive traits associated with the old rustic—is the manner in which Cicero describes his client's reaction to the wrongs done him by his enemies. According to Cicero,

---

9. Consider, for example, Menander's *geōrgos* (Edmonds, *Fragments,* vol. 3B.588–89, frag. 97), who says that he is a rustic "and not really experienced in city matters"; also Plaut. *Pers.* 169; Theophr. *Char.* 4; Ter. *Ad.* 544–47; Cic. *Red. sen.* 13–14; Quint. 12.10.53.

10. Pollux (*Onom.* 4.143–54) lists forty-four masks, including old men, young men, and an *agroikos;* Varro says that in the *Hypobolimaeus* of Caecilius a young man wears a leather-skin coat, while in a play of Terence an old man wears this rustic garb (*RR* 2.11.11). Since the hair color of the masked figure indicated whether he was young or old, we may conclude that the Roman audience of Cicero's time could readily identify the *senex rusticus* and the *adulescens rusticus* from the visual clues provided by mask and costume. On masks see Duckworth, *Roman Comedy,* 88–94; Beare, *Roman Stage,* 174–85, 293–99 (App. I); Webster, *Menander,* 191–92, 223–24.

the ignorant and innocent Roscius harbored no ill will or anger at the shocking treatment he had received, and he accepted the loss of his property and the destruction of his father's good name without protest. He asked only to be acquitted of parricide so that he might leave the court alive (128, 143–44). This extreme humility forms part of the positive stereotype of the young rustic, illustrated by such common phrases as *pudor subrusticus* and *modestia rustica*.[11] It is distinctly uncharacteristic, however, of the old rustic, whose chief trait is his fierce temper, instantly roused by an injury, whether imagined or real.

In the final section devoted to this *probabile ex vita* argument Cicero turns from drama to the Roman past. He summons up the image of the heroes of Roman history who had worked their own land, recalling the example of men such as Atilius, who had left the plow to lead the legions to victory. It was such individuals, he states, who had transformed the small and struggling Roman state into a great power (50). The orator then declares that since the greatest men in Rome had once dedicated themselves to cultivating their fields, surely Roscius might be forgiven for admitting that he too was a *rusticus* (51). Although Cicero here claims that the facts of Roscius's life were not to be compared with the deeds of such men, this is exactly what he has done. The early Roman state was a small agricultural community, and few cultures have guarded the memory of their simple beginnings as fiercely as did Rome. The man of Cicero's day who lived in the country and devoted himself to farming could therefore be depicted in the most positive terms. Cicero could claim that Roscius the farmer was a man of old-fashioned probity, formed—as Cato the Elder had said he was formed—by the thrift, hardship, and hard work of rural life.[12]

Following this part of the speech, Cicero reveals the paucity of argument and the absolute lack of evidence supporting the accusation

11. The phrase *pudor subrusticus* is found in Cic. *Fam.* 5.12.1; *modestia rustica* in Sen. *Cons. ad Helv.* 19.2. See also Bléry, *Rusticité et urbanité*, 27–29; Kier, *De laudibus vitae rusticae*, 75–82.

12. For C. Atilius Regulus Serranus, probably the consul of 257 B.C., see Cic. *Sest.* 72; Val. Max. 4.4.5; Pliny *HN* 18.20; Serv. ad *Aen.* 6.844. Roman legend included numerous stories of farmer-heroes: e.g., L. Quinctius Cincinnatus (Livy 3.26; Cic. *Sen.* 56); C. Fabricius Luscinus (Dion. Hal. 19.13.1–18.8); Manius Curius Dentatus (Cic. *Sen.* 55–56); M. Atilius Regulus (*De vir. ill.* 40). Cato is quoted by Festus (s.v. "*repastinari*"), 350 L. Cf. Plut. *Cat. Mai.* On the hardship and virtue of rustic life, see also Plaut. *Vid.* 31; *Merc.* 61–72; Ter. *Ad.* 45–46. Cf. Cic. *Sen.* 51–60; *Planc.* 22.

against his client. But before turning to the second of the three topics into which he had divided his case—that is, the plot against his client hatched by Magnus and Capito—Cicero makes a general statement concerning the arguments he has marshaled to support the defense of Roscius on the basis of *probabile ex vita*. According to the orator the strongest proof of Roscius's innocence was that "in rustic manners, in a frugal environment, in this rough and uncultivated way of life (75: *in rusticis moribus, in victu arido, in hac horrida incultaque vita*), crimes of this sort do not usually occur. Just as one cannot find every kind of plant or tree in every soil, so every kind of crime is not produced in every way of life." It is the city, he asserts, that creates excess (*luxuries*); and excess, in turn, produces greed (*avaritia*). From greed springs "boldness" (*audacia*) and, finally, all crimes and wrongdoings (75). The rustic life, which the prosecutor had termed "boorish" (74: *agrestem*), is in Cicero's view the teacher of "thrift, diligence, and justice" (75: *parsimoniae diligentiae iustitiae*).

Here we find an explicit connection of *ēthos* and *locus*, expressed through the assertion of the kind of geographical and social determinism familiar from the ethnographical treatises of the day. According to Cicero, the nature of a place determined the daily occupations of its inhabitants, and this variety of daily occupations, in turn, determined the virtues and vices to be found there. The range of vices of those who lived in the country is claimed to be more limited than that of city dwellers, and the reason for this, according to Cicero, lies in the availability in the city of nonessential goods and services (*luxuries*). The existence of such things leads to material desires (*avaritia*) that can grow so unbridled as to yield to none of the traditional constraints on behavior (*audacia*).

This attack on contemporary urban luxury and materialism as the source of vice was, of course, a commonplace, as was the assumption that the simple life of the small farmer represented an ideal. These ideas were prevalent in Cicero's day and appeared in works of various genres. For instance, both Stoic and Epicurean philosophers of the late Republic wrote that unrestrained desires led to the corruption of the individual and the destruction of the possibility of personal happiness, and they looked back to an earlier era as a model for a better life.[13] Roman his-

---

13. For the Epicurean idea of excessive desire as a disease of the mind, see, for example, Cic. *Fin.* 1.59 (*Animi autem morbi sunt cupiditates immensae et inanes divitiarum, gloriae, dominationis, libidinosarum etiam voluptatum*). For

torians of the period pointed to the flow of luxury goods into Rome following its foreign conquests as the reason for the destruction of the morally upright city of the *maiores* and for its subsequent corruption.[14] And Augustan poets would, in the coming years, rework the old Hesiodic theme of a simple agricultural Golden Age destroyed by greed and materialism.[15]

This section of the *Pro Roscio* serves as a bridge to the attack on the two Roscii, for Cicero will claim that the sordid manner in which Capito, Magnus, and Chrysogonus live makes their participation in the crime not only believable but inevitable, and he goes on to prove his accusations by attributing to the three the urban vices of which he has just absolved Roscius. The picture of Chrysogonus, for instance, focuses primarily on his *luxuries*. In the orator's first mention of him he says that Chrysogonus hoped to squander *per luxuriam* what he had obtained through crime (6). According to the scholiast, in the lacuna in the speech Cicero also made much of Chrysogonus's extravagance, describing his many amusements and possessions. This section is followed by an extended account of the excess that marks every aspect of Chrysogonus's life (133–35): his houses are numerous and opulently furnished; in addition to Delian and Corinthian vases he has quantities of silver, tapestries, paintings, and statues (133); he is accustomed to holding lavish banquets served by troops of effete slaves (134); and he is often seen "flitting about" (*volitet*) the Forum with a crowd of retainers (135).

The persona assigned to Chrysogonus thus forms an antithesis to that of Roscius, for the freedman's vices are the mirror image of Roscius's virtues: Roscius never goes to dinner parties (39, 52), while Chrysogonus is known for his lavish feasts; Roscius has not even one servant left to him (77, 145), while Chrysogonus has slaves to satisfy his every conceivable desire (134). Because of his lack of experience with the Forum and the courts, Roscius shrinks from the benches of the tribunal and from the city itself (88). The Greek freedman, on the other hand, is

Stoic condemnation of all *perturbationes animorum,* see *Fin.* 3.35; Long, *Hellenistic Philosophy,* 175–78, 206–7, 219–20.

14. Hampl, "Römische Politik"; Gruen, *Hellenistic World,* 1:274–78; Pöschl, "Die römische Auffasung der Geschichte."

15. E.g., Verg. *G.* 2.136–76; Prop. 3.22.17–42; Hor. *Carm.* 1.3.9–40; *Epod.* 16.63–66.

completely at home in Rome: he descends from his fine house on the Palatine into the Forum, where, surrounded by an entourage of Roman citizens, he flaunts his contempt for all (133–35). Roscius is a man devoted to the thrift and hard work of the country; Chrysogonus, to the luxury and excess of the city.

Capito and Magnus are depicted as villains of a similar sort. Having branded Chrysogonus with the vice of *luxuries,* Cicero constantly applies to these two the other vices to which the city gives rise, *avaritia* and *audacia.*[16] While the terms recur often in Cicero's attacks on his opponents in other speeches, the frequency of their use here is striking. As we have noted, after the *partitio* (29–34) he had spoken of the obstacles he had to overcome, dividing them into three. Capito and Magnus, he declares, have claimed for themselves the part of "boldness" (*audacia*). In the course of the argument (35–142), Cicero calls both men audacious and greedy several times. He asks the jury to consider who would be a more likely perpetrator of murder than Magnus, a man both "greedy" and "bold" (86: *avarus, audax*). He had proved his greed (87: *avaritiam*) by making a plot with a stranger against a fellow townsman and kinsman; his boldness (87: *audax*) was shown by the fact that he alone of the conspirators was unashamed to appear in court to support the false charge against Roscius. Cicero goes on to call Magnus a man "burning with greed" and "the boldest of brokers" (88). Capito shares these traits. According to Cicero, the reason that the crimes of the two have so easily been discovered is that they have been rendered blind to the transparency of their misdeeds by "desire, greed, and boldness" (101: *cupiditas et avaritia et audacia*). A little later Cicero tells the jury that in order to find the murderer of the elder Roscius they must simply look for examples of greed, boldness, depravity, and treachery (118). This will inevitably lead them to Magnus and Capito, who "are equal in greed, similar in their dishonesty, with the same shamelessness and boldness" (118: *par est avaritia, similis improbitas, eadem impudentia, gemina audacia*).

As was the case with Chrysogonus, the traits of Capito and Magnus are directly contrasted with Roscius's virtues. For instance, in section 88, each of the characteristics of Magnus is set against one of those attributed to Roscius in order to show which of the two would be a

---

16. For the contrast between the political and the nonpolitical use of the concept of *audacia,* see Wirszubski, "*Audaces.*" Cicero mentions that the term is a commonplace of abuse in the courts (*Phil.* 14.7).

more likely suspect in the murder. Magnus's present wealth is contrasted with Roscius's poverty; his greed, which had led him to attack a kinsman, is set against the description of Roscius as a man who knows only that profit that is the result of hard work (88: *semper ita vixerit ut quaestum nosset nullum, fructum autem eum solum quem labore peperisset*). The rural industriousness earlier ascribed to Roscius is here presented, therefore, as an antithesis to the *avaritia* of his enemy. Similarly, the *audacia* of the two is set against the humility of Sextus Roscius. As has been pointed out, Cicero claims that Roscius desires neither revenge nor the return of his property but only wishes to be acquitted of the charge against him. He thinks nothing that has happened to him is cause for indignation (143: *nihil indignum*); he accuses no one and does not seek his patrimony (128, 144); as a man of little experience, "a farmer and a rustic" (143: *agricola et rusticus*), he accepts without question all that has occurred under the laws and edicts of Sulla. Roscius's humility, then, appears to be a specifically rural trait, a natural concomitant of his identity as *agricola et rusticus*, just as the *audacia* of Magnus and Capito has been defined as an urban vice.

Cicero characterizes Magnus and Capito in yet another way as urban scoundrels whose traits are the opposite of those of his client. Both are called "brokers" (*sectores*). Magnus is *sectorum audacissimus* (88); Capito is *et sector . . . et sicarius* (103). Whether the term is taken in its technical sense to signify a broker of publicly seized property or, in a more general and metaphorical sense, to mean a cutthroat, it is an occupation specifically contrasted with Roscius's lack of urban experience. Cicero asks the jury to consider who would be a more likely murderer, "a man who is the boldest of brokers or one who, because of his lack of acquaintance with the Forum and the law courts, shrinks not only from these benches but from the city itself" (88). By implication, then, a *sector* is a man of experience in the city, a frequenter of the Forum, and a man who could easily take advantage of the rural naiveté of one such as Roscius.[17]

17. In other speeches of Cicero it can be observed that his urban scoundrels operate on a variety of levels of wealth and power, although they all share a lower-class morality. At the bottom level they are the auctioneers, cutthroats, and petty criminals who, like Naevius in the *Pro Quinctio*, frequent the "entrance to the market" (25) or, like Aebutius in the *Pro Caecina*, hang around the Regia (14) or, like the thugs referred to in the *Divinatio in Caecilium*, can be found near the Maenian column (50). These are men ready to broker stolen goods, bear false witness at a trial, or even contract to have a murder done. At a

IMAGE AND REALITY

In the *Pro Roscio* Cicero has presented his audience with a series of stark contrasts between the moral characters of those involved in the trial and has connected these mores with either the country or the city. It is natural to ask what relationship this picture bore to reality. The degree of idealization of country life in general can be gathered by comparing the *Pro Roscio* with the *Pro Cluentio,* a speech in which the country serves as a realistic setting rather than as a generic ideal. We have seen that in the earlier oration Cicero had pictured rural life as the teacher of simple virtue (75). Both Roscius and the local officials of Ameria were depicted as admirable men of the old school, and Cicero's recital of the attempts of the latter to right the wrongs done Roscius showed them to be, like the accused himself, virtuous men, albeit somewhat ineffectual and naive. Lumped together with these small townsmen as models of old-fashioned probity were the landholders of Umbria and the farmers from the old municipal towns. In the *Pro Cluentio,* however, we discover that the locals of a similar municipality, Larinum, are adept in practicing the entire range of human vices. Cicero speaks of multiple marriages motivated by hopes of large inheritances, of widespread use of poison, of attempted and actual murders undertaken out of greed or lust, and of rampant adultery, theft, fraud, and cruelty. In this speech the audience hears nothing of the nature of "the country" as a habitation, and nowhere is mention made of the common virtues of farmers or the shared excellences of the nobles of the "old municipal towns." It appears that in this speech we are closer to the pastoral environment portrayed by a Henry Fielding than the idyllic retreat painted in the *Pro Roscio.* Here, the country is a place where shepherds commit assault and battery (161), travelers are accused of beating up innkeepers (163), and the local estate holders are busy dispatching one another as

---

more elevated level are those like Chrysogonus who have risen to positions of power but remain creatures without breeding or scruple. Men such as Erucius, the professional prosecutor of the *Pro Roscio,* form an intermediate level. Cicero depicts such individuals as men of intelligence, cunning, and—in the case of Erucius—even of some education. They are not, however, "gentlemen" (*boni viri*), as their actions and words demonstrate. Finally, the city produces another class of villain, the sophisticated young men of good family and bad morals. The type is most familiar from the *Catilinarians,* where effete young men with long togas and pomaded hair are identified by Cicero as dangerous traitors residing within the body politic.

well as members of their own families. Although fourteen years separate
the two speeches, the radical disparity between the two pictures of the
Italian countryside owes more to the speeches' differing rhetorical strategies than to the moral degeneration that occurred during the interven-
ing decade and a half.

What, then, might have been the actual characters of the individuals
pictured in the *Pro Roscio?* While the answer to this question must remain speculative, a number of facts point to a difference between the
personae drawn by Cicero and the real situation. For instance, it seems
improbable that Roscius was actually the simple farmer Cicero makes
of him. In the first place, he and his father enjoyed close connections
with members of the Roman nobility.[18] At the beginning of the speech,
Cicero explains why he is speaking for the accused in spite of the fact
that his client is supported by "so many illustrious orators and aristocratic individuals" (1). The elder Roscius enjoyed not just *hospitium* but
even *domesticus usus* et *consuetudo* with the Metelli, the Servilii, and
the Scipiones (15). This is hardly surprising, since he was extremely rich
(6), an enthusiastic supporter of the cause of the *optimates* (16), and
an active participant in urban social life (52). One scholar has, in
fact, called the men who supported Roscius at his trial "die Regierung
Sullas selbst," the inner circle of the *optimates'* power.[19] Such connections call into question the picture of the younger Roscius as a simple
rustic.

The defendant was a landholder of Ameria, but this hardly proves his
lack of sophistication. Cicero states that Mallius Glaucia had, on the
night of the murder, been able to traverse the fifty-six Roman miles from
Rome to Ameria in ten hours (19), a feat made possible by the strategic
position of the town on the Via Amerina, an offshoot from the Via Cassia.[20] Although his principal holdings were at Ameria, the elder Roscius
was constantly at Rome with his second son, and he probably made the
short trip between the two places often. Ameria itself was an extremely
old foundation. Pliny states that Cato had dated its founding 963 years

18. See Afzelius, "Zwei Episoden," 214. Gruen, *Roman Politics,* 266, lists
the following as supporters of Roscius: Caecilia, daughter of Q. Caecilius Metellus Balearicus (cos. 123); Q. Metellus Celer (cos. 60) or Q. Metellus Nepos
(cos. 57); Q. Caecilius Metellus Scipio Nasica (cos. 52); M. Valerius Messala
Rufus (cos. 53) or M. Valerius Messala Niger (cos. 61).

19. Afzelius, "Zwei Episoden," 214.

20. Hülsen, "Ameria"; Pietrangeli and Ciotti, "Ameria"; Richardson,
"Ameria."

before the war with Perseus (that is, approximately 1134 B.C.).[21] At the time of the speech Ameria was a *municipium* enrolled in the aristocratic Clustumina tribe, which was also the tribe of Pompey.[22] Near a town itself strategically located on a high plain overlooking the Tiber, the estates of Roscius constituted the most important holdings in the district. The elder Roscius, according to Cicero, owned "thirteen estates, almost all of which touched the Tiber" (20). The orator also states that the younger Roscius did not simply live on the property but was the manager of this large group of holdings (44). It is hardly credible that the man who controlled the most important property in a strategic Roman *municipium* only one day's journey from the city and who enjoyed close ties to the most powerful families in Rome could be the simple rustic Cicero describes. We might note as well that the speech fosters the impression that Roscius, like Caecilius's Eutychus, was but a youth. It is with a start that we remember that Roscius was, in fact, a middle-aged man of more than forty (39).

There are also indications of a gap between the impression Cicero gives and reality in the case of Roscius's enemies. Chrysogonus may have been the depraved voluptuary Cicero describes, but at least the extent of his power can be called into question. Cicero calls him "perhaps the most powerful young man in the state at this time" (6). Yet only Cicero mentions him as such. No ancient historian attributes any significant undertaking to him. His *potentia* has probably been as much exaggerated as Roscius's has been underplayed. As for Magnus and Capito, one fact alone stands out: they, like Sextus Roscius, are Amerians. It is difficult to believe in both the rustic virtue of the defendant on the basis of his position as municipal landholder and the urban depravity of his opponents, who seem likewise to have been small-town landholders.

Cicero wrote many years later that this, his first oration delivered in a criminal case, had been a resounding success. Roscius was acquitted, and the young orator was the recipient of much favorable comment and many requests for his services (*Brut.* 312). That the personae created by Cicero seem to us fairly transparent after a careful reading of the speech should not cause us to be surprised at its success. Reading a speech is an experience quite different from attending the performance of an orator, and techniques that would fail to convince a thoughtful reader become

21. *HN* 3.114.
22. See Taylor, *Voting Districts*, 36–37, 83–84, 244–47, 271.

persuasive at the dramatic moment of delivery. The emotional impact of the *Pro Roscio* must have owed much to the voice and gestures of the orator and to the sight during the trial of the defendant, dressed in mourning and accompanied by his weeping wife and children.

The persuasive power of the speech, however, rested chiefly on Cicero's success in leading his audience to see the participants in the trial both as believable individuals and as stock types. The picture of Roscius is a subtle combination of the real and the fictional: vivid descriptions of events in Roscius's recent life, such as his flight to Rome and appeal to the noble Caecilia, are colored in the listeners' imaginations by similar scenes they have witnessed on the stage and of which they have been reminded by Cicero's allusions to Caecilius; appeals to the audience to consider the sentiments of "fathers of families . . . from the rustic townships" (43), men "from Umbria and from the old municipalities" (48), or the orator's own "fellow tribesmen and neighbors" (47) are interwoven with romantic images from Rome's past, called up by the mention of the *maiores* and the heroic Atilius. Cicero thus leads his audience to respond to Roscius both as an individual victim of particular circumstances of contemporary life and the pitiable *rusticus* subjected to the worst of fates: now destitute, he is attacked by men of wealth; innocent of the city, he must face the complexities of the Forum; schooled in rustic virtue, he is now victim of an urban villainy against which he has no defense.

In like manner, Cicero draws the negative traits of the "urban scoundrels" Chrysogonus, Capito, and Magnus in stereotypical terms but is careful to include references to contemporary reality. As a class these city types are all as clever and glib as their country cousins are naive and inarticulate, and they are as dedicated to luxury as simple farmers are to thrift. But in addition to creating this sort of general portrait Cicero adds the distinctive coloring that would allow his audience to summon to mind images from their own recent experience. Whatever Chrysogonus may have been in reality, in the trial Cicero successfully cast him as one of the foreign freedmen whose cleverness and unscrupulousness had allowed them to prosper during the aftermath of the civil war while freeborn Roman landowners lost home and property. Capito and Magnus likewise are identified as part of the army of cutthroats, war profiteers, and real estate brokers who had by this time become familiar and despised characters within the city.

A brief look at the employment of this same stereotype in another of Cicero's speeches points up the effectiveness of this technique. From various sources—including the remarks in Greek and Roman rhetorical treatises on *ēthos,* and the surviving training exercises of rhetoric (called *progymnastica*)—we can be sure that commonplaces concerning the character of the rural environment and regarding the traits of the inhabitants of that environment had long been part of the education of the orator.[23] While the *Pro Roscio* represents the most extensive use of the positive side of the topos, its outlines may be detected in a number of other orations, including the *Pro Quinctio,* Cicero's first extant speech.[24] Here he clearly wished his audience to see his client as a blameless man from the country and had assigned to Quinctius various stereotypically rustic characteristics, employing the familiar diction of the topos in doing so. For instance, Quinctius is said to live *inculte* and *horride;* his nature is called *tristis* and *recondita;* he is unacquainted with urban mores; and he is devoted to *parsimonia* and *officium* (59). At the end of the speech Cicero emphasizes Quinctius's *rusticana . . . atque inculta parsimonia* (92) and his devotion to duty, loyalty, and hard work (92–94). Further, there is again a suggestion that here, as in the *Pro Roscio,* the traits of the defendant are set in opposition to those of his urban enemy, Naevius, for Naevius is characterized as a wastrel and sharpster (11: *scurra*) who hangs around the public auction halls

23. See remarks by Ussher, *Theophrastus,* 9–10; Lausberg, *Handbuch,* 1:205 (§376.11: concerning arguments *a persona*); Quint. 1.9.3; 5.10.23–31; 6.2.17; 9.3.99. In discussing the practice theses often used in schools, Quintilian (2.4.24) gives the example of a debate over the relative merits of life in the city and life in the country. Theophrastus's sketch of the *agroikos* suggests that Greek rhetoric emphasized the negative traits of the typical rustic—boorishness, lack of cultivation, stupidity—rather than the positive ones. For discussion of rhetorical *ēthos,* see May, *Trials of Character,* 1–12. For development of ethical appeal in the *Pro Roscio,* see May, 12–31 (whose conclusions for the most part are in agreement with my own).

24. At a certain point in the *De lege agraria* 2, for instance, which is an extremely complex speech in terms of Cicero's presentation of the *ēthos* of those who inhabit Capua and the rich lands of Campania, the orator is intent on depicting the Campanians in a positive light. He therefore sees them not as a people whose characters have been formed by the special nature of this particular region, but simply as farmers who share the positive ethical characteristics of all farmers. They are "the finest and most unassuming" (84: *optima et modestissima*) of men, the kind who possess moral characters that make them the best of farmers and soldiers (84). See also *Planc.* 22: *Tractus ille celeberrimus Venafranus, Allifanus, tota denique ea nostra ita aspera et montuosa et fidelis et simplex et fautrix suorum regio se huius honore ornari, se augeri dignitate arbitrabatur.*

(12; 25: *atria Licinia*).[25] It is noteworthy that in the earlier speech there is nothing to suggest that the characterization of Quinctius is anything more than the application of a Greek rhetorical topos to a client who happens to be involved with rural pursuits; in the later speech, however, Cicero has made considerable efforts to Romanize the topos. His appeals to the audience to consider aspects of their own experience in judging the rural environment—the sentiments of landowners in Italian towns, the characters seen on Roman stages, and, most important, the heroes of Roman history and legend—constitute a much more sophisticated handling of the material.[26]

Cicero's success in the *Pro Roscio* was perhaps connected as well with the fact that the rural world depicted in the speech was, in large part, disappearing. The events that had taken place in Italy during the preceding two generations—including the decline in the number of free peasants, the conversion of large areas of productive land from small farms to grazing tracts, the constant increase in the use of slave labor, and the stunning growth of emigration to Rome—had worked revolutionary changes in the Italian countryside. By Cicero's day *Romanitas* was no longer implicitly connected with *rusticitas*. But this very fact contributed in no small measure to the attractiveness of the topos: its appeal was tied to the nostalgia felt by the Romans for a way of life commonly believed to have been the source of their military and moral superiority, a way of life that was now irretrievably lost.[27]

IN PRAISE OF THE CITY

THE STRATEGY OF THE *PRO CAELIO*

A close reading of the *Pro Caelio* makes plain that the prosecution in this case made use of much the same kind of topical material about old-

25. For the meaning of *scurra*, see Corbett, "Scurra"; Ramage, *Urbanitas*, 30–31. *Scurrae* are called *urbani assidui cives* by Plautus (*Trin.* 202).

26. Cf. Cic. *Verr.* II.2.7: *ea patientia virtus frugalitasque est ut proxime ad nostram disciplinam illam veterem, non ad hanc quae nunc increbruit.*

27. Even in the late first century B.C. it is estimated that three-quarters of the free population and half of the slave population were still rural. There had, however, been a marked decline in the numbers of the free peasantry and a huge growth in the population of the city of Rome. For a good general description of Roman society of the period written from a sociological perspective, see Wood, *Cicero's Thought*, 14–41.

fashioned virtue and contemporary urban vice that had served Cicero well in the *Pro Roscio Amerino.*[28] At the time of the trial M. Caelius Rufus was twenty-five years old, a sophisticated young man about town, familiar both with the legal skirmishes of the Forum and with the social moves of the smart set residing in the fashionable neighborhoods of the Palatine.[29] Just as Cicero had done in the *Pro Roscio,* Caelius's opponents had depended heavily on a *probabile ex vita* argument, supporting charges of sedition, assault, attempted murder, and murder by a demonstration of the immorality of Caelius's disreputable life in the city.[30] The seventeen-year-old prosecutor Atratinus, apparently with some embarrassment, accused the defendant of lewd behavior and used Caelius's support for Catiline in the consular elections for 62 B.C. to strengthen the charge. If such a strategy by the prosecution was successful, part of this success was owed to Cicero himself, who in the *Catilinarian* orations had created a vivid picture of the upper-class supporters of the conspiracy, in whom disloyalty to the Republic was wedded to moral corruption.

Atratinus's fellow prosecutors had evidently gone even farther in their attack on Caelius's morals. Cicero complains that the prosecution had droned on endlessly about "love affairs, adultery, . . . dinner parties, revelries, concerts," and the like (35). Herennius Balbus had used the supposedly decadent life of the defendant as a springboard from which to launch a passionate disquisition on the general corruption of

28. Recent studies of the speech include Classen, "Ciceros Rede für Caelius"; Stroh, *Taxis und Taktik,* 243–303 (with bibliography, 312–13); Wiseman, *Catullus,* 62–69; Gotoff, "Cicero's Analysis"; Craig, "Reason, Resonance, and Dilemma"; May, *Trials of Character,* 105–16; Ramage, "Strategy and Methods." A starting point in scholarly analysis of the speech has always been Heinze's "Ciceros Rede *Pro Caelio.*" While a number of its conclusions concerning the unity of the speech are now dated, Heinze's work contains powerful, and still valid, insights.

29. For a hypothetical reconstruction of Caelius's career and character based on the available evidence, see Wiseman, *Catullus,* 62–69; Austin, *Pro Caelio,* v–xvi.

30. Gotoff, "Cicero's Analysis," reminds us that we have only Cicero's description of what his opponents said, and this description is a crucial part of the orator's effort to persuade his audience of Caelius's innocence. As Gotoff and others (e.g., Leeman, Stroh, Classen) have affirmed, everything in a Ciceronian speech was "rhetorical"—that is, intended to serve the ultimate goal of persuasion.

the age and the immorality of contemporary youth.[31] This technique of "generalizing the case" was one of Cicero's own greatest strengths, and he remarks with tacit humor that if he too had only to inveigh against the wickedness of seduction, adultery, wantonness, and extravagance, daylight would surely fail him before he had finished (29). Although the topic of Balbus's diatribe was not specifically a comparison of the corruption of the city with the innocence of the country, this comparison is nevertheless implied by his subject matter. As noted above, since the Roman past was stereotypically viewed as a simple, rustic age, untainted by materialism or urban sophistication, any attack on the immorality of the present (30: *temporum vitia*) and praise for the virtue of the past carried with it implicit approval of the mores of the country and indictment of those of the city.

This leads us to consider what strategies were open to Cicero in responding to this aspect of the prosecution's attack. In the *Pro Roscio* he had defended a man who was "accused" of never going to dinner parties; now he was to speak on behalf of one who was guilty of "never refusing a dinner invitation" (27). Since his opponents had apparently praised the old-fashioned morality of bygone days and attacked the corruption of contemporary urban life, we might well expect Cicero to respond by exploiting the opposite side of the topos: that is, by ridiculing the outmoded standards of the rustic past and praising the more relaxed and sophisticated mores of contemporary Rome. As will be seen, this is a strategy that indeed appears at certain points in the *Pro Caelio*.

In the famous character impersonations (*prosopopoeiae*) of the central section of the work Cicero speaks in the voice of several personae who represent the strict morality of the past, and he carries off these impersonations in such a way as to lead his audience ultimately to reject the moral viewpoint represented by each as inappropriate to the present age. He first asks Clodia, on whose desire for revenge against her former lover he has claimed the prosecution depends, whether he should deal with her "gravely, harshly, and in the old-fashioned way" or "gently, mildly, and urbanely" (33: *severe et graviter et prisce . . . an remisse et leniter et urbane*). Choosing the former, he summons from the grave the

31. On what Balbus may have said, see Drexler,"Zu Ciceros Rede," 21; Reitzenstein, "Ciceros Rede für Caelius," 32; Austin, *Pro Caelio*, 78; Wiseman, *Catullus*, 73–74; and especially Gotoff, "Cicero's Analysis," 127–31, who provides us with a useful corrective to overambitious attempts to recreate the accuser's speech on the sole basis of Cicero's characterization of it.

austere persona of Appius Claudius Caecus, censor of 312 B.C., in order to rebuke Clodia. We learn from Quintilian that Cicero mimicked the sound and carriage of an irascible old man as he upbraided Clodia not simply for her scandalous public adventures but even for having had contact with any man other than her own relatives or those of her dead husband.[32] Raising the possibility that so forbidding a personage might turn his censure against Caelius as well, Cicero then dismisses the "harsh and almost boorish old man" (36: *senem durum ac paene agrestem*) and promises to deal more "urbanely" (36) with Clodia, whereupon he assumes the voice of her brother Clodius, who advises his sister against making a fuss over a lover who had kicked the traces.

In the second part of this series of dramatic personae Cicero addresses Caelius himself. Here, as in the first part, the orator alternates a strict with a lax moral viewpoint. The sentiments expressed by the "iron fathers" drawn from the plays of Caecilius are as rigid and unyielding as those put in the mouth of Claudius Caecus. As the latter had demanded to know how Clodia should have formed any connection with a man unrelated to her, so the Caecilian father demands to know why Caelius would not have fled from proximity to a woman of questionable virtue (37). And, just as the speech of Claudius Caecus was followed by one marked by a stark alteration in moral tone, so the "unendurable" fathers of Caecilius are here followed by the indulgent, city-dwelling father of Terence's *Adelphi,* who speaks in forgiving words (38).

The disagreeable personae created in these paired sections—Appius Claudius Caecus and the type of the rigid fathers of Roman comedy—are, at least obliquely, a means by which Cicero may question and even poke fun at the moral standards championed by the prosecutor. It is not surprising, therefore, that the section of the speech in which these stern patriarchs appear is immediately followed by one in which Cicero argues that the unbending moral standards of the rude past are inappropriate to the present and that indulgence ought especially to be granted to the behavior of the young (39–43). Despite his earlier assertion that he would refuse to seek refuge from the charges by pleading the excuse of Caelius's youth (30), this is exactly what he does. Here we find the orator claiming that the almost divine virtue of the heroes of the past was no longer to be found; that the Greeks, who at one time at least celebrated virtue in their writings if they could not practice it in their

---

32. Quint. 3.8.54; 12.10.61. See the discussion of *prosopopoeia* in Austin, *Pro Caelio,* 90–91.

lives, now taught that the wise did all for the sake of pleasure; that now-adays the individual who rejected all pleasures would be thought by most—if not by Cicero—to be cursed by the gods (42). The section ends with Cicero's plea to his listeners to "leave behind this road now deserted, neglected, and closed off by branches and brambles" (42). He asks them, instead, to grant a measure of freedom to youth and to observe a mean in pursuit both of pleasure and of virtue, neither allowing reason always to prevail nor allowing the desire for pleasure to recognize no limits.

There is much art in the way Cicero questions antique morality in these passages. We have only to remember the fate of Erucius in the *Pro Roscio* to realize that any sustained attack on the simple and strict mores of the past would have been a dangerous strategy. Cicero had prevailed in the earlier speech chiefly because he was able to convince the jury that the conviction of the innocent Roscius would have represented the acceptance of the violence and corruption of recent times, while Roscius's acquittal would be an affirmation of the simple Roman virtues of earlier days. It would have been shocking indeed if in the *Pro Caelio* Cicero seemed to be excusing the corruption of his own time and belittling the qualities that had made Rome great. Both his role of *pater patriae,* voted him by the Senate for his stern defense of the state during the Catilinarian crisis, and that of mentor to the young Caelius would have prevented him from pursuing such a strategy.[33]

Cicero, therefore, wishes to make it appear that the prosecution had championed not simply the higher ethical standard once common but a radical and uncompromising version of that standard, scarcely possible of attainment at any time. For this reason he has not summoned from the past figures like Scipio Aemilianus or Gaius Laelius to represent this ethical viewpoint—men who, according to tradition, balanced their devotion to their country with enjoyment of the pleasures of literature, philosophy, and friendship. Rather, he has called up the daunting figure of Appius Claudius Caecus, a model of rigidity even in his own day. The "almost boorish" (36) Claudius appears impossibly archaic, in the description both of his appearance and of his mores. And Cicero uses him to imply that only such a man—or a Camillus, a Fabricius, or a Curius—was capable of living the kind of life the prosecution demanded of Caelius. In like manner Cicero has carefully chosen as representatives of

33. Craig, "Reason, Resonance, and Dilemma," sees Cicero's use of the dilemma in this speech as another useful means of indirect attack.

this point of view the "iron fathers" (37) of comedy, those hard-bitten old rustic patriarchs who function in the plays as objects of ridicule rather than of respect. The orator goes on to equate this rigid moral standard with that held by those who practiced Stoic philosophy: both are said to have rejected all pleasures and devoted themselves solely to virtue. Cicero's tone throughout—humane, liberal-minded, experienced—is familiar from the *Pro Murena*, another speech in which he had used humor to disarm the moral seriousness of his opponent. In the earlier speech the orator's commonsensical approach to the challenge of living an honorable life in a naughty world had made an attractive alternative to the priggish and unrealistic Stoicism of Cato the Younger; similarly, in the *Pro Caelio*, Cicero labels this "ideal" life of unwavering seriousness and high moral purpose impossible of attainment for the majority of men.

Cicero faced another danger in questioning the moral standards of the past and arguing in favor of the more relaxed mores of the sophisticated present, one that can be readily understood by noting the way in which he was able to exploit an aspect of the prosecution's attack on Caelius. In seizing the moral high ground and excoriating Caelius for his immoral life-style, the prosecution had made themselves vulnerable to the counterattack by Cicero that the same arguments might be used to challenge the credibility of Clodia, whose life had likewise been a continuous round of "trips to Baiae, beach parties, dinner parties, revelries, concerts, musical entertainments, and boat parties" (35). And if Cicero was clever enough to understand that the sword that the prosecution wielded could cut both ways, he was also clever enough to understand that the arguments he might use in favor of a more lenient moral code of behavior could be used to excuse Clodia's actions as well those of Caelius. It should be kept in mind that Cicero's attempt to undermine Clodia's credibility in this speech was as important to its success as was his attack on Chrysogonus in the *Pro Roscio*. Both the foreign-born freedman and the emancipated widow were vulnerable targets; each would fill the role of bête noire, whose unmasking by Cicero would supposedly prevent the unjust conviction of an innocent victim. Cicero had, therefore, to couch his justification of Caelius in such a way as not to imply a justification of Clodia as well (and, conversely, to insure that accusations of Clodia's immorality could not also be used to blacken Caelius's name).

His escape from these difficulties is clever if not admirable. Since a straightforward attack on Clodia's morals might have led to uncomfortable questions about the consistency of Cicero's own ethical standards in defending Caelius's behavior, the orator executes the moral condemnation of Clodia for the most part through indirection, ridicule, and sarcasm.[34] As a result of Cicero's use of comic personification and his frequent recourse to double entendres, sly hints, and suggestive jokes, the jury is made to feel that they demonstrate their wide experience of the world and high degree of sophistication by recognizing Clodia as a *meretrix*, despite her wealth and nobility. In addition, Cicero is able to rely throughout the speech on a familiar double standard in arguing that Caelius's actions were innocuous, while Clodia's deserved condemnation. Since love affairs with prostitutes had traditionally been permitted to young men, but similar affairs were forbidden to women of any age, the orator is able to claim that Caelius's youthful indiscretions were within the bounds of acceptable behavior, even when judged by the strictest of standards, while at the same time suggesting that Clodia's actions cast her beyond the pale of polite society, even when these actions were viewed by the more relaxed standards of the present. The argument is both neat and cynical: Caelius's liaison with Clodia was morally excusable for the young man provided she was a *meretrix*, and she proved herself to be a *meretrix* by engaging in this and similar affairs.[35]

In the *Pro Caelio*, then, Cicero avoids falling into the trap of simply making use of a predictable response to the defense's exploitation of the theme of past virtue and contemporary vice. While he questions the moral standards of the past, he does so in large part indirectly—that is,

34. For the holiday atmosphere that made this kind of attack appropriate, see especially Geffcken, *Comedy in the Pro Caelio*, 1–8; May, *Trials of Character*, 115. For Clodia's vulnerability to attack, see Wiseman, *Catullus*, 52–53. For references to Clodia in connection with images of hiding and concealment, see Ramage, "Clodia," and "Strategy and Methods," 2–3, 6–8. Most scholars have not doubted the essential accuracy of Cicero's picture of Clodia; but see Dorey, "Cicero, Clodia and the *Pro Caelio*"; Skinner, "Clodia Metelli." I have argued elsewhere ("Personality and Power," 214) that one reason for Cicero's indirection in his attack on Clodia lay in his desire to avoid giving offense to powerful members of the Claudian *gens*. His efforts at diplomacy may be observed in his politic letters to Ap. Claudius Pulcher, Clodia's eldest brother (*Fam.* 3.1–13).

35. For further discussion of this strategy, see Stroh, *Taxis und Taktik*, 279–91. Classen, "Ciceros Rede für Caelius," 78–85, gives a particularly incisive account of how Cicero turns the attack on Caelius's morals against Clodia. The technical term for this strategy, also employed in the *Pro Roscio*, is *relatio criminis*.

by the comical and unattractive personae he chooses to represent these standards. In addition, he makes his audience understand that he rejects the mores of the past as a standard for the present only in their most unrealistic and rigid form, and goes on to argue that with the exception of such "semidivine" individuals as a Claudius Caecus Romans had always allowed young men to indulge in the innocuous pleasures of life.

AN IDEAL *PAIDEIA* OF THE CITY

The prosecution had made the urban life-style of the defendant a matter of reproach. Caelius's expensive apartment on the Palatine, his gay social life in the city, his trips to Baiae, were all part of the prosecution's picture of a young man who, like many of his day, had succumbed to the luxury and corruption of contemporary Rome. We hardly need look farther than Cicero's own denunciations of Chrysogonus or of Catiline's aristocratic young followers to reconstruct the line of the prosecution's attack. Cicero responds to this attack not only by questioning the antique and rigid moral standards championed by the prosecution but also by presenting his listeners with an alternate description of the city as ethical determinant. He uses the physical environment of the city and the training that could be secured within this setting to imply that—far from being simply a sink of corruption—only contemporary Rome could provide the conditions by which the state might produce for itself the best of men and the best of citizens.

The Urban Setting

The physical environment of the city figures in the *Pro Caelio* both as the actual setting of the speech and as the setting of many of the events described within the speech, and this environment is made to appear in a lurid and yet attractive light. In this most overtly dramatic of speeches, Cicero begins by asking the audience to see the trial as a performance carried on before the eyes of a visitor to Rome.[36] He asks them to imagine what a stranger would think if he came upon the scene of the trial.

36. See the crucial study of Geffcken, *Comedy in the Pro Caelio*. On Cicero's use of theatrical elements in general, see Wright, *Cicero and the Theater;* Austin, *Pro Caelio*, 141–43, 173–75; Pöschl, "Zur Einbeziehung anwesender Personen," 206–26; Vasaly, "Masks of Rhetoric," 1–4; and Cic. *Or.* 109; *De or.* 1.128–30; 2.192–94, 242; *Brut.* 290.

First he would note the festival atmosphere that prevailed at the time: the crowds, the noise, and the entertainments crowding the Forum.[37] Then, according to Cicero, he would wonder that a trial was taking place in the midst of all the merrymaking and would want to know what serious charge required the jury to spend the day in court when their fellow citizens were at play. This exordium encouraged the listeners (as well as the readers, if only imaginatively) to open their eyes and ears to the vitality, excitement, and energy of the world into which this imaginary stranger had been drawn. The jury was thereby encouraged by Cicero to relax their sense of serious purpose and participate in the diverting hubbub that existed everywhere about them. The allusion to the *otium* that all enjoyed is reminiscent of a passage in the *De lege agraria* 2. In this speech Cicero had warned against the possibility that his audience would be forced to leave Rome, and had advised them to "hold on to your influence, your freedom, your votes, your status; the city, the Forum, the games, festivals, and all your other enjoyments" (71). In the *Pro Caelio,* as in the earlier speech, Cicero reinforces his listeners' sense that the city was the center of all activities of value, whether serious or recreational.

This sense of the excitement and interest of the city continues in Cicero's vivid descriptions of various events and individuals. In spite of his feigned horror at the thunderings of the prosecution, the orator would have realized that his audience found tales of life among the demimonde titillating. Evidently, Cicero was not greatly dismayed by the prosecution's references to beach parties, dinner parties, boat parties, musical concerts, trips to Baiae, and the like, for he manages to repeat the catalogue twice himself.[38] His descriptions of Clodia's pleasure-filled days and nights, then, were not only intended to call forth moral condemnation; at the same time, tales of the rich and notorious widow would have seemed hugely entertaining. In fact, in his overall treatment of Clodia we have an excellent example of what Cicero defines early in the speech as *urbanitas:* that is, scurrilous gossip retailed with wit and humor (6). The audience hears that Clodia's gardens were the scene of assignations; her house, one in which mistress and slave lived in shock-

37. For the Megalenses, see Salzman, "Cicero, the *Megalenses* and the Defense of Caelius."
38. The prosecution's description of Caelius's life-style (35); Cicero's description of Clodia's life-style (49).

ing intimacy; and her grounds by the Tiber, a procuring place for the handsome young swimmers who frequented the beach. The story of the attempt to procure the poison in the baths (61–67) produces a variety of amusing images, including that of the group of elegant young men who are said to have hidden in the baths, then burst forth from their hiding places and set off in bumbling pursuit of their terrified quarry.

In the speech, then, Cicero makes the city appear to be the *locus* of all that is stimulating and amusing. While none of this presents Rome as a moral environment much better than that described in the *Pro Roscio,* the alteration in tone between the two speeches is of great importance. In the *Pro Roscio* we noted the audience's willingness to maintain the cultural myth of the superiority of the rustic over the urban environment, and Cicero was able to exploit that willingness by leading his audience to feel that in the case of Roscius reality intersected with myth. In this speech Cicero undercuts the prosecution's attempt to make use of a similar rhetorical topos by *identifying* it as a topos and arguing that his opponents, in exploiting it, had knowingly divorced themselves from reality (29). As part of this strategy of contrasting his own realistic attitude with the empty rhetoric of the prosecution, Cicero treats the audience throughout the speech as urbane and sophisticated individuals, who can see through the appearances and masks that might fool a more naive spectator. The orator speaks with the understanding that his listeners were the sort of people who could easily recognize the prostitute under the finery of the noblewoman, the dutiful son behind Atratinus's ill-cast role as accuser, or the underlying geniality of the orator Balbus, who had for the dramatic moment of the trial been forced to assume the role of unbending "uncle, censor, and teacher" (25).[39] Such men as the jury, Cicero implies, would realize that the quasi-rustic mores of an Appius Claudius or of the "iron fathers" of comedy were inappropriate to the present, and, although unwilling to countenance criminal or abandoned behavior, they would nevertheless be unlikely to condemn a fellow for "being good-looking" (6) or for "having seen Baiae" (27).

39. The characterization of Balbus as "censor" and as one who had castigated Caelius more severely than any father (25) is surely meant to be recalled in the references to Claudius, censor of 312 B.C., and to the harsh Caecilian fathers.

Scholars and Gentlemen

The *Pro Caelio* is a speech characterized by unusual generosity and civility, for—with the chief exception of Clodia—Cicero is full of praise
for a variety of individuals, even his opponents. An analysis of the kind
of praise Cicero accords these individuals reveals an ideal urban character and behavior. We are first introduced to the prosecutor, the young
Atratinus, whose dutifulness to his father, twice prosecuted by Caelius,
Cicero commends. The young man, who was probably about seventeen
at the time of the trial, is called *humanissimus atque optimus adulescens*
(2). Clearly this is an individual of merit, hoping to make his way by
taking on the prosecution of a man of status and experience. While Cicero is condescending towards the young man, his tone is indeed gentle:
he comments favorably upon his filial dutifulness, his industry, and his
eloquence. He is praised as well for his modesty, for he cannot speak
about the seamier sides of the indictment without a blush. Cicero's dis-
approval of Atratinus's speech is limited to the boy's embarrassed references to Caelius's moral dissipation: the experienced orator gives him
the fatherly advice that he ought to avoid ascribing to others the sort
of unsubstantiated charges that might as easily be lodged against himself (8).[40]

Among those mentioned approvingly by Cicero are two other *adulescentes*. The brothers Titus and Gaius Coponius were guest friends of
Dio, who had died under suspicious circumstances in their house. The
brothers, who are called to testify on behalf of Caelius, are termed *adulescentes humanissimi et doctissimi, rectissimis studiis atque optimis artibus praediti* (24), and they mourn Dio's death not simply because of
their acquaintanceship with the older man but because he was imbued
with a love of "learning and the liberal arts" (24: *doctrinae studio atque
humanitatis*). Cicero also speaks of Atratinus's coprosecutor, Lucius
Herennius Balbus, with respect. The orator claims that, like Atratinus,
Balbus has had to play a role in the case at odds with his real feelings;
his tirade against abandoned youth and the mores of the time was ill
suited to his temperament, which is actually "gentle" (25: *mitis*). Cicero
goes on to allude to the "attractiveness of his liberal manner, a quality
in which almost everyone now takes delight" (25: *hac suavitate human-*

---

40. Cicero thus begins the speech by assuming the role of the lenient (7:
lenius) father figure. Quintilian says of this speech: "[Cicero] seems to admonish
[Atratinus] almost like a father" (11.1.68). For the use of similar techniques by
Cicero in other speeches, see Craig, "*Accusator* as *Amicus*."

itatis, qua prope iam delectantur omnes). Lucius Lucceius, whose deposition on behalf of Caelius is read in court, is similarly described. He is not only a man whose testimony may be believed (54: *sanctissimum hominem et gravissimum testem*), he is one who is "endowed with liberality, . . . gentlemanly pursuits, . . . scholarly abilities, . . . and learning" (54: *illa humanitate praeditus, illis studiis, illis artibus atque doctrina*).

Cicero has led his audience to believe that all these men possessed certain characteristics in common. They are well read, well spoken, and, most telling, in the case of each Cicero uses some form of the word *humanitas*. The term is one that reappears throughout the orator's writings, and awareness of its implications is crucial to understanding the thrust of Cicero's praise here. As used in the speeches, *humanitas* refers to those qualities that combined the traditional virtues of the past with a new refinement of intellect and manner.[41] The word implies, first, the possession of a broad literary education, including familiarity with and enjoyment of poetry, as well as knowledge—although not a specialist's knowledge—of history and philosophy. *Humanitas* describes a quality of spirit as well, perhaps expressed in its most attractive aspect in the peroration of the *Pro Roscio,* where Cicero pleads eloquently for the return of the tolerance, pity, and humanity that had once existed in public life. The persona Cicero himself assumes throughout the speech—generous to the young Atratinus, tolerant towards the predictable excesses of youth, sophisticated in his "unmasking" of Clodia's real character—provides a further illustration of the meaning of the term.

41. The philosophical concept of "humanism" in Cicero's writings is much broader than the idea of *humanitas* as it appears in the speeches. The difference is well illustrated by a comparison of the wide-ranging implications attributed to Ciceronian "humanism" in Hunt, *Humanism of Cicero,* 188–205, and Clarke's description of a more narrowly conceived idea of *humanitas* (*Roman Mind,* 135–45). It is now asserted by many that the idea of humanism, even in Cicero's philosophical works, should actually be understood more narrowly and thus is closer to the conception found in the speeches. (Cf. Wood, *Cicero's Thought,* 79: "Just because Cicero conceives of men as belonging, by virtue of their reason and speech, to a single world commonwealth does not mean that his view is similar to the later benevolent idea of a common humanity or the Christian spiritual belief in the brotherhood of man. . . . Cicero's *humanitas* and *societas generis humani* (society of mankind)—both of Stoic derivation—have more to do with a common culture, a community of interests, or shared values originating in reason and speech than with an inner emotional feeling of universal love or kindness.") See also Snell, *Discovery of the Mind,* 253–55.

Finally, the word refers as well to a standard of style and external conduct: the wit, polished manners, and civilities of speech of which the *Pro Caelio* is itself an example. The concept of *humanitas*, then, describes an *ēthos* identified with the city rather than the country, and with the present rather than the past. As M. L. Clarke has noted, "Whatever its origins . . . its refinements belong . . . to a sophisticated, urban civilization with agreed standards of behavior and an appreciation of ease and polish in social relations and wit and style in conversation." [42]

Against this background of praise for the humane and sophisticated virtues of various individuals, Cicero describes the character and career of Caelius himself. The speech reveals him to have been the product of the uniquely Roman combination of educational training and active apprenticeship that was common among the upper classes in Cicero's day. [43] The family arose from a *municipium* in Picenum, and, while no doubt possessing estates there, Caelius's father resided principally in Rome. His son would have received literary training in both Greek and Latin and, like many of his class, might well have spent time in Athens, capping his earlier studies with attendance on the philosophers and rhetoricians who lectured there. An important, more traditional part of the education of a young man such as Caelius was a close and constant association with eminent older men of high standing in the state. From the wisdom and experience of such elder statesmen a young man was meant to profit, both by continual observation of their activities in public and private and by the intimate conversations that would lead to a close and enduring bond between them. Caelius's father had evidently been a Roman *eques* of some standing, as he was able to secure as mentors to his son two of the leading politicians and orators of the day, Cicero and Crassus.

In addition to being the recipient of this education, Caelius had especially devoted himself to the task of becoming a distinguished orator. This fact ultimately becomes part of Cicero's defense of the young man's character, for he supports his claim that Caelius's life could be justified

42. *Roman Mind*, 137. While it can be argued that elements of the Ciceronian conception of *humanitas* were based on tenets of Stoic philosophy, this standard of behavior stands in implicit contrast in the speech not only to the rustic mores of the past but also to the rigid Stoicism that Cicero equates with these antique mores (41).

43. See Bonner, *Education in Ancient Rome;* Stroh, *Taxis und Taktik,* 21; Clarke, *Roman Mind,* 8–11.

even to the strictest of judges by pointing to Caelius's rhetorical talent and training. His first reference to the defendant had described him as a young man of outstanding intellect, diligence, and influence (1: *illustri ingenio, industria, gratia*), and it is the second of these qualities that the orator emphasizes in his subsequent description of Caelius's public career. Cicero points to the eloquence shown by Caelius in his previous prosecutions of Antonius and Bestia and in his speech in his own defense at the current trial. This eloquence, Cicero argues, was not the result of natural ability alone (45: *ingenium*) but demonstrated "a method learned through study in the liberal arts and perfected through training and exercise" (45: *ratio et bonis artibus instituta et cura et vigiliis elaborata*). No young man who, like Caelius, had endured the discipline of body and mind required to attain such mastery of the art of persuasion could have lived a life devoted to pleasures. Cicero here seems to have altered Cato's well-known maxim, for instead of defining the orator in terms of the moral quality of the man (Sen. *Controv.* 1 *pr.* 9: *orator est . . . vir bonus dicendi peritus*), Cicero defines the man in terms of his accomplishment as an orator. He contends that if a man is a skilled orator, he proves himself to be a *vir bonus* as well, since this skill is, first of all, motivated by the noble desire to achieve glory and serve the state, and, second, it is perfected only by study and training so disciplined and rigorous that it leaves no opportunity for moral corruption.

In the last part of the speech (74–80) Cicero summarizes the chief arguments he has made in his defense of Caelius: the young man had early and long devoted himself through training in rhetoric to those activities and studies that would best prepare him for public office, honor, and prestige; his only fault had been an excess of youthful spirit and ambition that had led him—against Cicero's advice—to embark on the prosecution of Antonius and the second prosecution of Bestia; such energy and desire for glory, even though it may lead to errors in judgment, had always been the sign of a young man of great promise. If a shadow had been cast for a brief time over Caelius's personal reputation, it was due only to his unfortunate proximity to a hitherto unfamiliar temptation and to his inexperience of pleasures; this shadow was, however, soon dissipated by Caelius's complete break with Clodia.[44] The orator

---

44. Cicero's contention that "inexperience of pleasures" (75: *insolentia voluptatum*) had been partly to blame for Caelius's liaison with Clodia reminds one of Waugh's portrayal of Sebastian's legal defense in *Brideshead Revisited*,

ends by asking the jury to save Caelius for his aged father and for the Republic, to the service of which he would continue to devote his life.

This commendation of Caelius's education, style of life, and moral character clearly depends on a political and social viewpoint at odds with that found in the *Pro Roscio*. In the earlier speech, praise of the country and condemnation of the city had carried with it the understanding that rustic life was superior to urban life, that the past was better than the present, and that human history in general and Roman history in particular represented a gradual decay from an earlier ideal. The *Pro Caelio,* on the other hand, celebrates the possibilities to be realized in the modern and urban environment. It indicates that the *spes rei publicae* was not to be found in men like the rustic leaders of the past, who had been drawn from the plow to the consulship; rather, the hope of the state resided in the orator and statesman educated and trained in the sophisticated intellectual and political milieu of the city. This ideal statesman is pictured as a morally upright individual, and yet not one who has excluded all pleasures and forms of relaxation from his life; he is a man who, while not necessarily of noble birth, possesses native ability, and this ability has been carefully channeled and refined by a broad education, extensive experience, and personal application. The speech thus rejects the Roman commonplace that attributes moral corruption to the growth of sophistication by connecting intellectual development with moral worth. According to the *Pro Caelio,* it is the advanced education and training of the skilled orator that discipline his character, allow him to fulfill his potential as a citizen, and create the possibility that he may become the kind of leader most needed in a time of intense crisis within the Republic. In his first extant work on rhetoric, the *De inventione,* Cicero had pictured the orator as the individual who had raised his companions from savagery to civilization. At the beginning of the treatise he had stated that it had been due to the power of rhetoric that some great and wise man had been able to convince his fellows—who had hitherto lived in the fields like wild animals and had been ruled by their desires and by the power of violence—to come together in settled communities, to pursue useful occupations, and to keep faith and observe justice (1.1–3). In the *Pro Caelio* the orator has gone beyond the ideas found in this early and derivative work and has fore-

---

in which the young lord's drunken behavior is not severely punished because he is supposedly "unused to wine."

shadowed the conception found in his magnum opus on rhetoric, the *De oratore,* that the great orator embodies the culmination of the education and culture of the day. At the same time, he makes clear in the *Pro Caelio* that it is the city alone that is able to produce such an individual.

In utramque partem

The picture of the world that emerged from Ciceronian rhetoric was never simply black or white but was *both* black and white. That is, strong statements of the positive aspects of a place are often balanced at other times and in other speeches by equally strong statements in which the negative aspects of the same place are demonstrated. This was to be expected, in light of the varying exigencies of times and subjects, of the training in speaking *in utramque partem* designed to anticipate the arguments of one's opponent, and of the existence of commonplaces providing negative and positive positions on the same subject. This was also to be expected when we keep in mind that the orator was attempting to respond to his audience's prejudices about the world, and when we remember that the Roman audience of the late Republic had no single vision of reality. Like all of us, they were capable of entertaining various, often mutually inconsistent ideas about places and the people in them.

The necessity for such reversals of position, as well as the embarrassment they might cause, is referred to in the *Pro Cluentio.* Here the prosecution had read out a statement from an earlier case in which Cicero implied that his present client had been guilty of bribing a jury. Cicero defends himself by arguing that since any given speech of an advocate reflected the requirements of a specific case rather than his private opinions, consistency should not be expected.[45] In spite of this statement it

---

45. Cicero goes on to deflect attention from his own contradictory statements by recalling an incident in which L. Licinius Crassus, one of the greatest orators of the preceding generation, had been forced to listen to an opponent reading out passages from speeches he had made on two separate occasions, in one of which he had attacked the Senate, while in the other he had warmly praised it (*Clu.* 140). On the ethical question of defending the guilty, see Cic. *Off.* 2.51. Cicero cites no less an authority than Panaetius on the need sometimes to maintain the plausible rather than the true. On Cicero's blurring of the concept of *decorum* in the Stoic philosopher, see Neumeister, *Grundsätze der forensischen Rhetorik,* 59–60. As a philosophical Skeptic, Cicero was unin-

would be incorrect to assume that the orator's ability to argue both sides
of an issue signals that one or both of his positions must have been divorced from his privately held thoughts and opinions. The capacity to
adopt attitudes that, from a logical standpoint, were mutually exclusive
was one Cicero not only exploited in his audience but discovered in
himself as well. Surely when Cicero came to devise a strategy for the
defense of Roscius he drew not only on the commonplaces of rhetoric
but on his own deep attachment to the rural countryside and to the life
of the old municipal towns—an attachment best illustrated by the introductory passages of the second book of the *De legibus,* which are filled
with his delight in the sights and sounds of his native Arpinum.[46] Similarly, Cicero's celebration of the urban environment in the *Pro Caelio*
was at once a rhetorical strategy intended to manipulate the feelings of
his audience and at the same time the autobiographical expression of a
man whose attachment to the city was so intense that he seemed unable
to conceive of any meaningful existence outside of Rome.[47]

It should also be remembered that arguing *in utramque partem* was
not only an important part of the training of a young orator; it was also
intimately related to the philosophical technique for determining truth
advocated by the "New Academy," to which Cicero acknowledged al-
legiance. According to Carneades and his followers, it was impossible
for an individual to decide what was true in an absolute sense; condi-
tional truth, however, could be rationally determined by setting forth
arguments on either side of an issue and weighing their comparative
validity. Of the two sides, that which appeared more probably true
might be assented to as true for all practical purposes. This skeptical
calculus was so close to the exercises of rhetorical training that Cicero
called this system of philosophy one "that gives birth to fluency in
speaking" (*Para.* 2: *quae peperit dicendi copiam*).

In addition to demonstrating Cicero's adeptness in exploiting two
contrasting points of view vis-à-vis the rural and the urban environ-

---

clined to assume that humans possessed the ability to discover the ultimate truth
about their world; his experience, emotions, and intellect revealed to him not a
single, unvarying Truth but rather a variety of competing truths.

46. See above, pp. 30–33.

47. Cicero may have admired the Stoic courage of a Rutilius Rufus, who
after his notoriously unjust conviction lived out his life in exile, but he himself
proved incapable of emulating this discipline of mind. Cicero's letters from exile
are rivaled only by the exilic poetry of Ovid as a record of despair.

ments, the *Pro Roscio* and the *Pro Caelio* show Cicero's ability to identify himself with two very different clients.[48] In the earlier speech, delivered at a time when the orator was still relatively unknown, he was able to adapt his own persona to that of the defendant. He therefore depicted himself, like Roscius, as a man of limited talent and few resources, struggling against the overwhelming power and influence of his opponents.[49] By the date of the *Pro Caelio,* however, Cicero was a man of authority, influence, and—at the moment—wide popularity. In the speech, therefore, he uses his own public image as the model on which to form the persona assigned to Caelius. In reality Caelius seems to have been an ambitious, even ruthless young man of few scruples, but in the speech his background, training, dedication to oratory, political loyalties, and devotion to the Republic are claimed to mirror Cicero's own.[50] Caelius's infatuation with Catiline, like his affair with Clodia, is depicted as a youthful error within a life otherwise devoted to the same goals and ideals as those of Cicero, and Caelius's willingness to prosecute Antonius and Bestia against Cicero's advice is likewise portrayed not as an action separating the two men in principle but as proof of the ambition and spirit of the younger man.[51] In the peroration Cicero, pledging that Caelius will never deviate from the principles that have guided his own life, goes so far as to ask the jury to base their judgment of Caelius on their assessment of his own services to the Republic (77: *promitto hoc vobis et rei publicae spondeo, si modo nos ipsi rei publicae satis fecimus, numquam hunc a nostris rationibus seiunctum fore*). Again, as in the case of Cicero's treatment of the rural and urban environments, this plea is "rhetorical" in that its raison d'être was to induce

48. See May, "Rhetoric of Advocacy," and *Trials of Character,* passim.
49. Cicero claimed to be a man of little talent (*Rosc. Am.* 1, 5, 9, 59) who could speak without fear only because of his youth and lack of authority (*Rosc. Am.* 1, 3, 9, 31).
50. For Caelius, see Vell. Pat. 2.68.1; Macrob. *Sat.* 3.14.15; and above, p. 173 n. 29.
51. Cicero makes even this a point of identity by confessing that he himself had almost mistaken Catiline's true nature (14). For connections between the orator and Caelius, see 4–5 (both *equites*); 6 (similar municipal background); 9–10, 72 (Cicero as mentor to the young Caelius); 18 (Caelius's move to the Palatine in part motivated by a desire to be close to Cicero's house); 44–47 (description of a life devoted to oratory); 77, 80 (shared political principles); 78 (implicit comparison: unjust harrassment of Cicero by Clodius's adherents and unjust prosecution of Caelius instigated by Clodia).

the jury to acquit Caelius. But without denying this rhetorical intent, we may observe that Cicero has judged that the most effective strategy for making the defendant acceptable to his audience was to construct Caelius's persona in his own image.

Evidently Cicero did not misjudge his audience in pursuing this strategy, for Caelius was indeed acquitted. The glory of this victory, however, would be short-lived, as the surge of power and popularity Cicero experienced in the years immediately following his return from exile in 57 B.C. would soon subside before the renewed *amicitia* among Caesar, Crassus, and Pompey and the subsequent dissolution of the state into chaos, violence, and, ultimately, civil war. Thus the *Pro Caelio* would be Cicero's last great victory until the death of Caesar signaled the beginning of the final act in the orator's political and oratorical career.

CHAPTER SIX

Ethnic Personae

To paraphrase a cynical maxim of our own day, no Roman orator ever came to grief overestimating his audience's prejudices towards ethnic minorities. Not only Latin rhetoric but Latin literature of various genres is replete with allusions to the treachery of the Carthaginians, the debility of the Asians, the barbarism of the Gauls, the cruelty of the Spaniards, the duplicity of the Greeks.[1] In forensic rhetoric—that is, the rhetoric of the law courts—appeal to these stereotypes was constant when cases involved the defense of provincial governors accused of malfeasance in office. The permanent court dealing with these cases (*de repetundis*) dated back to 149 B.C. and was the first standing court instituted in Rome. The orators who defended ex-magistrates in cases heard before this court would have expended much time and energy on attempts to impeach the credibility of the witnesses for the prosecution. In the case of witnesses who were not Roman citizens doing business abroad but members of a subject people, the most obvious strategy pursued by the defense would have been to impugn the character of the entire race to which the witnesses belonged. The provinces from which these complainants came had, for the most part, entered the *imperium Romanum* through force of arms. Therefore, the same prejudices that had helped stir the Roman people to wage war against Carthaginians, Asians, Gauls, Spaniards, or Greeks could later be fanned in order to discredit

1. See Balsdon, *Romans and Aliens*, 30–76; Haarhoff, *Stranger at the Gate*, 189–221. See also above, p. 137 n. 13.

the character of representatives of these peoples when they came to Rome to complain of the abuses suffered under Roman rule.[2]

As many of his speeches bear witness, Cicero was not above pursuing such strategies. Three speeches can be usefully singled out for study. Two, the *Pro Flacco* and the *Verrines,* offer a special opportunity for comparison. Cicero's defense of the former provincial governor L. Valerius Flaccus and the approach he used in prosecuting Gaius Verres, a man accused of similar misconduct, illustrate yet again his ability to argue forcibly *in utramque partem,* since in the speech for Flaccus Cicero provided counterarguments to the same sort of attack he had himself launched earlier in the speech against Verres. In the third speech, the *De lege agraria* 2, a deliberative oration that was delivered in the year of his consulship, Cicero spoke against passage of a popular bill for land distribution. The oration is of particular interest here because of the somewhat surprising tack Cicero decided upon to persuade the Roman people to reject the proposal—that is, the exploitation of a centuries-old ethnic stereotype concerning the dangerous character of the Campanians in general and of the Capuans in particular. Although this strategy depends on a timeworn topos, Cicero's handling of it is strikingly effective. A closer look at the three speeches, therefore, has much to reveal concerning Cicero's methods of manipulating stereotypes connected with geographical locations.

GOOD GREEKS AND BAD GREEKS

In his capacity as attacker of provincials Cicero appears in an unfavorable light, exploiting the vulnerabilities of those who could be made to appear outside the pale of what continued to be, at least in its upper echelons, a narrow, conservative society.[3] It is particularly fortunate for

---

2. While the establishment in 149 B.C. of the *Quaestio de rebus repetundis* (known as the "extortion court") demonstrated Roman willingness to provide an opportunity for provincials to seek redress for ill treatment received at the hands of their governors (whose authority during the period of magistracy abroad was all but absolute), nevertheless the long history of this court points as well to the severity and continuity of Roman abuse of provincials. For a political and legal analysis of the functioning of such courts, see Gruen, *Roman Politics.* (Gruen, App. E, 304–10, gives a summary of trials between 149 and 78 B.C., including *de repetundis* cases.)

3. On the composition of society in Cicero's day, see Wood, *Cicero's Thought,* 14–41.

our study of Cicero's manipulation of arguments relating to ethnic character (if not for our belief in Cicero's unwavering high-mindedness) that among the orator's extant works there is one, the *Verrines*, in which the orator assumed the role of defender of the rights of Greek provincials, while in the *Pro Flacco* we see him defending a Roman governor accused of trampling on those same rights. A comparison of these works is also of special interest here because in them Cicero used geographical determinants to distinguish Greeks whose character was supposedly consonant with the prevailing negative stereotype from those whose admirable traits made them exceptions to the rule. Before embarking on an analysis of these speeches, however, let us turn briefly to two other orations in which, as in the *Pro Flacco*, Cicero was asked to defend the former governor of a province. Although the *Pro Fonteio* and the *Pro Scauro* were concerned with impeaching the credibility of the Gauls and Sardinians rather than the Greeks, these speeches provide a revealing introduction to the general strategies used by Cicero in attacking non-Romans—strategies that could be adapted for use against a variety of ethnic opponents.

In the *Pro Fonteio*, dated 69 B.C., Cicero defended Marcus Fonteius, who was accused of misconduct during his two-year praetorship in Gaul. Cicero praises Fonteius as a military man of outstanding talents, one of an increasingly rare breed on whom the Republic depended for its safety, a worthy heir to the seasoned campaigners of previous generations (42–43). Against the valiant Fonteius stand the Gauls, ranged before him now in court as once they had been on Gallic battlefields. These barbarian witnesses, according to Cicero, are incapable of providing trustworthy evidence, since they have no sense of the enormous burden of giving sworn testimony. One has only to compare the behavior on the witness stand of even the lowliest Roman to the most honorable of Gauls to realize the truth of this statement. The Roman is filled with anxiety lest he seem to betray the modesty and good faith (28: *pudoris ac religionis*) required of him; the Gaul, on the other hand, is unconcerned with his reputation and speaks with a boldness that betrays his unreliability. This willingness to disregard the sanctity of the oath is hardly surprising, Cicero points out, as the Gauls are a race distinct from all others, feeling neither fear of nor respect for the immortal gods. Cicero supports this contention by reminding his listeners of the attack on Delphi by Gallic raiders in the third century and of the Gallic sack of Rome at the beginning of the fourth century, and by referring to the Gauls' "savage and barbaric custom" (31: *immanem ac barbaram consuetudinem*) of sacrificing human beings to placate their angry gods (30–31).

While claiming that no scruples restrained the Gauls from violating their oath and giving false testimony against Fonteius, Cicero at the same time imputes to the foreigners a compelling motive for committing perjury: their implacable hostility to Roman rule. According to the orator, the Gauls harbor the resentment of the recently conquered and begrudge the money, men, and grain they are forced to render to their new masters (12–14, 17). This resentment is expressed with a ferocity that sets them apart from all other peoples. They are "most hostile and most savage" (41: *inimicissimis atque immanissimis*) and "the most implacable and most cruel enemies of the Roman people" (43: *inimicissimis populo Romano nationibus et crudelissimis*). The repetition in different forms of the words *iracundia* (15), *iratus* (18, 21, 36), *cupidus* (21, 29, 32), *temere* (29), *libido* (4, 36, 49), *immanis* (31, 33, 41, 44), and *crudelis* (43) in connection with the Gauls further reinforces this image of a wild and threatening race, awed by neither men nor gods, consumed with a desire for revenge against their conquerors. And because the prosecution apparently had presented no hostile witnesses from among the Roman citizens resident or doing business in Gaul, Cicero is able to claim that the case could be seen as a battle between all those loyal to the state and the barbarian hordes. On one side are the Gauls, traditional enemies of Rome, once more to be seen parading about Rome in their absurd garb, uttering threats against the Republic in the very Forum of the Roman people (33). Ranged on Fonteius's side—that is, on the Roman side—are all the Roman citizens of Gaul, the Roman colony of Narbo Martius, and the friendly Greek city-state of Massilia (14–15, 45–46). Even the other provinces oppose this Gallic attack on the homeland, for protecting Fonteius on one wing, says Cicero, stands Macedonia, which owes a debt of gratitude to the accused for his successful campaigns against its Thracian enemies; on the other wing is Further Spain, which "is able to resist the passion (*cupiditati*) of these [Gauls] not only by its loyalty (*religione*) but is able to refute the perjury of these wicked men by its testimony and praises" (45).[4]

A somewhat different, but no less damning, picture of provincial wit-

4. For Roman stereotypes of Gauls see Balsdon, *Romans and Aliens*, 65–66, 214–15.

nesses can be found in the *Pro Scauro*.[5] Although the speech is preserved
only in two large fragments, enough of the oration is extant for us to
trace the orator's plan of attack in dealing with the Sardinian witnesses
whose testimony formed the mainstay of the prosecution's case. Cicero
prefaces his remarks on the Sardinians with a commonplace elevating
the importance of argument over the evidence of witnesses (15–16).[6] He
then declares that in this case in which the witnesses are all of "one
complexion, one voice, and one nation" (19: *unus color, una vox, una
natio*), he will not attempt to take them on individually but will confront the whole army in a single great encounter. This he proceeds to
do, after revealing that the impetus for the case had actually been supplied by the consul, Appius Claudius Pulcher. According to Cicero, Appius had hoped that by encouraging the prosecution he could undermine the consular campaign of Scaurus and thereby secure the election
of his brother Gaius (31–37).

The attack on the testimony of the Sardinians occupies sections 38
through 45, which was, presumably, the central portion of the argument. Cicero begins by alleging that the unanimity of the Sardinian responses proved their testimony to be a fabrication, created out of greed
for the rewards promised them by Appius and the prosecution (38). He
then expands upon the failings of the race that would make these
charges of conspiracy and perjury believable. While disavowing any
prejudice against the Sardinians, Cicero remarks that even if they were
to come as honest witnesses, the "reputation of the race" (41: *gentis . . .
famam*) was such that they ought to be amazed whenever they were
taken at their word.[7] Cicero's audience is then presented with the orator's account of the history of racial degeneration that had produced the
Sardinian people. He declares:

> All the memorials and all the historical records of antiquity have revealed to
> us that the Phoenician race is the most deceptive of all (42: *fallacissimum*);

5. On Scaurus and the political background to the speech, see Henderson,
"The Career of Scaurus"; Courtney, "The Prosecution of Scaurus."

6. Quint. 5.7.3: *In actionibus primum generaliter pro testibus atque in testis
dici solet. Est hic communis locus, cum pars altera nullam firmiorem probati-
onem esse contendit quam quae sit hominum scientia nixa, altera ad detrahen-
dam illis fidem omnia per quae fieri soleant falsa testimonia enumerat.* Cf. Lausberg, *Handbuch*, 1:192–93 (§354).

7. For the negative stereotype of Sardinians, see Cic. *Fam.* 7.24.1; Tac. *Ann.*
2.85; Mart. 4.60.6; Paus. 10.17.1–7. See also Rowland, "Sardinians in the Roman Empire."

the Poeni, who sprang from them, proved by the many revolts of the Carthaginians and the many treaties they violated and broke that they had in no way declined from their ancestors; after elements of the African race were mixed in with this stock, the resulting Sardi were not led forth and settled in Sardinia but were rather marooned and exiled there by the Poeni. Wherefore, since there was nothing healthy in the pure stock of this race, how greatly corrupted should we judge it after so many such racial interminglings?

(42–43)

The orator hastens to note that there were certain Sardinians—notably those who were his own friends and those who were supporters of Scaurus—who, by their personal excellence, had overcome the shortcomings of their heritage; these men, however, were only exceptions to the generally recognized rule that the majority of Sardi were "without loyalty and without any bond or tie" (44: *sine fide, sine societate et coniunctione*) that connected them to the Roman people.

In the *Pro Fonteio* and the *Pro Scauro* Cicero has varied the type of ethnic attack with the peoples who are the target of the attack. The Gauls are made to seem by far the more formidable of the two races. They are a savage, cruel, and angry lot who believe they can intimidate the Roman judicial system with their fierce threats. Towards the Sardinians Cicero assumes a more contemptuous tone, speaking of their slavishness, sordidness, and moral worthlessness. In both cases, however, the final judgment is identical: neither race is capable of observing the *fides* and *religio* that guarantee the weight and credibility of their testimony.

These two terms, which appear several times in the two speeches, are of broad significance and are difficult of exact definition. *Fides* was used to describe the quality that produced the conviction that an individual could be trusted—whether as family member, friend, patron, client, business associate, magistrate, or witness—as well as to describe the conviction itself (thus it meant both "trustworthiness" and "trust"). A breach of *fides* between citizens was an offense on several levels: such an action could be grounds for social stigma and political attack; it could constitute the basis for an action at law; and it was a religious offense, a sin against the gods, even in cases where *fides* was not guaranteed by an explicit oath (although the close relationship between *fides* and oath was surely the basis for its religious aspect).[8] *Fides* was also a trait as-

---

8. See *Rosc. Am.* 116 for *fides* between partners. For a philosophical definition of *fides*, see Cic. *Off.* 1.23: *Fundamentum autem est iustitiae fides, id est*

signed to states as well as individuals: in the case of provinces and allies it signified the loyalty, trustworthiness, respect, and obedience the conquered owed their masters, at least in Roman eyes.[9] In the case of the Gauls, it is Cicero's contention that their fierce hostility to Rome in general and to its representative, Fonteius, in particular rendered them incapable of giving honest testimony.[10] Cicero thus ties their lack of *fides*—in the sense of attachment and loyalty to Rome—to their lack of *fides* or trustworthiness as sworn witnesses. The Sardi, who are likewise without *fides,* both in the sense of loyalty to Rome and credibility as witnesses, are not so because of anger or hostility at their lot but because they are a frivolous and contemptible race, motivated by greed. According to Cicero they believe that the difference between freedom and slavery is simply the opportunity to lie with impunity (38).[11]

The second term, *religio,* is perhaps even more difficult to define. It may be described in general as a scrupulousness derived from a sense of religious piety. *Religio* placed constraints on the actions of an individual towards people and things thought to be sacred or of concern to the gods. *Religio* guaranteed, for instance, the strict and solemn observance both of religious festivals and of honors to the deities; it also required that objects of public and private veneration be treated with respect; and it restrained the individual from lying under oath. The term is of particular importance in Cicero's attack on the Gauls. As noted, the orator attempts to create a picture of the race as a terrifying people who knew no fear, even of the gods. While other races fought *for* their divinities, declares Cicero, the Gauls alone "waged war against the immortal gods themselves" (*Font.* 30). No awe of divine prohibitions, therefore,

---

dictorum conventorumque constantia et veritas. Ex quo, quamquam hoc vide-bitur fortasse cuipiam durius, tamen audeamus imitari Stoicos, qui studiose ex-quirunt, unde verba sint ducta, credamusque, quia fiat, quod dictum est, appel-latam fidem. See also Heinze, "Fides"; Fraenkel, "Zur Geschichte des Wortes fides"; Earl, *Moral and Political Tradition,* 33; Latte, *Römische Religions-geschichte,* 237, 273.

9. On the application of the concept to international relations, see Badian, *Foreign Clientelae.*

10. Julius Victor *Ars rhet.* 15 (in Halm, *Rhetores Latini minores,* 423): *Licet etiam principales quaestiones in principio praecerpere, sed praecursu solo atque tactu, non ut de his quaeri videatur, quomodo pro Flacco et pro Fonteio Marcus Tullius, nihil agi illo iudicio, nisi ut magistratus in provinciis non audeant im-perare sociis, quod ex usu rei publicae sit.*

11. Slaves could give testimony only under torture.

could restrain them from exercising their hostility and anger against Fonteius by perjuring themselves under oath.

THE DEFENSE OF FLACCUS

The trial of L. Valerius Flaccus took place four years after Cicero's suppression of the Catilinarian conspiracy. The great swell of popularity that had carried him through the year of his consulship had ebbed during the following years, and by the time of Flaccus's trial in 59 B.C. Cicero and others who had been instrumental in bringing about the executions of the conspirators were being hard pressed by the attacks of the popular party. Flaccus could be numbered among this group, for, as praetor in 63 B.C., he had been responsible for the apprehension of Volturcius and the Gauls at the Milvian Bridge. The sealed messages seized at this time and later read before the Senate had provided the damning evidence that ultimately led to the conviction and death of the leading conspirators who had remained in Rome after Catiline's departure.

It is Cicero's allusions to Flaccus's participation in these earlier events that bind the speech together.[12] The *Pro Fonteio* makes clear that a common feature of the defense of provincial governors was an appeal to the military record of the accused. This appeal might focus on past campaigns that demonstrated the indispensable service the accused had rendered to the Republic and would again render if acquitted of the charges against him. Alternately, an orator might choose to praise his client's military record during the actual period of his provincial government in an attempt to convince a jury that disregard of the interests of their former enemies could be excused in one zealously devoted to maintaining the security of the state. In the case of Flaccus, this appeal to the military service of the accused does not focus primarily on Flaccus's foreign campaigns. Rather, the speech begins and ends with references to the role Flaccus played during the Catilinarian crisis (1–5, 101–6). This emphasis on Flaccus's actions in 63 B.C. serves an important purpose in

12. Humbert, *Les plaidoyers écrits*, 222–35, argued that the extant work represents a mélange. *Contra*, see Webster, *Pro Flacco*, App. A. The extant speech does not include a famous witticism that supposedly saved the guilty defendant: Macrob. *Sat.* 2.1.13 ([*Cicero*] *in quibus causis, cum nocentissimos reos tueretur, victoriam iocis adeptus est: ut ecce Pro L. Flacco, quem repetundarum reum ioci opportunitate de manifestissimis criminibus exemit. Is iocus in oratione non extat, mihi ex libro Furii Bibaculi notus est*). On Cicero's overall strategy in the speech, see Classen, "La difesa di Valerio Flacco."

addition to that of highlighting his martial prowess: in these passages Cicero draws on his *auctoritas* by reminding his audience once again of his role in saving the state. His listeners are led to recall that in the domestic campaign in which the accused had served so gloriously he had played the role of lieutenant to Cicero himself, the *dux togatus*.[13] At the same time, this tactic shows Cicero once more wedding himself to the character, career, and fate of his client. The jury who heard the case was asked to pass judgment not simply on Flaccus and his provincial command but also on Cicero and his conduct of the consulship of 63 B.C.

If the strategy pursued at the beginning and end of the speech is easily identifiable, the appeal made within the body of the speech is equally familiar from the *Pro Fonteio* and the *Pro Scauro*, for much of the oration is occupied with Cicero's attempt to undermine the credibility of the prosecution's evidence by an ethnic attack on the provincials who had supplied this evidence. Just as he had in the *Pro Scauro*, he argues that in the case of unknown foreign witnesses he has been compelled to discredit them as a group rather than individually (23); and, as in the *Pro Scauro*, he contends that in this case the evidence against his client has been provided by a race "least trustworthy of all in giving testimony" (23: *natio minime in testimoniis dicendis religiosa*). The orator begins his discussion of the testimony of the witnesses by asking his audience to recall that the one factor that was common among them was that they were Greeks (9). Declaring that there was no one less likely to be hostile to the Greeks than he, Cicero goes on to admit the excellence of the race in "literature, the knowledge of many arts, the charm of their discourse, the sharpness of their wits, and the copiousness of their speech" (9: *tribuo illis litteras, do multarum artium disciplinam, non adimo sermonis leporem, ingeniorum acumen, dicendi copiam*). He then states that for all their talents they were conspicuously lacking in one respect: they had no understanding of the religious scruples (*religionem*) or good faith (*fidem*) required of one giving testimony (9). In his attack on the Gallic witnesses in the *Pro Fonteio* Cicero had attempted to prove the unreliability of the witnesses by comparing the behavior of the Roman and the Gaul. Here, the same technique has been used in describing Greek witnesses. Whereas the Roman, says Cicero, schooled in traditional customs and discipline, is scrupulously honest

13. See *Cat.* 2.28 (*uno togato duce et imperatore*); 3.15, 23; *Sull.* 85; *Har. resp.* 49 (*togatum domestici belli exstinctorem*); and Nicolet, "Consul togatus," 240–45.

under oath and can hardly be induced to make hostile statements even against his enemies, the Greeks are concerned only with advancing their own interests and winning the verbal contest between themselves and their questioner. They choose as their representatives, therefore, neither the finest men nor the most respected but those who are the best talkers. To them, says the orator, "a sworn oath is a joke, giving testimony is a game, and their reputation before you but a shadow" (12). Cicero adds that his oration would indeed be without end if he were to dilate further upon the inconstancy (12: *levitatem*) of the whole Greek race in giving evidence.

In these remarks, and in similar passages made in reference to individual Greek witnesses, Cicero drew on the Roman stereotype of the Greeks and, indeed, of many of the inhabitants of the eastern Mediterranean. While the Gauls of the *Pro Fonteio* were pictured as savage and half-civilized, the Greeks were commonly attacked as overcivilized. They were said to be a people without scruples, a race of actors, ready to adapt their behavior to their ends. According to this stereotype, their failings were not of intellect but of character, so that even the talents for which Cicero had praised them at the beginning of the speech—cleverness, loquacity, verbal facility—formed part of the indictment against them. At several points Cicero hints that the motivation for the perjured testimony of the Greeks went beyond their inability to understand the sanctity of the oath; it expressed the "barbarian cruelty" and hostility towards Roman rule that had led them in 88 B.C. to embark on the mass slaughter of Roman citizens at the beginning of the First Mithridatic War (60–61). This line of argument, however—crucial to the *Pro Fonteio*—is soft-pedalled in this speech, and it is the *levitas* of the Greeks that becomes the theme repeated throughout, a *levitas* that is implicitly contrasted with the *gravitas* of the Romans.[14]

Cicero not only had to contend with the Greeks who journeyed to Rome to testify in person against Flaccus; he also had to undermine the effect of the resolutions against the defendant that had been passed by various towns within the province and introduced in evidence by the prosecution. Again, Cicero's strategy was to attack the entire race. As

14. See 12 (*levitatem*), 19 (*levissimi; levissimae nationis*), 24 (*levitate*), 36 (*nullam gravitatem*), 37 (*levitatem*), 38 (*leves*), 57 (*levitas*), 61 (*levitate*), 63 (contrasting the *gravitas* of the Massilians), and 71 (*levitate*). The word signifies untrustworthiness, mental mobility, lack of steadfastness, and infidelity. *Levitas* is a characteristic of all barbarians.

he had earlier in the speech compared the behavior of Roman witnesses when giving testimony with that of the Greeks, he also contrasts the wise arrangements for the debate and passage of public resolutions the Romans had inherited from their ancestors with those that prevailed in the Greek world. Whereas the Romans debated political questions on one day and voted on these same resolutions only three days later in orderly assemblies (*comitia*) in which the people were strictly divided according to rank, the Greeks allowed debate and voting to go on at the same meeting. Worse, they remained seated at such meetings and allowed the most crude and ignorant individuals to express their opinions. How was it surprising, then, if the prosecutor had been able to persuade the assemblies of the various states to pass rash and misleading resolutions against his client?[15]

Cicero supports this attack with several arguments that make use of the rhetorical figure called "the less and the more."[16] If Athens at its acme suffered from the effects of this disastrous system, he asks, how much more the Asian Greek states of Phrygia and Mysia (17)? And if political meetings had frequently been lashed by popular storms in Rome, "this most serious and restrained of states," a place in which the Curia, "the punisher of rashness and governor of our sense of duty," keeps watch upon the Rostra, how could one put any faith in the resolutions of the Greeks (57)? Alluding with disdain to the cobblers, belt makers, shopkeepers, and other "dregs of society" allowed to make public policy in these lands, Cicero declares to his audience that "when you hear these resolutions you are not hearing sworn testimony, but rather the rashness of the crowd, the voice of the most contemptible of citizens, the roaring of the ignorant, the impassioned assembly of the least trustworthy of races" (19).

The philosophical sources of this virulent attack on the Greek democratic system can be traced back to Greece itself. Cicero's condemnation of the fickle masses who are swayed by the oratory of the *imperiti* echoes Plato's attacks on rhetoric in the *Gorgias* and the *Phaedrus,* in which Socrates warns of the perilous condition of a state in which paid educators taught the tricks of persuasion without considering how those tricks might be used, and in which neither those who led nor those who were led understood the true nature of justice. The Platonic ideal

15. On the resolutions of the Greeks, see *Flac.* 15–19, 23, 57–58.

16. This is a form of the *locus a comparatione,* used in the *argumentum.* See Lausberg, *Handbuch,* 1:218–20 (§§395–97).

found in the *Republic*—of a state in which the governors were a special class, distinguished from the governed by birth, training, and education—was not realized in the Roman constitution, but Cicero indicates in the *Pro Flacco* that the superiority of the Roman system to that of the Greeks lay in the degree to which it repressed the whims of the ignorant masses and strengthened the control of the superior few. Thus the basic questions at issue in the passages dealing with the validity of the resolutions passed by the Greek assemblies had a long history in ancient political philosophy. Cicero's tone in these passages, however, is anything but philosophical. Fear and hostility are equally evident, a fact that reminds us that we are here reading not a single but a twofold indictment: in Cicero's view the seditious assemblies of the Greeks found their counterpart in the "great tempests" (57: *quantos fluctus*) aroused at the political rallies at Rome.[17] This attitude might at first seem surprising in a man who had risen to prominence through his skill in persuading these very masses. It should be remembered, however, that the *Pro Flacco* was delivered only a few months before Cicero was driven into exile, and perhaps we may detect within it the heartfelt sentiments of a man who was at the time feeling increasingly imperiled by the frequent displays of mass disorder and violence orchestrated by his enemies.

The section of the speech that treats the evidence both of individual witnesses and of the Greeks as a people ends with a broad condemnation of the race as untrustworthy (57: *levitas propria Graecorum*) and their political institutions as corrupt (57: *in contione seditiosa valeat oratio*). Cicero could hardly abandon the argument here, however, since a number of Greek communities had sent documents and witnesses *supporting* Flaccus. Some strategy had to be found that would induce the audience, on the one hand, to dismiss the evidence of the Greeks presented by the prosecution as the expression of the duplicity of the race, while, on the other, to accept the defense's evidence, which likewise had been furnished by a number of Greek states. Cicero's solution to the problem was to make distinctions between the trustworthy Greeks who supported the defense and the lying Greeks on whom the prosecution

17. For further discussion of Cicero's characterizations of Athenian democracy, see Soós, "Ciceros Betrachtungen über die Institutionen der athenischen Demokratie." Cicero also implies that it was the presence of Jews and other foreigners that was turning the Roman assemblies into a mirror of those of the Greeks (66). On the negative characterization of Jews and Judaism, see also 67 (*barbarae superstitioni*) and 69.

relied. He had also made distinctions in the case of the Sardinians in the *Pro Scauro* by stating that through a personal achievement of character certain Sardinians had overcome the debased heritage of their people. Here, however, it is chiefly geography that matters. In sections 62–66 Cicero attempts to oppose the character and habits of the Asian Greeks to those of the European Greeks. He begins with several *laudes urbium,* praising Athens for its invention of "civilization, learning, religion, agriculture, justice, and law" (62: *humanitas, doctrina, religio, fruges, iura, leges*), Sparta for the bravery of its citizens and the antiquity of its laws and customs, and Massilia (Marseille), which, in spite of being cut off from other civilized states and surrounded by the barbaric tribes of Gaul, was so well governed by the wisdom of its best citizens (63: *optimatium consilio*) that it surpassed not only Greece but all other places on earth in its customs and eminence (63: *disciplinam atque gravitatem non solum Graeciae, sed haud sciam an cunctis gentibus anteponendam*).[18] He then goes on to prove the "worthlessness, unreliability, and greed" (66) of the Asians by quoting a number of Greek proverbs that expressed contempt for Phrygians, Carians, Mysians, and Lydians.[19]

Cicero's elevation of the mainland and western Greeks over Asian Greeks stands in sharp contrast to passages in other speeches where praise of Greece is scanty and nearly always restricted to the glories of the past. Here, however, it is implied that the inhabitants of the mainland have not degenerated greatly from the nobility of their ancestors. Although in the case of Athens allusions to contemporary achievements are conspicuously absent, nevertheless it is the differences in character between "European" Greeks (64: *locum . . . Europae tenet*) and Asian Greeks on which the argument turns, not the difference between the Greeks of the past and those of the present. This ethnographical opposition between Europe and Asia is one that was common in Greek literature and that probably arose first in the period of the Persian wars, as the Greeks, and especially the Athenians, attempted to articulate the grounds for their moral and military superiority over their Asian enemies.[20] We have noted how stereotypes contrasting the bravery of the Greeks and the slavish weakness of the Asians were supported by pseu-

18. On *laudes urbium,* see Classen, *Die Stadt,* esp. 4–5. For similar praises of Athens, cf. Isoc. *Paneg.* and *Panath.*

19. For an objective account of early interactions between Greeks, Lydians, and Carians, see Carratelli, "Europa ed Asia," 7.

20. See Carratelli, "Europa ed Asia," 5–9.

doscientific theories within the corpus of the Hippocratic writings.[21] What makes Cicero's adoption of this distinction striking is that to the Roman the world was commonly divided in ethnological terms between East and West, with Greece often seen as part of the corrupt East, where weakness, dishonesty, and chicanery prevailed; within the *Pro Flacco,* however, Cicero has resuscitated the ancient Greek point of view, focusing on the ethical contrasts between Europe (which included Greece) and Asia. It is to be remembered as well that the topos as it appears in ancient Greek literature (including the proverbs quoted by Cicero) generally depended on a contrast between the non-Greek and the Greek, while Cicero has used the same topos to posit an ethical distinction between Greek and Greek.

Having pronounced a blanket condemnation upon Asian Greeks, Cicero was faced with the necessity of giving his listeners a reason to believe the testimony of the people of the Lydian town of Apollonis who had sent depositions in support of Flaccus. He describes the inhabitants of Apollonis as the people who are "in all Asia the most thrifty, the most pious, and the most removed from the luxury and unreliability of the Greeks" (71: *tota ex Asia frugalissimi, sanctissimi, a Graecorum luxuria et levitate remotissimi*). They are further described as "fathers of families who are satisfied with what they have, farmers, and rustics" (71: *patres familias suo contenti, aratores, rusticani*). While the Apollonians' land is indeed rich, it is through "hard work and cultivation" (71: *diligentia culturaque*) that it is made better. This description of the Apollonians as stereotypically virtuous farmers exempts them from the racial attack that Cicero has launched against their neighbors. The contrast with the stereotype of the Asian Greek he has played on in the rest of the speech could not be greater. While the ordinary Greek is untrustworthy because of his quick and deceptive mind and tongue, the Apollonians, who seem to inhabit a kind of isolated, Golden Age land where justice prevails, have no share in such negative traits.

Both the distinction between European and Asian Greeks and that between the Apollonians and the majority of Asian Greeks are reiter-

---

21. See above, pp. 142–45. For Roman attitudes towards Greeks (and further bibliography), see Balsdon, *Romans and Aliens,* 30–54. For Cicero's attitude, see Clavel, *De Cicerone Graecorum interprete;* Trouard, *Cicero's Attitude towards the Greeks;* Guite, "Cicero's Attitude to the Greeks." In some sources the division between East and West was cast as a division between Asia and Europe; see Varro *LL* 5.4; cf. Luc. *Phars.* 9.411.

ated in the peroration. As in the *Pro Fonteio,* Cicero depicts state ranged against state, province against province. On one side are Flaccus's enemies, the majority of the Greek city-states in Asia, whose faithlessness has been amply demonstrated. On the other side are the good Asians (that is, the farmers of Apollonis); the provinces of Gaul, Cilicia, Spain, and Crete; the Massilians, Rhodians, Spartans, and Athenians; as well as Achaea, Thessaly, and Boeotia—all of whom, says Cicero, stand in opposition to the Lydian, Phrygian, and Mysian Greeks (100).

THE PROSECUTION OF VERRES

Speeches like the *Pro Flacco,* the *Pro Fonteio,* and the *Pro Scauro* make clear that attacks on foreign ethnic groups were a staple of Ciceronian and presumably Latin rhetoric. It is with a certain sense of relief that we turn from the barrage of ethnic bigotry that played such an important part in these speeches to a further consideration of the strategy of persuasion found in the *Verrines.* Here the results of my earlier analysis of Cicero's indictment of Verres for his theft of statues and precious works of art—an analysis that focused almost exclusively on the fourth part of the Second Action—can be incorporated into a consideration of Cicero's exploitation in the work as a whole of certain commonplaces, especially those that depended on ethical and ethnic stereotypes.

The prosecution of Verres occurred in 70 B.C., early in Cicero's career but not nearly so early as, for instance, the prosecution of Caelius was in the career of young Atratinus. At the time of the trial Cicero was thirty-six years old, a mature and experienced orator, well prepared to prosecute the case that would establish his preeminence in forensic oratory and launch his political career. The *Verrines* represents the only extant speech in which Cicero's powers of persuasion were brought to bear on the side of provincials seeking redress for the abuse they had suffered under Roman rule, and the orator himself was justifiably proud of his handling of the case.[22] Even in the midst of an attack on the

22. Even in the case of the execrable Verres, there have been modern attempts at rehabilitation. See Martorana, "La Venus di Verre." Dilke, "Divided Loyalties in Eastern Sicily," argues that Cicero's rhetorical exaggeration has hidden the degree of support enjoyed by Verres in certain parts of Sicily. *Contra,* see Pritchard, "Gaius Verres." For the identities of those who aided Verres' crimes in Sicily, see Classen, "Verres' Gehilfen in Sizilien." For the importance of the case in establishing Cicero's dominance in forensic oratory, see Smallwood, "The Trial of Verres."

Fig. 4.   The Roman World, 63 B.C. At this time the *imperium Romanum* included the provinces of Sicily, Sardinia and Corsica, Cisalpine Gaul, Narbonese
Gaul, Nearer Spain, Further Spain, Africa, Asia, Macedonia and Achaea, Illy-
ricum, Bithynia, Cyrenaica and Crete, and Cilicia (probably including Pamphylia). At the conclusion of the Third Mithridatic War (62 B.C.), Pompey orga-

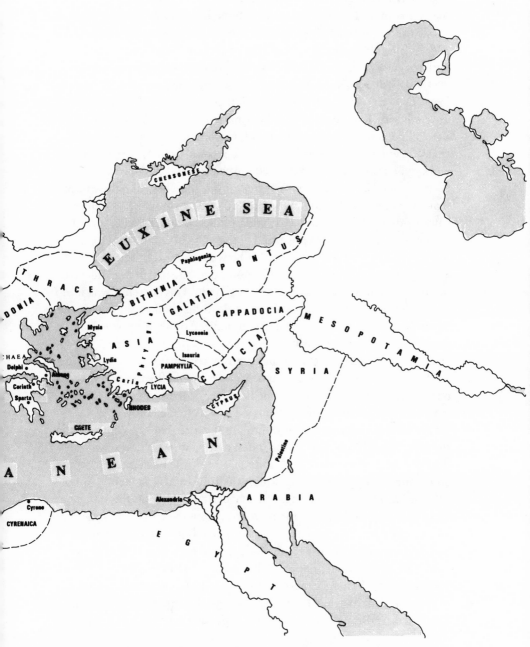

CHERSONESE

E U X I N E   S E A

THRACE

DONIA

Paphlagonia

P O N T U S

BITHYNIA

GALATIA

CAPPADOCIA

M E S O P O T A M I A

Mysia

A S I A

Phrygia

Lycaonia

CHAEA

Delphi

Lydia

Isauria

PAMPHYLIA

CILICIA

S Y R I A

Athens

Caria

Corinth

Sparta

LYCIA

RHODES

CYPRUS

CRETE

A E G E A N

Palestine

A N E A N

Cyrene

Alexandria

A R A B I A

CYRENAICA

E

G

Y

P

T

nized the new provinces of Bithynia-Pontus (including Paphlagonia) and Syria.
Gaul from the Rhine to the Pyrenees became a Roman province as the result of
Julius Caesar's campaigns of 58–50 B.C. In 63 B.C. Mauretania, Numidia,
Egypt, Cappadocia, and Galatia were nominally independent client kingdoms.

evidence of Sardinian provincials in the *Pro Scauro* he refers proudly to the events preceding Verres' trial, recalling how he had made his way in harsh winter through the valleys and hills of Agrigentum and how he had "visited the cottages of the Sicilian farmers" and had even spoken with the men in the fields as they stood sweating at the plough (25).

The *Verrines* is a massive work, comprising, together with the preliminary *Divinatio in Caecilium,* over 450 pages in the Oxford Classical Text edition. It is divided into two parts: the First Action, at which Verres had actually been present and which had preceded the introduction of evidence at the trial; and the Second Action, a much longer work, whose five parts summarized the charges and evidence against the accused. The Second Action was one of the speeches (like the *Pro Milone* or the second *Philippic*) that Cicero published but never delivered, since prior to its delivery the defendant had gone into exile, forced by the mountain of evidence presented in the first part of the trial to realize his conviction would be inevitable if he were to remain in Rome.[23] The Second Action maintained the illusion, however, that it was delivered orally and that Verres was present to hear it. This pretense was in no way an attempt on Cicero's part to mislead his readers. In fact, so far from trying to deceive them, he has capitalized on their knowledge that what he states as fact within the speech was patently untrue. For instance, when Cicero declared that many were surprised to see the defendant in court since it was assumed Verres would flee the city after the damning evidence presented in the first part of the trial (II.1.1), he was making use of irony: irony of the same sort as that employed by a playwright whose audience is allowed to know more than the characters in the play. Again, when the orator stated that he was grateful that Verres' presence had necessitated the continuation of the trial, since it would allow him the opportunity to exhibit the fruit of his long labors on the case (II.1.2), Cicero's ancient readers clearly understood the statement as an explanation both for the pretense within the speech that the trial had actually gone forward and for Cicero's publication of the work.

The *Verrines* as published, then, depended on a fiction, and my analysis, both here and in chapter 3, has acquiesced in this fiction. Cicero would have his readers believe that the Second Action was a continuous oration similar to what he would have given if the trial had actually continued, and my discussion of it accepts this premise and goes on to

23. On events subsequent to the First Action, see Venturini, "La conclusione del processo di Verre."

consider how Cicero went about persuading his hypothetical audience. My confidence that this is a sensible way of reading the speech grows out of the observation that its rhetorical strategy is closely related to that found in the *Pro Scauro, Pro Fonteio,* and *Pro Flacco,* speeches that actually were delivered. This does not mean, of course, that one finds the same arguments in the *Verrines* as those advanced in the speeches in which Cicero defended provincial governors; rather, it is the opposite side of the coin, the *counter*arguments to those discussed above, that Cicero exploits in the prosecution of Verres.[24]

While arguments relating to ethnic stereotypes will be the focus of my discussion, it is instructive to note that a number of other commonplace arguments, which figure prominently in the speeches on behalf of provincial governors, have also been treated from an opposite viewpoint in the *Verrines.* In his speeches in defense of provincial governors, for instance, Cicero not only attempts to discount the evidence of individual witnesses; he also makes use of commonplaces questioning the importance of witnesses in general by elevating the relative position of argument through probabilities as a means of proof.[25] In the *Pro Fonteio* (21–27) Cicero devotes a long passage to the need for jurors to assess critically, rather than simply to credit without question, the testimony of witnesses; in the *Pro Scauro* he calls argument "the voice of

24. It is argued that the unusual length and literary elaboration of the Second Action of the *Verrines* reveals its artificiality. But many of the orations that Cicero actually delivered represented only part of the case for the defense or the prosecution, since several defenders or accusers frequently spoke in sequence during a case. If the *Verrines* had gone forward, Cicero's would have been the sole prosecuting speech, and perhaps its length and elaboration are, in fact, much closer to what would have been delivered than hitherto imagined. *Contra,* see, among others, Fuhrmann, "Tecniche narrative," 41–42. Fuhrmann also argues that Cicero's narrative technique, in which he chooses to turn the oration into a series of exemplary and representative stories, reveals the literary, rather than the forensic, nature of the Second Action. It seems to me, however, that what Fuhrmann is describing is the only possible manner in which Cicero could have effectively organized such an extensive mass of evidence. Fuhrmann's objection that Cicero repeats in exposition material that would have been familiar to the jury from the First Action lacks force, unless we assume the jurors (who would have heard the Second Action only after an extended recess) possessed powers of memory and organization as prodigious as Cicero's own.

25. Quintilian mentions the commonplace concerning the relative value of witnesses and argument in his criticism of orators who simply memorized such topoi and used them unaltered in numerous cases (2.4.27).

reality, the token of nature, the imprint of truth" (16) and demeans the reliability of witnesses, who may easily be "driven, swayed, formed and diverted" (15). In rhetorical theory, evidence from witnesses, documents, legal precedents, tortures, and the like was termed "inartificial proof." While such proofs were simply "found" by the orator, the arguments that constituted "artificial proofs" were "invented" by him. Somewhat surprisingly to the modern, ancient rhetoricians often maintained the superiority of argument over evidence. Aristotle in particular gave short shrift to the subject of inartificial proof, reflecting the belief that such proofs were an adjunct rather than an integral part of rhetoric and that the handling of them was self-evident.[26] Even in Aristotle's time, however, it was realized that the impact of inartificial proofs could be strengthened or undermined by rhetorical argument, and as early as the fifth century B.C. a number of commonplaces had been evolved to aid the orator in inventing ways to deal with them.

Cicero was well prepared to adopt the Aristotelian point of view— that argument from probabilities was superior to direct evidence— when it suited him. He subscribed to the view that "witnesses could bend the truth, documents could be altered, slaves might lie under torture, but the rational force of argument from probability was irrefutable" in speeches such as the *Pro Fonteio* and *Pro Scauro,* in which the bulk of the inartificial proof told against his client.[27] In the prosecution of Verres, however, we see Cicero arguing the opposite side of the question. The orator had proved his case in the First Action by forgoing the customary extended opening speech and instead proceeding quickly to the presentation of direct evidence. In spite of the fact that the Second Action is the script for a highly elaborated performance, making use of the entire panoply of rhetorical weapons to rouse the passions of the audience, the orator wished to make it appear that he continued to rely primarily on objective, rather than subjective, proof. He therefore bypassed the usual inquiry into the private life and habits of the accused, a standard strategy of proof through probability, and restricted himself to

26. Aristotle's disdain for the subject would have stemmed from the philosopher's desire to found the art of rhetoric on the basis of rational predictability. According to this point of view, the proof through argument that an event should have occurred was superior to proof by direct evidence that it did (Arist. *Rhet.* 1.2.2 (1355b35–39), 1.15.1–33 (1375a22–1377b12); Kennedy, *Aristotle,* 108–18). See above, p. 25.

27. Cf. *Flac.* 23.

the discussion of specific crimes committed in public office, making frequent references to the witnesses and documents he had introduced to prove his contentions.[28] Cicero's attitude here, so different from that found in the trials in which he defended provincial governors, is summarized in his remark to Verres' advocate, Hortensius: "In this kind of trial, when someone is said to have stolen or appropriated something, who in the world pays attention to us? Is not the entire attention of the judges focused on either the documents or the witnesses?" (II.1.27).

A similar attempt to anticipate the arguments of the defense also appears when Cicero treats the topic of the interest of the state vis-à-vis that of the accused. As has been shown, a key element in the defense of Roman governors accused under the *de repetundis* laws was the presentation of the case as one that pitted the interests of the Roman state, represented by the accused, against the supposed interests of an isolated group of provincials who claimed to have suffered abuse at the hands of the accused. This tactic, which represents a variation on commonplaces concerning expediency and justice and which was traditionally assigned by ancient rhetoric to the province of deliberative oratory, is of great importance in forensic speeches of this kind.[29] While no ancient orator would have claimed outright to favor injustice towards conquered peoples, he may well, as in Cicero's defenses of Fonteius and Flaccus, have argued the patriotic necessity of the actions of the accused, whatever the complaints of the resentful provincials. In the *Verrines* Cicero employs a variety of tactics to prevent his opponents from exploiting this strategy.[30] He points out to anyone who might claim that Verres should be acquitted because the Roman citizens of Sicily supported him that the extortion court had been instituted specifically for the purpose of hearing the complaints of Rome's allies, not its citizens (II.2.15). He

28. Quintilian states that it required the greatest force of eloquence to refute inartificial proofs, and goes on to give general advice to the orator faced with the need to deny or mitigate such material (5.1.1–2).

29. Quint. 3.8.1–3, 30; cf. Cic. *Off.* 3.40.

30. The second speech of the Second Action even includes Cicero's ironic reference to the commonplace of the defendant's counsel, "Save this man for the Republic" (II.2.76: *Retinete, retinete hominem in civitate, iudices; parcite et conservate ut sit qui vobiscum res iudicet qui in senatu sine ulla cupiditate de bello et pace sententiam ferat*). For a general analysis of Cicero's exploitation (in the *Divinatio in Caecilium* and *In Verrem* I) of the political circumstances that surrounded this trial, see Neumeister, *Grundsätze der forensischen Rhetorik*, 35–46.

then hastens to add that, in fact, it was not the provincials alone who complained of Verres' conduct but a large number of Roman citizens residing and doing business in Sicily. The orator then declares that if Verres' administration had been satisfactory to any race, whether Sicilian or Roman, or to any order, whether farmer, stockbreeder, or merchant, he would be content to see the defendant freed.

Perhaps most important to Cicero's efforts to prevent the case from turning into a matter of "us versus them" was his refusal to base his demand for Verres' conviction simply on the sympathy and pity owed the abused Sicilians; at every point he connects the idea of justice for the Sicilians with the larger issue of the interests of the Roman state. At the very outset of the First Action he warns the jury that a corrupt verdict in the case would bring about the final discredit of senatorial juries and the transfer of the extortion court to the *equites* (I.3). He introduces numerous witnesses and documents to prove that Verres had committed crimes not only against provincials but also against Roman citizens throughout his career as legate in Asia, praetor in Rome, and propraetor in Sicily.[31] In the third part of the Second Action, Cicero complains as much about the harm done to Rome by the disruption of the Sicilian grain supply and the collection of taxes as about the sufferings of the Sicilians.[32] In the fourth part, as has been shown, he constantly attempts to transform the artworks stolen by Verres into symbols of the just, stable, and profitable Roman rule that had existed before Verres' tenure of power. Finally, to prevent the prosecution from implying that Verres' assault on human rights in Sicily was justified by the exigencies of the military situation there, Cicero charges in the fifth part of the Second Action that Verres has been criminally incompetent in his attempts to secure the island from piratical activity and even suggests that the former governor had colluded with the pirates.[33]

The Character of Verres and of the Sicilians

One sees from the above how adroitly Cicero as prosecutor anticipated and undermined the strategies that his opponent Hortensius might have used to defend Verres and that Cicero himself would later call on in

31. II.1.9, 14, 90–94, 104–14; 2.17, 30, 166; 3.6, 93–96; 4.26, 37, 42, 46, 58; 5.69, 72–75, 77, 136–37, 139–73.

32. II.3.11, 43, 48, 82–83, 120, 122, 127, 137, 201, 226.

33. II.5.60–79, 82. On pirates, cf. II.1.9.

defending clients like Fonteius, Scaurus, and Flaccus. But of all the strategies he could have anticipated from the defense, the most predictable and potentially the most dangerous was a racial attack against the Greeks in Sicily along the same lines as that which he would himself launch against the Asian Greeks in the *Pro Flacco*. How did Cicero forestall such an attack? One method was to anticipate the thrust of the defense's attack and to turn it back against his opponents. We have seen that in the speeches on behalf of provincial governors Cicero focused on the lack of *fides* and *religio* to be expected from foreign witnesses. In the *Verrines* Cicero counters this anticipated tactic from his opponents by attacking Verres on just these issues: throughout the First and Second Actions Cicero depicts Verres as a tyrant to whom human and divine laws were without force and whose entire public career represented a series of outrages against the obligations he owed to both.

Cicero's indictment of Verres for his violations of *fides* operates on a number of levels. In the first speech of the Second Action (devoted to Verres' career before his governorship of Sicily) he speaks of the defendant's betrayal of the trust placed in him by his superiors, describing his embezzlement of money when serving as quaestor in Gaul under the consul Cn. Carbo and of his later abandonment of this post (II.1.34–40). He refers as well to Verres' betrayal of the man whom he then served under as legate and proquaestor, Cn. Dolabella (II.1.41–102). Since the assignment of the quaestors to their provinces was made by lot, and since the lot was believed to be divinely guided, the orator presents the betrayal of the relationship between Verres and his superiors as both moral and religious corruption. Verres is, in addition, stigmatized for his violations of *fides* towards those under his magisterial power. Cicero implies, in fact, that Verres was at his worst in his treatment of those who were most dependent on his good faith. In the course of the account of Verres' career in the East Cicero frequently chooses to expand upon those crimes that show the accused preying upon provincials, especially women and children. The story of the affair at Lampsacus, in which Verres' lust for a young woman leads to the death of the father and brother who try to protect her, and the account of the legacy of the boy Junius fit into this pattern of exploitation of the vulnerable.[34] Such incidents also form a prelude to the revelation in parts 2 through 5 of the Second Action of Verres' greatest betrayal of *fides:* his abuse dur-

---

34. Lampsacus affair: II.1.63–85; story of Junius: II.1.129–54.

ing his provincial governorship of the Sicilians, whose well-being had been entrusted to him by the state.

In chapter 3 I noted Cicero's attempt to paint Verres in the colors of the rhetorical tyrant. This strategy overlaps with the orator's attacks on Verres as a man without religious scruples, for the tyrant is a despiser not only of human beings but of the gods as well. Throughout the *Verrines* Cicero accuses Verres of a veritable war against the gods, repeatedly making use of the term *religio* in doing so.[35] One crucial part of this attack turns on the defendant's appropriation of statues and works of art in the eastern Mediterranean and in Sicily. Since most of these were objects of veneration taken from temples or from shrines within private homes, their theft could be characterized as a religious offense. This strategy is introduced in the *Divinatio in Caecilium,* a speech in which Cicero argued his own claims to represent the Sicilians in the prosecution of Verres over the claims of a certain Caecilius. He begins the oration with the statement that the Sicilians could hardly appeal to their gods for help, as they had already been stolen by Verres. According to Cicero, the defendant had removed "the holiest images from the most sacred shrines" (*Div. Caec.* 3: *simulacra sanctissima . . . ex delubris religiosissimis*). The idea is prominent as well in the First Action, a summary of the crimes of the accused, in which Cicero alludes to Verres' plundering of the holy places of Asia and Pamphylia, as well as of Sicily. In the *prooemium* of the Second Action, Cicero voices the theme that will resound throughout all five parts of the work: that it is the gods themselves who seek justice in the trial of Verres. He declares:

35. *Verr.* II.1.6: *multa enim et in deos et in homines impie nefarieque commisit;* 4.72: *ita sese in ea provincia per triennium gessit ut ab isto non solum hominibus verum etiam dis immortalibus bellum indictum putaretur;* 5.188: *ceteros item deos deasque omnis . . . quorum templis et religionibus iste . . . bellum sacrilegum semper impiumque habuit indictum.* Cf. *Font.* 30. In his indictment of the defendant's offenses against various divinities, Cicero had to deal with the fact that Verres had fostered a close connection between himself and the powerful shrine of Venus Erycina in northwestern Sicily. Cicero solves this problem by focusing on the Sicilian cult of Ceres at Henna and by depicting Verres' devotion to Venus and Cupid as a mask for his greed and an expression of his libidinousness. See della Corte, "Conflitto di culti"; von Albrecht, "Cicero und die Götter Siziliens"; Martorana, "La Venus di Verre." Martorana, unlike della Corte and von Albrecht, sees Verres' support of the cult of Venus Erycina as a patriotic attempt to maintain and strengthen the link between the island and Roman *imperium.*

The gods of our fathers are taking him away for punishment because he was a man who could tear sons from the embrace of their parents in order to execute them and even demand that the parents pay him a price in order to bury their children. The holy rites and ceremonies of all the violated shrines and temples, the images of the gods, which were not only taken away from their temples but even allowed to lie hidden and neglected in the shadows, do not allow his mind any rest from madness and insanity. . . . We not only seek that this man be condemned so that property might be restored to those from whom it was stolen; the violated sanctity of the immortal gods must also be expiated.

(II.1.7–8)

Cicero then presents within the Second Action a seemingly unending catalogue of outrages against religious sensibilities.

At the same time that he was attempting to create for his audience a vivid picture of Verres as a man devoid of any sense of duty to men or to the gods, Cicero hoped to characterize the Sicilians as a race especially distinguished by such sensibilities, praising in particular their trustworthiness as allies and their pious respect for what they conceived of as their religious obligations. The introduction to the entire excursus on the crimes committed by Verres in Sicily begins with a passage devoted to the island's special bonds to Rome. Sicily is praised as the first province to be acquired by the Republic, the "jewel of the empire" (II.2.2: *ornamentum imperi*). Once the island had been reduced, says Cicero, it never wavered in its loyalty (*fides*) and goodwill (*benevolentia*) towards the Roman people. For this reason Africanus had adorned its cities after the fall of Carthage, and Marcellus had allowed even hostile Syracuse to remain standing. This "storehouse of the Republic" had long fed and equipped the Romans and their armies, even during the dark days of the Social War. Cicero refers also to the fact that Sicily had proved a source of extensive profits both to those who exploited its riches from afar and to the many Roman citizens who had settled there. It is a great advantage to many citizens, he states, that they may repair to this province, which is "close at hand, loyal, and rich in resources" (II.2.6: *propinquam fidelem fructuosamque provinciam*). The source of Sicily's outstanding loyalty to Rome is then revealed to be the character of its inhabitants. Cicero claims that the Sicilians are nothing like other Greeks, whose vices include laziness and excess (II.2.7: *desidia . . . luxuries*); rather, they possess the virtues of endurance, bravery, and frugality (II.2.7: *patientia virtus frugalitasque*), traits that remind the orator not of the Romans of the present but of those of the past. He goes on to praise the great industriousness, thrift, and diligence of the Sicilians (II.2.7: *summus labor . . . summa parsimonia summa diligentia*). They also are unassuming individuals who bear injustice and oppression without murmur (II.2.8–10). Only the outrages perpetrated by Verres have forced them to seek legal redress, and if this desperate plea for justice fails, they will simply abandon their homes. The diction and thought of such passages are clear enough: as with the Apollonians of the *Pro Flacco*, the virtues of the Sicilians are the stereotypical virtues of farmers, a class that Cicero says constitutes the heart both of the Republic as a whole and of the island of Sicily in particular (II.2.149). Although it is true that within the corpus of the *Verrines* Cicero characterizes the inhabitants of Sicily in various ways, depending on shifts in emphasis and changes in rhetorical goals, this attribution of stereotypical rustic virtues to the Sicilians recurs throughout. In one passage we even discover the scene, familiar from the *Pro Roscio*, of the innocent and confused countryman in the city. When Cicero is challenging the intent of a clause in a tax law allowing farmers to sue in disputes with tithe collectors he accuses Verres of "dragging men from the field to the forum, from cultivating the earth to the benches of the law courts, from the familiarity of rustic affairs to the unknown milieu of litigations and legal judgments" (II.3.26: *Ex agro homines traducis in forum, ab aratro ad subsellia, ab usu rerum rusticarum ad insolitam litem atque iudicium*).

Cicero's strategy in the Second Action, then, was to forestall the defense's anticipated attack on the witnesses as untrustworthy foreigners by characterizing the Sicilians as typical farmers rather than typical Greeks. This strategy was surely an obvious one, since Sicily was blessed with an abundance of rich farmland and was renowned in antiquity for its rich agricultural produce. As Cicero remarks, "The entire utility and advantage of the province of Sicily insofar as it relates to the interests of the Roman people consists chiefly in the matter of grain" (II.3.11). The strategy was also one that could be easily exploited in the third part of the Second Action, an extensive part of the speech dealing with the crimes committed by Verres against Sicilian farmers (divided by the orator into sections dealing with the tithe on grain, the purchase of grain, and grain commutation).

When Cicero came to the fourth part of the Second Action he faced a more difficult task, since he was compelled to speak at length about the various statues and works of art stolen or extorted by Verres from Sicil-

ian city-states and individuals. As previously noted, the accusations of
Verres' appropriation of cult statues from the very temples of the gods
added great force to Cicero's depiction of the defendant as an impious
tyrant. The difficulty such material raised, however, was that the complainants here could not be portrayed as simple farmers but were clearly
men of means and sophistication. The Sicilian witnesses who accused
Verres of removing precious works of art belonging to them or their
cities might therefore have served to reinforce the negative stereotype of
all Greeks as a race characterized by *luxuria* and *vanitas*. Cicero solves
this problem by depicting the desire of the Sicilians for the return of
their property as an expression not of *luxuria* but of a special sort of
religio. As has been demonstrated, the passages dealing with particular
objects removed by Verres emphasize their value as religious or patriotic
symbols rather than as precious works of art. The strategy is best articulated in a passage in which Cicero speaks in general of the attachment
of the Greeks to statues, paintings, and works of this sort, objects that
he and his audience deemed of little worth (II.4.124, 132–34). He
states:

> All [the Greeks] are affected by religious scruples (*religione*) and believe that
> the [statues of] their ancestral gods, handed down from their ancestors,
> should be carefully kept and worshipped by them. And further, these orna-
> ments, these works and artistic objects, statues, and pictures, afford the
> Greeks an unusual degree of pleasure. Therefore, when we hear their com-
> plaints we can understand why these events seem so bitter to them while we,
> perhaps, view them as insignificant trifles.
>
> (II.4.132)

The tone throughout the passage is unmistakably condescending. Yet it
should be seen that Cicero has effectively stolen the defense attorney's
thunder. He has agreed to the proposition that the Sicilians, like all
Greeks, placed an inordinate value on ornamental objects, statues,
paintings, and the like. But he converts this attachment to such "trifles"
into the non-Roman expression of one of the most Roman of virtues,
religio.

CAPUA AND THE THREAT TO ROME

The speeches surveyed show Cicero's cleverness in adapting and manipulating stereotypes of other races and cultures, whether he was intent
on attacking provincial witnesses or defending them. The creativity of

the orator in handling the connection between *ēthos* and *locus* resided in his intelligent choice, deft arrangement, and subtle manipulation of the commonplaces that were the inheritance of Latin rhetoric in this period. The *De lege agraria* 2 is a work that has been criticized for its recourse to well-worn ethnic stereotypes. At first blush, Cicero's dependence in the speech on a topos dating from the third century B.C. concerning the treachery of the Capuans appears to give the criticism force. But a closer study of the orator's strategy demonstrates that in the oration familiar commonplaces have been refashioned and adapted to carry new meanings.

In the discussion that follows I have employed a slightly different approach to the material in the speech. In the introduction to this work I argued that real understanding of particular parts of a Ciceronian oration—such as those that exploit ethnic prejudice—can be won only through constant reference to the role played by such passages within the overall strategy of persuasion found in the speech in which they occur. Perhaps no speech illustrates this point better than the *De lege agraria* 2. Cicero has constructed this particular work so tightly and coherently that if we hope to understand the intended effect of the references to the character of the Capuans and Campanians that occur at the end of the oration (and the methods that have been employed to achieve that effect), then it is absolutely necessary that we "hear" this part of the speech in the way it was meant to be heard: first, as the end point in a linearly developed structure of representation of the world and, second, as the culmination of certain crucial themes developed throughout the course of the speech. Thus before we consider passages dealing explicitly with *ēthos* and *locus* we will analyze the progression of arguments leading up to these passages.[36]

THE ART OF ARRANGEMENT

The *De lege agraria* 2 was delivered in 63 B.C. from the Rostra to the assembled people. By it Cicero hoped to induce his audience to abandon their support of a bill proposed by the tribune Rullus that would distribute land to a proportion of the urban citizens, and in this he was suc-

36. For a reconstruction of the provisions of the bill, see Jonkers, *De Lege Agraria*. For a political analysis and recent bibliography, see Mitchell, *Cicero*, 184–205. Most historians see the bill as an attempt by Caesar and, perhaps, Crassus to strengthen their position at the expense of Pompey.

cessful.[37] Cicero was, of course, in control of the material he would treat and the way in which he would treat it. In the speech, however, one of Cicero's tactics was to mask the degree to which the presentation of Rullus's bill was being rhetorically manipulated. He therefore gives his listeners the impression that the topics he discusses and the order in which he discusses them are simply determined by the content and arrangement of Rullus's bill. He says that he has found, after examining the document "from the very first to the very last provision" (15), that its only aim is tyrannical power for its inceptors. After declaring that he will make known the reality that lies behind this seemingly popular legislation (16), the orator discusses in order the first four articles of the law (16: *primum caput;* 18: *capite altero;* 29: *tertio capite . . . quarto*). At this point his audience is led to assume that, just as Cicero himself had studied the provisions of the law from beginning to end, he will go through the law with them in sequence, revealing the true meaning of each article from first to last. This impression is reinforced by the use of words such as *consequuntur* (38) and *sequitur* (47, 56), which suggest that the topic dealt with occurs next in sequence among the provisions of the bill.

There is no reason for us to accept without question the impression Cicero gives. It seems clear that the framers of the bill left the content vague in order to allow themselves the widest latitude in exercising their powers. Cicero complains often that the articles of the law were ambiguous.[38] This ambiguity can be seen, first, in the sections of the proposal dealing with the land to be sold by the decemvirs to procure money. Cicero says that the law orders (38: *iubet*) the decemvirs to sell the *ager*

---

37. Cf. Classen, *Recht, Rhetorik, Politik,* 304–67, who provides an exhaustive comparison of the *De lege agraria* 2 with the first agrarian speech (delivered before the Senate). I believe that my own conclusions concerning invention and arrangement complement and expand upon Classen's exploration of the subtle interrelation of *inventio* and *elocutio*.

38. See 35, 36, 38, 39, 41, 55, 56, 57, 66, 67, 73, 74. The idea that Cicero must expose the hidden intentions of Rullus is repeated often: 7 (*insidiosas . . . simulationes*), 10 (*quiddam obscure moliuntur*), 12 (*clam . . . privatos quosdam . . . coetus occultos noctem adiungere et solitudinem*), 15 (*ego . . . reperio*), 28 (*ita malitiosum ut obscurum*), 36 (*obscurum atque caecum*), 41 (*ut occulte latet, ut recondita est, ut furtim*), 44 (*caecis tenebris et caligine*), 49 (*patefacio vobis quas isti penitus abstrusas insidias*), 55 (*in Paphlagoniae tenebris atque in Cappadociae solitudine*), 66 (*obscura spe et caeca exspectatione*), 68 (*hoc carmen . . . non vobis, sed sibi intus canit*), 75 (*obscure*), 100 (*insidiisque*). Cf. *Leg. agr.* 1.1 (*occulte cuniculis*) and 3.12 (*sub hoc verbo furtum . . . latet*).

publicus outside Italy that had been acquired during or after 88 B.C.
This reference to a chronological formula to determine *ager publicus*
indicates that the framers of the bill were unwilling to tie themselves
down to the sale of particular lands. Since there was hardly a Roman
province during this period that had not been involved in sedition or
war, Cicero was free to argue that a great number of lands might be
liable to such sale. When he suggests that Pergamum, Smyrna, Tralles,
Ephesus, Miletus, Cyzicus, and all Asia might be sold (39), the choice of
places named is surely made by him, not dictated by Rullus's bill.[39] The
same may be said of the references to Bithynia (40), Mytilenae (40),
Alexandria, and all of Egypt (41, 43–44), since the phrasing used by
Cicero makes clear that these places were not explicitly named in the
proposal.[40]

Cicero also speaks of the tax lands—*vectigalia*—to be sold. He di-
rects the herald to read a list of specific places in Italy and Sicily that
had been named by Rullus (47: *vendant nominatim*) and that, he says,
the law "demands and requires" (47: *cogit atque imperat*) the decemvirs
to sell. The orator then states that Rullus orders (50: *iubet*) a great number of other lands to be sold, mentioning Attalia, Phaselis, Olympus,
Apera, Oroanda, Gedusa, royal lands in Bithynia, the Chersonese, Macedonia, Corinth, Cyrene, Paphlagonia, Pontus, and Cappadocia, as
well as New Carthage and Carthage (50–51). Since the herald had been
told to read the *vectigalia* to be sold within Italy and Sicily, the listener
would naturally assume that the lands next named by Cicero were the
vectigalia outside Italy and Sicily that the bill explicitly required the decemvirs to sell. There is little real basis for this assumption. A statement
introducing the section of the speech dealing with *vectigalia* outside of
Italy indicates that Rullus had not specified any of them in the bill: Cicero had here stated that he would make his listeners see and understand what he himself had already understood, thereby implying that
what followed was a revelation of specifics disguised by the language of
the bill.[41] It is probable that Rullus had not explicitly named any of the

39. Cicero states that it will be "convenient" (39: *commodum*) for Rullus to
say that these lands are the property of the Roman people.

40. The orator asks what would prevent Rullus from saying that these places
should be sold (40–41).

41. He makes a similar statement later in the speech: after saying that the
law empowered the decemvirs to buy land but did not specify where those lands
would be located, Cicero declares that he does not want the people to remain in

vectigalia outside Italy to be sold and that the choice of places mentioned was Cicero's own.

The bill must also have been ambiguous in those sections dealing with the acquisition of land on which colonists would be settled. Although Rullus had limited these allotments to Italy (66), no sites were actually named. Cicero complains that Rullus would not specify the lands on which he intended to settle colonists either because these lands were barren and unhealthy (66–70) or because they would be used as seats of opposition to Rome (73–74). When the orator suggests that land will be bought at certain specific sites in central Italy (66), the choice of places reflects nothing found in the Rullan bill. Similarly, when Cicero states that colonies might be implanted at Sipontum or Salapia (71) or that an armed *praesidium* might be located on the Janiculum (74), he is making a rhetorical choice based on the persuasive force of the material.

One should also view with scepticism the impression Cicero gives that the arrangement of topics within the speech follows the order of provisions in the law. After citing the first four articles of the bill, Cicero quotes from the document six times (31, 38, 56, 59, 67, 74), but in none of these passages does he specify exactly which article of the law he is referring to. It is logical to assume that the bill moved from sections dealing with (*a*) the election of the decemvirs to (*b*) the procurement of money to (*c*) the purchase of land for colonization. In general this is also the order of subjects in the speech. It should not be assumed, however, that Cicero would have tied himself to a fixed sequence of specific topics dictated by the order in which they occur in the bill.

The section dealing with Capua and Campania (76–97), for instance, constitutes the climax of the speech, but it is most unlikely that all the provisions concerning this area occurred at the end of the agrarian bill. These provisions would have involved two subjects: the sale of Campanian public lands and the establishment of a new colony at Capua. Mention of the sale of the Campanian *ager publicus* would have come under those articles at the beginning of the bill dealing with the acquisition of money. As for the creation of a colony at Capua, Cicero's complaint that Rullus had refused to name potential sites for colonies

---

ambiguous hope and blind expectation (66). He then suggests specific areas where land might be bought, none of them named by Rullus.

Representations

(66) makes it unlikely that Capua was specifically mentioned in the bill as the site of a new colony.[42] There is little reason to suppose that the topic that would provide a vehicle for Cicero's most strenuous objections to Rullus's plan coincided with the provision named last in the measure. Rather, Cicero places his treatment of Capua and Campania, as he does the other topics of the oration, in that part of the speech where it will be most persuasive.

The choice of places mentioned in the *De lege agraria* 2 and the sequence in which they occur are not the result of a strict adherence by Cicero to the content and arrangement of the measure proposed by Rullus, even though Cicero gives his audience that impression. Although he wishes to disguise the fact, the orator has profited from the ambiguity and inexactitude of the articles of the law to mention only those places he wishes and to mention them at exactly those points in the speech where he judges their impact will be greatest. A careful examination of the choice and arrangement of this material, therefore, reveals much about the strategy of the speech.

Orbis terrarum

A study of the references to places in the *De lege agraria* 2 indicates that Cicero has attempted in the speech to control his listeners' conception of geographical space—which, in turn, forms the backdrop to the actions attributed to the decemvirs. In the early sections of the speech the orator induces his audience to envision the power of the decemvirs operating throughout "the whole world" (*orbis terrarum*).[43] In section 15, for instance, Cicero declares that the purpose of the Rullan bill is to create "ten kings of the treasury, of the revenue-producing lands, of all the provinces, of the whole Republic, of the kingdoms, of free peoples, and of the whole world" (*decem reges aerari, vectigalium, provinciarum omnium, totius rei publicae, regnorum, liberorum populorum, orbis denique terrarum*). This idea of the all-embracing power of the decemvirs is then reiterated several times. The power of the decemvirs is termed

42. The idea of a Campanian colony had been discussed at the January 1 meeting of the Senate, for it was there that Rullus said he would begin distribution of these lands with the rural tribes (79). It was perhaps also at this meeting that the figure of five thousand colonists had been suggested (76).

43. For the phrase *orbis terrarum*, see 15, 26, 37, 45, 64, 98. Cf. 1.2 (*orbis terrae*), 9, 15.

"unlimited" (33: *infinita*) like that of kings or tyrants, and it operates over "the world and all its peoples" (33: *orbis terrarum gentiumque omnium*). Cicero complains that the land commissioners will be able to remain at Rome or "wander wherever they wish" (34: *vagari ut liceat*), and, in assessing the harm that they will bring to foreign nations, he predicts that they will leave the city and bring disgrace on the Roman name as they "wander throughout the entire world" (45: *cum hinc egressi sunt . . . per totum orbem terrarum vagabuntur*).

This power, derived from the assembly at Rome and exercised throughout the world, is also pictured turning back upon the city. Cicero says in section 47: "When they have gorged themselves on the blood of the allies, of foreign nations, and of kings, they would cut the sinews of the Roman people, lay violent hands on the revenue-producing lands, and break into the treasury" (*cum se sociorum, cum exterarum nationum, cum regum sanguine implerint, incidant nervos populi Romani, adhibeant manus vectigalibus vestris, inrumpant in aerarium*). The sequence of places in this list reverses the order of that found in section 15, which progressed from the *aerarium* to the *orbis terrarum*. Here, the sentence is divided into two parts that move in the opposite direction. The first three phrases in the sentence, connected by anaphora, culminate in the verb *implerint* and contain the idea that the exercise of decemviral power will first burden the world at large. The second tricolon, using three striking verbs that ascend in violence, moves the attention of the listeners from a focus on the outside world to Rome and its financial revenues. The *vectigalia*, the "sinews of the Roman people," are made to appear so crucial to the financial health of the city that the decemvirs' action is likened to an attack on the treasury itself.[44]

In addition to these, six other passages contain lists composed of parts of the Roman world (34, 39, 62, 71, 72, 98).[45] All of these serve

44. Cf. Cic. *Imp. Pomp.* 19 for the connection between *vectigalia* and Roman finances.

45. 34 (*omnis provincias . . . liberos populos . . . regnorum*), 39 (see below, p. 224), 62 (*omnes urbes, agri, regna denique, postremo etiam vectigalia vestra*), 71 (*omnis urbis, agros, vectigalia, regna*), 72 (*vectigalibus abalienatis, sociis vexatis, regibus atque omnibus gentibus exinanitis*), 98 (*urbis, nationes, provincias, liberos populos, reges, terrarum denique orbem*). Cf. 1.2 (*urbes pacatae, agri sociorum, regum status*), 8 (*provinciis, regnis, liberis populis*), 11 (*provincias, civitates liberas, socios, amicos, reges*), 15 (*orbem terrarum . . . vectigalia . . . aerarium*), and *Imp. Pomp.* 31 (*omnes orae atque omnes terrae gentes na-*

to reinforce the audience's image of the decemvirs' insidious power let loose upon a defenseless *imperium*. A study of the content and arrangement of the lists shows a strong preoccupation with style, for in each the orator chooses a number of elements from a set vocabulary (*urbes, agri, gentes, nationes, liberi populi, regna, reges, vectigalia, provinciae, socii*) and arranges them in a careful sequence determined as much by sound as by meaning.[46] A good example of this emphasis on style can be seen in a passage in which Cicero declares of one of the articles of the bill: "By this article, citizens, I say that all peoples, nations, provinces, and realms are entrusted and handed over to the dominion, judgment, and power of the decemvirs" (39: *hoc capite, Quirites, omnis gentis, nationes, provincias, regna decemvirum dicioni, iudicio potestatique permissa et condonata esse dico*). The sentence is carefully modeled. After *Quirites* four nouns follow, and after *decemvirum*, three nouns and then two verbs follow, giving the sequence of coordinated elements the shape of an inverted pyramid. The selection of *gentis, nationes, provincias,* and *regna* is chiefly determined by the weight and sound of the words, just as is the use of three synonyms for power (*dicio, iudicium, potestas*) and two for entrusting (*permitto, condono*). Although certain elements are marked by special emphasis, in general, lists such as this depend less on the specific meaning of their constituent parts than on an overall weightiness of diction and the general sense given that every part of the world will come under the sway of the land commissioners. The use of the adjective *omnis* at the beginning of four of these lists (34, 39, 62, 71) reinforces this impression.

The repetition of the types of places in which the decemvirs will hold power is interspersed with the mention of a great number of specific places. In section 39 Cicero speaks of Pergamum, Smyrna, Tralles, Ephesus, Miletus, and Cyzicus.[47] A little later he mentions Bithynia and Mytilenae (40) and speaks in detail of Alexandria (41–44). This is followed by references to Attalia, Phaselis, Olympus, Apera, Oroanda, and

---

tiones, maria denique omnia cum universa tum in singulis oris omnes sinus atque portus).

46. Such pleonasm and alliterative effects were also characteristic of early Latin; see, for example, prayers quoted by Cato *Agr.* 141.

47. Jonkers, *De Lege Agraria,* 81–82 (ad 2.39), names these as "the wealthiest cities in Asia."

Gedusa (50);[48] to the lands of Attalus in the Chersonese, of Philip and Perses in Macedonia, and of Apion in Corinth and Cyrene; to the cities of New Carthage and Carthage and to the lands of Mithridates in Paphlagonia, Pontus, and Cappadocia (50–51).

Cicero had various reasons for naming these places. It is unlikely that his listeners had a clear idea of the location and nature of any but the most famous of these sites. Much of the eastern *imperium* had, in fact, been won by Pompey and others only in the decade and a half before this speech. Cicero's audience would, perhaps, have known of Pergamum, Miletus, Alexandria, and Carthage but could hardly have been acquainted with places such as Apera, Oroanda, and Gedusa. References to many strange and foreign lands would simply have left the listener with the sense that the scope of the power granted by the bill would be limitless. Further, such a multiplicity of references would have promoted confusion as to the exact contents of the measure. At the end of this part of the speech the ancient (like the modern) audience would have only the dimmest idea of which lands were going to be sold, which might be sold, and which were outside the jurisdiction of the decemvirs. This confusion is surely intentional, for the orator uses no such tactics in his Senate speech opposing the bill. There, speaking before an audience with much wider knowledge and experience, Cicero limits mention of specific places to a discrete number, carefully connecting each with the name of its heroic Roman conqueror (1.5–6).[49]

The mention of the lands dominated by Philip and Mithridates and of Corinth and Carthage is significant, since each of these summoned up the memory of formidable opponents to Roman rule. In fact, at the time of the speech Mithridates was still alive and, as long as he was, still viewed as a threat to Roman security (52). The idea that the decemvirs would exercise power in these places would have suggested to Cicero's audience that decemviral power might well be linked to military opposition to the state. This is particularly clear in the references to Carthage. Here Cicero states that Scipio Aemilianus was not as "conscien-

48. Attalia was in Pamphylia, Phaselis and Olympus. in Lycia. Apera (emended from [*agrum*] *Agerensem*) and Oroanda (emended from [*agrum*] *Orindicum*) are uncertain readings. Zumpt, *De lege agraria,* 88 (ad 2.50), substitutes Eleusa (an island off the coast of Cilicia) for Gedusa, which is unknown.

49. See the discussion of this technique in Classen, *Recht, Rhetorik, Politik,* 323–24, 361, 364. For exaggeration in the speech before the people, see also Dilke, "Cicero's Attitude to the Allocation of Land."

tious" (51: *diligens*) as Rullus, for Scipio had consecrated the site of Carthage to serve as a reminder of an unsuccessful attempt by a city to contend in power with Rome, while Rullus would sell the site and allow resettlement. The passage foreshadows the extensive section near the end of the speech dealing with the colonization of Capua. In the case of Capua, as with Carthage, Rullus intended (according to Cicero) to disregard the wise provisions made by the *maiores* for the security of the state by reviving the site of its former enemy; the result will be that in the future, as in the past, that city will become a seat of opposition to Rome.

In addition to the practical arguments Cicero advances concerning the danger that would be posed if the decemvirs were to exercise power over certain strategic areas, or the loss in taxes that would result from divestiture, Cicero applies to these places a symbolic value. The lands possessed by the *populus Romanus* were not only a source of revenue and a guarantee of security, they were a source of *dignitas*.[50] Describing the public land of Sicily, Cicero speaks of the farmland and cities that their ancestors had left to the people of Rome (48: *maiores nostri proprium nobis reliquerint*). He speaks as well of the places that had come into the possession of the people through the victorious campaigns of P. Servilius Vatia Isauricus (50: *imperio et victoria . . . vestra facta sunt*). Since Servilius's campaigns had taken place only in the preceding decade, it may be assumed that the obscure locations in the East mentioned in this passage would have been unfamiliar to Cicero's audience. The diction of the passage (*vestra facta sunt*) points to the fact that the significance of these places lay chiefly in the Roman sense of pride in their possession. All the lands mentioned, whether known or unknown, whether of great or little value, were a common inheritance handed down to the people of Rome by the *maiores* of the past and the *principes* of the present. Their retention was a source of honor, for every Roman citizen derived *dignitas* through the *imperium* of the state as a whole and, conversely, could be disgraced by the loss of these lands. Rullus, therefore, could be pictured as a spendthrift son (48: *luxuriosus . . . nepos*) who would rob his family of their patrimony.

50. For the elevation of *dignitas* over *utilitas* in a public address, see Cic. *De or.* 2.334: *Ergo in suadendo nihil est optabilius quam dignitas; nam qui utilitatem petit, non quid maxime velit suasor, sed quid interdum magis sequatur, videt.* This appeal is also used (albeit to a limited extent) in the case of the Campanian lands (see *Leg. agr.* 1.21; 2.84).

Tota Italia

While the first part of the oration concentrates on the harm that the decemvirs will do if they are allowed to exercise power outside of Italy, the middle of the speech encourages its audience to focus their attention on Italy and the actions of the land commissioners there. The idea that the decemvirs would "fill all Italy with their colonies" (34: *totam Italiam suis coloniis ut complere*) is introduced early in the speech,[51] but it is the pattern of topography Cicero creates later that gives the idea a concrete topographical form in the listener's mind.

Rullus had not explicitly named the lands on which he would settle colonies (66), and Cicero capitalizes on this fact to suggest a number of possibilities that will be certain to alarm his audience. Moving down the Appian Way, he mentions the "Alban, Setian, Privernian, Fundian, Vescian, Falernian, Liternian, Cumaean, and Nucerian lands."[52] Proceeding from the "other gate" (66), he refers to the "Capenan, Faliscian, Sabine, Reatine, Venafran, Allifaean, and Trebulan lands." The decemvirs, according to the orator, will possess wealth so great that they will be able to purchase all these lands as well as others. With this list Cicero has named the sites of some of the richest farmland in central Italy.[53] When the orator mentions these fertile agricultural areas around Rome, he encourages his audience to believe that such lands could not be destined for them but were intended by the framers of the proposal to be kept for themselves. Cicero reinforces this impression by telling his audience that Rullus saw them as the "sewage" of the republic (70: *sentina*) and that for them Rullus planned settlements in the dry lands of Sipontum or the

51. For the phrase *tota Italia* see also 75 (*totam Italiam suis praesidiis obsidere atque occupare; in omnia municipia, in omnis colonias totius Italiae; totam Italiam suis opibus obsidebunt*), 98 (*omnia municipia coloniasque Italiae*). Cf. 1.16 (*totam Italiam inermem tradituros existimasti*), 17 (*totam Italiam vestris coloniis complere voluisti; totam Italiam militibus suis occuparint*).

52. Nuceria (an emendation proposed by A. C. Clark) replaces the codices' [*ager*] *Ancasianas*, which is clearly in error. Zumpt, *De lege agraria*, 106 (ad 2.66), has *Acerranus*.

53. The *ager Capenas* was perhaps allotted in part to Caesar's veterans (Cic. *Fam.* 9.17.2). For the settlement of veterans under Vespasian at Reate, see *CIL* IX.4682–85. Venafrum was the site of a colony under Augustus (*CIL* XI.4894). There also seems to have been a colony founded at Allifae under the triumvirs (*CIL* IX.2354). Jonkers, *De Lege Agraria*, 104 (ad 2.66), calls the list of towns "the most attractive lands in the proximity of Rome."

swamplands of Salapia in Apulia (71, 98). He even suggests the possibility that no lands whatsoever would be given them (72).

Both the identity of the towns and cities Cicero mentions in this part of the speech and the order in which they are named are significant. The first list includes the centers of the most important farming districts as one proceeds south from Rome. The first four sites—Ager Albanus, Setia, Privernum, and Fundi—are encountered as one travels south on the Via Appia, while the sequence Ager Vescinus, Ager Falernus, Liternum, Cumae, Nuceria represents a movement along the Campanian coast to a region just south of Capua. The omission of Capua itself would have been noted, since it was the terminus of the earliest construction of the Appian Way and the chief city of Campania and would thus have been a fitting end point in a list of fertile and strategic areas south of Rome.

The second list of towns mentioned for possible purchase by the decemvirs contains a peculiar feature. Cicero says that these towns are reached "from the other gate" (66). By this he must mean the Porta Flaminia, for the first places mentioned, Capena and the Faliscan territory (associated with the town of Falerii), were reached by exiting the city north and traveling up the Via Flaminia. The Sabine land was to the east of this region, and in this district, on a high, well-watered plain, stood Reate. Although the reference to Reate represents a departure from the implied directional guidepost of the Flaminian Way, it is nevertheless an important agricultural area to the north of Rome. But the next area mentioned on Cicero's list, Venafrum, is a complete departure from the implied organization of the whole, for it lies on a branch of the Via Latina in Samnium, *south* of Rome.[54] Allifae is situated even farther south in a fertile valley of Samnium, while Trebula, in Campania, lies less than five Roman miles from Capua.

Two spatial patterns have been created here. First, each time Cicero names a sequence of places ending in Campanian sites close to Capua without mentioning Capua itself he makes the city conspicuous by its absence, for it was the most important agricultural area in all Italy and the location of the last extensive holdings of *ager publicus* near Rome. Through the creation in both lists of a topographical pattern that points to Capua but suspends mention of it, Cicero subtly prepares his listeners for the long section at the end of the speech in which Capua is made to

54. The Oxford Classical Text attempts to solve the directional problem by adding the words *ab alia* [i.e., *porta*] before Venafranus.

1	Ager Albanus
2	Setia
3	Privernum
4	Fundi
5	Ager Vescinus
6	Ager Falernus
7	Liternum
8	Cumae
9	Nuceria
A	Capena
B	Falerii
C	Ager Sabinus
D	Reate
E	Venafrum
F	Allifae
G	Trebula

Fig. 5. Italy and Sicily. The map illustrates in proper sequence the two lists of places mentioned by Cicero in *De lege agraria* 2.66.

appear the culmination of all the dangers posed by the settlement of decemviral colonies in Italy. Second, by naming important sites in an arc to the north, east, and south of Rome, Cicero touches on a potent and continuing Roman fear, that of encirclement by hostile forces. Rullus's new settlements are depicted not as peaceful colonies to be filled with the dispossessed poor of the city but as armed camps that will provide their commanders with strategic positions from which to launch an attack on Rome.

The fear that Rullus's plans for colonization might endanger the city of Rome is further aroused by Cicero's suggestion that the bill would allow the creation of a settlement even on the Janiculum. He asks what would prevent Rullus from settling a colony there, "a garrison upon our head and necks" (74: *praesidium in capite atque cervicibus nostris*). The ridge of the Janiculum was the most crucial point in the western defenses of the city. Livy states that it had been fortified by Ancus Marcius not because the city required more space but because he realized that this area must never be controlled by an enemy (1.33.6: *ne quando ea arx hostium esset*). During meetings of the Comitia Centuriata in the Campus Martius a red flag was displayed on the heights as a sign that the area was secure and the city therefore not endangered.[55] Cicero's suggestion of the possibility that a *praesidium* might be located here would surely have been a frightening thought for his audience.[56]

The central section of the speech, then, uses the arrangement of references to places in order to create a topographical image of the danger posed by the agrarian bill. While at the beginning of the speech Cicero pictures the whole world at the mercy of the decemvirs, here he predicts that all Italy will be filled with Rullus's *coloniae* and *municipia*. By mentioning areas for these settlements to the north, east, and south of Rome and by picturing a *praesidium* on the western heights of the city, the orator graphically suggests to his audience the direct military threat to the city posed by the bill. Cicero has thus moved his listeners from concern for the status of allies and dependent nations (a concern based for the most part on financial interests) to anxiety for their own security.

55. Cassius Dio reports that the trial of Rabirius was stopped when the red flag on the Janiculum was lowered (37.27–28).

56. The passage would also have summoned up the image of Lars Porsenna, whose encampment on the Janiculum represented one of the great military crises in Rome's early history (Livy 2.10–14).

Only one element is lacking to exploit this anxiety fully: a focal point of opposition to Rome.

Altera Roma

In the final section of the speech before the peroration (76–97) Cicero takes up the question of the sale and allotment of Campanian land and the establishment of a colony at Capua. He begins by speaking of utility and honor (76: *de commodo/ ad amplitudinem et dignitatem*), topics we should expect to appear in a deliberative oration. Yet, in spite of his promise to address himself to "those who are upset by the indignity of the matter" (76), the orator devotes scant attention to *honestas;*[57] it is, rather, the self-interests (*commoda*) of his audience to which he chiefly appeals. Allusions are made to these interests in a number of areas: for instance, much is made of the reliability of Campanian tax revenues, of the security of its grain export, and of the military resource represented by the area.[58] Such arguments, however, are secondary to one that concerns the actual distribution of the land: Cicero contends that no gain can be realized by the people through passage of Rullus's bill because they will never actually possess any of the Campanian land (77, 78, 79, 82, 85–97). Both the land and the colony at Capua will instead fall to

57. The people are reminded that the Campanian holdings constitute a patrimony inherited from their ancestors and that it would be dishonorable therefore to lose such lands (see 81–82, 84–85); the injustice of depriving the present holders of their farms is alluded to in section 84. The latter passage, while ostensibly focusing on the issue of *iustitia,* is not entirely divorced from that of self-interest, since Cicero also reminds his audience of the vital role played by the present inhabitants of Campania in their feeding and protection.

58. See, for example, 80: *unumne fundum pulcherrimum populi Romani, caput vestrae pecuniae, pacis ornamentum, subsidium belli, fundamentum vectigalium, horreum legionum, solacium annonae disperire patemini?* The approach is very similar to that found in the *De imperio Cn. Pompei,* in which the argument from self-interest centers on the *vectigalia* from Asia. See esp. *Imp. Pomp.* 6: *aguntur certissima populi Romani vectigalia et maxima, quibus amissis et pacis ornamenta et subsidia belli requiretis;* 14: *de maximis vestris vectigalibus agatur* and *Asia vero tam opima est ac fertilis ut et ubertate agrorum et varietate fructuum et magnitudine pastionis et multitudine earum rerum quae exportantur facile omnibus terris antecellat.* (In the *Verrines,* of course, it had been Sicily, rather than Campania or Asia, that had been pictured as the granary of the Republic.)

the control of the rich (78, 82) and of those who will use it as a base of operations from which to overthrow the Republic.[59]

In sections 77–84 the orator makes frequent references to the seditious and violent men destined to settle the new foundation at Capua.[60] These references prepare the listeners for the long subsequent section (85–97) in which Capua is depicted as the focal point of opposition to the state, the "anti-Rome." [61] Here Cicero elaborates on the threat to Rome of the proposed colony at Capua both by referring to the dangerous individuals whom he expects to receive allotments if Rullus's bill passes and by equating this future colony with the independent Capua of the third century B.C. The present holders of Campanian lands, he argues, are good and loyal farmers, dedicated to their rural occupa-

59. A detailed political analysis of the results of passage of the bill is beyond the scope of the present study, but this much is clear: that Campania was a strategic area in Italy, that patronship of a large number of colonists there would represent a potent political tool, and that decemviral control of the allotment of the Campanian *ager publicus* would have weakened Pompey's ability to provide land for his veterans. Gabba, *Republican Rome*, 56–59, argues that Capua was at this time a hotbed of Marian and Italian opposition to the state. But Hardy, "Rullan Proposal," 254–55, claims that there was no threat of sedition. For Capua as the seat of hegemony over Italy, see Heurgon, *Capoue préromaine*, 3. Inscriptional evidence is treated by Frederiksen, *Campania*, 285–318. See also Hülsen, "Capua"; Beloch, *Campanien*, 295–374; Stillwell, *Princeton Encyclopedia*, s.v. "Capua," 195–96.

60. See 77 (*sed si quinque hominum milibus ad vim, facinus caedemque delectis locus atque urbs quae bellum facere atque instruere possit quaeritur, tamenne patiemini vestro nomine contra vos firmari opes, armari praesidia, urbis, agros, copias comparari?*), 82 (*Primo quidem acres, ad vim prompti, ad seditionem parati qui, simul ac decemviri concrepuerint, armati in civis et expediti ad caedem esse possint*), 84 (*his robustis et valentibus et audacibus decemvirum satellitibus agri Campani possessio tota tradetur*).

61. The phrase *altera Roma* ("the other Rome") occurs at *Leg. agr.* 1.24 and 2.86 and *Phil.* 12.7, the latter passage referring to the colony later founded at Capua by Caesar. For a historical overview of the topos, see Ceausescu, "Altera Roma." Cf. *Leg. agr.* 1, in which the colony at Capua is depicted as a danger as great as that posed by the creation of a *praesidium* on the Janiculum. In this speech Cicero had asked how Rullus would be prevented from placing a colony on the Janiculum and thereby "pressing and harassing this city with another" (1.16: *ne urbem hanc urbe alia premere atque urgere*). A similar phrase appears a little later when the orator describes the colonization of Capua. He states that "that city will again stand against this city" (1.18: *illam urbem huic urbi rursus opponere*).

tions and devoid of political ambition (84). The new colonists, on the other hand, will resemble the arrogant and treacherous Capuans of old, who, like the Carthaginians and Corinthians, contended with Rome for world empire. But whereas Rome had destroyed Carthage and Corinth, Capua continued to exist, ready to rise again if political power were restored to its citizens.

Cicero supports his arguments concerning the dangerous ambitions of the Capua of the past and, if Rullus has his way, of the Capua of the future by drawing on a theory of environmental determinism similar to that exploited in his account in the *Pro Roscio Amerino* of the differences in temperament between country and city dwellers.[62] He here asserts that the character of each people is determined by the means nature provides them to sustain life (95). The Carthaginians, he says, became a duplicitous, greedy, and crafty race because the site of their coastal city exposed them to the influence of merchants and strangers.[63] The harsh and unforgiving geography of Liguria, on the other hand, had made its people hardy rustics. Cicero then recounts why in the case of the Campanians "the place itself [had given rise] to haughtiness" (92: *locus ipse adferat superbiam*). The fertility of their land, the abundance of their crops, and the excellence of their chief city, he asserts, had led the Campanians to become affluent, and this affluence, in turn, had inevitably given birth to overweening pride and dangerous ambition (95–97). The section ends with Cicero's contention that any new colonists would not only share in the characteristics of the Capuans of old, but, because of their unfamiliarity with luxury, they would become even more corrupt (97).[64]

62. *Rosc. Am.* 75.
63. Cf. similar sentiments in *Rep.* 2.7–10.
64. Cicero's explanation for the temperament of the Campanians reflects theories found in contemporary authors, such as Caesar and Strabo (see above, pp. 148–51). Diodorus Siculus, drawing on earlier sources, several times observes that nature teaches human beings to adapt to whatever opportunities are at hand for sustaining life (see above, pp. 146–47 nn. 30 and 31). More specifically, Cicero's and Diodorus's accounts of the Ligurians are similar (Diod. Sic. 5.39.1–8), and Cicero's account of the growth of decadence in a place blessed with agricultural fertility is paralleled by Diodorus's comments on the land of the Etruscans (5.40.1–5). Connections between fertility and decadence, on the one hand, and scarcity and virtue, on the other, can be traced back to fifth-century commonplaces about the differences between Europe (i.e., Greece) and Asia (usually focusing on the Persians).

Clearly Cicero intends that these references to Capua should serve as the logical end point of the topographical sequence he has created, moving from the *orbis terrarum* to *Italia* to the *altera Roma*. In the following pages I shall indicate briefly how Cicero has also made his handling of the topic the culmination of the major themes of the oration. These themes were introduced in the very first lines, in which Cicero had stated that as a *novus homo* he owed his elevation not to the nobility but to the people and would therefore be a truly *popularis* consul by making his chief concerns the true interests of the people. These he had defined as *otium, libertas,* and *pax* (9). All three are said to be an inheritance from the *maiores:* it was by the labor of their forefathers, says Cicero, that the Roman people were able to live in peace without danger (9: *impune in otio*); liberty also had been handed down to the Roman people by their ancestors, who had won it "with much sweat and blood" (16: *plurimo sudore et sanguine maiorum vestrorum partam vobisque traditam libertatem*); that *pax* was also an inheritance can be seen in the references to Roman heroes such as Africanus, who, by their bravery (51: *virtute*), had brought the Mediterranean world under Roman rule. Cicero, as consul, defines his own role as preserver of what had been given by these men into his safekeeping (9: *in patrocinium mei consulatus*), and his constant objections throughout the speech that the provisions of Rullus's bill would depart from precedent are therefore made to appear an expression of his desire to safeguard the blessings of *pax, libertas,* and *otium.*

Of the three concepts named above, *pax* plays a less important role than either *otium* or *libertas*. The term is defined by the orator as *externa,* as opposed to *otium,* which is *domesticum* (9). External peace was the province of men such as Pompey, but it was the consul who had to deal with civil strife. Although the speech contains praise for the *maiores,* who had acquired the far-flung *imperium* of Rome (50–51), and for Pompey, who had extended and protected it (25, 46, 52), its chief concern is not with the disturbance of *regna, socii, provinciae,* or *amici* but with the danger decemviral power posed to *otium* or internal peace. In Cicero's mind this danger constituted the real threat to the continued existence of the Republic, a view that he would repeat in several other orations of his consular year.[65]

---

65. *Cat.* 2.11; *Mur.* 84; also *Rab. per.* 33.

Otium   In his thematic development of the idea of *otium* Cicero plays on a number of different meanings of the word.[66] The term can signify a wide range of ideas, including private idleness, retirement from official duties, and civic peace. In the proem, Cicero asks: "What is so popular as *otium*, a thing so pleasant that you and your ancestors and the bravest men think that great exertions (9: *maximos labores*) should be undertaken to be able, at some time, to live in peace (9: *in otio*), especially with authority and dignity (9: *imperio ac dignitate*)?" In this section the orator alludes to both a private and a public ideal. Not only can the goal of certain individuals be defined as retirement with the influence and respect won through service to the state, but the state as a whole looks to the possession of civic peace, won through great sacrifices and bringing as its reward rule (*imperium*) and honor (*dignitas*). Although Cicero says that his listeners believe that great labor should be exerted to secure this *otium*, he also makes clear that the present generation has not, in fact, been responsible for the tranquillity they enjoy. As mentioned, it was due to the labor of the *maiores* that the Roman people live *impune in otio* (9). The ideal of private *otium* to which Cicero alludes is one to which only the ruling classes could aspire; the common people, however, may at least possess this public *otium* as an inheritance from their ancestors, and by this inheritance they also possess a share in the *imperium* and *dignitas* of the state.

The introduction of the concept of *otium* in the first part of the speech prepares the audience for Cicero's crucial manipulation of the idea in his discussion of Rullus's plans for Capua. Cicero states that the *maiores* had transformed Campanian pride and fierceness (91: *adrogantiam atque intolerandam ferociam*) into lassitude and inactivity (91: *inertissimum ac desidiosissimum otium*) by removing contention for political power. These two traits (arrogance and sloth) were integral parts of a stereotypical view of Capua and Campania that had existed for many generations before Cicero's time.[67] The Roman perception

66. See the discussion of *otium* in Mitchell, *Cicero*, 198–99; and Wirszubski, "Cicero's *cum dignitate otium*."

67. For praise of the natural environment, see Polyb. 3.91; Strabo 5.4.3, chap. 242; Pliny *HN* 3.60; Flor. 1.16.3; Livy 7.30.16, 7.31.1. For connection of the Campanian character with the natural environment, see Strabo 5.4.13, chap. 250; Polyb. in Ath. 12.528a. It is probable that the connection of Carthage, Corinth, and Capua was also a commonplace (Flor. 33.18.1), as was the

that the city had betrayed its alliance with Rome by opening its gates to
Hannibal gave rise to the tradition that the Campanians were arrogant
and treacherous, while the productivity of the land and the sophistication of the town, coupled with the story that Hannibal's troops had been
corrupted by their stay there, must have been the source of the topos
concerning the debilitating effects of Capuan riches.[68]

Although both arrogance and sloth were stereotypical traits, Cicero's
separation of the two represents a clever manipulation of the tradition.
In other ancient sources the two traits go hand in hand, but here Cicero
claims that pride was changed to lassitude by the removal of Capua's
political rights after 211 B.C. This can be viewed as a logical improve-
ment upon the topos, since Campanian treachery and arrogance would
have appeared less dangerous if accompanied by weakness and inactivity. By presenting his argument in this way, the orator could expand
upon the dangerous propensities of the Campanian character of old
while arguing that the present occupants of the land were virtuous farmers and not to be feared.[69] Only a Capua with revived political power
could corrupt its inhabitants; without that power, the natural abundance and beauty of the place led to *otium* rather than *superbia*.

It is also clear that Cicero's reference to Campanian *otium* in this
section (91) has a double significance. Because of the adjectives used
(*inertissimum ac desidiosissimum otium*) and because of their familiarity with the commonplaces about Campania, his listeners would at first
understand this use of *otium* as referring only to sloth, a personal and
moral trait. The passage, however, carefully attributes the creation of
this *otium* to the "plan and thought" (91) of the *maiores,* and Cicero
later asks if they should not be venerated as gods for this action (95).
This ties the concept directly to the remarks on *otium* made earlier in
the speech, in which Cicero had said that it was by the labor of the
maiores that *otium* (i.e., domestic peace) had been secured for the Roman people, and for this the *maiores* were owed the greatest praise and
thanks (9). The listener would thus be led to see Campanian *otium* not

---

comparison of the site of Rome with the sites of those cities that contended with
Rome (Cic. *Rep.* 2.5–7, 10–11).

68. Livy 7.31.6; 23.45.4; see also Cic. *Red. sen.* 17 and Cicero's reluctance
to connect Pompey explicitly with the Caesarian colony in *Red. sen.* 29.

69. *Leg. agr.* 2.84: *Totus enim ager Campanus colitur et possidetur a plebe,
et a plebe optima et modestissima; quo genus hominum optime moratum opti-
morum et aratorum et militum ab hoc plebicola tribuno plebis funditus eicitur.*

just as an ethnic characteristic of the inhabitants of the area but as a description of the political stability enforced on Capua after 211. Cicero has, then, subtly conflated two meanings of the term: the slothful inactivity (*inertissimum ac desidiosissimum otium*) imposed on the area by the actions of the *maiores* has guaranteed its political quiescence (*otium*). The orator goes on to suggest that if this condition were to be changed, the *otium* of the Republic as a whole would also be destroyed.

In the peroration Cicero creates an astonishing summary of variations on the theme of *otium,* repeating again and again the terms that—along with *libertas*—function as the political catchwords of the oration:

> There can be nothing so "popular" as that which I, the "popular consul (*consul popularis*)," bestow on you for this year: external peace, tranquillity, and domestic peace (*pacem, tranquillitatem, otium*). . . . Not only will you, who have always desired it, be at peace (*in otio*), but I shall also render most calm and most peaceful those to whom domestic peace is hateful (*quietissimos atque otiosissimos quibus odio est otium*). For there are those who are accustomed to obtaining offices, power, and riches from anarchy and civil discord; you, whose influence depends upon your votes, whose liberty upon the laws, whose rights upon the law courts and the fairness of the magistrates, and whose property depends on external peace (*pace*), you must at all costs hold on to domestic peace (*omne ratione otium retinere debetis*). For if those who live in peace on account of their inactivity (*propter disidiam in otio vivunt*), even in their disgraceful indolence (*in sua turpi inertia*), yet derive pleasure from peace itself (*ex ipso otio*); how blessed will you be if, in this status which you possess, you hold on to a tranquillity (*otium*) that has not been acquired by your indolence (*ignavia*) but won through bravery (*virtute*), my fellow citizens!
>
> (102–3)

Here Cicero reiterates the changing nuances of the concept, and in so doing he ascribes to sections of the Roman population exactly those types of *otium* implied by his discussion of the Capuans. In the first lines of the passage he refers to the idea of *otium* as inactivity that is forced on seditious citizens by the exercise of the power of the state. Cicero promises to force tranquillity on those whose interests reside in civil discord, just as the *maiores* had tamed the treacherous Capuans through the power of the Roman prefect sent to govern the city. Attempting to disassociate the majority of the audience from such political anarchists, Cicero reminds his listeners that their voting, judicial, and property rights depended upon the peaceful functioning of the political machine.

He goes on to refer to *otium* as sloth or laziness. He states that even those whose tranquillity was the result of their idleness have benefited from peace, as did his audience, who had won it through their bravery. This attempt to exclude his audience from the despised ranks of the inactive should not obscure the fact that he had earlier reminded them that bravery had not been required of the present generation (16: *partam . . . libertatem nullo vestro labore*); it was not due to their own efforts but to those of their ancestors that they were allowed to live in peace (9). Further, an earlier reference to the games and amusements enjoyed by his audience (71) suggests that inactivity and lassitude were in the orator's view as characteristic of the city populace of his own time as of the Capuans after 211. And, as in the case of the Capuans, this inertia helped to guarantee the internal security of the state.

Through the development of this theme, then, Cicero—a *novus homo* lacking consular forebears—presents himself as a direct link with the semidivine Roman politicians of the past. These men had guaranteed the security of Rome by "pacifying" the proud and treacherous Capuans; Cicero, by his opposition to Rullus's bill, ensures that this salutary condition will continue and forces a similar tranquillity on seditious Romans of his own time. The *maiores* had, through great exertions and sacrifice, secured peace for the Republic, transforming the arrogance of the Campanians into inactivity and sloth; Cicero, whose consulship can be carried on only by means of *summus labor ac difficillima ratio* (6), declares that he will retain the blessings of domestic peace for the slothful and energetic alike.[70] Cicero is at some pains to avoid insulting his listeners, but it is clear that through his development of the theme of *otium* he has likened sections of the city population to the Capuans of old, and he has done so in order to cast himself in the same role as that of the *maiores*—guardian of peace.

Libertas   Like those who listened to Rullus's first *contio* and thought that his speech had something to do with an agrarian bill but were not sure exactly what (13), any Roman in Cicero's audience would have thought that what he had to say concerned *libertas*, for by sheer repetition the concept would have impinged on the minds of the audience. In discussing the election of the land commissioners at the beginning of the speech the orator returns again and again to the idea that passage of the bill would destroy Roman freedom by giving the commissioners unlimited power, and in the speech as a whole the word *libertas* is repeated

70. Cf. his self-description in section 100: *vigilanti homini, non timido, diligenti, non ignavo.*

some twenty-one times, in nine occurrences qualified by the adjective *vestra*.[71] Cicero clearly wished to convince his audience that the ultimate threat posed by the disturbance of *otium* was the loss of their freedom, and his strategy involved an attempt to present this danger as one that could strike from within as well as from without.

In order to make the agrarian bill appear to be a threat to *libertas* from within the state, Cicero draws on a well-worn strategy. In the late Republic the term *libertas* was a political catchword, used by *optimates* and *populares* alike.[72] While popular leaders publicly dedicated themselves to defending the freedom of the people from the danger posed to it by the actions of an oligarchic faction, conservatives from the days of the Gracchi onward branded popular leaders as potential despots who were setting plots to take over the government and enslave the people.[73] Cicero has used numerous elements of the latter topos: Rullus and his backers are would-be tyrants who, while seeming to espouse the interests of the masses, are aiming at absolute power; their sacrilegious disregard of precedent and of the manifest will of the gods can bring only disaster to the state; once they have secured power—a power that is described as regal—the commissioners will be free to resort to violence and intimidation.[74] In addition, Cicero's references to the future land commissioners as "ten kings" would surely have reminded the audience of the notorious story of the tyranny exercised by the second decemvirate under Appius Claudius, when Roman *libertas* was lost through the actions of a board of ten that had at first seemed popular in character.[75]

Cicero also depicts the bill as an external threat to Roman freedom. He does so, first of all, by identifying Rome as the embodiment of *libertas*. This idea is introduced in a passage in the middle of the speech in

71. For warnings against the potential power of the commissioners, see 15, 16, 20, 22, 24, 25, 29, 32. For *libertas*, see 9, 15, 16, 17, 20, 24, 25, 29, 71, 75 (*libertas vestra; libertas vestra; vestram libertatem; vestrae libertatis*), 86, 102. Cf. *Leg. agr.* 1.21, 22. Note that in the passage that precedes the long section on Capua and Campania (75), Cicero uses the phrase *libertas vestra* four times.

72. See, among others, Wirszubski, *Libertas;* Syme, *Roman Revolution,* 154–55; Weinstock, *Divus Julius,* 133–35; Hellegouarc'h, *Le vocabulaire latin,* 542–65. Cf. Hellegouarc'h's discussion of *popularis,* 518–44.

73. Caes. *B.Civ.* 22.5; Sall. *Cat.* 20, 28, 33, 52, 58.

74. For references to the kingly ambitions of Rullus and the future decemvirs, see 15 (*reges*), 20 (*regia potestas*), 21 (*dominos*), 22 (*dominis*), 24 (*regnum*), 25 (*dominationem*), 29 (*reges*), 32 (*regiam*), 33 (*regum*), 35 (*potestatem regiam*), 43 (*dominus, rex . . . regni*), 57 (*iudicium . . . regium*), 61 (*dominos*).

75. Livy 3.33–58.

which Cicero states that in addition to the other benefits that the people will lose if they leave the city they will lose their freedom (71: *libertas*). The city, then, is the *locus* of freedom. A little later Cicero identifies the danger to the city posed by Rullus as a threat to *libertas*. As has been shown, he creates an image of the city surrounded on all sides by the forces of the decemvirs: all the strategic sites around Rome will be adapted to the violent ends of the decemvirs, even the heights of the Janiculum; from these bases they will surround and oppress the Roman people (74); all Italy will ultimately be occupied and beset by their garrisons (75: *totam Italiam suis praesidiis obsidere atque occupare cogitet*). What hope or chance will remain for recovering liberty, asks Cicero, "once they hold your freedom shut in by their garrisons and colonies" (75: *vestram libertatem suis praesidiis et coloniis interclusam tenebunt*)? It can be seen in the quote above that *libertas* has replaced Rome in the military metaphor and has become the conceptual equivalent of Rome, for when the city is shut in and surrounded by the forces of the decemvirs, *libertas* is likewise hemmed in and surrounded.[76]

If Rome is made to appear the embodiment of *libertas*, then the spearhead of future opposition to Rome, Capua, is necessarily transformed in the listeners' minds into the greatest external threat to Roman freedom. As mentioned, Cicero draws on a centuries-old stereotype in order to paint in the minds of his audience a frightening picture of a revived Capua, controlled by the forces of the decemvirs: the city will be the seat of a new *regnum* (8, 75), from which Rullus and his cohorts will prepare to wage their war against the state (77: *locus atque urbs quae bellum facere atque instruere possit*); the new colonists will be soldiers rather than farmers (77), and like their masters they will be men of violence and greed, ready for crime and murder (77); once these men have formed an army, ready to attack whenever the decemvirs give the signal (82), then the Capuan standard will once more be lifted, and the *altera Roma* will rise against *hanc Romam* (86).

The strategy employed here is not without precedent. The opposition mounted against Gaius Gracchus's planned resettlement near ruined Carthage must have provided the blueprint for the orator's attack.

---

76. A similar metaphor is repeated in the peroration, where Cicero says that Rullus will surround the Republic with his soldiers, cities, and garrisons (99: *omnem rem publicam vestris militibus, vestris urbibus, vestris praesidiis cingeretis*).

Gracchus's enemies had alarmed the *plebs* with stories of the unfavorable omens reported from the site of Junonia, and they doubtlessly predicted that the new colony would rise to challenge Rome's supremacy.[77] Even as Cicero praises Gracchus in the speech (10) he employs the scare tactics that had been used so effectively by Gaius's opponents. This line of attack was to be used as well against Caesar and, with even more effect, by Octavian in his propaganda against Antony, who was accused of planning to raise up Alexandria as an imperial capital.[78]

Although in the *De lege agraria* 2 Cicero has employed a predictable conservative strategy to undermine a land distribution bill, his mastery of its structure and themes has made this an unusually persuasive and effective speech. In it the orator has set out to create in the minds of his listeners a psychological map of the Roman world; but unlike the map of the *imperium Romanum* that Agrippa would later erect in the Campus Martius, Cicero's verbal map is able to order—even to control—its audience's images of the world temporally through a carefully controlled sequence of representation.[79] He begins with a roll call of names of far-removed places—in most cases with no specific connotations for his listeners but simply intended to create a sense of the enormity and complexity of a far-flung empire and of the danger of decemviral intervention in this system. Although Cicero did not invent the idea of the "whole world" as the stage upon which Roman power was now exercised, its development here before a popular audience is a significant

77. Plut. *C. Gracch.* 10.3, 11.1.

78. Suet. *Iul. Caes.* 79.3; Nic. Dam. F 130.68 (Jacoby *FGrH*, 2A.404); Plut. *Ant.* 54.3–55.1. See the discussion by Ceausescu, "Altera Roma," 81–90, who notes the important part played by Cleopatra in making credible to the Roman people the rumors of the transfer of the capital to the East.

79. On the question of linear sequence in description, see Fowler, "The Problem of Ekphrasis," 29–30 (responding to Levelt's discussion, "The Speaker's Linearization Problem"). On Agrippa's map and its explanation through *commentarii*, see Nicolet, *Space, Geography, and Politics,* 95–114. As Nicolet explains, this map would also have manipulated its audience's image of the world, but the *degree* to which the artist can depend on controlled sequence and progression to carry out this manipulation is of necessity smaller in the visual than in the literary text. (Even if the images representing the *imperium* were meant to be viewed in a particular sequence, what would have prevented people from viewing it in some other way? We cannot, however, when listening to a speech, take in the end before the beginning; and even when reading, especially from a papyrus roll, it would be difficult to start, say, at the middle of the text.)

step towards what would become an Augustan commonplace.[80] In enlarging on this theme the orator could draw on his audience's pride in their share in the Roman *imperium,* on their concern for the maintenance of just and profitable foreign relations, and on their fears that unreasonable power might accompany the decemvirs' activity in the Mediterranean world.

In the central part of the speech, Cicero moves his listeners' attention to Italy, and here the emotional impact of the material would have increased along with the audience's familiarity with the places mentioned. In these sections of the speech the mere mention of each place would have stimulated in the Roman listener a complex web of remembered experience and current feeling, and to these images and emotions Cicero links a sense of imminent danger arising from his prediction that all the districts surrounding Rome would ultimately be controlled by the decemvirs. At the same time, he carefully exploits his audience's emotional attachment to Rome itself, reminding them of the pleasures they enjoyed and the influence they wielded by living in the center of power, and suggesting that Rullus's bill would ultimately remove them from the city.

The last part of the speech provides the culmination of a pattern of representation in which Cicero has described three spheres of decemviral power in succession: the *orbis terrarum,* Italy, and, finally, Capua. Here Rullus's bill is made to appear particularly threatening, as the Campanian city is verbally transformed into the seat of a future insurrection against Rome directed by Rullus and his powerful supporters. Cicero accomplishes this transformation of Capua not only by placing his treatment of it at the end point of a carefully developed geographical sequence but also by vividly depicting the future occupants of the city. The Capuans of Cicero's day appear in the speech to be the direct heirs of the ethnic characteristics possessed by the Capuans of old. While the orator draws on the familiar traits of a generations-old stereotype of the Campanians as arrogant, treacherous, luxurious, and indolent, at the same time he subtly alters this traditional stereotype by specifically

80. Nicolet, *Space, Geography, and Politics,* 29–56, has an excellent discussion of the development of this conception, although he surely slights Cicero's contribution in the *De imperio Pompei* and here. It seems to me probable that Pompey's and Caesar's exploitation of these ideas after their successful campaigns in the East and the West owed much to Cicero's previous popularization of them.

connecting the military threat inherent in the Campanian character with the political status of the region. Indolence and inactivity are thus linked to a politically emasculated Capua, while treachery and arrogance are associated only with a politically potent Capua. Cicero is then able to argue that if Rullus renews Campanian power and independence, the new inhabitants of the region will inevitably exhibit the vices that had made the Campanians of the third century B.C. so dangerous to Rome. Violent and seditious, they will be used as an army to upset the *otium* forced on this dangerous city by the *maiores* and, ultimately, to destroy the *otium* and *libertas* of the Roman people. Thus Cicero leads his audience to believe that all the dangers to be feared from passage of Rullus's proposal will culminate in a military threat to the state posed by a revived Capua, the *altera Roma*.

Conclusion

Rerum memoria propria est oratoris; eam singulis personis
bene positis notare possumus, ut sententias imaginibus,
ordinem locis comprehendamus.

A memory for the concrete is the unique possession of the
orator; we are able to imprint this memory on our minds
when the individual "masks" have been well ordered, so that
we assimilate ideas by means of images and their sequence by
means of places.

Cicero, De oratore 2.359

THE CHARACTER OF THE ORATOR

As early as the third century B.C. Roman historians had begun to employ the techniques of fiction to create compelling tales out of the un-
adorned scraps of information handed down to them from earlier generations. Drawing on recognizable personae and familiar narrative
patterns, they transformed the bare names and scanty records associated with the earliest days of the city into a rich historical tapestry,
illustrating the triumph of Roman virtue over the challenges that were
faced from within and without. This study has shown the degree to
which Cicero engaged in a similar, although not identical, kind of embellishment. By fitting to the features of various individuals treated in
his speeches the masks of stereotypical characters, by narrating events
in such a way as to reinforce these stereotypes, Cicero created in his
oratory a reflection of the world that was both familiar and credible to
his audience. As we have seen, when assigning these ethical masks to
various individuals, Cicero frequently had recourse to stereotypes dependent upon place. And, in spite of the presence of passages purporting
to explain why the Capuan was arrogant, the Greek deceptive, or the
farmer honest, this appeal was ultimately directed to the emotions, not
to reason. By locating the specific issues of an argument within the
larger universe of Roman assumptions about how *ēthos* and *locus* were

connected, the orator hoped to draw on his audience's unexamined but deeply rooted prejudices, both negative and positive.

Modern historians have often found fault with their Roman counterparts for their exploitation of the techniques of fiction.[1] If something of the same sort went on in Cicero's speeches, that is, if Ciceronian rhetoric frequently involved a fictionalization of the real world and the people in it, are we not entitled to condemn the orator at least as strongly as we do the historian? After all, it was not the long-dead figures of the antique past whose reputations and fortunes were affected by Cicero's speeches but living men and women—citizens of a nation that, for most of Cicero's oratorical career, tottered on the edge of moral and political collapse. Was it not ethically irresponsible of Cicero to practice a rhetoric that depended upon appearances rather than reality, upon popular prejudices rather than unpopular truths, upon the emotionally potent rather than the logically persuasive? In 155 B.C., the Academic philosopher Carneades scandalized some and delighted many when on an embassy to Rome he delivered lectures on successive days demonstrating first the justice and then the injustice of Rome's empire. Cato the Elder, we are told, realizing the potential danger to the state of such a performance, attempted to hurry the Greek philosopher out of town.[2] Is Cicero not to be considered an equally dangerous character?

There is no doubt that at various points in his oratorical career Cicero lied, successfully defended those guilty of the crimes with which they were charged, exploited his audience's ethnic and gender prejudices, and constantly attempted to control his audience's perceptions of reality through emotional appeals. But as the case against Cicero on all of these charges has been forcefully articulated and extremely influential, especially among modern scholars, let me attempt to argue briefly the case for the defense. It is recorded that, in the fifth century B.C., when the Sicilians Corax and Tisias attempted to systematize various aspects of the rhetorical art, they had stressed the primary importance of the argument from probability. Plato later depicted Socrates as demonstrating the immorality of one of Tisias's better-known illustrations

1. Although many would agree with Luce, who, in his analysis of Livy's "free hand" in narrating the history of early Rome, observes: "Since [that history] was uncertain and suspect, what else could he do?" ("Design and Structure," 301–2).

2. Plut. *Cat. Mai.* 22; Cic. *De or.* 2.155; Aul. Gell. 6.14.8–10; Pliny *HN* 7.112.

of the need to argue the probable rather than the true. In the *Phaedrus* (273b), Socrates states that if a strong but cowardly man was assaulted and robbed by a weak one and thereafter sought remedy through a lawsuit, according to Tisias the strong man should not tell the truth, since no one would believe him. Instead he should claim that the small man had not been alone when he had assaulted him. Although Socrates emphatically rejects this kind of argument, nevertheless the case is a good illustration of the fact that the truth, simply by being true, is not necessarily persuasive to a popular jury. A case cited by Cicero himself adds another dimension to the question of whether or not it is ethical to make use of certain kinds of arguments. In the *De oratore* Antonius states that Publius Rutilius Rufus had roundly condemned an orator who prostrated himself before his judges and used emotional pleas to secure an acquittal. Rutilius, says Antonius, though completely innocent, rejected any such appeal when he himself was arraigned. He "not only refused to supplicate his judges but did not wish that his case should make use of any rhetorical embellishment more than the simple truth of the matter required" (*De or.* 1. 229). The outcome, Antonius goes on, was the same as in the case of Socrates—a wise and blameless man was condemned.

Cicero's point in alluding to the condemnations of Socrates and Rutilius Rufus involved the question of means and ends. Should not an innocent individual when defending himself or herself against a false accusation make use of whatever legal means exist to win the case? While Socrates and Rutilius Rufus would have said no, Cicero argued in the *De oratore* that an orator, because he had to practice in the real world and not in the ideal republic of Plato, ought to base his rhetorical strategy upon "what his fellow citizens . . . think, feel, believe, and hope for" (*De or.* 1.223) rather than upon the tenets of philosophy. And once we grant that the kind of rhetoric that both bends the truth and clouds the judgment of its audience is morally justified in the case of the defense of an innocent person, may we not grant as well that the same techniques may be used "to bring help to the suppliant, to succor the afflicted, to grant men their safety, to free them from danger, to retain them as citizens, . . . to attack the wicked, and to take vengeance on those who have harmed us" (*De or.* 1.32)? In practice, once we have deemed permissible the use of these techniques in some cases, we deem them permissible in many others.

It should be kept in mind that Cicero himself operated under several self-imposed restraints in using the rhetorical weapons at his command.

When the orator was constrained to speak against his own friends and political allies, as in his defense of Lucius Licinius Murena when prosecuted by Servius Sulpicius Rufus and Marcus Porcius Cato, he chose with great care the sort of criticisms he thought might be safely leveled at his two antagonists, conscious of the subtle rules that dictated what a Roman orator could say in support of his client without meriting the lasting enmity of the opposition. Cicero acknowledged as well that he was more comfortable exercising his oratorical prowess in defense of those accused than in the prosecution of his enemies, since a successful lawyer for the defense might be guilty of freeing a wrongdoer but could not be charged with destroying an innocent man.[3] The greatest restraint on Cicero's handling of any rhetorical situation, however, was his desire to say or do nothing that, in his opinion, might ultimately injure the Republic. For Cicero and for every other orator of importance in ancient Rome, public speaking was not a profession in itself; rather, it represented one aspect of their activities as magistrates, leaders, and politicians. The cases a man chose to prosecute or defend, the speeches he made for or against various bills or senatorial motions, even the funeral orations he pronounced, were part of an attempt to further his political goals. Cicero, unlike certain of his contemporaries, was no demagogue. His ultimate goal was not self-promotion but rather the preservation of a system of government he considered superior to all alternatives. It is my opinion that, with the possible exception of a period in the middle fifties following his return from exile, Cicero never intentionally allowed his rhetorical handling of the arguments he made in any speech to contradict this goal.[4] Thus, while we find him arguing *in utramque partem* on a variety of issues, we never find him arguing in

---

3. See *Div. Caec.* 1 for Cicero's habit of speaking for the defense and Cic. *Off.* 2.49–51 for a more extended discussion of why it was preferable to defend rather than to prosecute. A legal bias on behalf of the defense exists in our own system and is reflected by the fact that the law allows much wider latitude to the defense than to the prosecution in the use of emotional appeals.

4. Cf. *De or.* 1.34: *Sic enim statuo, perfecti oratoris moderatione et sapientia non solum ipsius dignitatem, sed et privatorum plurimorum et universae rei publicae salutem maxime contineri. Quam ob rem pergite, ut facitis, adulescentes, atque in id studium, in quo estis, incumbite, ut et vobis honori et amicis utilitati et rei publicae emolumento esse possitis.* For a perceptive, and just, assessment of Cicero's political activity, see Habicht, *Cicero the Politician,* esp. 87–99.

such a way as to suggest that autocracy was to be preferred even to the fatally compromised Republic of his day.[5]

It is possible to mount a defense of Ciceronian rhetoric on grounds other than simply the fact that, in many cases, laudable ends could justify less than admirable means. The very nature of what can be considered truth in oratory provides another basis for defending Cicero's persuasive strategies. In the *Gorgias* Socrates had argued that all of the speakers of his own and earlier times could be likened to cooks—that is, they were men who earned their living by flattering other men's tastes rather than by attempting to further their true health and well-being. Socrates had compared the true orator (whose like had never yet been seen in Athens) to a physician, for he was one who gave his fellow citizens what was good for them rather than what they merely wished for. And as the physician was able to do this because of his knowledge of the basic causes of health and sickness, so the true orator was able to serve his fellow citizens because he based his oratory on knowledge of what was, in a Platonic sense, true and false. For the Socrates of the *Gorgias*, then, the only true orator was the philosopher, as only he could persuade through knowledge (*epistēmē*) rather than opinion (*doxa*); and the orator who was, in reality, a philosopher would make his audience better by the practice of his craft, since it would, of necessity, aim at leading them to knowledge and virtue.

If the notion of truth found in the *Gorgias* is a realistic standard for the orator, then Cicero was surely to be condemned for failing to meet that standard. But even Aristotle, who had in his *Rhetoric* fulfilled many of the requisites Plato lists in the *Phaedrus* for the creation of a true "art" (*technē*) of persuasion, denied that it was possible for popular oratory to deal in absolute truths. He argued that since rhetoric deals with human actions, which are governed by no systematic rules, and since it takes place before an audience that may be assumed to be incapable of following a complex chain of logical argumentation, it follows that the orator deals for the most part only with what appears to be probably and generally true, not with what is of necessity true.[6] The point was echoed by Cicero himself in the *De oratore*. In reproducing the arguments of Charmadas, Antonius states that no systematic art of rhetoric exists, since what deserves to be termed an "art" deals with

5. Cicero did believe, however, that autocracy was preferable to civil war.
6. *Rhet.* 1.2.11–17 (1357a1–b10).

incontrovertible facts, while all those matters treated by oratory "are doubtful and uncertain" due to the fact that orators themselves do not grasp these matters clearly (1.92). Cicero went even farther in denying the applicability of the absolute truths of the philosophers to persuasion. While philosophy might supply the orator with commonplaces concerning friendship, justice, moderation, and the like, what use is it, he asked, for the orator to know "whether the *summum bonum* resides in the mind or in the body, whether it is to be defined as virtue or pleasure," or whether, in fact, anything at all can be known for certain?[7] "The greatest fault in oratory," he declared in one of the opening passages of the *De oratore* (1.12) "is to depart from the ordinary way of speaking and to shrink from the habits of common sense." And in book 2 (223–24) he continues: "[The orator] must feel the pulse of each class, each age group, each rank; he should taste the thoughts and sensibilities of those before whom he is pleading or intending to plead. But he should keep his philosophy books for the rest and relaxation of places such as this Tusculan estate."

It has been noted that Cicero, as a Skeptic, was not inclined to believe that human beings were able to achieve absolute certainty about the facts of experience. He was a man whose most ingrained habit was to question, to weigh each side of a proposition, to search not for the unquestionably true but for the more convincing, the more probable, of various alternatives. In March of 49 B.C., shortly after Caesar had crossed the Rubicon and the civil war had been set in motion, we find him debating, Hamlet-like, *in utramque partem* the question of whether or not one ought to remain in one's country when it is ruled by a tyrant and whether or not it is required of the citizen to risk every danger for the sake of freedom.[8] This tendency to see the world not as black and white but in shades of gray continued to the very last, for his inability in 43 B.C. to decide whether it was better to flee Italy or to remain allowed the agents of the triumvirs to part him from his head and hands. If we see the reality that lay behind Cicero's speeches as unequivocal, then Cicero's constant manipulation of that reality looks like an effort to undermine the truth. But, as Renato Barilli has written,

> Matters appear quite different if we proceed from the supposition that, at least in the realm of human actions, no secure and unequivocal "truth" can triumph; there exist only more or less probable arguments; it is therefore

7. *De or.* 1.56, 222.
8. *Att.* 9.4.

both the right and the duty of one who is convinced of the goodness (*bontà*) of his or her own arguments to make them "better," more competitive, to make them acceptable to others.[9]

Even if we are willing to grant that there is such a thing as an unequivocal truth about a person, an event, or a situation, what is the clearest way this truth can be expressed? Are there not certain kinds of truths which are more readily understood through fiction than through the recital of facts? In his brilliant account of the literary history of the First World War, Paul Fussell writes of the difficulty veterans encountered in attempting to reproduce the "truth" of their experiences. He quotes a young airman in the Second World War who had hoped that in his daily diaries he might retain an accurate account of what had happened to him. The flyer had written:

> From all the quite detailed evidence of these diary entries I can't add up a very coherent picture of how it really was to be on a bomber squadron in those days. There's nothing you could really get hold of if you were trying to write a proper historical account of it all. . . . No wonder [historians] have to erect rather artificial structures of one sort or another in its place. No wonder it is those artists who re-create life rather than try to recapture it who, in one way, prove the good historians in the end.[10]

In referring to this quote I am not attempting to excuse Cicero for those times when he simply misrepresented facts; rather I am contending that in some instances a fiction that appeals to the emotions and imagination may represent reality more accurately than an objective account. No better illustration of this can be found in Ciceronian rhetoric than the account of the theft by Gaius Verres of the statue of Ceres from Henna. Cicero's digressive narrative of the crime would surely not be allowed if the case were to be tried in a modern courtroom. Yet if one assumes, as do most historians, that Verres was guilty of the gross offenses with which he was charged, then the narrative is a striking example of the

9. R. Barilli, translated from *La retorica*, 8. Cf. *La retorica*, 3: "In the rhetorical universe the notion of a 'truth,' which could relate to external principles to be discovered in the nature of things or in discourses themselves or in some transcendental entity, is invalid. This, however, does not mean that all arguments are of equal force. In fact, some are more credible than others. But the ultimate right of determining the relative truth of an argument belongs to the *demos,* to the community, to the assemblage of politicians, of judges, of participants in a meeting or a debate."
10. "Mercury on a Fork," *Listener,* 18 February 1971, 208, quoted in Fussell, *The Great War,* 311.

kind of quasi-fictional treatment by which, in the end, Cicero was able to "re-create" reality rather than "recapture" it.

THE CHARACTER OF CICERONIAN ORATORY

Oratory in ancient times was an oral art, in which a speaker could depend only to a limited degree on written reminders. Even an orator with as prodigious a memory as Cicero, therefore, had constant recourse to a "formulaic language" of rhetoric—taught both by schooling and experience—and consisting of familiar diction, oft-repeated phrases, more or less set passages, and commonplace arguments (topoi), all ordered within a more or less predictable structure. The survey of speeches in this book has shown the degree to which the ability to exploit and adapt various kinds of commonplaces figured in Cicero's representation of external reality.

The commonplaces of ancient rhetoric were of two kinds: those that applied to general sources of argument, such as "the less and the more" (seen in Cicero's comparison of the political institutions of the Athenians and those of the Asian Greeks in the *Pro Flacco*), and those that dealt with more specific topics (for instance, "the value of the military leader to the state"; "the perfidy of the Gauls"; "the simple virtue of rustic life"; or "the superiority of proof through witnesses to proof through argument").[11] Cicero himself compares the general commonplaces to the letters of the alphabet:

> For whenever we must write some word, we do not need to search strenuously in our thoughts for the letters of this word; similarly, whenever we must plead a case, we ought not to turn to a set of arguments stored up for this case, but rather to have certain [general] commonplaces, which, just like the letters for writing a word, immediately come to mind for setting out the case.
>
> (*De or.* 2.130)

Familiarity with the topoi was only a beginning, then, for if it is true that they constituted a key part of the formulaic language of rhetoric, it is also true that their effectiveness turned on how this language was used. Simply memorizing a series of topoi did not, in itself, give an orator the ability to persuade; specific arguments had to be created from the general topics and the specific arguments themselves had to be adapted to a particular rhetorical occasion. As Cicero writes:

11. The general topoi are catalogued in Cicero's *Topica*.

For you may bring me a man as educated, incisive, intelligent, and articulate as you wish, and if the same man is a stranger to the traditions, precedents, and customs of the state, and to the mores and character of its citizens, then the commonplaces from which proofs are derived will be of little use to him.[12]

(*De or.* 2.131)

Clearly, the creation of persuasive oratory through the use of general and specific topoi required subtlety of invention, stylistic judgment, and, ultimately, the ability to gauge the effect of a particular strategy upon a particular audience.[13] Furthermore, it should also be clear that simply recognizing that an orator has made use of a topos (or even a stereotype) in a speech does not constitute proof of either its truth or its falsity in a particular instance; nor does it say anything about whether this strategy was employed effectively or not.

Another observation concerning commonplaces that has emerged, especially from the second part of this work, is that justifications of topoi connecting place and character had, by Cicero's day, become part and parcel of the topoi themselves. Like his contemporaries whose writing touched on ethnography, Cicero appended to his descriptions of the world a variety of explanations for the characteristics imputed to the people in it: racial mixing and degeneration explain the character of the Sardinians in the *Pro Scauro;* in the *Pro Flacco* Cicero implies that exposure to the decadent and slavish cultures of the East is the reason for the cultural and moral debasement of the Asian Greeks as compared with the European Greeks; and the effect of geography and resources on ways of life and, ultimately, on human temperament is alluded to in a number of speeches to explain the admirable character of country folk, as well as the negative traits of the proud and treacherous Campanians of the *De lege agraria* 2. Only in the *Pro Fonteio* does the orator rely on

12. Cicero is here speaking of the general topoi, but the argument applies to the specific as well. Cf. the crucial idea of *decorum* in the employment of commonplaces in *Or.* 123–26.

13. Quintilian (2.1.12) compares commonplaces to weapons that are always available to be used when the occasion demands. He notes, however, that since no commonplace is so universal as to fit perfectly within any actual case, it is a sign of weakness in an orator simply to memorize a specific commonplace and then trot it out repeatedly (2.4.27) or to employ a commonplace because he has prepared it rather than because it is apt (2.4.30–31). The employment of a commonplace, he states, requires that the orator create a connection (*vinculum*) between it and the case at hand (2.4.30: *vix ullus est tam communis locus qui possit cohaerere cum causa nisi aliquo propriae quaestionis vinculo copulatus*).

an appeal to negative prejudice unsupported by any arguments as to the grounds for that prejudice.

Comparison of the *Pro Roscio Amerino* with the *Pro Caelio* and of the *Pro Flacco* with the *Verrines* has also shown the degree to which Cicero exploited commonplaces on both sides of an issue (*in utramque partem*) in his representations of the world. We have seen that appeals to one set of images of places and the people who inhabit them are made in one speech, only to be abandoned or even reversed in another. As I have argued in the introduction to this work, awareness of these contradictions is crucial to understanding the spectrum of viewpoints to be found among Cicero's listeners. But even within the shifting topoi studied in this work a certain consistency can be observed in Cicero's frequent exploitation of the commonplace of the *rusticus bonus*. Arguments concerning the value of rural life and the virtues of rustic landowners appear in the *Pro Flacco,* the *Verrine* orations, and the *De lege agraria* 2; in the *Pro Quinctio* and the *Pro Roscio Amerino* such arguments are central to Cicero's rhetorical strategy. Time and again when the orator wished to characterize a client, supporter, or friendly witness in positive terms he turned to this tactic. While this would clearly have been a futile strategy when he was faced with the necessity of creating a credible and attractive persona for an individual of recognized power and influence, when it came to portraying the outsider— the stranger who lived in a small Italian municipality or the unknown witness or litigant who came from a Roman province—the most effective positive stereotype Cicero could draw on was evidently that of the humble, honest farmer.

This book has fallen into two parts: the first dealing with specific places and monuments, both seen and unseen, and the symbolic roles assigned to them in various speeches; the second focusing for the most part on more general representations of place and the link forged in Cicero's speeches between place and character. One might well ask at this point what one has to do with the other and, further, whether Cicero's frequent recourse to both strategies reveals something important about the character of his oratory. I shall use the closing pages of this work to suggest an answer to such questions.

I believe that both of these strategies of persuasion were part of Cicero's effort to create within his oratory an impression of objectivity. Allusions to the visual ambiance, descriptions of places and things not seen by the audience, creation of believable settings for characters and the actions they perform, invest what are actually subjective arguments with some of the same credibility as that derived from the presentation of documents, exhibits, and witnesses. It seems probable that the combined effect of Aristotle's cursory treatment of inartificial proof and the existence of commonplaces elevating arguments from probabilities above this sort of proof has led us to underestimate its importance in Latin oratory. Cicero's remark in the *Verrines* that when something had been stolen or appropriated the whole focus of the trial was on documents and witnesses (II.1.27) and Quintilian's observation that most forensic arguments dealt with inartificial proofs (5.1.2) might be more accurate reflections of the actual role played by evidentiary proof in Roman courts. As already noted (above, p. 25), the places, monuments, and topography referred to in Cicero's speeches did not actually constitute inartificial proofs, but such references must have produced an effect on an audience similar to that produced by the use of inartificial proofs.[14] Both general references to places as an explanation of character and allusions to and descriptions of specific places and things were a vital part of the orator's attempt to convince his audience that all of his arguments and appeals were ultimately grounded in a potentially discernable and verifiable reality.

Another connection between the various kinds of representation analyzed in this work appears when we consider these strategies in light of the theatrical nature of Ciceronian oratory. In the speeches Cicero creates a number of figures who play their roles against a variety of backgrounds. Both the stereotypical masks assigned to the characters and the milieux in which they perform function on a superficial level as locations of meaning: that is, the success of the dramas created by the speeches depended in large part on the orator's choice of characters, "props," and settings and on the power and persuasiveness of the symbolic values he assigned to these signifiers.

The passage from *De oratore* quoted at the beginning of this chapter makes us wonder whether Cicero himself might not have understood some of the strategies he employed in just this way. Here he states that through the use of the mnemonic art it is possible to "imprint" (*notare*) the mind. The verb used, *notare,* carries the sense of something impressed, as, for instance, marks on a writing table. It may also refer to the creation of an emblem or symbol, since *notatio* can designate a kind of shorthand in which letters stand for complete words. In the passage,

14. For inartificial proofs, see Arist. *Rhet.* 1.2.2 (1355b35–39); 1.15.1–33 (1375a22–1377b12); Kennedy, *Aristotle,* 108–18.

the final clause defines both what is imprinted and what the imprints stand for: through images the mind apprehends ideas, and through the memory *loci* it takes in the sequence of these ideas. It is, however, the phrase that precedes this which is most interesting and most relevant to our effort to connect the two halves of this study. In it Cicero refers to the orator's need to create a clear sequence of *loci*, observing that the images must be "well placed" (*bene positis*). In alluding to the *imagines* themselves Cicero employs an unusual term: *personae*, or "masks." A. S. Wilkins explains: "The mnemonic images are compared to the masks in a theatre, behind which were the facts or thoughts which they represented." [15] Cicero's use of the term *personae* in this context reminds us that images of persons as well as of things served as memory stimuli for the orator. It suggests as well that Cicero's connection of ideas with specific places and objects, as well as his manipulation of ethical stereotypes, might both have figured in his application (whether conscious or unconscious) of the principles of the *ars memoriae* to the task of manipulating the thoughts and feelings of an audience.

It has long been a truism among scholars of the ancient world that the Greeks were gifted abstract thinkers and the Romans a plodding folk, extraordinarily tied to the world of things rather than of ideas. [16] This study of Cicero's speeches has, to a great extent, confirmed the accuracy of the second half of this judgment, although I see no reason to couch the observation in the pejorative terms frequently used. Ciceronian oratory was indeed characterized by its constant allusions to "things." Whether Cicero at any given point in a speech was relying chiefly on an appeal to *logos, ēthos,* or *pathos,* he consistently grounded these appeals in concrete reality: logical proofs demonstrating guilt or innocence included frequent recourse to *probabile ex vita* arguments in which the character of various places provided a setting and an expla-

15. *De oratore,* 405 (ad 2.359).
16. See, for instance, Rose, *Religion in Greece and Rome,* 157: "The Greeks were keen, original thinkers, bold experimenters, capable of breaking with their past, if they thought it advisable, to a far greater degree than most nations. They had, moreover, a gift for abstract thought, and a remarkably high proportion of them had logical minds and were ready to follow their own ideas to the uttermost consequences. . . . But the Romans were a much slower-witted people. Orderly and legalistic, willing to learn but at the same time extraordinarily tenacious of the past, . . . they neither struck out any new lines for themselves nor ever quite abandoned the old, half-savage practices which they had inherited from simple ancestors, peasants and herdsmen of prehistoric days."

nation for the character of individuals; the ethical traits of friends and enemies were illustrated through dramatic narrations of events in which the setting of a scene often played a crucial role in the actions described and in the interpretation of them; and in his most memorable attempts to engage the emotions of his audience Cicero consistently linked appeals to his audience's patriotism and piety to specific places and objects. But while this study has thus reinforced the stereotype of the orator and his audience as closely wedded to the real world, it has also shown that this constant reliance on the visual and the concrete was but the Roman gateway to the world of ideas.

Abbreviations

AAT	*Atti dell'Accademia delle Scienze di Torino, Classe di Scienze morali, storiche e filologiche*
AJP	*American Journal of Philology*
AnnInst	*Annali dell' instituto di corrispondenza archeologica*
ANRW	*Aufstieg und Niedergang der römischen Welt*
ArchCl	*Archeologia classica*
BC	*Bullettino della Commissione Archeologica Communale di Roma*
CB	*Classical Bulletin*
CIL	*Corpus inscriptionum Latinarum*
CJ	*Classical Journal*
CP	*Classical Philology*
CQ	*Classical Quarterly*
CW	*Classical World*
DialArch	*Dialoghi di archeologia*
FGrH	F. Jacoby, ed., *Fragmente der griechischen Historiker*
G&R	*Greece & Rome*
HSCP	*Harvard Studies in Classical Philology*

InvLuc	*Invigilata lucernis*
JP	*Journal of Philology*
JRS	*Journal of Roman Studies*
MAAR	*Memoirs of the American Academy in Rome*
MAL	*Memorie della Classe di Scienze morali e storiche dell' Accademia dei Lincei*
MD	*Materiali e discussioni per l'analisi dei testi classici*
MDAI(R)	*Mitteilungen des Deutschen Archäologischen Instituts (Röm)*
NAWG	*Nachrichten der Akademie der Wissenschaften in Göttingen*
OpArch	*Opuscula archaeologica*
PBSR	*Papers of the British School at Rome*
RAL	*Rendiconti dell'Accademia Nazionale dei Lincei, Classe di Scienze morali, storiche e filologiche*
RE	Pauly-Wissowa, *Real-Encyclopädie der classischen Altertumswissenschaft*
REA	*Revue des études anciennes*
REL	*Revue des études latines*
RevUniv	*Revue Universitaire*
RFIC	*Rivista di filologia e di istruzione classica*
RhM	*Rheinisches Museum*
RMM	*Revue de métaphysique et de morale*
SDHI	*Studia et documenta historiae et iuris*
StRom	*Studi romani*
SVF	H. von Arnim, ed., *Stoicorum veterum fragmenta*
TAPA	*Transactions of the American Philological Association*
WS	*Wiener Studien*
YCS	*Yale Classical Studies*

Bibliography

Adcock, F. E. *The Roman Art of War under the Republic.* Cambridge, Mass., 1940.

Afzelius, A. "Zwei Episoden aus dem Leben Ciceros." *Classica et mediaevalia 5* (1942):209–17.

Alexander, M. "Hortensius' Speech in Defense of Verres." *Phoenix* 30 (1976):46–53.

Alföldi, A. *Die trojanischen Urahnen der Römer.* Basel, 1957.

———. *Early Rome and the Latins.* Ann Arbor, 1965.

Alfonsi, L. "Tra l'ozio e l'inerzia." *Aevum* 28 (1954):375–76.

Aly, W., ed. *Strabonis geographica.* Bonn, 1957.

Arnim, H. von, ed. *Stoicorum veterum fragmenta.* 3 vols. Leipzig, 1903–5. Vol. 4, indexes by M. Adler. Leipzig 1924.

Austin, R. G., ed. *M. Tulli Ciceronis pro M. Caelio oratio.* 3d ed. Oxford, 1960.

Axler, J. "Tribunal-Stage-Arena: Modelling of the Communication Situation in M. Tullius Cicero's Judicial Speeches." *Rhetorica* 7 (1989):299–311.

Bacon, H. *Barbarians in Greek Tragedy.* New Haven, 1961.

Badian, E. *Foreign Clientelae (264–70 B.C.).* Oxford, 1958.

———. "Agis III." *Hermes* 95 (1967):170–92.

———. *Roman Imperialism in the Late Republic.* 2d ed. Oxford, 1968.

Baldry, H. C. *The Unity of Mankind in Greek Thought.* Cambridge, 1965.

Balsdon, J. P. V. D. "History of the Extortion Court at Rome, 123–70 B.C." *PBSR* 14 (1938):98–114.

———. "Auctoritas, Dignitas, Otium." *CQ* 10 (1960):43–50.

———. *Romans and Aliens.* London, 1979.

Bardon, H., and R. Verdière, R., eds. *Vergiliana.* Leiden, 1971.

Barilli, R. *La retorica.* Milan, 1983.

Barthes, R. "The Reality Effect." In *The Rustle of Language,* translated by R. Howard, 141–48. New York, 1986.

Beare, W. *The Roman Stage*. 3d ed. London, 1977.

Beckmann, F. *Geographie und Ethnographie in Caesars Bellum Gallicum*. Dortmund, 1930.

Beloch, J. *Campanien: Geschichte und Topographie des antiken Neapel und seiner Umgebung*. Breslau, 1890.

Berger, P. *Cicero als Erzähler: Forensische und literarische Strategien in den Gerichtsreden*. Europaïsche Hochschulschriften 15, Klassische Philologie und Literatur 12. Bern, 1978.

Bianchi Bandinelli, R. *Rome: The Center of Power, 500 B.C. to A.D. 200*. Translated by P. Green. New York, 1970.

Bianchi Bandinelli, R., and M. Torelli. *L'arte dell' antichità classica*. 2 vols. Turin, 1976.

Blake, M. E. *Ancient Roman Construction in Italy from the Prehistoric Period to Augustus*. Washington, D.C., 1947.

———. *Roman Construction in Italy from Tiberius through the Flavians*. Washington, D.C., 1959.

Bléry, H. *Rusticité et urbanité romaines*. Paris, 1909.

Blickman, D. R. "Lucretius, Epicurus, and Prehistory." *HSCP* 92 (1989): 157–91.

Boatwright, M. T. "The Pomerial Extension of Augustus." *Historia* 35 (1986):13–27.

Bömer, F. *Rom und Troja: Untersuchungen zur Frühgeschichte Roms*. Baden-Baden, 1951.

Bonner, S. F. *Education in Ancient Rome: From the Elder Cato to the Younger Pliny*. Berkeley, 1977.

Bonnet, M. "Le dilemme de C. Gracchus." *REA* 8 (1906):40–46.

Bornecque, H. *Les Catilinaires de Cicéron*. Paris, 1936.

Borza, E. "The End of Agis' Revolt." *CP* 66 (1971):230–35.

Botsford, G. *The Roman Assemblies from Their Origin to the End of the Republic*. New York, 1909.

Bréguet, E. "Urbi et orbi: Un cliché et un thème." In *Hommages à Marcel Renard*, edited by J. Bibauw, 1:140–52. Brussels, 1969.

Brilliant, R. *Visual Narratives: Storytelling in Etruscan and Roman Art*. Ithaca, N.Y., 1984.

Bringmann, K. *Studien zu den politischen Ideen des Isokrates*. Göttingen, 1965.

Brink, C. "Cicero's *Orator* and Horace's *Ars Poetica*." *Ciceroniana* n.s. 2 (1975):97–106.

Brunt, P. A. *Italian Manpower, 225 B.C.–A.D. 14*. Oxford, 1971.

———. "Patronage and Politics in the 'Verrines.'" *Chiron* 10 (1980):273–89.

Bruwaene, M. van den. *La théologie de Cicéron*. Louvain, 1937.

Buchheit, V. "Chrysogonus als Tyrann in Ciceros Rede für Roscius aus Ameria." *Chiron* 5 (1975):193–211.

Canter, H. V. "Praise of Italy in Ancient Authors." *CJ* 33 (1938):457–70.

Caplan, H. "Memoria: Treasure House of Eloquence." In *Of Eloquence: Studies in Ancient and Mediaeval Rhetoric*, edited by A. King and H. North, 196–246. Ithaca, N.Y., 1970.

Carratelli, G. "Europa ed Asia nella storia del mondo antico." *La parola del passato* 40 (1955):5–19.

Castagnoli, F. "Gli edifici rappresentati in un relievo del sepolcro degli Haterii." *BC* 69 (1941):59–69.

———. "Il tempio dei Penati e la Velia." *RFIC* 74 (1946):157–65.

———. "Note sulla topografia del Palatino e del Foro Romano." *ArchCl* 16 (1964):73–99.

———. "Per la cronologia dei monumenti del Comizio." *StRom* 23 (1975):187–89.

Catalano, P. "Aspetti spaziali del sistema giuridico-religioso romano." *ANRW* 2.16.1 (1978):440–553.

Ceausescu, P. "Altera Roma: Histoire d'une folie politique." *Historia* 25 (1976):79–108.

Clarke, M. L. *Rhetoric at Rome: A Historical Survey.* London, 1953. Reprint with corrections. 1966.

———. *The Roman Mind: Studies in the History of Thought from Cicero to Marcus Aurelius.* 2d ed. Cambridge, Mass., 1960.

Classen, C. J. "Ciceros Rede für Caelius." *ANRW* 1.3 (1973):60–94.

———. *Die Stadt im Spiegel der Descriptiones und Laudes urbium in der antiken und mittelalterlichen Literatur bis zum Ende des zwölften Jahrhunderts.* Hildesheim, 1980.

———. "Verres' Gehilfen in Sizilien nach Ciceros Darstellung." *Ciceroniana* n. s. 4 (1980):93–111.

———. "Ciceros Kunst der Überredung." In *Eloquence et rhétorique chez Cicéron,* edited by W. Stroh, 149–92. Fondation Hardt, Entretiens 28. Geneva, 1982.

———. "La difesa di Valerio Flacco, un' orazione di Cicerone." In *Studi in onore di C. Sanfilippo,* 1:115–29. Milan, 1982.

———. *Recht, Rhetorik, Politik: Untersuchungen zu Ciceros rhetorischer Strategie.* Darmstadt, 1985.

Clavel, V. *De M. T. Cicerone Graecorum interprete.* Paris, 1868.

Cloché, P. *Isocrate et son temps.* Paris, 1963.

Coarelli, F. "La Sicilia tra la fine della guerra annibalica e Cicerone." In *Società romana e produzione schiavistica,* edited by A. Giardina and A. Schiavone, 1:2–18. Bari, 1981.

———. *Il Foro Romano.* Vol. 1, *Periodo arcaico.* Rome, 1983. Vol. 2, *Periodo repubblicano e augusteo.* Rome, 1985.

Cole, A. T. *Democritus and the Sources of Greek Anthropology.* APA Monographs 25. Chapel Hill, N.C., 1967.

Conte, G. B. *The Rhetoric of Imitation: Genre and Poetic Memory in Virgil and Other Latin Poets.* Ithaca, N.Y., 1986.

Corbett, P. B. "The Scurra." In *Hommages à André Boutemy,* edited by G. Cambier, 23–31. Brussels, 1976.

Cossarini, A. "Il prestigio dell' agricoltura in Sallustio e Cicerone." *Atti dell' Istituto Veneto di Scienze, Lettere ed Arti* 138 (1979–80):355–64.

Courtney, E. "The Prosecution of Scaurus in 54 B.C." *Philologus* 105 (1961):151–56.

Craig, C. "The Role of Rational Argumentation in Selected Judicial Speeches of Cicero." Ph.D. diss., University of North Carolina at Chapel Hill, 1979.
————. "The *Accusator* as *Amicus:* An Original Roman Tactic of Ethical Argumentation." *TAPA* 111 (1981):31–37.
————. "Cato's Stoicism and the Understanding of Cicero's Speech for Murena." *TAPA* 116 (1986):229–39.
————. "Reason, Resonance, and Dilemma in Cicero's Speech for Caelius." *Rhetorica* 7 (1989):313–28.
Crawford, M. *Roman Republican Coinage.* 2 vols. Cambridge, 1974.
Criniti, N., ed. *Bibliografia catilinaria.* Milan, 1971.
Culler, J. *The Pursuit of Signs: Semiotics, Literature, Deconstruction.* Ithaca, N.Y., 1981.
Davies, J. C. "Was Cicero Aware of Natural Beauty?" *G&R* 18 (1971): 152–65.
De Coulanges, F. *The Ancient City.* Translated by W. Small. Boston, 1874.
Della Corte, F. "Conflitto di culti in Sicilia." *Ciceroniana* n. s. 4 (1980):205–9.
Della Morte, P. M. *Studi su Cicerone oratore.* Naples, 1977.
Desmouliez, A. "Sur l'interpretation du 'De Signis.' " *RevUniv* 58 (1949): 155–66.
Detlefsen, D. "De Comitio romano." *AnnInst* 32 (1860):128–60.
DeWitt, N. "Litigation in the Forum in Cicero's Time." *CP* 21 (1926):218–24.
Diels, H., ed. *Doxographi Graeci.* Berlin, 1879.
Dihle, A. "Zur hellenistischen Ethnographie." In *Grecs et barbares,* edited by H. Schwabl et al., 207–32. Fondation Hardt, Entretiens 8. Geneva, 1961.
Dilke, O. A. W. "Cicero's Attitude to the Allocation of Land in the *De Lege Agraria.*" *Ciceroniana* n. s. 3 (1978):183–87.
————. "Divided Loyalties in Eastern Sicily under Verres." *Ciceroniana* n. s. 4 (1980):43–51.
Diller, H. "Die Hellenen-Barbaren-Antithese im Zeitalter der Perserkriege." In *Grecs et barbares,* edited by H. Schwabl et al., 39–82. Fondation Hardt, Entretiens 8. Geneva, 1961.
————, ed. *Hippocrates, Über die Umwelt.* Berlin, 1970.
Dirkzwager, A. *Strabo über Gallia Narbonensis.* Leiden, 1975.
Dobesch, G. *Der panhellenische Gedanke in 4 Jh. v. Chr. und der "Philippos" des Isokrates."* Vienna, 1968.
Dodds, E. R. *The Greeks and the Irrational.* Berkeley, 1951.
————. *The Ancient Concept of Progress.* Oxford, 1973.
Dorey, T. A. "Cicero, Clodia and the *Pro Caelio.*" *G&R* 5 (1958):175–80.
Douglas, A. E. "The Intellectual Background of Cicero's Rhetorica: A Study in Method." *ANRW* 1.3 (1973):95–138.
Downey, G. "Ekphrasis." In *Reallexikon für Antike und Christentum,* 4:921–44. Stuttgart, 1959.
Draheim, H. "Die ursprüngliche Form der katilinarischen Reden Ciceros." *Wochenschrift für klassische Philologie* 34 (1917):1061–71.
Drexler, H. "Zu Ciceros Rede *pro Caelio.*" *NAWG,* 1944, 1–32.
Duckworth, G. *The Nature of Roman Comedy: A Study in Popular Entertainment.* Princeton, 1952.

Dumézil, G. "Remarques sur la stèle archaïque du Forum." In *Hommages à J. Bayet,* edited by M. Renard and R. Schilling, 172–79. Brussels-Berchem, 1964.

Dunkle, J. R. "The Greek Tyrant and Roman Political Invective of the Late Republic." *TAPA* 98 (1967):151–71.

———. "The Rhetorical Tyrant in Roman Historiography." *CW* 65 (1971): 12–20.

Earl, D. *The Moral and Political Tradition of Rome.* Ithaca, N.Y., 1967.

Eco, U. *Semiotics and the Philosophy of Language.* Bloomington, Ind., 1984.

Edmonds, J. M., ed. *The Fragments of Attic Comedy.* 3 vols. in 4. Leiden, 1957–61.

Eliade, M. *Cosmos and History: The Myth of the Eternal Return.* Translated by W. Trask. New York, 1959.

———. *Images and Symbols: Studies in Religious Symbolism.* Translated by P. Mairet. New York, 1961.

Engmann, J. "Imagination and Truth in Aristotle." *Journal of the History of Philosophy* 14 (1976):259–65.

Fantham, E. *Comparative Studies in Republican Latin Imagery.* Toronto, 1972.

———. "Quintilian on Performance: Traditional and Personal Elements in *Institutio* 11.3." *Phoenix* 36 (1982):243–63.

Fears, J. R. "The Cult of Jupiter and Roman Imperial Ideology." *ANRW* 2.17.1 (1981):3–141.

Fehling, D. "Das Problem der Geschichte des griechischen Weltmodells vor Aristoteles." *RhM* 128 (1985):195–231.

Ferry, J. J. "The Art of Cicero." *CJ* 63 (1968):201–4.

Fowler, D. P. "Narrate and Describe: The Problem of Ekphrasis." *JRS* 81 (1991):25–35.

Fowler, W. W. "Mundus patet." *JRS* 2 (1912):25–33.

Fraenkel, E. "Zur Geschichte des Wortes *fides.*" *RhM* 71 (1916):187–99.

Frank, T. *Roman Buildings of the Republic.* Rome, 1924.

Frederiksen, M. W. *Campania.* Edited by N. Purcell. London, 1984.

Fredouille, J. C. "Lucrèce et le 'double progrès contrastant.'" *Pallas* 19 (1972):11–27.

Freudenthal, J. *Über den Begriff des Wortes FANTASIA bei Aristoteles.* Göttingen, 1863.

Friedländer, P. *Johannes von Gaza und Paulus Silentiarius.* Leipzig, 1912. Reprint. Hildesheim, 1969.

Frye, N. "Myth, Fiction and Displacement." In *Fables of Identity: Studies in Poetic Mythology,* 21–38. New York, 1963.

Fuchs, H. "Eine Doppelfassung in Ciceros catilinarischen Reden." *Hermes* 87 (1959):463–69.

Fuhrmann, M. "*Cum dignitate otium:* Politisches Programm und Staatstheorie bei Cicero." *Gymnasium* 67 (1960):481–500.

———. "Tecniche narrative nella seconda orazione contro Verre." *Ciceroniana* n.s. 4 (1980):27–42.

Fussell, P. *The Great War and Modern Memory.* New York, 1975.

Gabba, E. *Republican Rome, the Army and the Allies*. Translated by P. J. Cuff. Berkeley, 1976.

Gaillard, J. "Que représentent les Gracques pour Cicéron?" *Bulletin de L'Association G. Budé*, ser. 4 (1975):499–529.

Garnsey, P. D. A., and C. R. Whittaker, eds. *Imperialism in the Ancient World*. Cambridge, 1978.

Geffcken, J. "Saturnia Tellus." *Hermes* 27 (1892):381–88.

Geffcken, K. *Comedy in the Pro Caelio*. Leiden, 1973.

Gelzer, M. *Caesar: Politician and Statesman*. Translated by P. Needham. Cambridge, Mass., 1968.

———. *Cicero, Ein biographischer Versuch*. Wiesbaden, 1969.

Genette, G. "Boundaries of Narrative" (translated by A. Levonas). *New Literary History* 8 (1976):1–13.

Gioffredi, C. "I tribunali del Foro." *SDHI* 9 (1943):227–82.

Gjerstad, E. "Il Comizio romano dell' età repubblicana." *OpArch (Acta Instituti Romani Regni Sueciae)* 2.2 (1941):97–158.

———. *Early Rome (Acta Instituti Romani Regni Sueciae* 17.3), 3:217–59. Lund, 1960.

Goar, R. *Cicero and the State Religion*. Amsterdam, 1972.

Gotoff, H. C. "Cicero's Analysis of the Prosecution Speeches in the *Pro Caelio*: An Exercise in Practical Criticism." *CP* 81 (1986):122–32.

Grant, M. *The Jews in the Roman World*. London, 1973.

Greenidge, A. H. J. *The Legal Procedure of Cicero's Time*. Oxford, 1901.

Griffin, M. T. "The 'leges iudiciariae' of the Pre-Sullan Era." *CQ* 23 (1973): 108–26.

Grimal, P. "Cicéron et les tyrans de Sicile." *Ciceroniana* n.s. 4 (1980):63–74.

Gruen, E. *Roman Politics and the Criminal Courts, 149–78 B.C.* Cambridge, Mass., 1968.

———. *The Last Generation of the Roman Republic*. Berkeley, 1974.

———. *The Hellenistic World and the Coming of Rome*. Berkeley, 1984.

Gsell, S. *Histoire ancienne de l'Afrique du Nord*. 8 vols. Paris, 1913–28.

Guite, H. "Cicero's Attitude to the Greeks." *G&R* 9 (1962):142–59.

Guthrie, W. K. C. *The Greeks and Their Gods*. London, 1950.

———. *In the Beginning: Some Greek Views on the Origins of Life and the Early State of Man*. London, 1957.

———. *A History of Greek Philosophy*. Vol. 3, *The Fifth-Century Enlightenment*. Cambridge, 1969. Vol. 4, *Plato, the Man and His Dialogues: Earlier Period*. Cambridge, 1975.

Haarhoff, T. J. *The Stranger at the Gate: Aspects of Isolationism and Cooperation in Ancient Greece and Rome*. 2d ed. Oxford, 1948.

Habicht, C. *Cicero the Politician*. Baltimore, 1990.

Hahm, D. E. "Early Hellenistic Theories of Vision and the Perception of Color." In *Studies in Perception: Interrelations in the History of Philosophy and Science*, edited by P. K. Machamer and R. G. Turnbull, 60–95. Columbus, 1978.

Hall, U. "Voting Procedure in Roman Assemblies." *Historia* 13 (1964):267–306.

Halm, K., ed. *Rhetores Latini minores*. Leipzig, 1863.

Halm, K., and G. Laubmann, eds. "Ciceros Reden gegen L. Sergius Catilina." In *Ciceros ausgewählte Reden*, 3:1–100. Berlin, 1891.

Hammond, M. "Ancient Imperialism: Contemporary Justifications." *HSCP* 68–69 (1948):105–61.

Hampl, F. "'Stoische Staatsethik' und frühes Rom." *Historische Zeitschrift* 184 (1957):249–71.

———. "Römische Politik in republikanischer Zeit und das Problem des 'Sitten-verfalls.'" *Historische Zeitschrift* 188 (1959):497–525.

Hansen, W. F. "Odysseus' Last Journey." *Quaderni urbinati di cultura classica* 24 (1977):27–48.

Hardy, E. G. "The Policy of the Rullan Proposal in 63 B.C." *JP* 32 (1913): 228–60.

———. *The Catilinarian Conspiracy in Its Context*. Oxford, 1924.

Harris, W. V. *War and Imperialism in Republican Rome, 327–70 B.C.* Oxford, 1979.

Haury, A., ed. *Orationes in Catilinam*. Paris, 1969.

Heibges, U. "Cicero—A Hypocrite in Religion?" *AJP* 90 (1969):304–12.

———. "Religion and Rhetoric in Cicero's Speeches." *Latomus* 28 (1969): 833–49.

Heinze, R. "Auctoritas." *Hermes* 60 (1925):348–66.

———. "Ciceros Rede *Pro Caelio*." *Hermes* 60 (1925):193–258.

———. "Fides." *Hermes* 64 (1929):140–66.

Heitland, W. E. *Agricola: A Study of Agriculture and Rustic Life in the Greco-Roman World from the Point of View of Labour*. Cambridge, 1921.

Hellegouarc'h, J. *Le vocabulaire latin des relations et des partis politiques sous la république*. 2d ed. Paris, 1972.

Henderson, C. "The Career of the Younger M. Aemilius Scaurus." *CJ* 53 (1958):194–206.

Henderson, M. I. "The Process de repetundis." *JRS* 41 (1951):71–88.

Heurgon, J. *Recherches sur l'histoire, la religion et la civilisation de Capoue préromaine des origines à la deuxième guerre punique*. Paris, 1942.

Hillard, T. W. "The Seventies, the Senate, and Popular Discontent: A Background to the First Verrine." *Ancient Society* 11.3 (1981):12–21.

Hinds, S. "An Allusion in the Literary Tradition of the Proserpina Myth." *CQ* 32 (1982):476–78.

Hopkins, K. *Conquerors and Slaves*. Cambridge, 1978.

Horsfall, N. "Some Problems in the Aeneas Legend." *CQ* 29 (1979):372–90.

Hülsen, C. "Das Comitium und seine Denkmäler in der republikanischen Zeit." *MDAI(R)* 8 (1893):79–94.

———. "Ameria." *RE* 1² (1894):1826–27.

———. "Capua." *RE* 3² (1899):1555–61.

———. *Forum und Palatin*. Munich, 1926.

Humbert, J. *Les plaidoyers écrits et les plaidoiries réelles de Cicéron*. Paris, 1925.

Hunt, H. A. K. *The Humanism of Cicero*. Melbourne, 1954.

Huxley, G. L. "Zeugma." *Liverpool Classical Monthly* 6 (1981):219.

Imholz, A. A. "Gladiatorial Metaphors in Cicero's *Pro Sex. Roscio Amerino.*"
   CW 65 (1972):228–30.
Izzo, P. F. "Cicero and Political Expediency." *Classical Weekly* 42.11 (1948–
   49):168–72.
Jacoby, F. *Die Fragmente der griechischen Historiker.* Berlin and Leiden,
   1923–58.
Jal, P. "Hostis (publicus) dans la littérature latine de la fin de la République."
   REA 65 (1963):53–79.
Jauss, H. R. "Literary History as a Challenge to Literary Theory." Translated
   by E. Benzinger. In *New Directions in Literary History,* edited by R. Cohen,
   11–41. Baltimore, 1974.
———. *Towards an Aesthetic of Reception.* Translated by T. Bahti. Minneapo-
   lis, 1982.
Johnson, H. D. *The Roman Tribunal.* Baltimore, 1927.
Jonkers, E. J. *Social and Economic Commentary on Cicero's De Lege Agraria
   Orationes Tres.* Leiden, 1963.
Jordan, H., and C. Hülsen. *Topographie der Stadt Rom im Alterthum.* Vol. 1.3.
   Berlin, 1871–1907.
Kähler, H. *Rom und seine Welt: Bilder zur Geschichte und Kultur.* Munich,
   1958.
Kennedy, G. *The Art of Persuasion in Greece.* Princeton, 1963.
———. "The Rhetoric of Advocacy in Greece and Rome." *AJP* 89 (1968):
   419–36.
———. *The Art of Rhetoric in the Roman World.* Princeton, 1972.
———. *Aristotle on Rhetoric: A Theory of Civic Discourse.* New York and
   Oxford, 1991.
Kessler, J. *Isokrates und die panhellenische Idee.* Paderborn, 1911.
Kier, H. *De laudibus vitae rusticae.* Marburg, 1933.
Kinsey, T. E. "The Case against Sextus Roscius of Ameria." *L'antiquité clas-
   sique* 54 (1985):188–96.
Klotz, A. "Geographie und Ethnographie in Caesars *Bellum Gallicum.*" *RhM*
   83 (1934):66–96.
Knauss, E. "Unterrichtliche Behandlung von Cicero *in Verrem* 2.4.27–83 als
   Einführung in die römische Wertewelt." *Der altsprachliche Unterricht* 5
   (1962):67–85.
Knoche, U. *Vom Selbstverständnis der Römer.* Heidelberg, 196ᴢ.
Köstermann, E. "Das Problem des römischen Dekadenz bei Sallust und Taci-
   tus." *ANRW* 1.3 (1973):781–810.
Krieger, M. *Ekphrasis: The Illusion of the Natural Sign.* Baltimore, 1992.
Kühner, R., and C. Stegmann. *Ausführliche Grammatik der lateinischen
   Sprache.* 2 vols. Munich, 1962.
Landgraf, G. *Kommentar zu Ciceros Rede Pro Sex. Roscio Amerino.* 2d ed.
   Leipzig, 1914.
La Piana, G. "Foreign Groups in Rome during the First Centuries of the Em-
   pire." *Harvard Theological Review* 20 (1927):183–403.
Latte, K. *Römische Religionsgeschichte.* Munich, 1960.

Laurand, L. *Etudes sur le style des discours de Cicéron*. 3 vols. 4th ed. Paris 1936–38. Reprint, Amsterdam, 1965.

Lausberg, H. *Handbuch der literarischen Rhetorik*. 2 vols. Munich, 1960.

Leach, E. W. "Ekphrasis and the Theme of Artistic Failure in Ovid's Metamorphoses." *Ramus* 3 (1974):102–42.

———. Review of *La Villa dei Papiri ad Ercolano: Contributo alla ricostruzione dell' ideologia della nobilitas tardorepubblicana*, by M. Wojcik. *AJA* 92.1 (January 1988):145–46.

———. *The Rhetoric of Space: Literary and Artistic Representations of Landscape in Republican and Augustan Rome*. Princeton, 1988.

Lee, E. N. "The Sense of an Object: Epicurus on Seeing and Hearing." In *Studies in Perception: Interrelations in the History of Philosophy and Science*, edited by P. K. Machamer and R. G. Turnbull, 27–59. Columbus, 1978.

Leeman, A. D. *Orationis Ratio: The Stylistic Theories and Practice of the Roman Orators, Historians and Philosophers*. 2 vols. Amsterdam, 1963.

———. "The Technique of Persuasion in Cicero's *Pro Murena*." In *Eloquence et rhétorique chez Cicéron*, edited by W. Stroh, 193–236. Fondation Hardt, Entretiens 28. Geneva, 1982.

Leeman, A. D., and H. Pinkster, eds. *M. T. Cicero, De oratore libri III*. Heidelberg, 1981–89.

Leen, A. "Cicero and the Rhetoric of Art." *AJP* 112 (1991):229–45.

Leon, H. J. *The Jews of Ancient Rome*. Philadelphia, 1960.

Levelt, W. J. M. "The Speaker's Linearization Problem." In *The Psychological Mechanisms of Language*, edited by H. C. Longuet-Higgins, J. Lyons, and D. E. Broadbent, 305–14. London, 1981.

Levine, E. B. *Hippocrates*. New York, 1971.

Lintott, A. W. *Violence in Republican Rome*. Oxford, 1968.

———. "The leges de repetundis." *Zeitschrift der Savigny-Stiftung für Rechtsgerichte* 98 (1981):162–211.

Long, A. A. *Hellenistic Philosophy*. London, 1974.

Long, A. A., ed. *Problems in Stoicism*. London, 1971.

Long, A. A., and D. N. Sedley, eds. *The Hellenistic Philosophers*. 2 vols. Cambridge, 1987.

Long, T. *Barbarians in Greek Comedy*. Carbondale, Ill., 1986.

Lovejoy, A. O., and G. Boas. *Primitivism and Related Ideas in Antiquity*. 2d ed. New York, 1965.

Lucas, F. L. *The Greatest Problem and Other Essays*. London, 1960.

Luce, T. J. "Design and Structure in Livy: 5.32–55." *TAPA* 102 (1971):265–302.

Luck, G. *Ovid's Tristia*. Vol. 2, *Kommentar*. Heidelberg, 1977.

Lugli, G. *I monumenti antichi di Roma e suburbio*. 3 vols. and suppl. Rome, 1930–40.

———. *Roma antica: Il centro monumentale*. Rome, 1946.

———. *Monumenti minori del Foro Romano*. Rome, 1947.

———. *Fontes ad topographiam veteris urbis Romae pertinentes*. 7 vols. Rome, 1952–69.

————. *Itinerario di Roma antica.* Milan, 1978.

McDermott, W. C. "The Verrine Jury." *RhM* 120 (1977):64–75.

Madvig, J. N. M. *Tulli Ciceronis de finibus bonorum et malorum libri quinque.* 3d ed. Copenhagen, 1876. Reprint. Hildesheim, 1963.

Magdelain, A. "Le pomerium archaïque et le mundus." *REL* 54 (1976):71–109.

Malcovati, H., ed. *Oratorum Romanorum fragmenta liberae rei publicae.* 2d ed. Turin, 1955.

Marchetti, S. "L'avvocato, il giudice, il reus: La psicologia della colpa e del vizio nelle opere retoriche e nelle prime orazioni de Cicerone." *MD* 17 (1986):93–124.

Maróti, E. "Die Piratenwesen um Sizilien zur Zeit des Proprätors C. Verres." *Acta antiqua* 4 (1956):197–210.

Martorana, G. "La Venus di Verre e le Verrine." *Kokalos* 25 (1979) [1981]:73–103.

May, J. "The Rhetoric of Advocacy and Patron-Client Identification: Variation on a Theme." *AJP* 102 (1981):308–15.

————. *Trials of Character: The Eloquence of Ciceronian Ethos.* Chapel Hill, N.C., 1988.

Mazzolani, L. Storoni. *The Idea of the City in Roman Thought.* Translated by S. O'Donnell. Bloomington, Ind., 1970.

Metaxaki-Mitrou, F. "Violence in the Contio during the Ciceronian Age." *L'antiquité classique* 54 (1985):180–87.

Meyer, H. "Cicero und das Reich." Diss., Cologne, 1957.

Michel, A. *Les rapports de la rhétorique et de la philosophie dans l'oeuvre de Cicéron.* Paris, 1960.

Mitchell, T. N. *Cicero: The Ascending Years.* New Haven, 1979.

Mitchell, W. J. T. *Iconology: Image, Text, Ideology.* Chicago, 1986.

Modrak, D. K. W. *Aristotle: The Power of Perception.* Chicago, 1987.

Momigliano, A. *Alien Wisdom.* Cambridge, 1975.

Moorton, R. F. "The Innocence of Italy in Vergil's *Aeneid.*" *AJP* 110 (1989):105–30.

Morgan, M. G. "*Imperium sine finibus:* Romans and World Conquest in the First Century B.C." In *Panhellenica: Essays in Ancient History and Historiography in Honor of Truesdell S. Brown,* edited by S. M. Burstein and L. A. Okin, 143–54. Lawrence, Kans., 1980.

Most, G. "Seming and Being: Sign and Metaphor in Aristotle." In *Studies in Science and Culture,* 3:11–33. Newark, 1987.

Nash, E. *Pictorial Dictionary of Ancient Rome.* 2 vols. London, 1968.

Neuhauser, W. *Patronus und Orator.* Innsbruck, 1958.

Neumeister, C. *Grundsätze der forensischen Rhetorik gezeigt an Gerichtsreden Ciceros.* Munich, 1964.

Nicolet, C. "Consul togatus: Remarques sur le vocabulaire politique de Cicéron et de Tite-Live." *REL* 38 (1960):236–63.

————. *Space, Geography, and Politics in the Early Roman Empire.* Ann Arbor, 1991.

Nissen, H. *Templum.* Berlin, 1869.

Norden, E. *Die antike Kunstprosa.* 2 vols. Leipzig, 1898.

———. *Die germanische Urgeschichte in Tacitus Germania.* 5th ed. Stuttgart, 1971.

Nordh, A. *Libellus de regionibus urbis Romae* (*Acta Instituti Romani Regni Sueciae,* ser. in 8°). Lund, 1949.

North, H. *From Myth to Icon: Reflections of Greek Ethical Doctrine in Literature and Art.* Ithaca, N.Y., 1979.

North, J. A. "The Development of Imperialism." *JRS* 71 (1981):1–9.

Oehler, K. "Der consensus omnium als Kriterium der Wahrheit in der antiken Philosophie und der Patristik." *Antike und Abendland* 10 (1961): 103–29.

Ogilvie, R. M. *A Commentary on Livy, Books 1–5.* 2d ed. Oxford, 1970.

Orelli, I., J. G. Baiter, and K. Halm. *M. Tulli Ciceronis opera quae supersunt omnia.* Vol. 2.2. Zurich, 1856.

Pais, E. M. *Ancient Legends of Roman History.* Translated by M. E. Cosenze. New York, 1905. Reprint. Freeport, N.Y., 1971.

Palmer, R. E. A. *The King and the Comitium: A Study of Rome's Oldest Public Document.* Historia Einzelschriften 11. Wiesbaden, 1969.

Panofsky, E. "Et in Arcadia Ego." In *Philosophy and History: Essays Presented to Ernst Cassirer,* edited by R. Klibansky and H. J. Paton, 23–54. Oxford, 1936. Reprint. New York, 1963.

Paoli, U. E. *Cicerone, De signis.* 5th ed. Florence, 1959.

Pape, M. *Griechische Kunstwerke aus Kriegsbeute und ihre öffentliche Aufstellung in Rom.* Hamburg, 1975.

Pariente, A. "Stator, teóforo y nombre común." *Durius* 2 (1974):57–66.

Parry, A. "Landscape in Greek Poetry." *YCS* 15 (1957):3–29.

Paul, G. M. "*Urbs Capta:* Sketch of an Ancient Literary Motif." *Phoenix* 36 (1982):144–55.

———. *A Historical Commentary on Sallust's Bellum Jugurthinum.* Liverpool, 1984.

Pease, A. S. *Cicero, De divinatione.* Chicago, 1921.

Perelli, L. "La storia dell' umanità nel V libro di Lucrezio." *AAT* 101 (1967):117–285.

Perl, G. "Der Redner Helvius Mancia und der Pictus Gallus (Cic. *De Or.* 2.266)." *Philologus* 126 (1982):59–69.

Petrochilos, N. *Roman Attitudes to the Greeks.* Athens, 1974.

Picheca, C. "Un esempio di *moderatio* ciceroniana: La presentazione di L. Sempronius Atratinus nella *Pro Caelio.*" *InvLuc* 2 (1980):41–51.

Piderit, K., and O. Harnecker, eds. *Cicero, De oratore.* 6th ed. Leipzig, 1886–90.

Pietrangeli, C., and U. Ciotti. "Ameria." In *Enciclopedia dell' arte antica, classica e orientale,* 1:317. Rome, 1958.

Platner, S. B., and T. Ashby. *A Topographical Dictionary of Rome.* Oxford, 1929.

Poe, J. P. "The Secular Games, the Aventine, and the Pomerium in the Campus Martius." *Classical Antiquity* 3 (1984):57–81.

Pollitt, J. J. *The Ancient View of Greek Art: Criticism, History, and Terminology.* New Haven, 1974.

―――. *The Art of Rome, c. 753 B.C.–A.D. 337: Sources and Documents.* 2d ed. Cambridge, 1983.

―――. *The Art of Ancient Greece, 1400–31 B.C.: Sources and Documents.* 2d ed. Englewood Cliffs, N.J., 1990.

Pöschl, V. "Die römische Auffassung der Geschichte." *Gymnasium* 63 (1956):190–206.

―――. "Zur Einbeziehung anwesender Personen und sichtbarer Objekte in Ciceros Reden." In *Ciceroniana: Hommages à K. Kumaniecki,* edited by A. Michel and R. Verdière, 206–26. Leiden, 1975.

Primmer, A. "Historisches und Oratorisches zur ersten Catilinaria." *Gymnasium* 84 (1977):18–38.

Pritchard, R. T. "Gaius Verres and the Sicilian Farmers." *Historia* 20 (1971):224–38.

Ramage, E. S. "City and Country in Menander's Dyskolos." *Philologus* 110 (1966):194–211.

―――. *Urbanitas: Ancient Sophistication and Refinement.* Norman, Okla., 1973.

―――. "Velleius Paterculus 2.126.2–3 and the Panegyric Tradition." *Classical Antiquity* 1 (1982):266–71.

―――. "Clodia in Cicero's *Pro Caelio.*" In *Classical Texts and Their Traditions: Studies in Honor of C. R. Trahman,* edited by D. F. Bright and E. S. Ramage, 201–11. Chico, Calif., 1984.

―――. "Strategy and Methods in Cicero's *Pro Caelio.*" *Atene·e Roma* 30 (1985):1–8.

Rambaud, M. "Le *Pro Fonteio* et l'assimilation des Gaulois de la Transalpine." In *Mélanges P. Wuilleumier,* edited by H. Le Bonniec and G. Vallet, 301–16. Paris, 1980.

Rankin, H. D. *Celts and the Classical World.* Portland, Oreg., 1987.

Ratkowitsch, C. "Ein 'Hymnus' in Ciceros erster Catilinaria." *WS* 94 (1981):157–67.

Rawson, E. *Intellectual Life in the Late Republic.* Baltimore, 1985.

Rees, D. A. "Aristotle's Treatment of *phantasia.*" In *Essays in Ancient Greek Philosophy,* edited by J. P. Anton and G. L. Kustas, 491–504. Albany, 1971.

Reinhold, M. *Diaspora: The Jews among the Greeks and Romans.* Sarasota, Fla., 1983.

Reitzenstein, R. "Ciceros Rede für Caelius." *NAWG,* 1925, 25–32.

Reynen, H. "Ewiger Frühling und goldene Zeit." *Gymnasium* 72 (1965): 415–33.

Richardson, E. H. "The Etruscan Origins of Early Roman Sculpture." *MAAR* 21 (1953):77–124.

Richardson, L. Jr. "Cosa and Rome, Comitium and Curia." *Archaeology* 10 (1957):49–55.

―――. "The Tribunals of the Praetors of Rome." *MDAI(R)* 80 (1973): 219–33.

———. "Ameria." In *Princeton Encyclopedia of Classical Sites,* edited by R. Stillwell, 49. Princeton, 1976.

Richter, F. *Ciceros catilinarische Reden.* Leipzig, 1878.

Rizzo, F. P. "'*Principes Civitatis*' nelle Verrine: Realtà civica e idealità Ciceroniana." *Ciceroniana* n. s. 4 (1980):211–21.

———. "La invidia nobilium nelle Verrine." In *Scritti sul mondo antico in memoria di F. Grosso,* edited by L. Gasperini, 527–42. Rome, 1981.

Robin, L. "Sur la conception épicurienne du progrès." *RMM* 23 (1916): 697–719.

Romano, D. "Cicerone e il ratto di Proserpina." *Ciceroniana* n. s. 4 (1980):191–201.

Römisch, E. "Mensch und Raum, Gedanken zur Behandlung von Cicero, *de leg.* II.1–8." *Anregung,* 1962, 223–33.

———. "Cicero." In *Interpretationen lateinischer Schulautoren,* edited by H. Krefeld, 43–65. Frankfurt, 1968.

———. "Ovid." In *Interpretationen lateinischer Schulautoren,* edited by H. Krefeld, 173–74. Frankfurt, 1968.

———. "Satis Praesidii, Gedanken zur Behandlung der catilinarischen Reden." *Der altsprachliche Unterricht* 11 (1968):48–61.

———. "Umwelt und Atmosphäre, Gedanken zur Lektüre von Ciceros Reden." In *Cicero, Ein Mensch seiner Zeit,* edited by G. Radke, 117–35. Berlin, 1968.

Rose, H. J. *Religion in Greece and Rome.* London, 1948 (originally published as *Ancient Greek Religion* and *Ancient Roman Religion*). Reprint. New York, 1959.

Rose, P. W. "Sophocles' *Philoctetes* and the Teaching of the Sophists." *HSCP* 80 (1976):49–105.

Rowland, R. J. "Sardinians in the Roman Empire." *Ancient Society* 5 (1974):223–29.

Russell, D. A. *Criticism in Antiquity.* Berkeley, 1981.

Rykwert, J. *The Idea of a Town.* Princeton, 1976.

Salmon, E. T. *Roman Colonization under the Republic.* Ithaca, N.Y., 1970.

———. "Cicero Romanus an Italicus anceps." In *Cicero and Vergil: Studies in Honor of Howard Hunt,* edited by J. R. C. Martyn, 75–86. Amsterdam, 1972.

Salzman, M. R. "Cicero, the *Megalenses* and the Defense of Caelius." *AJP* 103 (1982):299–304.

Sandbach, F. H. "Phantasia Kataleptike." In *Problems in Stoicism,* edited by A. A. Long, 9–21. London, 1971.

Scanlon, T. *The Influence of Thucydides on Sallust.* Heidelberg, 1980.

Schick, T. "Cicero and the Pathetic Appeal in Oratory." *CB* 42 (1965):17–18.

Schofield, M. "Aristotle on the Imagination." In *Aristotle on Mind and the Senses,* edited by G. E. R. Lloyd and G. E. L. Owen, 99–140, Cambridge, 1978; and in *Articles on Aristotle.* Vol. 4, *Psychology and Aesthetics,* edited by J. Barnes, M. Schofield, and R. Sorabji, 103–32. London, 1979.

Schrijvers, P. H. "Invention, imagination et théorie des émotions chez Cicéron et Quintilien." In *Actus: Studies in Honor of H. L. W. Nelson,* edited by J. den Boeft and A. H. M. Kessels, 395–408. Utrecht, 1982.

Scullard, H. H. *Roman Politics, 220–150 B.C.* Oxford, 1973.
———. *Festivals and Ceremonies of the Roman Republic.* Ithaca, N.Y., 1981.
Scully, S. "Cities in Italy's Golden Age." *Numen* 35 (1988):69–78.
Seager, R. "Cicero and the Word *popularis.*" *CQ* 22 (1972):328–38.
Shatzman, I. "The Roman General's Authority over Booty." *Historia* 21 (1972):177–205.
Sherwin-White, A. N. "Poena Legis Repetundarum." *PBSR* 17 (1949):5–25.
———. "The Extortion Procedure Again." *JRS* 42 (1952):43–55.
———. *Racial Prejudice in Imperial Rome.* Cambridge, 1967.
———. *Roman Foreign Policy in the East, 168 B.C. to A.D. 1.* London, 1984.
Showerman, G. "Cicero's Appreciation of Greek Art." *AJP* 25 (1904):306–14.
Skinner, M. B. "Clodia Metelli." *TAPA* 113 (1983):273–87.
Skutsch, O. *The Annals of Ennius.* Oxford, 1985.
Smallwood, M. "The Trial of Verres and the Struggle for Mastery at the Roman Bar." *Ancient Society* 1.3 (1981):37–47.
Smethurst, S. E. "Cicero and Roman Imperial Policy." *TAPA* 84 (1953): 216–26.
Snell, B. *Discovery of the Mind: The Greek Origins of European Thought.* Translated by T. G. Rosenmeyer. Oxford, 1953.
Snowden, F. M. *Blacks in Antiquity: Ethiopians in the Greco-Roman Experience.* Cambridge, Mass., 1970.
———. *Before Color Prejudice: The Ancient View of Blacks.* Cambridge, Mass., 1983.
Solmsen, F. "The Aristotelian Tradition in Ancient Rhetoric." In *Kleine Schriften,* 2:178–215. Hildesheim, 1968.
———. "Aristotle and Cicero on the Orator's Playing upon the Feelings." In *Kleine Schriften,* 2:216–30. Hildesheim, 1968.
———. "Cicero's First Speeches, A Rhetorical Analysis," in *Kleine Schriften,* 2:231–45. Hildesheim, 1968.
Soós, I. "M. T. Ciceros Betrachtungen über die Institutionen der athenischen Demokratie." *Oikumene* 4 (1983):710–79.
Spengel, L. *Rhetores Graeci.* 3 vols. Leipzig, 1854–85.
Staveley, E. S. *Greek and Roman Voting and Elections.* London, 1972.
Steiner, W. *The Colors of Rhetoric: Problems in the Relation between Modern Literature and Painting.* Chicago, 1982.
Stillwell, R., ed. *Princeton Encyclopedia of Classical Sites.* Princeton, 1976.
Strasburger, H. "Poseidonius on Problems of the Roman Empire." *JRS* 55 (1965):40–53.
Stroh, W. *Taxis und Taktik: Die advokatische Dispositionskunst in Ciceros Gerichtsreden.* Stuttgart, 1975.
Syme, R. *The Roman Revolution.* Oxford, 1939.
———. *Sallust.* Berkeley, 1964.
Taylor, L. R. *Voting Districts of the Roman Republic.* Rome, 1960.
———. *Roman Voting Assemblies.* Ann Arbor, 1966.
Thomas, R. *Lands and Peoples in Roman Poetry: The Ethnographical Tradition.* Cambridge, 1982.
Thompson, L. A. *Romans and Blacks.* Norman, Okla., 1989.

Torelli, M. "Un *templum augurale* d'età repubblicana a Bantia." *RAL* 8.21 (1966):293–315.

———. *Typology and Structure of Roman Historical Reliefs*. Ann Arbor, 1982.

Trouard, M. A. *Cicero's Attitude towards the Greeks*. Chicago, 1942.

Trüdinger, K. "Studien zur Geschichte der griechisch-römischen Ethnographie." Diss., Basel, 1918.

Tuan, Yi-Fu. *Topophilia: A Study of Environmental Perception, Attitudes, and Values*. Englewood Cliffs, N.J., 1974.

———. *Space and Place*. Minneapolis, 1977.

Ussher, R. G. *The Characters of Theophrastus*. London, 1960.

Van Deman, E. B. "The Sullan Forum." *JRS* 12 (1922):1–31.

Van Deman, E. B., and A. G. Glay. "The Sacra Via of Nero." *MAAR* 5 (1925):115–26.

Vasaly, A. "Transforming the Visible." *Res* 6 (1983):65–71.

———. "The Masks of Rhetoric: Cicero's *Pro Roscio Amerino*." *Rhetorica* 3 (1985):1–20.

———. "Personality and Power: Livy's Depiction of the Appii Claudii in the First Pentad." *TAPA* 117 (1987):203–26.

———. "*Ars Dispositionis:* Cicero's Second Agrarian Speech." *Hermes* 116 (1988):409–27.

Venturini, C. "La conclusione del processo di Verre." *Ciceroniana* n. s. 4 (1980):155–75.

Verbeke, G. "Le stoïcisme, une philosophie sans frontières." *ANRW* 1.4 (1973):3–42.

Verzar, M. "L'umbilicus urbis: Il mundus in età tardo-repubblicana." *DialArch* 9–10 (1976–77):378–98.

Vogt, J. *Orbis*. Tübingen, 1929. Reprint. Freiberg, 1960.

———. *Ciceros Glaube an Rom*. Stuttgart, 1935.

———. *Ancient Slavery and the Ideal of Man*. Translated by T. Wiedemann. Cambridge, Mass., 1975.

Von Albrecht, M. "Cicero und die Götter Siziliens (*Verr.* II.5.184–189)." *Ciceroniana* n. s. 4 (1980):53–62.

Von Staden, H. "The Stoic Theory of Perception and Its 'Platonic' Critics." In *Studies in Perception: Interrelations in the History of Philosophy and Science,* edited by P. K. Machamer and R. G. Turnbull, 96–136. Columbus, 1978.

Walter, E. V. *Placeways: A Theory of the Human Environment*. Chapel Hill, N.C., 1988.

Warry, J. *Warfare in the Classical World*. London, 1980.

Watson, G. *The Stoic Theory of Knowledge*. Belfast, 1966.

———. "*Phantasia* in Aristotle, *De Anima* 3.3" *CQ* 32 (1982): 101–113.

———. *Phantasia in Classical Thought*. Galway, 1988.

Watson, G. R. *The Roman Soldier*. Ithaca, N.Y., 1969.

Webster, T. B. L. M. *Tulli Ciceronis pro L. Flacco oratio*. Oxford, 1931.

———. *Studies in Menander*. 2d ed. Manchester, 1960.

Weinstock, S. "Mundus patet." *MDAI(R)* 45 (1930):111–23.

———. "Templum." *MDAI(R)* 47 (1932):95–121.

———. *Divus Julius.* Oxford, 1971.

Werner, R. "Das Problem des Imperialismus und die römische Ostpolitik im zweiten Jahrhundert v. Chr." *ANRW* 1.1 (1972):501–63.

White, K. D. *Roman Farming.* London, 1970.

Wilkins, A. S., ed. *Cicero, De oratore libri tres.* 3 vols. Oxford, 1888–92. Reprint in one volume. Hildesheim, 1965.

Williams, R. *The Country and the City.* New York, 1973.

Wirszubski, C. *Libertas as a Political Idea at Rome.* Cambridge, 1950.

———. "Cicero's *cum dignitate otium:* A Reconsideration." *JRS* 44 (1954): 1–13.

———. "*Audaces:* A Study in Political Phraseology." *JRS* 51 (1961):12–22.

Wiseman, T. P. "Topography and Rhetoric: The Trial of Manlius." *Historia* 28 (1979):32–50.

———. *Catullus and His World: A Reappraisal.* Cambridge, 1985.

———. "Monuments and the Roman Annalists." In *Past Perspectives: Studies in Greek and Roman Historical Writing,* edited by I. S. Moxon, J. D. Smart, and A. J. Woodman, 87–100. Cambridge, 1986.

Wisse, J. *Ethos and Pathos from Aristotle to Cicero.* Amsterdam, 1989.

Wojcik, M. R. *La Villa dei Papiri ad Ercolano: Contributo alla ricostruzione dell' ideologia della nobilitas tardorepubblicana.* Rome, 1986.

Wood, N. *Cicero's Social and Political Thought.* Berkeley, 1988.

Wright, F. W. *Cicero and the Theater.* Smith College Classical Studies 11. Northampton, 1931.

Yates, F. *The Art of Memory.* Chicago, 1966.

Zanker, G. "Enargeia in the Ancient Criticism of Poetry." *RhM* 124 (1981):297–311.

Zanker, P. *The Power of Images in the Age of Augustus.* Translated by A. Shapiro. Ann Arbor, 1988.

Ziegler, K. "Palatium." *RE* 36^2 (1949):1–81.

———, ed. *M. Tullius Cicero, De legibus.* 2d ed. Heidelberg, 1963.

Zumpt, A. W. *Orationes tres de lege agraria.* Berlin, 1861.

General Index

Places and monuments in Rome are designated under "Rome, places and monuments" and are in boldface type. References to illustrations are in italics.

109n35; called foreigner, 138; called *peregrinus rex*, 138n15; concept of ideal statesman, 186–87; condemnation of Greek democracy by, 201–2; as *consul popularis*, 74; and definition of rhetoric, 13; as *dux togatus*, 52, 52n22, 199; ethical character of oratorical methods, 245–52; identification with clients, 188–90, 189n51, 199; influence of speeches in antiquity, x; as *pater patriae*, 80, 80n82, 176; published form of speeches, 8–9, 9n11, 38–39, 38n41, 38n42, 38–39; reasons for publication of speeches, 9–10, 9–10n12; *supplicatio* decreed to honor, 78; value in studying speeches of, x–xi
—works: *Academica* (2), 92–94; *De finibus*, 29–30, 31, 32, 63, 100; *De imperio Cn. Pompei*, 25, 88; *De inventione*, 4, 155, 186; *De lege agraria* (1), 36; *De lege agraria* (2), 88, 171n24, 180, 217–43, 253, 254; *De legibus*, 28n20, 29, 30–33, 35, 58, 188; *De oratore*, 3, 6n9, 26–29, 27n18, 28n20, 31, 102n25, 187, 247, 249, 250, 255; *De provinciis consularibus*, 88; *Divinatio in Caecilium*, 36, 110, 166n17, 208, 214; *In Catilinam* (1), 8, 38–39, 49–59, 49–50n16, 74, 86–87, 99; *In Catilinam* (1), setting of, 41–49, 59, 74, 86–87; *In Catilinam* (3), 8, 38–39, 75–87, 99, 116n39; *In Catilinam* (3), setting of, 60–75, 86–87; *In Catilinam* (4), 35, 36, 69; *In Verrem* (I), 110; *In Verrem* (II.1), 25, 108, 129, 255; *In Verrem* (II.2), 105, 109; *In Verrem* (II.4),103, 104–28; *Orator*, 60; *Philippic* (2), 208; *Philippic* (6), 142n22; *Post reditum in senatu*, 38n41; *Pro Balbo*, 88; *Pro Caecina*, 36, 166n17; *Pro Caelio*, 4–5, 156, 172–90, 254; *Pro Caelio*, setting of, 179–80; *Pro Cluentio*, 167–68, 187; *Pro Flacco*, 192, 193, 198–205, 216, 252, 253, 254; *Pro Fonteio*, 193–94, 196–98, 199, 205, 209, 253; *Pro Milone*, 4, 8, 9–10, 22, 23–24, 38n41, 57, 88, 208; *Pro Murena*, 6, 177; *Pro Plancio*, 34n33; *Pro Quinctio*, 36, 166n17, 171–72, 254; *Pro rege Deiotaro*, 34; *Pro Roscio Amerino*, 36, 156–72, 167n17, 173, 174, 176, 177, 178n35, 181, 186, 189, 216, 233, 254; *Pro Scauro*, 37–

38, 101, 102–3n25, 193, 194–97, 199, 203, 205, 209–10, 253; *Pro Sestio*, 36; *Verrines*, 105, 109, 119, 122–23, 205–17, 254; *Verrines*, artificiality of, 8, 208–9, 209n24
Cicero, Q. (brother of Marcus): in *De finibus*, 29, 30; in *De legibus*, 31, 33
Cilicia, 205, 206–7, 225n48
Cincinnatus, L. Quinctius, 162n12
Cincius Alimentus, L., 18n3
Cinna, L. Cornelius, 73
Clarke, M. L., 184
Classen, C. J., 6
Claudius, Appius (*decemvir*), 122n50, 239
Claudius Caecus, Appius, 24, 175, 176, 179, 181
Claudius Marcellus, M. *See* Marcellus
Claudius Pulcher, Appius (cos. 54 B.C.), 178n34, 195
Claudius Pulcher, C., 106n29, 112
Claudius Pulcher, C. (brother of Ap. Claudius Pulcher, cos. 54 B.C.), 195
Clodia, 174, 175, 177–78, 178n34, 180, 182, 183, 185, 189
Clodius Pulcher, P., 22, 23, 24, 57, 67, 88, 175
Coarelli, F., 40, 62
Colonus (Attica), 29
Comitia Centuriata, 230
Comitia Curiata, 70–71
Comitia Tributa, 70
Commonplaces, rhetorical, 5n5, 25, 77, 123n50, 163, 171, 186, 187–88, 195, 205, 209, 211, 218, 252–54, 255. *For specific commonplaces, see* Topoi, rhetorical
Corax, 1, 246
Corfinium ("Italia"), 135n11
Corinth, 106, 206–7, 220, 225, 233, 235n67
Corinthians, 233
Cornelius Balbus, L., *See* Balbus, L. Cornelius
Cornelius Cossus, A., 73
Coruncanius, Ti. (cos. 280 B.C.), 138n15
Cosa, 62n39
Cotta, C. Aurelius, 27
Crassus, C. Licinius (tr. pl. 145 B.C.), 71n62, 74n71
Crassus, L. Licinius (orator), 187n45; in *De oratore*, 27, 28, 34–35n33, 106n29
Crassus, M. (Dives), 184, 190, 218n36
Crete, 205, 206–7
Culler, Jonathan, 12

Greeks, 109, 145, 256. *See also* Stereo-
    types, rhetorical, Greeks; Topoi, rhe-
    torical, East vs. West

Hannibal, 73, 236
Heius, C., 111–14, 123, 125, 126
Henna (Sicily), 111, 120, 121, 122, 125,
    126, 229, 251
Hercules, 60–61, 139n17, 147; statue of
    (Messana), 112, 114. *See also* Rome:
    places and monuments, Hercules
Herennius Balbus, L. *See* Balbus, L. Her-
    ennius
Hermagoras, 21
Herodotus, 146
Hieron I, 1
Hippocrates, *On Airs, Waters, Places,*
    142–45, 146, 204
Homer, 111, 133n6; *Iliad,* 5; *Odyssey,* 5
Horatii, tombs of the (Via Appia), 18n3
Horatius, P., 17–18, 23
Hortensius Hortalus, Q., 211, 212
Hostilius, Hostus, 43, 72. *See also* Rome:
    places and monuments, Hostus Hos-
    tilius
Hostilius, Tullus, 73
Humanitas, 119, 182–84, 183n41,
    184n42

Iberians, 148
Ichthyophages, 139n16
Ilissus River (Attica), 32n26
Imagines, mnemonic, 100–102, 102–
    3n25, 256
Inartificial proofs (*atekhnoi pisteis*). *See*
    Proofs
India, 147n31
Invention (*inventio*), 4, 19n5, 128
Isles of the Blessed, 138
Isocrates, 143n25
Italy, 25, 30, 88, 106, 134, 134n6, 206–
    7, 220, 229, 242
Ithaca, 33n28

Julius Victor, C., 18
Junonia (Africa), 241
Jupiter, 16, 135; Invictus, 58; Latiaris,
    23, 57; Latiaris, temple of (Alban
    Mount), 69n57; Optimus Maximus,
    43, 68, 83, 84, 85, 87, 99, 115–16,
    126; Stator, 43, 45, 46, 48, 50–51,
    51n19, 53–59, 87. *See also* Rome:
    places and monuments, Jupiter, co-
    lossal statue of; Rome: places and
    monuments, Jupiter Stator; Rome:
    places and monuments, temples, Ju-
    piter

Laelius, C., interest of, in literature and
    philosophy, 176
Lampsacus (Troad), 123, 213
Lares, 48
Larinum, 167
Latiaris, Mount, 23
Leeman, A. D., 6
Lentulus, P. Cornelius, 77, 78, 79
Levitas, barbarian, 150n39, 200, 202
Libertas, 149, 239; in *De lege agraria*
    (2), 234, 237, 238–40, 243; ple-
    beian, 68
Liguria, 233
Liternum, 228, 229
Livy, *Ab urbe condita:* battle with Sa-
    bines in, 43–46, 47–48, 53; Camil-
    lus in, 33n30, 37, 80, 135–36; Cice-
    ronian influence on, x, 33n30; and
    fortification of Janiculum, 230; P.
    Horatius in, 17, 18, 23; Manlius
    Capitolinus in, 15, 16, 23
Logos, 6n9, 256
Longinus, on *phantasia,* 97n15
Lucceius, L., 183
Luceria, 46
Lucretius, *De rerum natura:* and ethnic
    characteristics, 153; and human an-
    thropology, 140n19
Lucullus, L. Licinius, in *Academica* (2),
    92–94
Lucullus, M. Terentius (cos. 73 B.C.), 68–
    69n57
Lupercalia, 48
Luscinus, C. Fabricius, 162n12, 176
Lusitanians, 148
Lycia, 225n48, *206–7*
Lydians, 203. *See also* Stereotypes, rhe-
    torical, Asian Greeks
Lysias, 143n25

Macedonia, 194, *206–7,* 220, 225
Maenius, C., 63, 66
Manlius Capitolinus, M., 15–16, 23,
    45–46, 73
Marcellus, M. Claudius, 107, 107n32,
    119, 123n50, 215
Marcius, Ancus, 230
Marius, C., 73, 79, 138n15
Massilia (Gaul), 194, 203, *206–7*
Medes, 147
Memory (*memoria*), 4, 128
Memory, artificial (*ars memoriae*),
    100–102, 102–3n25, 127–28,
    255–56
Menander, *Dyskolos,* 160, 161
Messala, M'. Valerius (cos. 263 B.C.),
    61n37

Messala Niger, M. Valerius (cos. 61 B.C.), 168n18
Messala Rufus, M. Valerius (cos. 53 B.C.), 168n18
Messana (Sicily), 107n31, 109, 110, 111, 112, 113, 113n38, 114, 123, 125, 229
Metapontum, 29
Metella, Caecilia. *See* Caecilia Metella; Caecilia Metella, in *Pro Roscio Amerino*
Metellus, L. Caecilius, 38, 102n25
Metellus Celer, Q. Caecilius (cos. 60 B.C.), 168n18
Metellus Nepos, Q. Caecilius (cos. 57 B.C.), 168n18
Metellus Pius Scipio, Q. Caecilius (cos. 52 B.C.), 118–20, 120n46, 168n18
Mettius Curtius. *See* Curtius, Mettius
Miletus (Ionia), 220, 224, 225
Milo, T. Annius, 22, 23, 70n60, 88
Milvian Bridge, 198
Minerva, 123; temple of (Syracuse), 123
Mitchell, Thomas N., ix
Mithridates, 225
Mummius, L., 107n31, 107n32, 112, 113, 119
Murena, L. Licinius, 248
Myron, 109
Mysia, 201, 206–7
Mysians, 203. *See also* Stereotypes, rhetorical, Asian Greeks
Mytilenae (Lesbos), 220, 224

Narbo Martius (Gaul), 194, 206–7
Nasica, P. Scipio. *See* Scipio
Nasica Corculum, P. Cornelius Scipio. *See* Scipio Nasica Corculum
Nature and custom (*physis-nomos* debate), 141, 144
Navius, Attus, 67. *See also* Rome: places and monuments, Navius
New Carthage (Spain), 206–7, 220, 225
Nicolet, Claude, 13, 14
Nuceria, 227n52, 228, 229
Numidians, 147

Octavian. *See* Augustus
Octavius, Cn., 68. *See also* Rome: places and monuments, Octavius
October Horse, 72
Odysseus, 33n28, 133n5, 133–34n6
Oedipus, 29
Olympus (Lycia), 220, 224, 225n48
Oratio pridie quam in exsilium iret, 58–59, 83n85
Oratory, performance aspects of, 5, 6–7,

10–11, 34, 34n32, 40–41, 169–70. *See also* Delivery (*actio*)
Orcus, 124
Oroanda, 220, 224, 225, 225n48
Otium, in *De lege agraria* (2), 234, 235–38, 239, 243
Ovid, 47, 48, 104, 188n47; *Metamorphoses*, 23

Palladium, 38, 102n25. *See also* Rome: places and monuments, Palladium
Palmer, R. E. A., 72
Pamphylia, 214, 206–7, 225n48
Panaetius, 187n45
Panhellenism, 143
Paphlagonia, 206–7, 220, 225
Papirius Cursor, L. *See* Cursor
Pathos, 6n9, 20, 24, 36, 97, 97n15, 256. *See also* Emotional appeal in oratory
Penates, Di, 36, 48. *See also* Rome: places and monuments, Penates
Perception. *See* Sensory perception
Pergamum (Mysia), 220, 224, 225
Pericles, 29
Perses (Perseus), king of Macedon, 169, 225
Personae. See Stereotypes, rhetorical
Phalaris, 117n42
Phantasia/phantasiai, 93, 95–97, 95n13, 95–96n14, 97n15
Pharsalus (Thessalia), 51n19
Phaselis (Lycia), 220, 224, 225n48
Philip II, 152n43
Philip V, 225
Philippus, Q. Marcius (cos. 186 B.C.), 61n37
Phoenicians. *See* Stereotypes, rhetorical, Poeni
Phrygia, 201, 206–7
Phrygians, 203. *See also* Stereotypes, rhetorical, Asian Greeks
Picenum, 184
Pillars of Hercules, 138
Piso, M., in *De finibus*, 29, 30, 63, 100
Plancius, Cn., 34n33
Plato, 29; criticism of Sophistic rhetoric by, 1; *Gorgias*, 201, 249; on natural character of ethnic groups, 141, 141n21; *Phaedrus*, 27–28, 27n18, 28n20, 201, 246–47, 249; and *phantasia*, 95n13; *Republic*, 202
Plautus, 104; *Curculio*, 35–36
Pliny the Elder, 61–62, 105, 168
Plutarch, 105n27
Polybius, 133–34n6
Polyclitus, 109

rope), 143–45, 145n26, 152, 200,
203–4, 253; expediency vs. justice,
118–119, 211, 231; general and specific, 252–53; immorality of the
young, 173–74; indulgence for the
behavior of the young, 175–77; "the
less and the more," 201, 252; the
military achievements of the accused, 198–99, 211; North vs.
South (Scythians vs. Aethiopians),
145n26; "refounding" of the city
(*urbs restituta*), 77, 77n77; the reliability of witnesses, 209–11; subcategories of, 21; "them vs. us," 137–
38; the tyrant and his career, 117,
122–24, 122–23n50, 213–15, 217,
239
Topothesia, 20, 90n3
Torquatus, L. Manlius, 138n15
Tralles (Caria), 220, 224
Trebula, 228, 229
Triptolemus, statue of (Temple of Ceres,
Henna), 122
Troy, 48, 117
Tullus Hostilius. *See* Hostilius, Tullus
Turdetani, 148
Tusculum, 27

Umbria, 167, 170

Varro, 47, 142n23
Veii, 135, 136

Venafrum, 227n53, 228, 229
Venus Erycina, 121n48
Vergil, 111; *Aeneid,* 37, 60–61, 119,
140n19
Verres, C., 84n87, 89, 104–30 passim,
192, 205–17 passim, 251; as *alter
Orcus,* 124; statues of (Sicily),
105n27, 119n44. *See also* Rome:
places and monuments, Verres
Vesta, 37, 135
Vestals, 79
Via Amerina, 168
Via Appia (Appian Way), 17, 24, 42, 88,
228
Via Cassia, 168
Via Flaminia, 17, 228
Via Latina, 17, 228
Vitruvius, 142–43n23
Vivid description, 19–20, 91–104, 111,
127–28. See also *Ekphrasis; Enar-
geia; Evidentia*

Walter, E. V., 60
Wilkins, A. S., 256
Wood, Neal, ix

Xenophon, on barbarians, 150n38

Yates, Frances, 100–101

Zanker, Paul, 13, 14

Index of Ancient Authors

Aphthonius (ed. Spengel, *Rhetores Graeci*
 2)
  Progymnasmata
  46–49: 91n4
Appian
  (B. civ.) Bella civilia
  1.8.71: 73n70
  1.10.94: 73n70
  1.11.97: 68n56
  (Lib.) Libyca historia
  69: 120n46
Aristotle
  (De an.) De anima
  3.8 (432a7–11): 98n18
  (De insomn.) De insomniis
  460b1–8: 97n16
  461a15–25: 98n17
  461b22–23: 97n16
  (Mem.) De memoria
  450a31: 92n6
  (Rhet.) Rhetorica
  1.2.2 (1355b35–39): 25n14,
   210n26, 255n14
  1.2.11–17 (1357a1–b10): 249n6
  1.14.6 (1375a11–13): 22n13
  1.15.1–33 (1375a22–1377b12):
   25n14, 210n26, 255n14
  3.11.1–4 (1411b22–
   1412a9): 91n5
Arnobius
  4.3: 55n26
Asclepiades of Prusa (ed. Diels, *Doxographi Graeci*)
  443–44: 142n23

Asconius
  ad *Mil.* 35: 70n60
Athenaeus
  12.528a: 235n67
Augustine
  (De civ. d.) De civitate dei
  3.13: 46n8
Augustus
  Res gestae
  19: 48n15
Caesar
  (B. civ) De bello civili
  3.88–95: 51n19
  22.5: 239n73
  (B. Gall.) De bello Gallico
  1.1: 149n37
  1.31: 149n35
  1.32: 149n35
  1.33: 149n35
  1.36: 149n37
  2.1: 150n39
  2.19–27: 51n19
  3.8: 150n39
  3.10: 149n36
  3.19: 150n39
  4.1: 150
  4.2: 149
  4.3: 149n37
  4.5: 150n39
  5.14: 148n34, 149n37
  5.27: 149n36
  5.29: 149n36
  5.54: 149n36
  6.24: 149

Cicero: orations (*continued*)
6:   231n58
14:   231n58
19:   223n44
30–31:   25
31:   223–24n45
53:   134n9
(*Leg. agr.*) De lege agraria
1.1:   219n38
1.2:   222n43, 223n45
1.5–6:   225
1.8:   223n45
1.9:   222n43
1.11:   223n45
1.15:   222n43, 223n45
1.16:   227n51, 232n61
1.17:   227n51
1.18:   36, 134n9, 232n61
1.21:   226n50, 239n71
1.22:   239n71
1.24:   232n61
1.26:   76n76
2.6:   238
2.7:   219n38
2.8:   240
2.9:   74n73, 234, 235, 236, 238, 239n71
2.10:   219n38, 241
2.12:   219n38
2.13:   238
2.15:   219, 219n38, 222, 222n43, 223, 239n71, 239n74
2.16:   219, 234, 238, 239n71
2.17:   239n71
2.18:   219
2.20:   239n71, 239n74
2.21:   239n74
2.22:   239n71, 239n74
2.24:   239n71, 239n74
2.25:   234, 239n71, 239n74
2.26:   222n43
2.28:   219n38
2.29:   219, 239n71, 239n74
2.31:   221
2.32:   239n71, 239n74
2.33:   223, 239n74
2.34:   223, 223n45, 224, 227
2.35:   219n38, 239n74
2.36:   219n38
2.37:   222n43
2.38:   219, 219n38, 221
2.39:   219n38, 220, 220n39, 223, 223n45, 224, 224n47
2.40:   220, 224
2.40–41:   220n40
2.41:   219n38, 220
2.41–44:   224

2.43:   239n74
2.43–44:   220
2.44:   219n38
2.45:   222n43, 223
2.46:   234
2.47:   219, 220, 223
2.48:   226
2.49:   219n38
2.50:   224–25, 225n48, 226
2.50–51:   220, 225, 234
2.51:   225–26
2.52:   225, 234
2.55:   219n38
2.56:   219, 219n38, 221
2.57:   219n38, 239n74
2.59:   221
2.61:   239n74
2.62:   223, 223n45, 224
2.64:   222n43
2.66:   219n38, 221, 221n41, 222, 227, 227n52, 227n53, 228
2.66–70:   221
2.67:   219n38, 221
2.68:   219n38
2.70:   227
2.71:   180, 221, 223, 223n45, 224, 228, 238, 239n71, 240
2.72:   223, 223n45, 228
2.73:   219n38
2.73–74:   221
2.74:   219n38, 221, 230, 240
2.75:   219n38, 227n51, 239n71, 240
2.76:   222n42, 231
2.76–97:   221, 231
2.77:   231, 232n60, 240
2.77–84:   232
2.78:   231, 232
2.79:   222n42, 231
2.80:   231n58
2.81–82:   231n57
2.82:   231, 232, 232n60, 240
2.84:   171n24, 226n50, 232n60, 233, 236n68
2.84–85:   231n57
2.85–97:   231, 232
2.86:   232n61, 239n71, 240
2.91:   235, 236
2.92:   233
2.95:   233, 236
2.95–97:   233
2.96:   134n7
2.98:   222n43, 223, 223n45, 227n51, 228
2.99:   240n76
2.100:   219n38, 238n70
2.102:   53n23, 239n71

II.4.105:   121
II.4.105–15:   111, 120
II.4.107:   30n21, 121n49
II.4.108:   121
II.4.109:   122
II.4.110:   122
II.4.111:   122, 124
II.4.114:   122, 127
II.4.115:   108n32, 120n45, 123n50
II.4.116:   123
II.4.120–23:   108n32, 120n45
II.4.122:   107, 119
II.4.123:   117n42, 123
II.4.124:   109, 110, 217
II.4.126:   106n29
II.4.129:   108n32
II.4.130:   108n32, 120n45
II.4.132–34:   109, 217
II.4.133:   106n29, 108n32
II.4.134:   110, 120
II.4.137–44:.   113n38
II.5.60–79:   212n33
II.5.69:   212n31
II.5.72–75:   212n31
II.5.77:   212n31
II.5.82:   212n33
II.5.84:   108n32, 120n45
II.5.115:   120n45
II.5.124:   108n32, 120n45
II.5.136–37:   212n31
II.5.139–73:   212n31
II.5.143–45:   122
II.5.145:   117n42
I.5.186:   84n88
II.5.188:   117n41, 214n35
Cicero: philosophical works
(Acad.) Academica
  2.17:   94n11
  2.100:   93
(Amic.) De amicitia
  96:   71n62
(Div.) De divinatione
  1.20:   80n82
  1.21:   81n83
  1.31–33:   67n50
  1.107:   55n26
  2.46:   81n83
(Fin.) De finibus
  1.59:   163n13
  2.88:   56n28
  3.35:   164n13
  5.2:   29, 63, 100, 103n25
  5.3:   30
  5.4:   30
  5.5:   29
(Leg.) De legibus

1.1–4:   28n20
2.1–8:   35
2.2:   31, 32n25
2.3:   31n24, 33
2.4:   31
2.5:   32, 32n28
2.28:   58
2.33:   67n50
(Nat. d.) De natura deorum
  3.63:   48n15
(Off.) De officiis
  1.23:   196–97n8
  1.36–38:   151n41
  2.26–29:   141n20
  2.49–51:   248n3
  2.51:   157n3, 187n45
  3:40:   211n29
(Para.) Paradoxa Stoicorum
  2:   153n45, 188
(Rep.) De republica
  2.5–7:   236n67
  2.5–11:   134n7
  2.7–10:   233n63
  2.10–11:   236n67
  2.31:   71n64
  2.36:   67n50
  3.41:   141n20
  6.21:   134n7
(Sen.) De senectute
  51–60:   162n12
  55–56:   162n12
  56:   162n12
(Tusc.) Tusculanae disputationes
  1.18:   120n46
  2:57:   56n28
  4.64:   56n28
  5.5:   139n17
  5.66:   56n28
  5.87:   56n28
  5.90:   150n38
Cicero: rhetorical works
(Brut.) Brutus
  79:   120n46
  185:   30n22
  212:   120n46
  276:   30n22, 99n20
  279:   30n22, 99n20
  290:   179n36
  312:   169
  322:   30n22, 99n20
(De or.) De oratore
  1.12:   250
  1.17:   30n22, 99n20
  1.24–29:   27
  1.32:   247
  1.33:   139n17

3.38–42: 134n6
3.60: 235n67
3.114: 169n21
6.84–91: 139n16
7.60: 66n47
7.112: 246n2
7.212–15: 61n37
15.77: 67n52
16.236: 67n52, 67n53
18.20: 162n12
33.19: 67n49, 67n53
34.1–93: 105
34.20: 66n47
34.21: 67n48, 67n51
34.22: 66n48, 68n54
34.23: 68n54, 68n56
34.24: 62n38, 68n56
34.26: 62n38, 66n44, 67n49
34.30: 67n49
34.30–31: 105
34.36: 105
34.39–43: 68–69n57
34.93: 68n54
37.201: 134n7
Plutarch
(Mor.) Moralia
17f: 100n21
58b: 100n21
346f: 100n21
(Quaest. Rom.) Quaestiones Romanae
63: 72n65
—Vitae Parallelae
(Ant.) Antonius
54.3–55.1: 241n78
(Cam.) Camillus
42.4: 83–84n87
(Cat. Mai.) Cato Maior
19: 105n27
22: 246n2
27.1–2: 120n46
(Cic.) Cicero
16.3: 41n2
(C. Gracch.) Gaius Gracchus
5.4: 74n71
10.3: 241n77
11.1: 241n77
(Num.) Numa
8.10: 67n49
(Publ.) Publicola
16.7: 66n48
(Rom.) Romulus
4: 67n52
11.1–2: 48n13
18.2–7: 43n6
18.7: 46n8
(Sull.) Sulla

14.2–5: 77n78
30.5: 117n40
33: 73n70
Pollux
(Onom.) Onomasticon
4.143–54: 161n10
Polybius
3.36.8: 147n32
3.91: 235n67
5.21.4–9: 147n32
6.16.5: 74n71
Porphyrion
ad Epod. 16.13: 72n66
ad Sat. 1.3.21: 66n47
Propertius
3.22.17–42: 134n6, 164n15
Ps. Acron
ad Epod. 16.13: 68n55, 72n66
ad Sat. 1.3.21: 66n47
ad Sat. 1.6.119–21: 70n60
Ps. Asconius
ad Div. Caec. 50: 66n47
Ps. Cicero
Oratio priusquam in exsilium iret
24: 41n2, 58–59, 83n85
Ps. Sallust
Invectiva in Ciceronem
7: 54n24
Quintilian
1.7.12: 66n47
1.9.3: 171n23
2.1.12: 253n13
2.4.24: 171n23
2.4.27: 209n25, 253n13
2.4.30–31: 253n13
2.4.32: 10n13
3.6.1–104: 21n10
3.7.26–27: 26
3.8.1–3: 211n29
3.8.30: 211n29
3.8.54: 175n32
4.1.6–10: 34n31
4.2.19: 121n47
4.2.63: 90n3
4.2.63–65: 20n6
4.2.123: 20n6
4.3.12–13: 124
4.3.13: 121n47
5.1.1–2: 211n28
5.1.2: 255
5.7.3: 195n6
5.10.23–31: 171n23
5.10.37: 22n11
5.10.37–41: 21n10
5.10.39: 22n13
5.10.41: 23, 24, 89, 89n2, 128n54

Compositor: Graphic Composition, Inc.
Text: 10/13 Sabon
Display: Sabon
Printer: Thomson-Shore, Inc.
Binder: Thomson-Shore, Inc.